THE LAND IS FULL

THE LAND IS FULL

Addressing Overpopulation in Israel

Alon Tal

Yale

UNIVERSITY

PRESS

New Haven & London

Yale University Press books may be purchased in quantity for educational, business,
or promotional use. For information, please e-mail sales.press@yale.edu (U.S. office)
or sales@yaleup.co.uk (U.K. office).

Set in Electra and Trajan types by Westchester Publishing Services.
Printed in the United States of America.

Library of Congress Control Number: 2015958261
ISBN 978-0-300-21688-2 (hardcover : alk. paper)

A catalogue record for this book is available from the British Library.

This paper meets the requirements of ANSI/NISO Z39.48-1992 (Permanence of Paper).

10 9 8 7 6 5 4 3 2 1

This book is dedicated to
Marshall Brinn, Noah Efron, Joe Kruger, Bill Slott,
and Josh Star-Lack:
"Liquid Plummer"—a brilliant band of brothers and lifelong friends
sporting a collective total fertility rate of 2.2—not bad!

CONTENTS

FOREWORD: A NEGLECTED DIMENSION OF THE MIDDLE EASTERN (AND WORLD) DILEMMA

Paul R. Ehrlich and Anne H. Ehrlich

A scorpion sat by the edge of the Suez Canal. He said to a frog sitting next to him, "Hey, I need to get to the other side. Will you swim me over?" The frog said, "Hah! If I carry you over, you'll sting me and I'll die." The scorpion replied, "Don't be silly. If you die, I'll drown; you'll be perfectly safe." The frog said, "You are right—let's go." Halfway across, the scorpion stung the frog. As the frog went under, he gasped, "Are you nuts? Why did you do it? Now we'll both die." The scorpion replied, "You must remember: this is the Middle East."

This allegory resonates with regard to any number of substantive areas of conflict. It surely is symbolic that both sink because of the excess baggage. Most countries in the Middle East are committing ecological suicide on account of their rapidly growing populations and by ignoring opportunities to cooperate for their mutual benefit.

The area has long been a geopolitical mess, especially since Britain, France, and the United States started interfering there to control energy sources after the Ottoman Empire died. Oil has been at the center of the controversy, and even before Israel formally became a state, petroleum has been a significant node in the mess.

Although the region's conflicts continue, the area's grim environmental future, like that of global civilization, is largely neglected. Ecological conditions are truly dire, but not considered nearly as important as the political situation and access to the region's energy resources. This is especially true of the huge demographic problems that are central to the rapidly darkening prospects for regional sustainability. If there is any glimmer of light, it is this brilliant book by Alon Tal, Israeli environmental scientist and politician. As he has in the past, Tal focuses attention on his nation's ecological predicament—in this case its vast overpopulation. He shows that at least some Middle Easterners understand their environmental peril, even if most U.S. politicians in the American empire do not.

Population is often referred to as the "elephant in the room," largely ignored even though it is the biggest driver of civilization toward collapse (overconsumption by the rich is its only competition). Israel has no need of elephants. It is a desert nation, by 2015 home to 8.3 million people, unable to feed itself now, "planning" to increase to about 14 million inhabitants by midcentury. That would take its population density, now nearly twice that of well-watered western Europe, to far beyond that of even the Netherlands. The Palestinian Territory is almost twice as crowded and is also due to double by 2050. Similar grim prospects face most of the rest of Israel's desert neighbors. Despite substantial bloodletting, before the recent civil war Syria was projected to grow 50 percent or more in the next thirty-five years, as are Jordan, Kuwait, Oman, and the United Arab Emirates. Saudi Arabia will come close to that increase, and Iraq will much more than double its numbers. All that growth will be happening in a dryland region short of arable land with chronically scarce water resources!

Besides the biophysical challenges the population situation presents, Israel also faces the demographic challenge of incredible overreproduction by myriad religious and ethnic groups. Many of them contain extreme elements that already threaten peaceful solutions and the country's democratic culture. Should these groups become politically dominant, they could destroy Israel's main advantage in the region: its modern, evidence-oriented culture. Many Israelis have told us they are more afraid of Orthodox extremists than of enemy Arab states. It is not a hopeful sign for the nation that should start taking a sensible approach to its security by establishing peace in the region.

The time in which Israel could move toward sustainability is likely past, but there may still be hope. Its economic dependence on oil is not as direct as that of its Arab neighbors. Israel's high-tech competence, as illustrated by its great advances in agriculture, solar energy, and other areas might allow it to start feeding itself and to help its neighbors do the same—if the population monster could be slain.

Unhappily, however, Israeli politicians and economists have pretty much surrendered to the idiotic notion that economic growth can continue forever. Unless such ideas can be killed locally and globally, the entire point of this essay and, indeed, of this book will become moot.

Suppose instead, someday soon Israel's leaders realize that perpetual growth is the creed of the cancer cell and start to promote population and economic shrinkage, sustainability, efficiency, and equity? Suppose the Israelis stopped seeking to assert numeric dominance over their Arab citizens and helped the Palestinians to forge a prosperous future? Jointly, the Israelis and Palestinians might be able to lead their environmentally challenged region toward population reduction and sustainability. They might, as everyone must, leave the past behind them to secure a decent life for their descendants. If such miracles could occur—and many people see Israel as a land of miracles—Israeli citizens might hope to dodge the bullet of collapse, as long as other nations do the same.

Although in terms of geographic and demographic scale Israel is insignificant, it may play the same role in international politics as it has played in advancing desert agriculture. The fate of civilization may even hang on Israel's population situation, which if left unchanged, likely will play an expanding negative role in that nation's behavior. That's why *The Land Is Full* is such an incredibly important book.

PREFACE

The first time I visited Israel, in 1965, I was but five years old. Back then, there were only 2.5 million people there. I retain vague recollections of driving from Rehovoth to Jerusalem through a countryside that seemed somewhat barren and undeveloped. The landscape was entirely different from the forested North Carolina suburbs I called home, but surprisingly compelling.

Fifteen years later I immigrated to Israel. It felt like a grand adventure to link my life to the trials and errors of the incipient Third Jewish Commonwealth. It still does. By then there were already almost 4 million Israelis, a significant increase to be sure—but less than half of the country's present population.

Joining the army thirty-two days after arriving, I soon began to think about the subtleties of demographic densities. As part of an infantry unit, most of our time was spent outdoors and in the field. These inaccessible military training grounds were far from civilization. There I came to appreciate the unembellished beauty of the country's drylands. As we ran up and down parched hillsides, the vast plains never seemed to end. After simulating a charge up some rocky knoll, we invariably were rewarded by stunning vistas or skies as starry as any mortal has ever admired.

Yet our officers were forever yelling at us to spread out and take advantage of these open spaces. Their concern was that we not be caught in clusters, allowing a shell to take out a group in a single, unlucky shot, as tragically happens in battle from time to time. Apparently, in stressful situations, even hardened soldiers take comfort in being close to other people.

Therein lay the paradox of density and soldiering for me. Living on sweeping prairies, the army was actually the most crowded experience I ever encountered. Camping out during maneuvers, we'd sleep in pairs: two sardines, squeezed side

by side inside a tiny pup tent. Piling into the armored personal carrier often re-
minded me of adolescent competitions during my youth, when record numbers
of kids were packed into sundry car models. Inside these military vehicles for
hours and often days on end, previous notions of personal space were soon forgotten. The resulting dynamics involved plenty of annoyances, jostling, banging, and yelling. But on the whole, those nineteen-year-olds were some of the
best folks I have ever met. We all adapted.

People, it turns out, find all sorts of ways to adapt to crowded conditions.
Once, well into my service, while waiting in line for dinner at the field kitchen,
I noticed a friend with his head buried in a book. It was an unusual sight given
the setting. He explained to me that reading was the best way to stay sane in the
army. That's why he always kept a shabby paperback buried deep in his pants
pocket. He could pull it out whenever he felt the need for diversion.

It sounded like an inspirational idea. Beginning with *Of Human Bondage*, I
soon kept a modest stack of books in my tent, with one stashed in my baggy
green trousers. A year later, a taxi showed up at Kibbutz Ketura at 1:00 A.M. to
take me to what later was called the First Lebanon War. Knowing I'd be gone
awhile, I pinched ten volumes from the kibbutz library. There were plenty of
distractions and horrors on that journey, but the books kept me largely indiffer-
ent to the heat and congested conditions in the half-track, all the way to the
eastern suburbs of Beirut. In retrospect, reading gave me a set of psychological
wings; it allowed me to fly away, whenever density became too much.

Healthy folks invariably do find ways to adjust to crowding, especially when
conditions are temporary. Today's youth have iPods or get lost in texting friends
thousands of miles away. An imaginative twenty-one-year-old can dream himself out of a congested reality for a while. Over time, however, it is not a sustainable solution. It is not sustainable because most people are not hardwired for
the crowded conditions of the urban twenty-first century. The physical evolution of *Homo sapiens* did not take place in metropolitan centers. Frequently,
humans seek closeness, but there are limits. Most normal people need some
space in which to retreat.

Israel is among the most crowded countries in the Western world. It is getting
more so very quickly. Even without the obvious environmental and social side
effects, there are psychological consequences, which we have long since stopped
noticing. Finding space for a bit of respite gets harder all the time. I fear there
will come a time when young Israelis will not be satisfied finding relief by flying
away from their congested homeland through reading and will opt for one way
El Al tickets, never to return. Israel's mammals are also feeling the congestion.
But they have no wings and nowhere else to go. So they slowly disappear.

Twenty years after the war, I finished writing my first book, *Pollution in a Promised Land*, in which I chronicled Israel's sundry environmental afflictions. By then there were over 6 million people in Israel. The manuscript finished with a thorough description of the dismal state of Eilat's coral reefs that grace Israel's southernmost coastline, on the Red Sea. What had once been a magical playground of psychedelic corals and fish was rapidly disappearing: 75 percent of coral cover and abundance were already gone. "People, not tankers, have brought large areas of the reef to the brink of extinction," I wrote then. "The cumulative impact of well-meaning swimmers and divers probably constitutes the single greatest cause of coral destruction." The policy dilemma seemed a no-brainer at the time: either promulgate strict constraints on accessing the coral while there was still some left, or continue allowing unrestricted diving until all remaining specimens were extirpated.

Against all odds, an aggressive management program was implemented some fifteen years ago. Conditions on the ground changed completely. Long pedestrian bridges were built from the beach into the deeper waters, preventing snorkelers and divers from walking on the sensitive coral floor; a daily ceiling was placed on the number of visitors allowed into the coral coast reserve; potential hazards imposed by human activities from aquaculture and shipping were abated. In short, the heavy footprint of human activity was reduced.

Nature's response has been encouraging. A national monitoring program indicates that collapse has been averted, replaced by modest but undeniable progress: there are more fish; coral is rebounding; water quality has improved. Once again, the simple truth about ecosystems with overloaded carrying capacity has become clear: "Less is more." The experience also confirms a personal motto that has kept me going through thirty years of environmental advocacy, activism, and academia: "Trend is not destiny."

Since I wrote that book, I have spoken of Eilat's coral reefs as a metaphor for Israel's environmental situation. While running an advocacy group representing environmental interests in the 1990s, the pace of ecological destruction and contamination grew ever more relentless. The scope of the insults became increasingly overwhelming. There was always something new, and crises never let up. It took some time to realize that I was addressing symptoms triggered by a much deeper cause. Real environmental progress would only be possible if the number of people pressuring the country's limited resources stabilized.

Trying to solve ecological problems with a rapidly growing population evokes images of "The Sorcerer's Apprentice," Goethe's 1797 poem immortalized with music by Paul Dukas in Disney's *Fantasia*. Mickey's desperate efforts to stop the deluge are doomed to fail, given the rising water levels and unyielding pails of water fetched by the enchanted and irrepressible brooms. This is much like the rising tide of environmental hazards, which engulfs us mortals today. For those who prefer a more-classical analogy, there is always Sisyphus, the Greek mythological king of Ephyra. We too are afflicted with the impossible task of rolling the giant boulder of sustainability up the mountain, knowing full well that no matter how hard we push, it will roll back down. The forces pushing back are simply too great. In our failed efforts to make Israel a clean, healthy, and just society, it is time that we recognize that force for what it is: population growth.

At a macro level, reality in many ways remains as it was when Thomas Malthus asserted two fundamental truths in his 1798 *Essay on the Principle of Population*: "First, that food is necessary to the existence of man. Secondly, that the passion between the sexes is necessary and will remain nearly in its present state." Ostensibly, of course, everything has changed. As a fairly prudish clergyman, Malthus could not have imagined the marvelous ability of contraception to offer convenient controls over the product of human passions. And our extraordinary resourcefulness in food production undermined his ominous "arithmetic" agricultural calculations.

Yet, the laundry list of despair produced by overpopulation actually seems to grow longer with time: the staggering disappearance of species, the increase in greenhouse gas emissions, the explosion of refugees, water shortages, famine, human discomfort, and foregone quality of life. In the global discourse, those who are insouciantly dismissive of Malthus's pessimism are probably only vaguely aware of the scores of people on the planet who die every day from hunger-related diseases. My recent professional interest in desertification, land degradation, and food security suggests that there are more places than ever on the earth where Malthus's grim predictions have come true.

Hunger around the planet is on the rise. The most recent assessments by the United Nations estimate that more than one in four people in Africa are undernourished. Some 10 million people die each year due to hunger-related illnesses or acute starvation. Of course, efficient food distribution systems could prevent much of this suffering. The failure to do a better job at this is our generation's collective disgrace. But it is also true that had these unimaginable numbers of forlorn people been luckier and been born into societies with stable populations (rather than societies that double every twenty-five years), most would be alive.

My friend, the renowned ecologist Paul Ehrlich, often talks about the "nonlinearity" of population growth's environmental impacts. Even as demographic proliferation on the planet slows, each additional person on the planet does more harm than the previous 7 billion. As open spaces vanish, habitats dwindle, and resource scarcity becomes more acute, producing the same amount of food, energy, fiber, and quality of life will cause increasingly egregious damage to the environment. This is particularly true in a small country.

Nobody is going to die of hunger for the foreseeable future in Israel. But there are myriad ways that the country becomes poorer as the number of people proliferates. Lost quality of life can be found in the crowded roads, schools, hospitals, courts, and housing market. We try hard to build an exceptional society and restore our environment, but the water level keeps rising and the boulder keeps rolling down.

It took another decade, a massive national social protest, and a stint as chairman of the Green Movement—Israel's green party—for me to realize how much Israel's social crises were part of the same dynamic. The vast majority of poor Israelis live in large families. How can we even think of eradicating poverty without putting this delicate issue on the table? Education will always be substandard in elementary school classrooms with over forty children. How can we speak of pedagogical excellence without addressing the growing numbers attending schools in crowded classrooms?

There are many smart people living in Israel. But we seem to suffer from a collective blind spot, imagining that if we could just grow the population enough or expand the economy or increase the housing stock or build more highways, then everything would be fine. It won't. Albert Einstein's oft-quoted observation seems particularly germane when considering Israel's population dynamics: "We can't solve problems by using the same kind of thinking we used when we created them."

One way our thinking has to change involves our time horizons. Facing a relentless litany of existential crises since national independence, Israelis find it hard to think twenty or thirty years ahead, much less centuries. It is hard for Jews and Arabs to think about family planning without lapsing into the rhetoric of nationalist conflict. Only seventy years after the Holocaust, it is especially difficult to talk about strategies for limiting the number of Jews. But our thinking must change. That is why I wrote this book.

As a professor of public policy, I actually prefer a second, less-familiar Einstein quote: "If I had an hour to solve a problem, I'd spend 55 minutes thinking about the problem and 5 minutes thinking about solutions." During my writing, I never intentionally divided up the relevant topics so that 91 percent of the text would be dedicated to the problem and 9 percent to solutions. Nonetheless, it was clear to me that meaningful answers to the population conundrum meant getting the questions right, a more-challenging endeavor than merely restating solutions, many of which, like empowerment of women, are self-evident. That's why many of the chapters take on a distinctly "historical" flavor. I couldn't imagine mapping the way forward without describing how we got into the mess in the first place. Nonetheless, if readers have the stamina to reach chapter 12, they will get some answers about what must be done.

As an incurable optimist, I know solutions are available. Innumerable national successes demonstrate swift transitions in demographic forces when the right way of thinking meets the right policies and government incentives. At the same time, Israel's circumstances are decidedly idiosyncratic. Although I am not a professional demographer, I hope that the book tells this country's arcane but fascinating demographic story clearly and objectively, so that the happy ending we can still achieve sounds persuasive.

Coming clean to readers, I should acknowledge that although this is an academic work with hundreds of references and almost an obsessive commitment to peer review, when distilled down to its essence, this book is designed to be a polemic. Technically this means "a harsh criticism of someone or something, using language." Hence, I want to make it clear what I am criticizing.

This book is not an anti-Zionist diatribe or attempt to tarnish the astonishing achievements of the dedicated folks who built my country. On the contrary: I am still motivated by the same love of the land and people of Israel—the same radical Zionist idea that brought me here thirty-five years ago. Nor is the book intended to be an attack on Haredi or Bedouin societies, practices, and values, about which I try to write with respect. Nonetheless, I do believe that their high fertility is a significant part of Israel's demographic problem and needs to be reined in. Local pathologies will worsen if the population continues to grow unceasingly. I criticize policies and people who continue to promote high fertility.

Because so many Israelis cannot yet see that their "land is full," I try to make the case. Accordingly, I hope that the book will be understood as "tough love." Israel's impressive success is due to a historic ability to nimbly shift to new paradigms and norms as circumstances evolve. The country is no longer a sparsely populated province. Reality has changed. We can, too. The same society that creates an Iron Dome system in which *Star Wars* technology neutralizes missiles, revolutionizes desalination membranes, and rocks the high-tech world can adopt smart demographic policies.

More than 8 million people live in Israel today. Demographic projections tell us that the least we can expect in a matter of four or five decades is 15 million. I write this book with the hope that it will help Israelis and those who care about Israel to ask themselves—and decision makers—whether it makes sense to reach 30 million. To me that seems a rhetorical question. Life in Israel is good. There are many areas where we are starting to reach Genesis "Monday morning" levels of "very good." But we also have many problems. Millions more people will not make it easier to solve them. On the contrary, stabilizing the population will. So this book is written in the context of a national consensus that has always seen Israel's existence as a miracle and living proof that *trend indeed need not be destiny.* Hopefully, it will galvanize people to embrace a new and more sustainable way of thinking about Israel's future and what it will take to get there.

Acknowledgments

Seventeen years ago I first started speaking openly about the futility of environmental protection in Israel without a strategy to slow population growth. The issue gave me no rest, and I spoke often about Israel's worrying demographic trends. But I never had the opportunity to fully consider demographic history, the minutiae of present policies and alternative routes. It would take the tranquility of a sabbatical and the unique resources of Stanford University to make that happen.

The many expressions of gratitude that I would like to offer, therefore, begin with Professor Paul Ehrlich—and his partner for so many years, Anne Ehrlich. Their writing inspired me since I first stumbled onto the field of environmental protection, and long before we became friends it found its way into required reading lists for many of my classes. Paul was more than an official host during my stay in Stanford in 2013–2014, when this book was written. To spend significant chunks of time, innumerable lunches and "drool farm" dinners with him was an intellectual adventure and a very good time. His encouragement, unparalleled familiarity with the field, insights, and endless arsenal of off-color jokes made a daunting academic project a far more pleasant endeavor. The hospitality he and Anne extended to our family was among the highlights of the year, and their foreword is surely one of the highlights of this book.

The cheerful environment created by my Stanford office mates, Professor Nick Haddad and Professor Jian Wu, often created the happy sensation of being back in graduate school. I want to thank Nick for patiently sharing his deep understanding of ecology and university sporting events, as well as for his weekly editions of *The Economist*. Jian never grew tired of sharing her knowledge about different aspects of China's environmental strategies, including her fascinating explanations about life with the "one-child policy." It was wonderful to spend time with them and their families. Thanks to Gretchen Dailey, who in absentia orchestrated the whole thing.

Among our friends in Palo Alto, it is hard to say too much about the welcome provided by the Star-Lacks, for all practical purposes our extended California family. The football games, tennis matches, Eagles concerts, and countless meals with Josh, Sylvia, Russell, and Maya remain treasured memories for my family and me. Grueling but wonderful runs up and down the dish with Jay Hirsch punctuated and enhanced my mornings.

Certain Israeli scholarship proved to be particularly valuable. Professor Sergio Della Pergola's research and commentaries during his long career at Hebrew University as Israel's preeminent demographer constitute vital references. His unfailing patience in answering my steady stream of trivial questions while writing is much appreciated. My good friend at the Technion—the Israel Institute of Technology—Dr. Daniel Orenstein, dived into the environmental-demographic interface long before I did, and his publications are particularly insightful. Rhoda Ann Kanaaneh's *Birthing the Nation* broke new ground a decade ago in describing the complex issue of fertility among Israeli Arabs, and it stands the test of time. Arnon Soffer has written much about Israel's demography. The sabbatical finally allowed me the time to read and to consider his ideas. Few people are neutral about Arnon's work. I am surely a fan and appreciate the forthrightness and refusal to pull punches in his analysis. The insightful writing of his colleague Evgenia Bystrov constitutes another important voice in the discourse. To understand the evolution of Israel's policies, past volumes by Dov Friedlander and Calvin Goldscheider, along with *Fertility Policy in Israel* by Jacqueline Portuguese are deserving of mention. And, of course, Roberto Bachi's early scholarship set a standard in the field. Finally, I join the chorus of commendation for Alan Weisman's most recent work, *Countdown*, and its fascinating update about demographic trends in twenty countries.

The Land is Full pushed me onto new ground, making friendly reviews more significant than ever before. Scores of friends and colleagues agreed to take a look at different chapters or passages. Among these friendly reviewers are Dr. Alon Ben-Gal, Rabbi David Boothe, Professor Sergio Della Pergola, Dr. Mousa Diabat, Dr. Noah Efron, Professor Paul Ehrlich, Ms. Rachel Feit, Dr. Uri Givon, Professor Nick Hadad, Dr. Efrat Hadas, Dr. Steven Klein, Attorney Tziona Koenig-Yair, Mr. Michael Maze, Tal Nishri, Dr. Daniel Orenstein, Professor Michelle Rivkin-Fish, Dr. Yonina Rosenthal, Ms. Manar Saria, Mr. Misha Shauli, Mr. Bill Slott, Dr. Aliza Stark, Professor Ken Stein, Dr. Gila Stopler, Dr. Barbara Swirski, Dr. David Tal, Ms. Robyn Tal, Professor Gil Troy,

Dr. Susan Warchaizer, and Professor Steve Zipperstein. Dr. Adi Inbar, now a researcher for Israel's Knesset, worked closely with me in preparing the Hebrew version of this book, offering countless excellent suggestions for improving the text. The book is far better and incalculably more accurate due to the time they shared. For this I am very grateful. Any errors that fell between the cracks are surely my own.

Bill Slott, my close friend for forty-five years now, read early versions of all the chapters. His comments were encouraging, thoughtful, provoking, and entertaining. As has been the case with all my previous books, the most fastidious (and critical) reviewer of my writing is my mother, Dr. Yonina Rosenthal. I have always known that I was blessed with a mother who is exceptionally intelligent, opinionated, and devoted. Hopefully her uncompromising editorial standards are reflected in the quality and coherence of the writing.

At Yale University Press, Senior Executive Editor Jean Thomson Black believed in this book from the start and stuck with it through the undulated review process. I am lucky to be the beneficiary, for the second time now, of her exceptional experience and knowledge about how books should be written and why they are important. Samantha Ostrowski was consistently helpful and efficient in expediting this book's publication. Kate Davis was everything one could hope for in a copy editor and much, much more. Her careful corrections and smart suggestions were invaluable. Jeff Schier once again was a terrific help in shepherding the project along expeditiously as the press's in-house production editor.

Most of all, my appreciation goes to my family. Robyn and Zoe agreed to take leave of their lives in Israel and return to Stanford, California, and brave the extreme climatic conditions of Silicon Valley. As the chapters rolled off the printer, Robyn always got to read the roughest of drafts and was invariably charitable and usually diplomatic in making her excellent suggestions. When Yale University Press delivered the traumatic diagnosis that the manuscript was 25,000 words too long, it was Robyn who served as chief surgeon. I have never been more grateful for her wisdom, love, and partnership. Zoe suffered countless harangues and diatribes about overpopulation with astonishing forbearance. Apparently, she even listened: lately, she has started sending me links to newspaper articles about the effect of crowding on Israel's high school classrooms. Mika and Hadas, our two most intelligent officers, kept our country safe, our house standing, and our cars running during our absence. More than any other writing project, this book has left me thinking about their future and the wonderful homeland they so deserve.

THE LAND IS FULL

◆—◆

INTRODUCTION: TALKING ABOUT
DEMOGRAPHY IN ISRAEL

We can evade reality *but are not free to avoid*
the abyss we refuse to see.
—*Ayn Rand*, 1961 symposium "Ethics in Our Time"

In 1995, outside the environmental community, Dan Perry was relatively un-known among Israel's senior bureaucrats. As director of the country's Nature Reserve Authority, he cut a tall, striking figure with his full, dark beard and confident demeanor. A limp, resulting from an unfortunate meeting with a land mine while designing trails in the Golan Heights, enhanced his fighter persona.[1] As a ranger and conservation expert, Perry rose through the ranks of a highly professional and principled agency by offering an intelligent, clear, and uncom-promising voice for preservation. It was these qualities that led him to write a short introductory note in a local nature magazine about a newly proposed "2020 master plan" for the country. The piece brought his anonymity to an end.

Perry argued:

All of the program's assumptions about the number of residents in the state of Israel in 2020 are fed by data reflecting the rate of natural population growth and present immigration rates and their implications on the future. If the plan's point of departure is to sketch out desirable scenarios for our country, there is no avoiding yet another scenario, one that assumes that population numbers in the State of Israel in 2020 will, for example, be 7.5 million resi-dents and not 8.5 million—the planners' assumption. Such a supposition will only require a doubling of the constructed and developed areas in Israel and not a tripling, something of a revolution for the master plan. Planners have the obligation to propose ways to lower the rate of natural population growth in Israel from the level of developing nations to the accepted level in a developed country.[2]

Perry went on to emphasize that a policy to slow demographic expansion would need to challenge fundamental axioms that define life in modern Israel, including unlimited absorption of Jewish immigration and the extremely broad, legal definition of a Jew under Israel's Law of Return. Moreover, public policies designed to maximize fertility and encourage large families needed to be reconsidered. Such a reform would require fundamental changes in legislation and mind-sets.

He concluded:

> The meaning of such a comprehensive shift involves recognition of the fact that we have a very small country that is only able to carry a limited human load. To the extent that we increase the load, the relationship between the land and the number of people who use it will grow more severe. . . . In these days, when the entire world recognizes the fact that population growth is the central problem facing the human race, Israel cannot behave as if it is not part of the planet.

When word got out that a senior government official had articulated such a view, the "hue and cry" was thunderous. The leading Israeli daily, *Yedioth Ahronot,* reported calls by sundry Israeli politicians for Perry's resignation: "These are shocking and infuriating views," roared religious party parliamentarian Yitzhak Levy: "Woe is us if we reach a situation where we need to create an association: *'Let the Children be Born'* or *'Let the Jews Immigrate,'* because of nature and landscape loving missionaries—who are no lovers of humanity, and who cannot see the people for the trees."[3]

The hullabaloo in the media would take some time to subside. Today, Dr. Yehoshua Shkedi is the chief scientist overseeing Israel's nature reserves. He has vivid recollections of returning to Israel in 1995 after several years of postdoctoral research in ecology at Stanford University. By chance he turned on the television one evening and recounts:

> I remember watching channel two very clearly—because when I left for the states there had only been one Israeli television station and now there was a second one. It was an afternoon talk show about politics. Imagine my surprise to see Dan Perry, the Director of the Nature Reserve on the air, facing off against Yitzhak Levy, who would soon be Minister of Education. The topic was demography and there was Dan Perry saying that he thought it was high time that a public discussion take place about how many people we want living in

Israel. Levy was calm but firm in his opinion arguing that any public servant who after the Holocaust has the nerve to talk about limiting population should lose their job. Ever since then I always tell my students that overpopulation may be an important topic, but I am not talking about it.[4]

Today, Dan Perry has embraced a second career as an environmental planner, and while his beard has fully turned to gray, his views have not softened a bit:

> The demographic challenge today in the Middle East is not Egypt or Syria but Israel. Egypt's population bomb leaves it completely without hope. They simply do not have the resources to support themselves with dignity. Ours is a different situation. Israel can still support itself, but it comes at a price and that is our natural systems. Back in 1995 I said something very simple which has not changed: There is a connection between the number of people in Israel and the number of wild animals. As the former increases, the latter drops. With the pace of development, we are slowly creating islands—every city is an island to itself. And we know from island biogeography that as the island gets smaller, the number of species drops. This is no longer theory. Thirty years ago I started saying that if nature protection remains in a defensive mode, our reserves will be little more than flower pots. I had no trouble saying this in any professional forum, or at professional conferences. But I realized at the time that the politicians and I were not going to live in peace.[5]

Almost twenty years have passed since Dan Perry articulated what many Israeli citizens—and not just environmentalists—think. Yet, since that time, few advocates in government or in the public sphere have dared to express similar views so openly. Soon after he caused the stir, the overseeing minister of agriculture, Yaakov Tsur, requested and received Perry's resignation, ostensibly with no direct link to the demographic controversy. In his stead, Shaikeh Erez, a former military commander with no previous experience in conservation, was appointed.[6]

In the twenty years since Dan Perry resigned his post, Israel's populations grew by over 45 percent: There were 5.5. million people living in Israel in 1995. Within twenty-one years the number burgeoned beyond 8 million, reflecting the largest absolute annual population increase in the country's history. Local citizens are not conscious of the incremental transformation. Yet visitors surely notice how crowded life has become. While "overpopulation" is a concept typically associated with the pathology of poverty and despair in developing countries, the concept is increasingly germane in Israel, even though it is rarely

Dan Perry, as chairman of Israel's
Nature Reserve Authority, who dared to
speak out about the ecological implications of overpopulation. (Photograph
courtesy of Dan Perry)

discussed or understood. The quality of almost every aspect of life and surely
the environment are profoundly affected by the footprints of so many people
now filling this ancient land.

Israel's demographic trends are among the most dramatic in the world: since
the country was established sixty-seven years ago, its population has swelled
eightfold, adding a million people each decade and growing from 1 million to
more than 8 million. A simple chronological graph offers a clear picture of what
demographers mean when they talk about "geometric growth."

These numbers reflect massive immigration, which augmented the population between 1948 and 2000. They also are a function of a very high birthrate.
Israel is unique among Western countries, where typically totally fertility is only
1.6 children per family. Israel's TFR (total fertility rate) is estimated to be 3.0.[7]
More than 76 percent of Israeli women between ages forty-five and fifty, the age
when most women stop having children, have had two or more children. By
way of contrast, in the United States the percentage is 63 percent; in Italy and

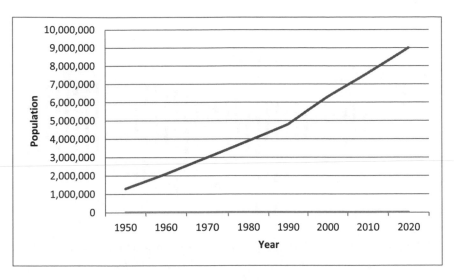

"Geometric growth": Israel's population increases from 1 million in 1950
to 8 million in 2013. (Source: Israel Central Bureau of Statistics)

Germany, it is only 51 percent.[8] More than 60 percent of Israeli women have
three or more children. Marriage is still a vaunted institution in Israel. In New
Zealand, only 59 percent of women are married.[9] Some 90 percent of women
in Israel get married—and 20 percent of those who aren't still have children.

During its sixty-seven-year history, the country was transformed from a
sparsely settled land to one of the most crowded nations on the planet. Population
density in Israel skyrocketed: from 43 people per square kilometer in 1948 to 347 in
2011.[10] This means that Israel is 1,000 percent more congested on average than
other countries in the Organisation for Economic Co-operation and Development (OECD).[11] But even this hardly reflects the true reality facing most Israelis. Relatively few people live in Israel's Negev southlands, even as it comprises
some 60 percent of Israel's lands. This means that the country's central heart-
lands actually have densities of 1,463 per square kilometer, while the Greater Tel
Aviv region has an astonishing 7,522 people per square kilometer. While many
people in Israel believe that this represents a significant problem, they are loath
to raise the issue.

There are any number of reasons why most Israelis are not comfortable talking about the phenomenal increase in their numbers as a negative phenomenon. One key factor is a shared, positive inclination toward large families. In a
country with no shortage of friction between the Jewish majority and the Arab
minority, a fundamentally pro-natal impulse constitutes a common value. The

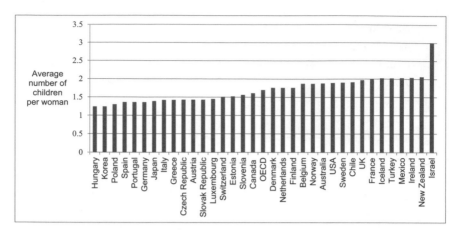

Unquestioned demographic champion among developed countries: total fertility rates in Israel versus OECD states. (Source: OECD, *Society at a Glance,* 2014)

first commandment in the Bible calls on humans to "Be fruitful and multiply and fill up the earth" (Genesis: 1:28). Jewish tradition not only presents this expectation as an individual obligation but as a collective mission.[12] While Jews have always cut corners with plenty of commandments, this is one "mitzvah" that historically was always taken seriously.

The inclination cuts across Israeli society today, so that even highly secular Jewish families increasingly have four children and more.[13] Indeed, the very Hebrew expression for a "large family" is value laden: a "family blessed with children." The word for a Jewish immigrant, *oleh,* literally means "he who has risen up"—connoting the prestige Hebrew language attributes to new arrivals.

At the same time, for more than a century Israel's Arab population was among the world's fastest growing communities. During the thirty years of the British Mandate (1918–1948), the Muslim Palestinian population of Palestine more than doubled from five hundred thousand to 1.1 million.[14] While migration from surrounding Arab lands undoubtedly furthered this exceptional annual increase[15] (over 2 percent per year), an estimated family size of six[16] was a critical contributing factor. As Arabs settled into their new minority status, even larger families became the norm. During the 1960s and 1970s, Muslim-Israeli families averaged nine children per family.[17]

With such pervasive cultural bias, more people is not typically seen as a problem but rather a triumph. Feminist authors decry the imperative of motherhood that hounds women who either cannot or prefer not to become mothers.[18] Rutti Gur, a founder of Israel's women's movement, explains that Israeli women who choose not to have children still face a largely belligerent society. Even the more tolerant elements will assume that something must be fundamentally wrong with the woman and view her with pity.[19] The rare call to reexamine the merits of geometric population growth is greeted by most Israelis with a mix of perplexity and indignation.

Another deterring factor involves the very virulence of attacks against anyone who challenges such a central principle in the country's code of ethics. Israel's national identity, economics, and ideological raison d'être from inception were founded on an unfettered commitment to maximal demographic growth. There is little tolerance for people who question the sagacity of this belief. In one typical instance, in 2000, Labor politician Yossi Beilin, serving as minister of justice, stated in an interview that large families constituted a burden on society, explaining that they cause their children distress, hardship, and discrimination. "Having many children in and of itself does not constitute a blessing," he suggested. Retribution was swift.[20] The vicious assaults that followed came from across Israel's diverse political spectrum, from Druze to Sephardic to Orthodox politicians, all assailing his elitism and calling for his resignation. In 2014, the minister of agriculture, Yair Shamir, called for "addressing the phenomenon of polygamy among the Bedouins and reducing their fertility" and elicited a barrage of condemnations impugning racist motives.[21] Geographer and population maven Arnon Soffer advises anyone who wants to even talk about local demographic policies openly to be prepared to be censured as an "anti-Zionist" by Israel's right wing or as a "fascist" by Israel's left wing.[22]

Moreover, the Holocaust still looms as a powerful factor. At the end of World War II the global Jewish population had been cut down to 11 million people. Since that time there has been a steady increase in the number of Jews worldwide. The increase of more than 8 percent between the years 2005 and 2015 was the greatest surge of any decade since the war. Nonetheless, as of 2015, when the most-recent calculations were made by the Jerusalem-based Jewish People Policy Institute, there were only an estimated 14.3 million Jews counted worldwide. (When people, largely in the United States, who define themselves as "partially Jewish" are added, the number goes up by another million.)[23] This is still significantly below the 16.5 million Jews assumed to be alive in 1939, before the Nazis launched their "Final Solution" and began the wholesale slaughter of European Jewry.[24] Even some of the world's leading Jewish environmentalists feel that the normal rules of demographic restraint should be suspended in the case of the Jewish people, at the very least until pre–World War II numbers are restored.[25]

While one would expect Israel's environmentalists to be united in their concern about the issue, in fact most green organizations avoid the issue compulsively.[26]

There are voices in Israel's environmental community that argue that it is not population growth but profligate consumption that is behind the unacceptably heavy ecological footprint of the Third Jewish Commonwealth. Acknowledging the role of population size on quality of life and the environment is perceived as implicit disapproval of disenfranchised and indigent societal sectors, who tend to have large families (for example, Bedouins or Haredim). There is profound discomfort among privileged, liberal intellectuals in criticizing less-fortunate communities when their sense of social justice suggests they should be championing them. Blaming consumption offers a politically correct "way out."

Hebrew University environmental philosopher Avner de-Shalit has often contended that his family of four's consumption leaves a larger footprint than an indigent religious family of fourteen. He writes, "One cannot deny that the population lobby's theory is reasonable, arithmetically speaking. . . . However, while the mathematics is right, the sociology is wrong. I would therefore argue that the impact of humans on the environment is a function of three parameters, the least significant of which is the size of the population."[27] De-Shalit maintains that racism is the real reason why environmentalists support policies to control demographic growth: "It can be argued that the population scare is very much a matter of an emotional aversion to and a dislike of the 'other' whose culture is different."[28]

Ben-Gurion University environmental expert Yaakov Garb is less judgmental but openly expresses concerns about the political conflicts that can infiltrate demographic debates in Israel. "A simplistic call of 'too many people' could become a dangerous flag to be raising in a region fraught with ethnic and religious tensions." He argues that population growth is "only one contribution to growing and unsustainable environmental impacts, which are due in a large measure to increased consumption. . . . In the short and medium term, however, high-consumption, low-fertility lifestyles may be as harmful as low consumption, high-fertility ones. . . . In several important spheres, the growth in environmental impacts over the coming 50 years may be predominantly a function of technology and lifestyle."[29] By creating a false dilemma between working to reduce consumption versus efforts to reduce population growth (even though clearly both are crucial), the awkwardness of demographic discussions can be evaded.

Then there is the view among some environmentalists who simply see discussions about demography as a tactical error. This position identifies encouraging trends and argues with considerable Pollyannaish optimism that, left alone, a steady reduction in future birthrates can be expected. An open societal debate over demographic policies could become a boomerang, politicizing individual decisions about family planning and undermining progress in the very natal-enthusiastic sectors targeted.[30] At the very least, the issue must be approached "obliquely."[31]

The truth is that Israel finds itself in a social and environmental crisis that is largely the result of its steadily escalating numbers. Rapid demographic growth exacerbates the poverty and inequality that have reached unprecedented dimensions in Israel. While public protesters demand social change, and while government ministries suggest sundry solutions, the proposed responses ultimately only address symptoms. The proximate cause of Israel's ailing social predicament is overpopulation: crowded classrooms, crowded hospitals, crowded highways, and crowded courtrooms are all manifestations of an infrastructure unable to keep pace with growing demand. The single greatest predictor of poverty in Israel is family size. While there are many instances in which the country may eventually be able to "catch up" and close this infrastructure gap, there are many instances in which resulting damage is irreversible.

Most ecological indicators show mounting contamination, dwindling natural resources, and a collapse of biodiversity—all of which are associated with population pressures. Data confirm that this tiny land, half the size of Costa Rica, is increasingly unable to support the growing number of people who live there. Today, Israel grows fewer than half the calories required to feed its citizens.[32] The depletion of natural resources, from groundwater to the Dead Sea— even sands that are mined for building roads or apartments—cries out that Israel exceeds local carrying capacity. With increasingly fragmented habitats due to steady encroachment by humans, the country's unique mammal, reptile, and amphibian wildlife may never recover. An increasing number of environmental conflicts involve dynamics in which sprawling populations face a variety of environmental insults, hazards, and nuisances.[33] During rush hours, commuters crawl at speeds approaching seven kilometers an hour, costing the country an estimated 20 billion shekels a year.[34] As more and more people seek housing and jobs, development comes at a price, with the sheer density literally sabotaging quality of life.

The damage to the landscape, natural resources, and general ambience has repercussions far beyond Israel's borders. It is important to remember that Israel is no ordinary land but one that is considered holy by billions of people around the planet. It is not just Israelis who are losing something profoundly meaningful when asphalt and concrete slowly erase a landscape that inspired prophets and pilgrims for millennia.

The trouble is . . . the decimation has just begun. One of the central metaphors that sustainable-population advocates employ to get people to think about exponential growth was promoted by the late University of Colorado physicist Albert Bartlett, involving a hypothetical strain of bacteria that divides into two every sixty seconds. Bartlett presented this thought exercise over seventeen hundred times to audiences around the world.[35] He described, a single bacterium put in a bottle at 11:00 A.M. Doubling every minute, within an hour the bottle is completely filled up. The first question Bartlett would ask is "When is the bottle half full?" Intuitively, many people would answer 11:30. But of course the correct response is at 11:59. The even more troubling query is "At one point might a bacterium start to realize that it is running out of space?" For most, who do not spend too much time thinking about the future, it might be around 11:58, when the bottle is 25 percent full, but by then it would be too late to organize the necessary changes for stabilization. It is unlikely that even the most prescient bacteria would realize they have a problem at five minutes before noon—when the bottle is only 3 percent full and 97 percent of the bottle is available, just waiting to be filled![36]

The parallel to Israeli demography is self-evident. Hebrew University professor Sergio DellaPergola is arguably Israel's foremost demographic expert. DellaPergola has been tracking population trends in Israel and the Jewish world for almost fifty years. His projections suggest that even if families miraculously moved overnight to "replacement levels" of two children, given the young age of Israelis (due to previous high birthrates), its population would still double.[37] Indeed, ten years after first running sophisticated population models in 2003, he stands by his predictions that show a very likely scenario of 23 million Jews and Palestinians by 2050; a higher, plausible scenario could reach 36 million people.[38] As Israelis begin to question the wisdom of obsessively pro-natal policies, they should at least be aware that population momentum alone means that today's existing density will soon double.

This book, therefore, seeks to answer the question that Dan Perry urged society to confront two decades ago. What should Israel's demographic objectives be, and what public policies are needed to attain them? It argues that while Israel has made remarkable efforts to accommodate its growing population, this extraordinary demographic expansion is ultimately unsustainable. Both the pace of demographic increase and the absolute pressures it creates produce pernicious social pathologies and egregious environmental impacts. It is time for a dispassionate evaluation of Israel's demographic policies; it is time to answer some hard questions.

The subsequent chapters in this book consider the implications of Israel's rapidly expanding population. What forces and policies have driven local demographic growth, and what are the dynamics behind the high fertility rates in the country's different ethnic and religious communities? If population cannot grow forever, how should the optimal size of Israel's population be determined? And what is worth leaning from other countries' public policies targeting demography? A critical issue involves the status of women in Israel and how it affects family-planning decisions. It is time to ask what changes are required to bring Israel onto a sustainable demographic course.

It is not surprising that the pathology of overpopulation in Israel is an extremely complicated one. It involves economics, religious norms, cultural traditions, national conflicts, gender inequalities, and of course politics. In a multicultural society, there is no single "story" that explains why people have so many children or why Jews choose to move to Israel. Any proposals need to be cognizant and sensitive to the values and traditions of disparate communities. To the extent possible, the demographic policy debate should seek to prevent the infiltration of the societal tensions, prejudices, and malice that make Israeli political discourse so toxic.

The complexities make any blueprint for progress particularly thorny. But this in no way means the problem should not be confronted and that solutions don't exist. International experience offers a rich menu of interventions and cautionary tales for addressing rapid population growth that have proven to be successful, empowering women and bettering societies. There are innumerable cases around the world where policies have been effective, and many are instructive. An informed and dynamic society can save itself from demographic disaster.

——◆——

OF POLLUTION, PAUCITY, AND
POPULATION PRESSURES

Overconsumption and overpopulation underlie every
environmental problem we face today.
—Jacques-Yves Cousteau

TONE IT DOWN

Senior Israeli police officers were bemused at the end of 2012 when they evaluated the criminal complaints filed during the year. One out of every four Israelis who submitted a formal grievance at a police station complained about noise pollution. As cities and towns swelled to new population densities, and as apartment residents huddled together ever tighter, unprecedented numbers of Israelis decided that the racket made by their neighbors had reached levels that were not only intolerable but unlawful. On three hundred thousand occasions the police sent out mobile units to investigate the commotions.[1] By way of context, there were over one hundred times more complaints requesting relief from noise disturbances than those directed against the next most vexing environmental problem: littering.

Noise has always been ranked by Israelis as the most bothersome environmental nuisance,[2] but the new dimensions of discomfort are unprecedented. "Israel's police force working on its own is unable to withstand this burden," explained Yitzhak Aharonovitch, then minister of internal security, apologizing for the apparent impotence of his law enforcers. "Police patrols cannot successfully arrive at every call and citizens simply suffer."

Seasonal timing offers an important insight into the cause of the phenomenon. It turns out that the public's affliction with noise pollution peaks between the months of May and October. These are warm months, when windows open to catch the occasional breeze and children are on vacation, taking leave of their packed apartments. Restless from the time indoors, they pour onto teeming sidewalks and streets. The timing suggests that noise pollution is one of the predictable results of crowded conditions, which have come to characterize life in modern Israel. Sociological research in Israel's cities confirms that there is a correlation between the frequency of a given noise exposure and the degree to which it is considered annoying.[3]

Israelis are living in closer quarters than ever before. At the new densities, there is an extremely fine line between reasonable human behavior and a nuisance. Israel's demographic growth pushes hundreds of thousands of citizens every year into unpleasant and sometimes confrontational situations with their noisy neighbors. The associated stress should surprise no one.

Literally hundreds of animal experiments show the negative effects of living under congested conditions and the resulting anxiety and aggressive behaviors.[4] Humans are also animals. There are numerous cross-cultural studies[5] that show that while some people successfully develop coping mechanisms, a positive correlation exists between crowding and human hostility and violence.[6] There is some evidence suggesting that the response to crowding is gender-specific. Faced with crowded environments, women are more likely to be depressed or to withdraw from social interactions, while males tend to respond more aggressively.[7] In settings from prisons[8] to homes,[9] overcrowding invariably creates stress and produces a high degree of irritability. Complaining about noise can actually be seen as a civilized response to the resulting frustration.

Problems caused by demographic pressures are often divided into social and environmental categories. In fact, many nuisances, like noise pollution or transportation gridlock, have interwoven social and environmental dimensions. They represent two sides of the same coin. For other hazards, the distinction is clearer. Production of garbage and greenhouse gas emissions, like the loss of biodiversity and open spaces, are part of Israel's present *environmental* crisis, caused primarily by demographic pressures. Overloaded schools, hospitals, courts, and roads, along with the lack of affordable housing, the growth of poverty, and income inequality are but a sampling of the related *social* problems to be discussed in the next chapter.

Regardless of their classification, when these social and environmental maladies are added up, the unavoidable conclusion is that a tipping point exists separating positive and negative demographic conditions. The dividing line is sometimes defined vaguely in physical terms as "carrying capacity." Whatever the line may be, in Israel it has long since been crossed. A review of these trends and their distinct (and aggregate) impacts suggests that Israel's environment already suffers acutely from population pressures that are only getting worse.

GARBAGE OUT

When Tel Aviv's citizens filed suit against the city's repulsive garbage dump in 1950, it was the first case of environmental litigation in the country's history. The municipal government realized things had to change. After consultation with the nascent Ministry of Health, the municipality eventually began to cart the city's three hundred daily tons of trash for disposal several kilometers to the east, on top of an abandoned village called Hiriya. By and by, Tel Aviv's population grew, so that in 1997 the entire metropolitan region was dumping three thousand tons of garbage a day on the site.[10] During the intervening years, a sixty-meter-high mountain of trash arose in the heart of Israel's coastal plains. Its leachate contaminated underlying groundwater. There were frequent fires at the site, and the resulting odors were a nuisance to thousands of residents who lived in the vicinity.

Eventually, it was not the mountain's instability nor the pollution but danger to air traffic from birds feasting on the rubbish that forced the closing of the facility. Birds were occasionally "sucked" into the engines of airplanes arriving at nearby Ben Gurion Airport, turning the landfill into a disaster in the making.[11] In 1998 Hiriya was officially declared to be full. But then a political struggle ensued about the fate of the site. After prolonged confrontation between environmental groups and land developers, it was decided that the old dump would eventually be converted into a park and an environmental education center rather than a commercial or apartment complex. The story ostensibly had a happy ending: in November 2004 plans for the Ariel Sharon Park were approved.

The problem, however, did not go away; there was still no alternative burial space for garbage within a hundred kilometers. The lion's share of Tel Aviv's trash was now transported down to the Dudaim landfill in the Negev desert.[12] Unfortunately, its capacity was also finite and projections at the time suggested that it would fill up within twenty years. Increasingly, entrepreneurial *pirate* operations carted the growing quantities of Israeli trash to Palestinian sites on the West Bank.[13]

Israel's solid-waste profile offers just one example of the environmental side of the overpopulation debit sheet and its synergistic interface with consumption patterns. Even though Israel enacted a "recycling law" in 1993,[14] the country still buries some 80 percent of its garbage.[15] This creates a significant problem.

In 2002, Israel's Ministry of Environmental Protection introduced a national strategy for managing solid waste that sounded the alarm: "Today, there exists a shortage in the available and approved burial space for 3,000 tons of garbage a day. . . . If all the solid waste were buried in institutionally approved garbage sites today, the available sites would be exhausted by 2003. The addition of two large sites, like the Efeh site planned for the Rotem Plains, has a capacity of 25 million tons. This will allow only adequate burial volume until the year 2008."[16] More than a decade since the landfill shortage was officially acknowledged, the amount of garbage produced by Israelis has increased at a rate of 3–5 percent a year.

An external international evaluation of Israel's waste management in 2011 offered a global context: "Population growth and rising standards of living resulted in a 15% increase in municipal waste generation during the last decade. The 610 kg of solid waste generated per capita per year is well above the OECD and OECD Europe averages."[17]

While conventional wisdom has for some time claimed that "solid waste" was a consumption problem and that wealthy Israeli communities are the main perpetrators of excessive trash generation, this turns out be imprecise and constitutes an overstatement. A recent, in-depth analysis of the solid-waste-disposal patterns in Israel's cities reached a different conclusion: "Regression analysis reveals that aggregate per-capita waste outputs of cities are only vaguely correlated with their socio-economic indicators. In fact, the apparent 'hedonic' waste of the richest cities, compared with the average ones, accounts for only about 2% of the total waste production."[18]

Idit El-Hasid, a solid waste "maven" and one of the country's leading "garbologists," is in charge of the new environmental education center at Hiriya. El-Hasid describes the throwaway epidemic affecting all sectors of Israeli society this way:

> We would have assumed that the Haredim [Israel's ultra-Orthodox] don't fall into the consumption trap, but Haredi society uses tremendous quantities of disposable items: cups, tablecloths, cutlery, diapers, aluminum pans. Bnei Brak, where garbage cans were for years a bastion of organic waste, has turned into an 'empire' of stores for disposable dishes that find their way into the garbage. A Shabbat meal is set on a disposable tablecloth, with disposable dishes, and at the end the housewife wraps everything in a disposable tablecloth, turns it into a garbage bag and throws it out. The same is true of Arab society and everywhere where women are trying to deal with the heavy burden of caring for a large family.[19]

Empirically, rich or poor, more people means more trash.

As they fill up, landfills are abandoned and Israel's municipal governments move on to the next location, vaguely aware that this strategy cannot go on forever. Although there is an expectation that closed sites should be rehabilitated, it has been difficult to enforce the high expense of environmental restoration. The many deserted garbage dumps offer a vulgar monument to a culture of consumption, fueled by steady demographic growth. At most recent count, only ten sites have been rehabilitated while another thirty are waiting.[20]

PARADISE LOST

Henry Baker Tristram was an eccentric British priest who visited Palestine on four separate occasions between the years 1858 and 1881. Tristram was a *reasonable* man of the cloth, but an *extraordinary* naturalist and prolific writer. As he traversed Ottoman Palestine he meticulously recorded the numerous creatures that he stumbled upon, many identified for the very first time. (Half a dozen of the bird species that he discovered and a few gerbils bear his name.) Then he returned to England and set about documenting his findings. Together these five voluminous tomes form a treasure chest of descriptions, drawings, and observations.[21] Sadly, today they mostly tell us what we have lost.

More than a century later in England, an important landmark in the international strategy to preserve global biodiversity involved the identification and demarcation of global "biodiversity hotspots." In 2000, a team from Oxford University published an article in the journal *Nature* mapping 12 percent of the planet that it recommended for preservation because the lands contained such a high percentage of the world's species. The natural world Tristram described lies entirely within the "Mediterranean Basin" prioritized for preservation.[22]

Prior to Israel's independence, unregulated hunting was rampant, leading to the disappearance of such species as cheetahs, crocodiles, and bears. But for the past sixty years, the State of Israel has made exceptional efforts to protect the 115 mammal species, 103 kinds of reptiles, 534 bird types, and 2,780 species of flowering plants it inherited.[23] A national master plan was enacted that designated almost a quarter of the country for nature reserves;[24] in 1995 an additional 10 percent of lands were zoned as forest; an extensive list of "protected natural assets" was assembled and afforded legal protection. A Nature and Parks Authority was established with the requisite manpower and legal authorities to pursue an ambitious preservation strategy.

Sadly, these bold measures do not seem to be enough. All recent surveys suggest that the vast majority of identifiable trends among flora and fauna populations in Israel are negative. When the OECD summed up the available data in

Habitat loss brings Israel's remarakble biodiversity to the brink.
(Photographs courtesy of Uri Shanas)

2011, it concluded that 33 percent of the country's vertebrate species were endangered, with particularly high losses among amphibian and mammal populations. More than half of the thirty-four species now listed as extinct used to live in the country's wetlands environment.[25] As humans increasingly filled the land and drained the swamps, 97 percent of these aquatic habitats were erased forever.[26]

When dire prospects for nature in Israel are compared with statistics in other countries, the role of population densities becomes self-evident. Israel has fifty-six mammal species that are threatened with extinction today. This is more than double those found in the vast and largely empty continent of Australia, which has only twenty-four endangered mammals, or the United States, with only seventeen. Nineteen Israeli bird species are dwindling and are on track to disappear. This is almost 50 percent more than endangered species in the massive United States (twelve species) or Australia (thirteen).

Although Israel signed the *United Nations Convention on Biological Diversity* and even adopted a National Biodiversity Strategy and Action Plan in 2010,[27] these formal commitments remain empty declarations that do little to stem the tide. Direct interactions with humans is not the only cause of nature's woes.

Indirect drivers also contribute, but ultimately, they are all associated with human activities. They include the crowding out of native plants and animals by invasive species and illegal hunting. Yet these are still not sufficiently widespread to lead to extinctions. *The central problem in Israel is loss of habitat, supplanted by people and development.*

The OECD analyzed the Israeli dynamics in its 2011 report: "Habitat fragmentation is mainly attributable to construction, infrastructure development and agricultural activities. Israel's population is projected to increase by 1.8% annually and to triple by 2050. Demographic changes are leading to increased demand for new dwellings and for more floor space. Taken together, these effects are increasing demand for new construction. Most of the construction is likely to take place in the non-desert areas which host higher amounts of Israel's biodiversity."[28]

One example of the shape of things to come is the mutually exclusive trade-offs between human population growth and Israeli wildlife, which is being played out in the young city of Modi'in. The city is set on the hills where, in 167 B.C., a four-year rebellion by the heroic Maccabees was launched against the occupying Greek regime. Its success is commemorated each year in Hanukah celebrations around the world. The town's convenient access to Jerusalem in the east—and Tel Aviv in the opposite direction—along with relatively moderate real estate prices makes it a particularly attractive community. Founded in 1996, in fewer than twenty years the city became home to eighty thousand residents.

Modi'in is located in the heart of Israel's crowded central region and fills an enormous swath of land that used to provide precious habitat to the country's idiosyncratic mix of African, Asian, and European mammals and reptiles. The hills just south of the city still constitute a critical ecological corridor for a rich variety of animals.[29] On any given morning, the quiet visitor can enjoy a *safari-worthy* display of gazelles, porcupines, and even the odd hyena. Little wonder: with a hermetically sealed fence separating Israel and Palestine to the east, and the urban barrier of stone and asphalt to the west, wildlife is increasingly squeezed into this tiny sliver of the Judean foothills, which may soon disappear.

Their future is grim. Haim Bibas was elected mayor of Modi'in in 2008 on an optimistic platform of development, defeating a candidate deemed to be somewhat more environmentally friendly. Yet during his first term as mayor, the young politician made his peace with the city's strong environmental community and local chapter of the Society for Protection of Nature in Israel (SPNI), the country's largest green NGO. Bibas has come to appreciate the unique ecological endowment that surrounds the city and sees it as a valued resource. But he tries to be pragmatic, caught in a seemingly insoluble dilemma.

If it was up to me—I would stop the city's growth at 120,000 people and not even touch the southern hills. They are magnificent. But I'm a realist and I know that in the not so distant future, a whole lot of people are going to want to move to Modi'in. And there's nothing that I, nor green advocates, can do to stop this. People need to live somewhere and in a democracy that means that a city like Modi'in is going to keep growing. So my suggestion to environmentalists is to try to prioritize what you might be able to protect. There will be 250,000 people in Modi'in before long. If we're pragmatic today, maybe we can save something for the future.[30]

Modi'in's situation is symptomatic of numerous other sites in Israel, like the cities of Beit Shemesh, Elad, or Jerusalem where population pressures threaten to destroy lovely landscapes and critical habitats. The SPNI recently published *Threats, 2013*, its most recent catalog of the 119 top menaces to Israel's open spaces.[31] This was during the heart of the national election campaign. Unfortunately, the warning went almost unnoticed by the competing political parties. The report describes development projects that would destroy extraordinarily diverse national treasures—from Mediterranean beaches to the Galilee hills to the scattered lonely vistas of the Negev desert.

The growing number of people and the development needed to support them are slowly but steadily devouring the lovely countryside that makes the land of Israel a magical, edifying place and a home to rich ecological communities. Just to provide the annual demand for 60 million tons of raw materials for construction and road pavement requires 1,450 dunams of open spaces each year.[32] Shortages are just a matter of time.

The population pressures not only leave little nature available for animals but also for human beings. By ten in the morning on major national holidays, the media broadcast the long list of nature reserves and forests that are already full to capacity.[33] Authorities beseech the public seeking a bit of respite from their jam-packed cities to simply stay away. Even before the 119 natural wonders cited by the SPNI are destroyed, there is not enough nature to go around.

GROWING GREENHOUSE GAS EMISSIONS

In December 2009, as part of the UN Convention on Climate Change, representatives of the international community assembled in Copenhagen. Israel participated in this international forum of 192 nations, including 115 heads of state. The goal was to chart a path toward global atmospheric stability. Expectations had been high for a dramatic breakthrough that would finally lead to progress.[34] On December 17, Israeli President Shimon Peres took the rostrum.

As part of its responsibility to global sustainability, Israel was expected to present the conference with a summary of its future, internal policies to mitigate global warming. In truth, the actual measures being considered were still amorphous. There had been unceasing haggling between officials on the Israeli delegation from the Ministry of Finance (who were evasive) and those from the Ministry of Environmental Protection (who were enthusiastic). Nothing had been resolved. So the president simply took matters into his own hands. Reading from a text, he called for action: "Copenhagen is a hope," Peres intoned. "It has to be realized. . . . Dear friends: In the Mediterranean, a growing population meets declining resources. The population has tripled from 150 million to over 400 [million] in thirty years. Water is diminishing. Energy is polluting."

After self-congratulatory comments about Israeli technological innovations in water and electrical cars, Israel's president got down to business, promising "By 2020, the government of Israel intends to make best efforts to reduce its CO_2 emissions by 20 percent compared to a business as usual scenario."[35]

To outsiders, it seemed that Israel was "stepping up to the plate" to do its part in the international efforts to address the planet's paramount ecological challenge. In fact, Peres's speech has come to represent a low point of hypocrisy in Israeli environmental diplomacy. Despite lip service to the significance of global warming, the rate of the country's greenhouse gas emissions is increasing and remains among the highest in the world.[36]

In 1992 when the *UN Framework Convention on Climate Change* was drafted in Rio de Janeiro, Israel choose to classify itself as a "developing country" and has clung to this status ever since, its economic prosperity notwithstanding.[37] This means that any promises to reduce emissions only constitute a voluntary commitment, anyway. The convention's Kyoto Protocol does not require mitigation activities from developing countries—only monitoring.

The "business as usual" scenario to which President Peres referred was based on projections made for the Israeli government just a few months earlier by McKinsey & Company, a leading international consulting agency.[38] The report, hastily prepared for the Copenhagen meeting, documented Israel's growing greenhouse emissions. It calculated that "business as usual" would result in a doubling of greenhouse gas emissions by the year 2030. The report explained that this increase was "higher than other developed countries, primarily due to Israel's relatively high growth in population and GDP per capita." At best, even fairly heroic policy interventions, involving low carbon energy sources and improved energy efficiency, meant that Israel would "only" *increase* its emissions by a third during a period when the international community expected countries to meaningfully *reduce* emissions. The relentless anticipated population growth, which in recent years held steady at 1.8 percent, would mean that the country had to run to stay in place. In other words, if over the next ten years, Israel could manage to curb "consumption" and increase energy efficiency by an impressive 20 percent (as Peres promised), the concomitant rise in population would erase any improvement.

Of course, the high-minded promises of Copenhagen were soon forgotten. But a modest program of loans along with investments in energy efficiency and renewable energy was adopted by an intergovernmental committee. Soon thereafter, however, in the face of a 2013 budgetary crisis, the program was frozen. The sad fact is that since 2009, energy demand has not gone down by 20 percent—but has actually increased by more than 20 percent within six short years.[39] Israel's Ministry of Energy and Water Resources now predicts a doubling of electricity demand within twenty years, a rate far faster than the McKinsey report had predicted. And because of the high relative costs of solar energy and low political will, as of 2015 Israel's renewable energy portfolio was stuck below 2 percent.[40] This embarrassing chapter in international double-talk highlights the fact that while changing consumption patterns are surely critical to improving Israel's environmental performance, it is not enough.

There are some environmentalists in the "consumption camp" that challenge the significance of population growth and constantly point to the higher carbon footprint of affluent Israeli families, who fly abroad, own multiple cars, and enjoy an electrical appliance–intensive lifestyle.[41] The consumption advocates call for "disaggregation" of the causes of environmental impacts to better identify those that are caused by rising population and those exacerbated by affluence and consumption.[42]

In fact, both overconsumption and overpopulation contribute to Israel's massive environmental degradation. Paul Ehrlich, the great Stanford ecologist, has compared the false dilemma implicit in spats over the relative importance of consumption versus population to a rectangle. It doesn't really matter which of the two sides are longer than the other two—the area in the figure remains the same.[43]

Individual perspective and bias drive selection of the relevant criterion for determining environmental performance. For instance, organic loadings in sewage (measured by biological oxygen demand) or disposable diapers are more affected by population growth than by consumption, as there are physical limits to how often even wealthy people go to the bathroom. Those who argue that "consumption is the problem," prefer to emphasize greenhouse gas emissions as the problem. In fact, statistics suggest otherwise.

Israel's Central Bureau of Statistics meticulously measures myriad environmental parameters and conforms to the United Nations' monitoring protocols regarding greenhouse gas emissions. While overall greenhouse gas emissions continue to rise—increasing 23 percent, from 62 million tons in 1996 to 76 million in 2010—per capita emissions during the same period actually dropped by 10 percent: from 11 tons per person to 10.[44] During this time, Israel's population grew from 5.6 million people to 7.5 million people, an increase of 34 percent. In other words, Israelis made some progress in adopting conservation measures, and the fleet efficiency of its cars improved. This led to a per capita drop in greenhouse gas emissions. But it did not affect the overall trend: the steady increase in Israel's carbon footprint can be attributed almost entirely to demographic growth. Indeed, Israel's Ministry of Energy and Water Web site attributes the increase in the country's electricity demand first and foremost to the expanding population, not its buying power.

Israel may want to continue to pursue a path of least resistance on climate policy, but it is unlikely that the OECD will allow it to do so.[45] As part of the preparations to the 2015 international gathering in Paris, the government submitted a plan to the *United Nations Framework Convention on Climate Change*, which pledged a 26 percent reduction below 2005 levels in greenhouse gas by the year 2030. It is not at all clear whether this goal of reducing 7.7 tons of CO_2 equivalent in per capita emissions will be more conscientiously pursued than previous empty promises.[46] The recent discovery of natural gas will slow some of the projected greenhouse increase, even as natural gas production has its own carbon footprint[47] and the methane associated with its production has a "carbon equivalent" twenty-three times higher than that of carbon dioxide.[48] Best estimates suggest that Israel will have to cut back even further. As voluntary lifestyle changes are unlikely to happen by themselves, taxes associated with inducing reduced carbon emissions will disproportionately fall on poor populations. When climate change policy makers in Israel are honest, they admit that population growth makes it almost impossible to become a responsible player in the world community.

HYDROLOGICAL OVERDRAFT

Israel is located in a region characterized by water scarcity. Malin Falkenmark, the Swedish hydrologist, wrote a report in 1976 that calculated that people need one thousand cubic meters of water (1 million liters) a year.[49] Countries that did not have rainfall sufficient to supply that level were characterized as suffering from "water scarcity." (Those that have seventeen hundred cubic meters a year were merely "water stressed.") In the Middle East, nine out of the fourteen nations have the parched status of "water-scarce countries." Israel is one of them.

In Biblical days, the young former shepherd David evaded a vengeful King Saul by hiding in the caves around the Ein Gedi oasis near the banks of the Dead Sea (1 Samuel 24:1). A thousand years later, King Herod, the prolific builder and despotic king, erected his magnificent Masada palace, which towered over its shoreline, as a highly fortified spa and resort.[50] For millennia, the deep blue waters encircled by the majestic dolomite and limestone cliffs offered inspirational scenery. But if these protagonists of old were to see the present condition of the Dead Sea, they would be aghast.

The "Dead Sea" has always been something of a misnomer. The "sea" is actually only a moderately sized, hypersaline lake. But it has characteristics so extraordinary that it was a finalist in the recent global vote selecting the "New 7 Wonders of Nature."[51] Located at the lowest point on the planet, with 33.7 percent salt content, the Dead Sea purportedly is also the saltiest water body in the world, containing water with ten times the salt concentration of the oceans. There is no misnomer associated with the adjective "dead," however. The hypersaline concentration makes the marine environment intolerable for almost all aquatic organisms, save some trace amounts of extremely hearty bacteria and microbial fungi.

Tragically, due to decades of abuse and demographic pressures, the Dead Sea seems to be disappearing. A third of the water is already gone, and during the coming decades another third will surely vanish.[52] The sea is dependent on Jordan River water, which receives the overflow from the Kinneret Lake in the Galilee. The River Jordan was never really chilly and wide, and it was always a little bit salty for freshwater. When it poured into the terminal lake, the scorching desert climate—over time—caused massive evaporation, leaving a salty broth of minerals.

Today, tourists on both the Israeli and Jordanian sides of the lake enjoy the salubrious properties of the mud and mineral-rich waters. The Dead Sea is a prized destination for people seeking treatment for dermatological conditions such as psoriasis and atopic dermatitis. This is because the exceptionally low altitude along with the scorching sun provide patients the ultraviolet rays they need to keep such diseases in remission, while naturally filtering out more damaging radiation. The elevated salt concentrations increase buoyancy so much that visitors can literally sit in the water and read a newspaper, creating the most popular selfie snapped by tourists in the Holy Land.[53] Many do not realize that this enormous saline bathtub is rapidly shrinking.

The 1960s saw the establishment of the National Water Carrier in response to the country's insatiable demand for water. For the past fifty years, the Kinneret hasn't really been sharing any of its water with the Jordan River, pumping all surplus waters from the lake directly into the pipeline and the national water grid. The carrier delivered the flow as irrigation and drinking water for the country's growing agricultural and urban centers, as far south as the highlands of the Negev desert.[54] Very often, during drought years, when there was no surplus water available, overpumping occurred. When too much water is drawn from the lake, water quality and aquatic life suffer. Due to the recent climate-change-induced drought, the past decade has seen the lowest levels ever recorded in this recreationally and spiritually significant water body.

Israel is not the only country that has been siphoning water away from the Lower Jordan River and the Dead Sea. During the past sixty years other riparian nations—Syria and Jordan—also witnessed astonishing population growth. Jordan's population has increased from fewer than .5 million in 1950 to 7.6 million people today; Syria's increased from 3.4 to over 20 million before the outbreak of its civil war.[55] This demographic surge was immediately translated into a amplified demand for water. Syria constructed dams along the watershed to the Yarmuk River and virtually emptied this major tributary of the watershed. The Hashemite Kingdom of Jordan, one of the most water-scarce nations on earth, captures whatever flow is left in Jordan for use by its struggling farmers.[56] The River Jordan was left with less than a tenth of its original flow.

By the end of the 1970s the Dead Sea's shoreline had begun to drop noticeably.[57] Only a pitiful trickle of putrid sewage and irrigation runoff reached the lake, while evaporation continued unrelentingly. The Dead Sea's water level fell at an average rate of one meter per year.

Such crass and colossal interference with the natural hydrological cycles of the region produced "unexpected consequences." The most spectacular of these came in the form of some three thousand "sinkholes," which have turned the local landscape into a virtual Swiss cheese.[58] These massive gorges in the earth are caused by a drop in the groundwater levels around the Dead Sea and the dissolving of the underlying salt rock. The surface collapses into cavities that can be as wide as thirty meters and fifteen meters deep.[59] The phenomenon evokes epic biblical legends of the earth swallowing wayward humans (Numbers 16:31–34). Today's sinkholes not only constitute substantial safety hazards, but threaten the viability of the local tourist industry.[60]

There have been several plans for saving the Dead Sea. The most high-profile proposal involves building a massive canal or "conduit" from the Red Sea, designed to replace the deficit in the freshwater flow. A 2012 World Bank assessment estimated the costs of this project at a "mere" $10 billion. Moreover, the environmental impact assessment did little to dispel the concerns of environmentalists about the possible dangers of seismic instability and the resultant effect of such a megaproject on surface-water chemistry.[61]

Unregulated withdrawal from the Jordan River to supply the region's growing population is drying up the Dead Sea. An aerial view shows the extent of the waterline's recent retreat. (Photograph courtesy of EcoPeace Middle East)

Whether or not Jordan, Israel, or the international community can find this kind of money remains unclear. A 2015 agreement signed in Jordan between the Israeli and Jordanian governments suggests that they have every intention of trying.[62] It is clear, however, that no one has discussed the real, underlying reason why the Dead Sea has been transformed from an international treasure into a natural resource disaster area: the ecological balance of a lake is based on a delicate equilibrium. Like central Asia's vanishing Aral Sea, the steady disappearance of the Dead Sea and the associated environmental insults implicitly stand as a sad testament to Israel's and its neighbors' exceeding their hydrological carrying capacity. People need water, and the Jordan River flow has been diverted to meet this demand. When the number of people living in a water-scarce region increases by 1,000 percent, nature cannot keep up.

The Dead Sea is just one example of overpopulation's impact on Israel's water resources. There are many more. The hydrological history of the country can be seen in the context of a "frontier" paradigm. Israel brought a pioneering spirit to its water management strategy, in which it set out to subjugate the natural resources. As more and more people became water consumers, existing freshwater was stretched to the last drop. There was not enough. So the country began to recycle its sewage during the 1960s and today boasts an unprecedented 86 percent wastewater reuse rate,[63] supplying the majority of irrigation for farmers and adding some 50 percent to overall supply.[64] Notwithstanding additional improvements in Israeli irrigation techniques and local agricultural efficiency, these innovations still were not enough to satisfy the demands of an ever-growing population.[65] Water scarcity problems continued to grow worse.

The *Mountain Aquifer* offers another case illustrating the perilous dynamics of scarcity. This groundwater resource is shared by Israel and Palestine. It has had a sustainable yield of 350 million cubic meters of water a year.[66] The ongoing drop in rainfall reduced this. One analysis shows that the recharge rate in the Mountain Aquifer fell by 5–7 percent in recent years. Wellheads and the aquifer water table in the region south of Jerusalem (for example, the Herodian and Bani Naim wells) dropped by as much as thirty to sixty meters, leading to acute shortages in the greater Hebron region. In 2008 only 64 percent of the usual rain fell in the West Bank, creating the most serious groundwater shortfall of the past decade. Palestinian hydrologists estimated that the drought caused an estimated shortfall of 69 million cubic meters.[67]

The UN World Health Organization (WHO) recommends a minimum of fifty to one hundred liters of water per person a day.[68] Palestinian water availability varies greatly across the West Bank, but the per capita average is seventy-three liters per person per day.[69] This means that there are many communities that fall below minimum acceptable levels. Israelis developed other water resources and enjoy roughly three times Palestinian supply per capita. But they still live in a nation defined as "water-scarce."[70] While interim pre–peace agreements seek to manage aquifer sustainability, the growth in population on both sides makes the original allocations irrelevant. There simply isn't enough groundwater to go around. And every year, per capita availability drops 2.0 percent, commensurate with the increase in population size.[71]

The only major freshwater resource that Israel enjoys that is essentially not transboundary and shared with neighbors is also its largest. The *Coastal Aquifer* runs beneath Israel's crowded coastal corridor, from Haifa to the Israeli border with the Gaza Strip. Dr. Sara Elchanani, the head of the Government Hydrological Service, recently reported that a full tenth of this aquifer is polluted from human activities, most notably salinization from overpumping. This constitutes a loss of 4,100 billion liters of water, which are forfeited for the foreseeable future.[72] For decades, water managers drew down the groundwater levels to meet the country's insatiable demands, and seawater from the Mediterranean rushed in to fill the resulting "vacuum."[73] Hundreds of wells were decommissioned due to the ensuing salinization. Unfortunately, this is just the tip of the iceberg. Israel's Ministry of Environmental Protection reports that thirty-three hundred sites were identified where soil is significantly contaminated with pollutants likely to corrupt the underlying groundwater in the future.

In 2002, the impending shortages pushed Israel's cabinet to reach a decision to build a series of four desalination facilities on the Mediterranean coastline. The project has changed Israel's "hydrological profile." The new facilities now provide 50 percent of Israel's annual freshwater supply and virtually all of its drinking water.[74] Most of the country's water is no longer transported from the north to the thirsty south and central regions.

This good news has some drawbacks, however. Desalination plants are energy intensive and contribute to even greater greenhouse gas emissions. (Some 3.5 kilowatt hours of energy are required to produce one thousand liters of water. The basic formula is that that each new desalination plant increases national electricity demand by 1 percent.). Technology appears to have provided a way out, at least temporarily, for Israeli domestic water use. But it makes Israel's water system highly vulnerable to terrorist or military actions that target infrastructure. Water prices have also become dependent on international energy markets. Most agricultural operations cannot afford the high cost of desalinated water and must depend on effluents, containing high levels of sodium, that cause long-term damage to the soil.[75] The Dead Sea will probably go on dying, as the Jordan River waters will be completely exploited. In the meantime, the collective thirst of Israel and its neighbors is only expected to increase upstream.

POPULATION GROWTH AND ELUSIVE ENVIRONMENTAL PROGRESS

Even if Israel's population had not grown geometrically, local ecological conditions today would hardly be pristine. Under ideal circumstances, it is very difficult to overcome millennia of neglect, desertification, and degradation and move toward meaningful ecological restoration. Like many other Israeli environmental problems—from pesticide exposures and hazardous chemicals to electromagnetic radiation and industrial meat production—incremental and site-specific progress can be made. It may be possible to temporarily reduce noise, garbage, water, and air pollution through greater societal commitment and smarter policies.

Nonetheless, two sobering facts are worth considering: if Israel were to consist of 2 million people today rather than 8 million, its environment would not be facing a crisis of significant dimensions. And without stable demographic conditions, it is unlikely that its environmental problems can be solved.

3

OF IMPAIRED PUBLIC SERVICES, POVERTY, AND POPULATION PRESSURES

I've never seen a problem that wouldn't be easier to solve with
fewer people, or harder, and ultimately impossible, with more.
—Sir David Attenborough, "Population Overload," BBC *Focus*

KEEPING UP

In a very small country, it is not just the magnitude but the swiftness of the
change that matters. Many of Israel's most pernicious problems can be traced
to the pace of demographic growth in Israel. In their book *The Stork and the
Plow*, Stanford ecologists Paul and Anne Ehrlich along with Gretchen Daily ask
rhetorically how life would be affected in the United States if the population
doubled every twenty-five years as it does in Africa: "In essence, every facility
the U.S. has for support of human life would need to be duplicated in a generation. We'd need to grow and process twice as much food and draw twice as
much fresh water. The number of physicians and teachers would need to be
doubled, as would the capacities of hospitals, schools and colleges. The capacities of highways, railroads and airlines would need to double. So would the number of homes, offices buildings, stores and theaters. So would the capacity of
the economy to absorb young workers."[1]

This scenario describes dynamics that have characterized Israel's brief history. Only worse: the country has had to face even faster doubling rates. The
effects are devastating, undermining heroic efforts across the land to build a
model, equitable society with a high quality of life for all inhabitants. There are
many social manifestations of Israel's high and growing density. Five striking
examples demonstrate the profound impact of Israel's phenomenal demographic

growth on society, its institutions, and quality of life: *transportation, housing, education, health, and poverty.*

GRIDLOCK AND AFFORDABLE HOUSING:
THE FUTILITY OF SUPPLY-DRIVEN POLICIES

Many environmentalists see transportation as essentially an environmental challenge due to the air pollution from mobile sources and the toll that highway construction takes on open spaces. Medical professionals certainly see the broad range of respiratory and other health insults caused by air pollution. The exceptionally high asthma and cancer rates in Israel's major cities can be traced in a large part to emissions from the many motor vehicles that crowd streets each day.[2]

But transportation is about moving *people* around. Before anything else, Israel's chronic traffic jams are a compelling social and economic issue. Without reasonable mobility, people cannot get to work, they forfeit valuable family time, they are late to appointments, and they are chronically high-strung. Every country with urban centers suffers some levels of traffic congestion. Israelis suffer more. A 2007 United Nations study reported that Israel's roads were the most crowded of any Western country participating in the study.[3] There is not enough room on the country's twenty thousand kilometers of paved motorways for the millions of people who use them. And for commuters living in the greater Tel Aviv region, morning travel into the country's largest employment center creeps along at an average speed below ten kilometers an hour.[4]

As population increases, road congestion only grows worse. Every year some 280,000 *new* automobiles are sold to the expanding pool of drivers.[5] When the natural attrition of old cars is figured in, the growing fleet of almost 3 million vehicles[6] precisely reflects the 100,000 additional people living in Israel each year: roughly 140,000 births minus 40,000 deaths.[7] Politicians sit in traffic jams, too, and are well aware of the situation. Thus, the government invests hundreds of millions of shekels in road infrastructure each year to meet increased demand. On average, over five hundred kilometers of road have been paved or widened every year since 2008. This has come at the expense of open spaces and the habitat they provide.[8]

The investment does little to relieve conditions on the road, which despite isolated improvements overall only grow worse. In 2009, Israel's Central Bureau of Statistics counted 62,200 cars driving through the Ben Shemen junction each day on the Jerusalem–Tel Aviv highway. Just four years later, the figure jumped to 82,900. During this same period the number of cars driving on the roads

Gridlock nation: Tel Aviv daily commuters crawl, averaging fewer than ten kilometers
per hour. Government projections suggest that during the coming sixteen years,
Israelis will spend an additional sixty minutes a day in their cars due to increasingly
crowded roads. (Photograph courtesy of Transport Today & Tomorrow, 2015)

increased in all but two of the country's thirty-five major intersections monitored.[9]
The good news is that during the same period—almost without exception—the
rate of accidents went down at these junctions.[10] Some of the accidents prevented can be attributed to the growing congestion. Like it or not, caught in
traffic, the public drives a whole lot slower.

Israelis do love their cars, though: About 80 percent of the vehicles on the road
are private automobiles. One of the reasons for this is the perverse incentives
granted to car owners. Israeli public policy encourages private vehicle usage by
allowing a major portion of workers' salaries to include "car maintenance payments" exempt from full income taxes. Additionally, many "high-end" companies provide vehicles with free gas and maintenance as "perks" to favored
employees, thereby giving many families an extra car. Other family members
are often allowed to use the company vehicle. No parallel incentives exist to take
a bicycle to work, and the value of reimbursed bus fares comes to only a fraction of the private-vehicle subsidy. This lenient pro-car policy apparently is a

function of the government's desire to collect extraordinarily high import taxes for automobiles, bringing in billions of dollars each year to the national coffers.[11] The sad truth is that with the exception of several train lines, public transportation utilization on the whole is down.

To be fair, Israel's motorization rate is among the lowest in the Western world—less than European countries' and less than half of the United States'.[12] But then Israel is a very small country. The population density in the center and north means that any new roads will only allow a greater number of cars to reach bottlenecks that clog the entrances to the country's major cities and attractions. Driving to popular Galilee recreation spots on Friday afternoons before the weekend break or major holidays has become unbearable. The insufferable crawl of traffic into major cities, and rush hours that stretch on for much of the day lead to unconventional ideas, such as "levitating sky trains,"[13] the banning of trucks during rush hour,[14] and a new generation of congestion sensitive GPS apps.[15]

For decades, transportation experts as well as environmentalists have argued that Israel cannot pave its way out of gridlock. Any temporary relief created by new highways and roads will soon be filled by the new influx of drivers. The need for "demand management" is widely accepted. Yet most Israelis trying to address the issue understand the slogan only as a reference to congestion fees or increasing rail and bus capacity.

Transportation budgets must be completely realigned to prioritize public transportation and cycling infrastructure.[16] Policy tools, such as congestion tariffs that worked so successfully in London,[17] may help reduce traffic in Tel Aviv, Haifa, and Jerusalem. But it is time to recognize that not only do a higher percentage of Israelis own cars today than twenty years ago, but that there are a whole lot more Israelis. Demand management should also include a concerted effort to create public policies that stabilize the number of people driving on the road.

HOUSING SHORTAGES

The same narrow thinking that won't go beyond symptoms characterizes national discourse about the country's housing shortage. During the summer of 2011 over a million Israelis took to the streets and called for social justice. The protests were fueled by young people who simply could not afford to rent or purchase apartments in the Greater Tel Aviv region where they work or study. The shortage is very real. At the end of 2013, there were 2,411,000 apartments in Israel—and 2,526,000 households.[18] About a quarter of Israelis live in rented apartments.[19] Real estate prices increased all over the country during the previous decade. In 2015 alone, housing prices continued to rise on average by 4.4 percent,[20] a modest increase relative to 6.3 percent in 2012. The prediction is that they will double in a decade.[21] The rental market is no different: In 2013, tenants in the center of Israel were paying 50 percent more to their landlords on average than they had five years earlier.[22]

Working middle-class citizens, on whose shoulders the brunt of the country's tax and military burden rests, will be increasingly unable to buy apartments unless they receive massive help from their parents or win the lottery. This frustration was apparent during Israel's 2015 election campaign; the Kulanu party's success was not just due to the charismatic personality of its chair, Moshe Kahlon. Rather, it was his promise to reduce the costs of housing. An Israeli needs to pay 191 months of the average national salary to buy a five-room apartment, twice the salaries it takes in other OECD countries and six times higher than in Sweden.[23]

Once again, the government's knee-jerk response focused on increasing the supply of housing through an easing of procedural barriers. It sought to stream-

Construction in the Tel Aviv metropolitan area: Prices keep rising as a nation races to keep up with demand for sixty thousand to eighty thousand new residential units a year. (Photograph courtesy of Dani Machlis, Ben-Gurion University)

line the process for zoning changes and construction permit applications, but often without the proper oversight necessary to preserve open spaces and create green areas. This approach would presumably expand the available *supply* of statutorily approved available building sites, especially in the high-demand central region. Laws of supply and demand suggest that if cities could only build fast enough, lower prices would result.[24] The government has done its part by maintaining an extremely low interest rate for mortgages.[25]

One thing is clear. Demographic pressures may not be the only reason for the phenomenal increase in Israel's housing market, but they are the main one. If the population were stable, prices would be too. Like the shortage of roads, there is a clear cause for the country's housing crisis: the relentless, rising demand of 1 million new people every decade who need a place to live.

JUSTICE DELAYED

Israel's legal system usually is a source of pride among the public and enjoys respect around the world for its impartiality and commitment to human rights. Israel's judges are highly professional due to an appointment system that marginalizes politics and makes legal prowess and competence salient criteria for selection. Nonetheless, Israel's court system has been sick for some time.

Morris Ben-Atar was a respected and beloved judge in Jerusalem's local court. Ben-Atar immigrated to Israel from Rhodesia when he was nineteen and attended law school. After working in a private law firm, he sought a career change that would give him a greater sense of public service and satisfaction.[26] Ben-Atar was a thoughtful, scholarly man who took special interest in the details of his cases so that he could make fair rulings and reach constructive solutions. Unfortunately, doing a good job was not what the Israeli legal system expected from him. It needed him to act quickly and efficiently. This does not always mean acting justly. Every year the number of legal actions that reaches Israel's courts grows: in 2012 alone some seven hundred thousand suits were filed.[27] Judges are expected to reach decisions expeditiously—regardless of the results.

Ben-Atar was taken to task and later formally reprimanded by the director of the Israeli court system and by the chief justice in the Jerusalem magistrate court for taking too much time to reach verdicts. He spent even longer hours trying to catch up. Despite working late each night, every room in his house became stacked with files that continued to pour in. Ultimately, he found the Sisyphean task impossible. Unable to face the humiliation of resignation, in February 2011 the fifty-four-year-old judge chose to commit suicide by asphyxiation, leaving behind a note: "The workload has defeated me."[28]

The courts are so overloaded that a 2013 Ministry of Justice report calculates that litigants who file civil suits in district courts wait an average of 20.2 months before receiving a decision. (Criminal rulings are somewhat faster.) Guaranteed at least one appeal to the Supreme Court of Israel, they can expect an additional delay there of 21.6 months. Israel's chief justice, Asher Grunis, publicly expresses pride that this timetable actually represents progress. The reality is that it takes 3.5 years to be tried and appealed. Individuals who are on the wrong side of that average can wait 5 or 6 years until their claims are resolved.

To be sure, part of the reason that Israel's courts are clogged has to do with an increasingly litigious public and the surfeit of lawyers who need to generate billable hours. But the truth is that there are more people than ever who expect to be served by a legal system that is increasingly unable to ensure quality control. As the *quantity* of cases reaching the courts increases, it is inevitable that the *quality* of the decisions handed down will decline.

A 2011 report to Israel's Ministry of Justice by retired Supreme Court justice Eliezer Goldberg considered different bureaucratic options for reducing the burden on Israel's judges. The common denominator involves a reduction in the fairness offered the public seeking its day in court or the competency of judges hearing the cases. Justice Goldberg was remarkably forthright in summing up the problem: "When I look at the amount of cases in the system, I don't see how we can overcome it. A judge who looks at the quantity of cases he is facing becomes stressed."[29]

The upshot is that a growing number of cases are resolved by plea bargains or court-imposed agreements, which may or may not be equitable. Forced solutions based on superficial impressions and without the benefit of testimony are increasingly becoming the norm. Research by Haifa University professor, Oren Gazal-Ayal, reports that 86 percent of all criminal cases today are resolved by plea bargaining. This is among the highest rate in the world.[30] Gazal-Ayal warns about the number of innocent defendants who are pressured into confessions by the very justice system that is supposed to be protecting their rights.[31] Faced with long waits and impatient judges, many *innocent* defendants are convinced that confessing offers the best deal available.

It is hard to blame judges who face an unbearable load and cannot afford the patience to do the job right. They resolve cases the best they can, as quickly as they can. The result is a diminished level of justice, which impoverishes the soul of Israeli society. Yet even such assembly-line adjudication may be preferable to the alternative—the interminable waiting, which characterizes so many legal actions. Ultimately, "justice delayed is justice denied." The problem, of course, is that the legal infrastructure will need to continue to grow exponentially if it is to offer even the existing, degraded level of adjudication to the growing number of litigants.

CROWDED CLASSROOMS

Another calamitous outcome of rapid growth can be found in Israel's education system.[32] Traditionally, Jews always made learning a paramount value, and Israel's many scholars on the forefront of the sciences, technologies, and humanities is a source of enormous national pride.[33] When Israel joined the OECD in 2011, it was a validation that the country had come of age economically.[34] Industrialists and politicians appreciated the financial opportunities associated with membership in this elite club of nations. Social scientists also stood to benefit from the requisite data collection and improved ability to compare local conditions with those in the thirty-four other developed countries monitored by the OECD. But when the comparisons were made, Israel often came out poorly.

Israelis were taken aback when the first OECD education reports including Israel were published. One area of societal *failure* was particularly conspicuous: Israel's classrooms are among the most crowded in the developed world.[35] Its elementary schools have 28 children *on average* in classrooms—as opposed to OECD averages of 21.2. This is some 30 percent higher than the classroom density found in most developed countries. In a parallel study in *The Marker*, an Israeli economic magazine, only two countries—China and Chile—were worse.[36] The crowding in Israeli middle schools was even higher, with an average of 29 children per class, leaving Israel third from the bottom. While Israel is very proud of its early childhood education program, preschools can be chaotic places: A 2014 OECD study showed that an average nursery school class in developed countries has 14 children per teacher. Israel's media never misses a chance to unearth superlatives associated with the country. It reported that with 27 children per teacher, local kindergartens are the most crowded in the world—a dubious distinction.[37]

It's not that there hasn't been a mad effort to increase supply and expand educational infrastructure. During the decade following mass immigration from the former Soviet Union, Israel increased the number of public schoolteachers by almost 50 percent: from 84,301 to 125,358.[38] But with a population growing that quickly, it was not enough. The numbers are an average, which means that for the children of most taxpayers, density is probably underestimated. This is because religious schools enjoy relatively small classes, whereas mainstream

Sixth-graders try to learn in a crowded classroom, Maccabim, Israel. A recent study of
reported that only China and Chile have classrooms that are more jam-packed.
(Photograph by author)

secular classes frequently exceed 40 pupils. This overcrowding makes many Israeli schools a chaotic, cacophonous, and sometimes violent place.

The negative effect of crowded classrooms on students and teachers is well
documented in the international professional literature.[39] Crowding is especially
problematic during elementary school years, when a caring, supportive relationship with a teacher can be critical for a successful educational experience.[40]
There is simply a finite amount of attention that a single teacher can dedicate
to students. When thirty-five hands are raised to answer a question, many will
never get a chance to participate. Psychological research confirms that crowded
environments amplify cognitive complexity, creating an "overload" that reduces
the amount of new information that can be processed.[41] Frequently, the child
who needs a little personalized assistance to "keep up" will not receive it. The
exceptional child will tune out, unchallenged by a teacher who has no time to
relate to individual potential. Rather than tailor lessons to the capabilities or interests of each child, teachers are forced into a "one size fits all" generic teaching style.

Creativity and pedagogically effective teaching suffer, but Israel's children are the real casualties. For those lucky enough to enjoy special attention at home, the neglect is probably not irreversible. But many may never get the chance to develop their true intellectual abilities.

There are international tests that allow societies to assess their schools' performance. One such test is the Program for International School Assessment (PISA), including examinations that evaluate basic reading and mathematics skills among fifteen-year-olds around the world.[42] Israeli students consistently perform in the lowest third. When the most recent results from PISA were published, the *Jerusalem Post* headline read, "PISA Test Results Show Colossal Failure of Israel Schools."[43]

Teachers suffer great frustration and disillusionment as overcrowded classrooms leave them settling for mediocrity. Attrition rates are high. Yoav Vaknin is the kind of teacher that any parent would want to attract to their neighborhood school. Vaknin is a graduate of the air force's elite pilot's course and was a combat navigator for six years, reaching the rank of major. But he felt that the real national challenges were to be found in the classroom. He enrolled in a special teacher-training program at Hebrew University and became a teacher of Israeli heritage and mathematics. He describes the classroom dynamics he discovered with concern: "After several years in the field, I have come to believe that there are two things you need for a successful educational experience: a teacher with integrity and small classrooms. That's the formula. It's all you really need. Most people go into teaching with great ideals, but I have seen statistics that suggest that as many as 40% leave after a year. Much of the attrition involves frustration with the crowded classrooms."

His own experience is unique but validates the argument. As part of the Hebrew University training program in 2006, participating schools were required to divide classes in two so that the teacher–student ratio would be reasonable. Vaknin recalls:

> Under those circumstances, let me tell you, during my first year I was convinced I was the greatest teacher that ever walked the earth. I could be completely engaged and in touch with all the children in my Jewish philosophy class.
>
> I had one boy who was only interested in the Jerusalem-Beitar soccer team. He wasn't even interested in soccer per se—just the Beitar team. At some point I realized that all my students had poor writing skills, so even though it wasn't a literature course, I started requiring book reports. But this kid refused to open a book: "I don't read books" he told me. So I went to the university library and found a book with stories about soccer in Israel. It was no literary

masterpiece, but it was a book. At first he refused to take it, but I pushed him
and he said he'd try it. When I spoke to him a week later I was delighted to
hear that he had read the entire thing. I know because I quizzed him about
the chapters. When I told the other teachers this boy had actually opened a
book, they were in shock. They assumed he was a lost cause. I'm telling you
I thought I was the world's greatest teacher. But I only had 18 kids in the classroom.

Imagine my surprise during my second year of teaching when we were
thrown into a normal-size class with 37 children. I had serious discipline problems. It was impossible to get to know the kids. Most of all, I couldn't inspire
them. I realized what a profound difference class size means for successful
education. A strict teacher might be able to maintain order with 37 children
and even get them to reach reasonable results on a standardized test. But he
won't have a chance to influence them individually or challenge them.[44]

What many children do learn in Israel's crowded classrooms are the laws of the
jungle and survival. Discipline problems and violent behavior increase in proportion to class size, as children "act out" in response to the shortage of personal
space or instructional attention.[45] It is not only the absolute number of children
sitting in a classroom but the *spatial density* that is associated with behavior
problems.[46] Many Israeli schools are unable to create a serene and stimulating
atmosphere of learning; instead, classrooms are jam-packed and noisy, with
teachers constantly interrupted by rowdy pupils or at times even intimidated by
bullies and troublemakers.

Unfortunately, these crowded schools have become training grounds for an
increasingly violent society. Hebrew University researchers recently conducted a
national survey of 15,961 Israeli public school students: one-third of elementary
and middle school students and almost a quarter of the high school students
thought that violence was a big or very big problem in their schools. The researchers summarized, "The majority of students reported that another student
had cursed them at least once during the past month. . . . About one-half of
the elementary and middle school students and 30 percent of the high school
students reported being seized and shoved on purpose at least once in the pre-
ceding month. Having their personal belongings stolen was equally reported
by elementary and middle school students . . . and slightly less reported (33.8
percent) by high school students."[47]

While it is hard to formulate a "big picture" from the Israeli media's sensa-
tionalistic reporting of crimes, including rape and even murder by juveniles,
more systematic evaluations suggest that the problem is severe. Looking at a
five-month period in 2005, for instance, the government reported that youth

crime increased at a rate of 34 percent. In just two months that year, 8,700 cases of knife attacks, murders, and sexual abuse committed by minors were reported to the police.[48] A recent 2011 report by the Israel Police stated that 15,194 criminal investigations involving juveniles took place annually in Israel. Roughly one-third of these involved violent crimes. Sexual violence showed a marked 15 percent increase.[49]

In a disturbing touch of irony, recently youth violence even reached Israel's solemn Holocaust museum, Yad Vashem, when a visiting band of high school students beat another child senseless as payback for an insulting comment.[50] Physical violence is not the only problem. As in other countries, psychological harassment through the Internet has victimized countless adolescents, causing at least one to commit suicide. This sparked a special investigation of the phenomenon by Israel's state comptroller.[51]

To make matters worse, the same Israeli teachers who face the daunting task of educating such large classes also happen to be among the worst paid in the Western world. Little wonder they find ways to avoid the headache of the crowded Israeli schoolroom. Most Israelis don't realize that in their middle schools, on average a teacher is present only 874 hours a year—28 percent below the OECD average of 1,219 hours.[52] In high schools the level is 100 hours lower!

When classes are overcrowded, both the quantity and the quality of teaching are diminished and a society's educational objectives cannot be attained. When more than three dozen desks are squeezed into a small classroom, schools will not be offering children a positive socialization experience. Nor can teachers create the positive association with learning that is so critical for a country that must produce a qualified, competitive workforce and the cultured citizenry necessary for a healthy society. As Israel's demographic train rolls on, the country's schools will continue to be crowded and often violent places, spinning out of control.

THE DIAGNOSIS: CROWDING

While Israel's classrooms are crowded, its hospitals are bursting. A headline in the leading daily newspaper *Yedioth Ahronot* announced its diagnosis—"The Illness: Crowding."[53] A 2011 OECD report showed how much crowding affects health care in Israel: the country has only 1.9 hospital beds for every one thousand people. This is the third lowest level in the entire OECD. Only Mexico (1.64) and Canada (1.73) are worse. While the average occupancy of hospitals in the OECD is 77 percent, in Israel it is 98 percent. Such a high average reflects many instances when full capacity is exceeded and the corridors of Israel's hospitals look like a World War I movie saga. Patients' most painful and personal moments are completely exposed as their beds line the hallways.

Just one of many examples is crowding in Israel's maternity wards. Rachel Feit has been a midwife in Tel Aviv hospitals for almost twenty years. Given the shortage of staff, an Israeli midwife will often be responsible for three women in labor simultaneously. She compares that to the situation in hospitals in the United States, where a midwife often has one patient at a time and at least one medical assistant. Feit describes her not-atypical day at Tel HaShomer, one of the city's leading medical centers: A woman in labor arrived, but the twelve beds set aside for delivering mothers at the hospital were full. Feit had to examine the patient in a room adjacent to admissions, without the benefit of a monitor or other basic diagnostic equipment. Fortunately, the birth was successful and the infant healthy, but it was conducted under undignified conditions and without proper equipment. Feit explains, "Basically, we operate under a constant dynamic of triage. I think that we do a phenomenal job, doing more with less. But clearly it's not ideal."[54]

Shortages, in Feit's opinion, could easily be amended by different funding priorities. But whatever the reason, in practice she hasn't seen any real growth in the Tel Aviv maternity wards' capacity over the past twenty years, even as the area's population has swelled significantly. There have been occasions where women in labor were simply turned away (after locating an alternative hospital) because there was no place to put them. Feit argues that ex post investigations conducted after unfortunate medical outcomes suggest that crowding rarely leads to medical mistakes. But there are times when it precludes the kind of "loving care" that health professionals would like to give at a time when it is most needed.

For people requiring surgery, shortages are even more acute—and problematic. In a socialized medical system it is not unusual for patients to wait as much as six months for elective surgery. In the orthopedic ward of the same hospital, there are times when so many emergencies requiring urgent attention arise, that days set aside for elective surgery, such as back surgery or hip replacements, are simply canceled with no warning. Even the most "patient" patient becomes irate (or despondent) when told that she must start the long wait again. In many cases, until the elective orthopedic surgery is completed, patients' families bear the burden of care and provide assistance for basic mobility for as long as a year. This is because hospitals are simply too crowded to provide treatment expeditiously.[55] In Tel Aviv's Ichilov Hospital, a 1,050-bed facility, it is not unusual for a patient to wake up from orthopedic surgery only to discover that there is not a single bed available in any ward for them to move to. Notwithstanding the pain

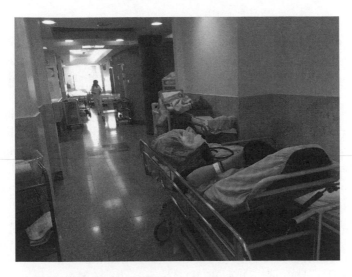

In Saroka Hospital, Beer Sheva, waiting for a room to become available, patients line the hallway, in a country with the most crowded hospitals in the OECD. (Photograph by author)

and the trauma, the patient must wait in a cold and crowded recovery room—sometimes for an entire day—until a bed can be found.

After receiving the 2011 OECD report, the overseeing deputy health minister, Yaakov Litzman, had to acknowledge the grave shortage of hospital beds. Litzman called for an additional 600 beds to be added to hospitals around the country during the next six years.[56] Unfortunately, that is but a drop in the bucket. By way of comparison, in 2018 Stanford University will open a new hospital for its local community with 1,200 beds.[57] Indeed, even though Israel added 699 hospital beds nationally, the actual rate of hospital beds per person dropped from 1.91 per thousand in 2010 to 1.86 in 2014.[58]

Crowding in Israel's hospitals is not just an issue of privacy. There are graver implications for the quality of care. Because hospitals are so full and new patients are literally banging on the door each day, Israelis are often released from hospitals earlier than they should be. An average hospital stay in OECD countries is 6.5 days. In Israel it is only 4.3 days.[59] Unnecessary relapses and protracted recovery due to insufficient treatment are the statistically significant results. Dr. Uri Givon, an orthopedic surgeon, describes a policy of clearing out as many beds on Thursdays as possible in order to make room for anticipated cases that pile up during the weekend. Many patients released prematurely are back in a few days, in much worse condition than when they left.[60]

The chronic shortages are also manifested in technology. Israel may be in the forefront of developing diagnostic high-tech innovations, but its hospitals don't have enough of them. One example is access to medical imaging: Israel has 2.5 MRI machines per 1 million people. This means that there are 8–9 nine working machines in the whole country at any given time, with appointments assigned through the night. The OECD typically has 18.7 on average, while Japan has 47 per million![61] People can wait for months just to be diagnosed, by which time tumors can metastasize. Unnecessary suffering is prolonged. Hospitals often send patients to take tests in community infirmaries, where waits can be notoriously long.[62] But premature babies have nowhere they can be outsourced. The present shortage in preemie wards has already cost lives.[63]

Israel also faces a shortage of doctors. Even though the aspiration of every Jewish (and Arab) mother may be to have her son or daughter go to medical school, in fact there are only 3.3 doctors per thousand people in Israel. This is among the lowest ratios in the OECD. There is also an acute nursing shortage: 4.8 nurses per thousand is a particularly abysmal statistic. The average number of nurses in other developed countries is twice that: 8.8 per thousand people. It means that health professionals are overworked and hospital patients often have long waits before receiving basic care.

Israel has managed to create a reasonably good public health system through a national insurance program and community infirmaries that *prevent* illness. Despite the many untimely deaths of citizens in car accidents, military-security casualties, and smoking-related illnesses, Israelis on average live long lives. At 80.4 years, Israeli men's average life expectancy is the fourth highest in the world—trailing only Switzerland, Iceland and Australia. Israeli women live longer, reaching 84.2 years on average, but are only fifteenth globally.[64] It could be even better, arguably the best in the world. Yet, Israel's health system simply cannot build the hospital wards, train the doctors and nurses, or purchase the machinery fast enough to provide the growing number of Israelis the health care they deserve.

POVERTY AND POPULATION

Poverty is an inevitable outcome for the many large families who fuel Israel's uncontrolled population growth. Two sectors in particular, the ultrareligious Haredi Jews and the Bedouins, have an average "total fertility rate" of more than six children. Most of them live below the poverty line.[65]

About ten thousand Bedouins founded Rahat in 1972. Today's Rahat is Israel's largest Bedouin city, with about sixty thousand residents. It holds two other records of dubious distinction: Growing at 2.7 percent a year, Rahat has the high-est birthrate of any city in Israel.[66] It is also the poorest city in Israel. Just over 60 percent of the population lives below the poverty line.[67] Over 60 percent of the population is under eighteen.[68] These parallel percentages are not coinci-dental. The two phenomena are integrally related.

The combination of large families and very low income (an *average* local in-come of thirty-five hundred shekels, fewer than one thousand dollars a month) produces considerable misery. When interviewed about her life in Rahat, one mother rhetorically asks, "How am I supposed to feed twelve children on a bud-get of 3500 shekels?"[69] The polygamous culture that increasingly defines famil-ial norms has much to do with this. With about one-third of the adult men marrying more than one wife,[70] families can be very large. There is a chronic housing shortage, and crowding can be extraordinary. Investigating a neighbor-hood where a despairing woman killed three of her children, a journalist un-covered one home where twenty-seven people live within a fifty-square-meter space.

Faiz Abu Sahiban, mayor of Rahat from 2008 to 2013, recognizes the cause and effect. He was a schoolteacher and later imam at one of Rahat's most popu-lar mosques. The position offered a political stepping stone to launch a success-ful election campaign in 2008, and at age forty-two he headed the Islamic Movement party's ticket. A thin, intelligent man with a well-groomed beard, "Faiz" is concerned about environmental issues. But it is economics that makes him a strong advocate of family planning: "The best way to reduce the poverty here is to decrease the number of children," he explains without hesitation. "People have too many children and they can't take care of them properly. So they end up getting into alcohol and drugs. It's amazing, but we actually have a problem with this in Rahat. We know that the way out of poverty is to have smaller families. That's just common sense. The question is—how do you do it?"[71] This view is universally held by mayors in other Bedouin towns.[72]

Similarly, the link between poverty and family size is conspicuous among Israel's ultra-Orthodox Haredi sector. This religious Jewish community com-prises 8 percent of adult Israelis. But with an average of 6.5 children per family, it is growing quickly.[73] Over half of Israel's Haredi families are poor and live below the poverty line.[74]

Statistics suggest that while there is an association, poverty is not ethnically driven: size matters. Indeed, family size matters a great deal. A family with four or more children in Israel has three times the likelihood of being poor and living below the poverty line than families with one to three children.[75] Only 14 percent of Haredi families with two children or fewer live below the poverty

line. This is also true among Arab families where 16 percent of families with
two or fewer children live below the poverty line.[76]

Mathematically, it's a fairly straightforward calculation: when you divide a
salary into eight it leaves half the disposable income per family member than
when it is divided by four. That means that there is less money available for
food and clothing. For families who aspire to more than the essentials, it also
means that there will be less money for everything else: less money for eye-
glasses, less money for orthodontia, less money for travel, less money for
computers, less money for air-conditioning, less money for books, less money
for music lessons, less money for tutors, and less money for the countless expenses that life in a prosperous Western society requires. The phenomenon is
universal: Research among fourteen hundred British children showed clearly
that those in larger families suffered from a reduced investment of parental
time and money, with inferior educational and physical development. Not only
did children with fewer siblings do better in school assessments, they were
likely to be taller than children from large families.[77]

A much-repeated societal platitude, expressed by Israelis of all political
persuasions, involves consternation about the steady increase in income disparity. This is for good reason. While Israel emerged as a society with a socialist ideology, the percentage of local wealth controlled by the "haves" rose
dramatically over the past thirty years.[78] A 2011 OECD document reported that
in Israel "the level of inequality is very similar to and even slightly exceeds
that of the United States." The absolute poverty rate in Israel, at 20.9 percent,
is the highest of any developed country, edging out even Mexico, with only
20.4 percent living in destitution. But analysis suggests that family size is driving the gap. Childhood poverty figures tell an important story: the average in
OECD countries is 13.3 percent; In Israel 28.8 percent of children live under the
poverty line.[79]

Sever Plotsker, Israel's leading popular economics correspondent, explains
the flip side of the dynamic: "The poverty levels among non-Haredi Jews are
similar to accepted levels in Western developed countries, with the exception
of Finland and Denmark."[80] In other words, for the most part, Israel's ethnic
and religious groups, whose members choose to have large families, remain
locked in a cycle of poverty and deprivation. This presents a problem. Highlighting this self-evident dynamic is politically incorrect and avoided unremittingly.

Far too often such straight talking is interpreted as an expression of scorn for
Israeli minority groups with high birthrates. It is also true that fertility is not the
only reason why Bedouins or Haredim tend to be poor. There are contributing
cultural, sociological, and economic factors, not the least of which is that Israel

has become a capitalist society with a laissez-faire orientation that accelerates gaps in income. But at the same time, even if these inequities are addressed, family size will continue to keep a shockingly high proportion of Israelis under the poverty line, whether this reality is acknowledged or not.

A breakdown of data from Israel's National Insurance Institute, whose mandate includes poverty reduction, shows that Haredi and Arab families with three children or fewer have per capita income that is twice that of families with seven or more children. As the graph shows, Israeli families with one to three children are universally better off than larger families. Sadly, many who seek a more-equitable society in Israel are loath to explore the implications of these dynamics: better to have Bedouin mayors say the obvious.

If a paramount objective of public policy is to ensure equality of opportunity for all, then Israel's pro-natal programs need to be reconsidered. The high number of children produced by these policies constitutes the single greatest driver of poverty. Not wishing to stigmatize already marginalized populations, many people of good will shy away from confronting this simple truth. But when demography is ignored, efforts to confront Israel's growing epidemic of dependence, poverty, and indigence may actually exacerbate the problem.

Professor Tomer Lev is one of Israel's most talented concert pianists. But he is also an outspoken social and environmental activist. Lev has compared Israel's environmental and social problems to the well-known proverb that tells of six blind Indian wise men who encounter an elephant. One blind man feels the tail and says he feels a rope; another touches a leg and claims he has found a pillar; the trunk suggests a tree branch; to another the tusk feels like a spike; to the others the ear feels like a fan, and the belly a low ceiling. In fact they are all very real, but different dimensions of the same beast. When Israelis complain about the traffic, the schools, the hospitals, the courts, the air emissions, the shrinking Dead Sea, or the poverty, they are as blind as the proverbial sightless Indians. They fail to see that what they have is a single phenomenon: demographic growth.[81] To start to address its problems, Israel must first confront the common, underlying cause.

4

THE RISE AND FALL OF ALIYAH: A BRIEF
HISTORY OF IMMIGRATION TO ISRAEL

At the moment of his immigration his [an immigrant Jew's]
only thought is not to starve. . . . It is like a natural force which
drives them and like a stream of water which seeks the
place of least resistance.
—Theodor Herzl, evidence before the Royal British
Commission on Immigration, 1902

ASCENT

"I'll tell you an historical fact: Never since the time the people of Israel went into exile have they wanted to return. This has been the case since the destruction of the first temple. When Koresh [Cyrus the Great of Persia] offered the Jews a chance to return to their homeland, most of them didn't want to come. He gave them more than a charter; he gave them logistical assistance. And how many came with Nehemiah and Ezra? Maybe a few hundred." A former tour guide, Avraham Duvdevani, chairman of the World Zionist Organization, sees Israeli immigration dynamics in a historic context. Like Theodore Herzl and Chaim Weizmann before him, Duvdevani's role is first and foremost ideological: to spread a buoyant vision of modern Jewish nationalism as a world movement. But he harbors no illusions about Israel's present ability to attract immigrants: "In the near future, most of the world's Jews will be in Israel. But not because of immigration. It will be due to assimilation. If one looks at the big picture and demographically significant movements, the only Jews who have ever come to Israel were those who were in distress. Jews immigrate when they are faced with economic or political adversity and they need to escape."[1]

46

A review of the chronicles of immigration during the past century confirms this somewhat unsentimental view of Israel's immigration story.[2] Moving to the "holy land" in fact has never been a particularly comfortable, convenient, or compelling option. Precisely because they could be given little else, Jewish immigrants were always accorded honor and esteem by the Zionist movement. There is a generic and fairly neutral Hebrew word for migration (*hagirah*). So a separate, implicitly prestigious word has always been used for *Jewish* immigration to Israel: *aliyah*—literally, "ascent." (This is a secular adoption of the traditional term for calling participants to ascend to *metaphorical heights* during prayers in front of the congregation when the Bible is read.)

Most immigrants who came to Israel over the years arrived from northern Europe. Based on latitudes, they traveled south. Some took a drop in their standard of living. Yet, the edifying effects of life in the ancient homeland presumably conferred a higher stature: immigrants to Israel "ascended." Israel's 1950 Law of Return retroactively conferred the status of *oleh* (Jewish immigrant; literally, one who has risen) on all Jewish inhabitants, lest they be deprived the opportunity to achieve this uplifting station.[3]

Marketing life in Israel to Jews around the world was always a hard sell. But Zionists learned to become very persuasive salesmen. One study by demographic experts characterized Israel's policies as "the most active pro-immigration program ever recorded—encouraging, stimulating and assisting immigrants in all stages of the immigration process."[4] All told, between 1918 and 2015 some 3.7 million Jews moved to Israel.[5] For most of Israel's history it was the single greatest engine for Israel's dramatic demographic growth. In recent years, however, subsequent to the end of the great influx of Jews from the former Soviet Union, immigration slowed significantly. The present number of immigrants is only slightly more than the Israelis leaving the country.[6]

Typically, demographers talk about a parallel "push" and "pull" informing individual decisions to immigrate. For millions of Jews living in hostile or indigent environments, the "push" was easy to identify. The "pull" that Israel exerted, however, was never as clear.

The ideological gratification gained from moving to the "Promised Land" counts for something. But the associated fulfillment only lasts so long. More concrete amenities, such as well-paying jobs, professional challenges, comfortable homes, pleasant neighborhoods, high quality health care, good schools—and of course personal security—are more sustainable components of the "pull" in most personal immigration equations. Learning a new language, enduring an oppressive climate, and surviving abrasive day-to-day interactions in a prickly society is not for everyone. Many find the prospects of annihilation, so constantly promised by Israel's neighbors, to be off-putting and do not want their children to grow up to be soldiers. Israel has always had a hard time competing with the West.[7]

The specific circumstances behind the "exodus" of the past century and the motivation of immigrants have been as diverse and colorful as the dozens of countries naturalized Israelis once called home. But a single pattern emerges. The majority of the people who came to Israel felt a "push" to leave their native land and had nowhere else to go. Most Jews living throughout the world, who didn't feel their personal circumstances to be untenable, never found the pull of Israel's magnetic field alluring enough to pick up and move there. Understanding how Israel's mass migration unfolded suggests that this dramatic, historic phenomenon has played itself out.

A CRITICAL MASS OF JEWS IN PALESTINE

When David Ben-Gurion learned of the astonishing dimensions of the Nazi Holocaust he was appalled but rarely spoke of it. It was not just the horrific loss of lives and the destruction of the world of his childhood that he mourned. He was equally upset about the implications for Jewish nationalism. As early as December 6, 1942, he confided his concerns to the Jewish Agency Executive in Jerusalem: "The extermination of European Jewry is a catastrophe for Zionism. There won't be anyone left to build the country!"[8]

A July 30, 1945, diary entry written as he sailed to Europe to meet with survivors is described by historian Tom Segev as resembling a "an accountant's ledger, all numbers: so many Jews lived in Europe before the war, so many were murdered, so many remained alive."[9] Ben-Gurion divided the surviving Jews into five blocs, calculating whether he had the necessary soldiers to fight for a sovereign Jewish state. In a 1954 essay, he wrote in retrospect, "Hitler harmed more than the Jewish people, who he knew and hated: he caused damage to the Jewish state, whose coming he did not foresee. He destroyed the country's main support and central force. The state appeared and did not find the nation that had awaited it."[10]

For the tiny group of activists who established the Zionist movement at the end of the nineteenth century, moving to Palestine not only solved the existential identity crisis facing Jewish Diasporas around the world. It also promised to provide the critical mass of people necessary to create an independent Jewish state. Encouraging the handful of Jews living in Ottoman Palestine to have large families was well and good but made for highly incremental population growth. At the same time, many Zionists believed that European Jewry was like a village sitting at the foot of a volcano, where the bubbling lava of imminent violence was growing perilously close.[11] For those who had tasted Polish and Russian anti-Semitism and, after 1933, the more-lethal German variety, there was literally no time to lose. Immigration was the key if Zionism was to make a successful play for Jewish sovereignty in the land of Israel.

Palestine at the twilight of the Ottoman rule appears in photographs and travelers' descriptions as a peripheral province where life was universally sparse and, for most people, short. The eroded lands were inhabited by only a fraction of the masses who filled the land in earlier days of old. The first reliable Turkish census figures were collected between 1891 and 1892 and released in 1893. It showed roughly half a million residents in Palestine. Eighty percent were Muslim.[12] The small and splintered community of forty-three thousand Jews in Palestine (known as "the Yishuv") was easily outnumbered by the fifty-seven-thousand-person Christian community. But for millions of beleaguered Jews in Europe and the Middle East, a derelict Holy Land was perceived as an opportunity. A "forlorn" land was waiting to be redeemed.

The impediments to realizing this vision of national restoration, however, were formidable. The immediate (but hardly most daunting) obstacle was a legal ban on Jewish immigration: in 1881, the Ottoman Council of Ministers granted Jews the right "to settle as scattered groups anywhere throughout Turkey excluding Palestine."[13] In practice, Jews trickled into Palestine despite the prohibition, and Ottoman authorities did little to stop them.

Long before a formal political movement was formed, Jews were finding their way to the Promised Land. These were times of pogroms and persecution for Jews in Europe. For Zionist immigrants, far more powerful than any "pull" the Holy Land exerted was the push of violence and discrimination in Europe.[14] The waves of immigration (*aliyot*), which continued until the establishment of Israel in 1948, reflected the fact that Jewish immigrants largely arrived in pulses, with different years delivering discrete geographic origins and ideological cohorts. In retrospect, the waves were sufficiently homogeneous to be given numbers and afforded stereotypes.

The "First Aliyah" (1882–1903) brought about twenty-five thousand Jews, largely from eastern Europe. Journalist Amos Elon describes the mentality of these late-nineteenth-century first settlers: "It was a fervor born of despair with societies that had made anti-Semitism official State policy. Theirs was weariness and a discontent born of oppression, dire need, and the hope, surely naive, of a better world."[15] This eclectic assemblage faced enormous hardships. Many left Palestine, overwhelmed by the tribulations. But with assistance from the philanthropy of French banker Edmond de Rothschild, a critical mass held on, successfully purchasing lands and establishing a series of rural villages across Ottoman Palestine.[16] The sixty "idealistic" youth "the Biluim," who in 1882 came to Palestine to become agricultural settlers, are instructive: only twenty-seven stayed in the country, and only half of these remained farmers.[17]

A second, somewhat larger aliyah (containing forty thousand to fifty-five thousand Jews) began to disembark at Jaffa Port in 1904 and continued flowing into Palestine until the outbreak of World War I.[18] Not unlike the first wave, most were young, single, middle-class Russian, Lithuanian, and Polish Jews of modest means.[19] A significant number—roughly estimated to be 16 percent of the group—saw themselves as Zionist "pioneers."[20] Socialist and self-righteous in their dogma, these young immigrants came to Palestine to change the world, and arguably they did. Their highest pioneering ideal involved working the land in collective settlements.[21] They also are credited with establishing a Jewish self-defense organization (HaShomer—"the Guardian"), renewing the Hebrew language and creating more *indistinguishable* political factions than the most fastidious historian could ever chronicle.

For many of the immigrants, the hot, inhospitable weather, constant fear of violence, unemployment, poverty, malaria, and homesickness were too much. It is estimated that at least half (and probably more) of these high-minded immigrants did not remain in Palestine.[22] Indeed, as a Second Aliyah veteran himself, David Ben-Gurion once exaggerated that 90 percent of his peers ultimately left the country.[23] The number of actual "dropouts" is comparable to the 70 percent of immigrants during this period who came to New Zealand and Australia (or 50 percent to the United States) and who would eventually pack their bags and return to Europe.[24] Like that of so many immigrants who changed their minds, these dropouts' ambivalence was enormous: they felt both a profound sense of failure and wonderful relief at being able to return to some semblance of a normal life, with less emotional and physical sacrifice.

When one considers the global migrations during this period that brought millions of Jews to the shores of North and South America, it is well to remember that only 3 percent of Jewish immigrants from Europe pursued the Zionist option.[25] At the eve of World War I, the Ottoman census reported the population in Palestine was close to 689,000, only 13 percent of whom were Jewish.[26] Jerusalem was the exception. Ever since the 1860s, when the city contained 22,000 residents, Jews constituted the largest single ethnic group.[27]

Given the English propensity for record keeping, it is much easier to trace the trajectory of Jewish immigration during the thirty years of British control in Palestine that extended from the end of World War I until 1948. The first of two comprehensive demographic inventories conducted during the Mandate period was the 1922 census, administered somewhat unsystematically by the new civilian regime. It showed 752,000 total residents in Palestine. Due to the objective adversities and expulsions by the Ottoman regime during the Great War, the Jewish community had actually shrunk to only 83,790, or 11 percent of the total population. This was a modest number to be sure. But it was already three times the size of the Jewish community, counted just thirty-eight years earlier, that had survived centuries of austere conditions under Ottoman rule![28]

During the Mandate, the Yishuv expanded steadily at an average annual rate of 9 percent.[29] By the time the much more meticulous 1931 Palestine census was conducted, Jewish numbers had more than doubled to 175,000. There was constant disappointment among Zionists with British immigration policies. Still, the rate of Jewish population growth was four times higher than that of local Arabs.[30] Like most international migrations of the time, newly arrived Jewish Palestinians were largely young, European, and had relatively few children with a modest surplus of males.[31] (In the 1930s, Tel Aviv was the only major city in Palestine with more women than men.)[32]

Given the pervasiveness of European anti-Semitism, it is natural to ask why so few Jews chose to come to Palestine during the British Mandate. Max Nordau, the eminent European intellectual and journalist, was Herzl's close friend and deputy chair of the Zionist organization. Nordau remained an esteemed figure in the Zionist world throughout World War I. In a series of ten articles published in Paris between September and November 1920, he publicly called for 600,000 Jewish immigrants to take advantage of the British foreign secretary Arthur Balfour's 1917 public declaration favoring a Jewish national home and move to Israel without delay.[33]

The gates after the war were wide open. When appointed as Palestine's first high commissioner, Sir Herbert Samuel became the first Jewish leader of Palestine in two thousand years. As a tactical measure after the Arab riots in Jaffa in 1921, he placed temporary limitations on immigration. Yet Samuel had always believed in the fundamental morality of a Jewish national home in Palestine and imposed no real constraints on immigration, even as he tried very hard to govern Palestine impartially.[34] Presciently, Nordau warned that such favorable policies would not last for long and should be exploited immediately to create a Jewish majority in Palestine. The "Nordau Plan," however, did not resonate with the millions of Jews in Europe or the United States and was never taken very seriously by the Zionist movement itself, from which he soon resigned in frustration.[35] During this period, Jews around the world who chose to emigrate preferred to pursue their dreams in America, South Africa, New Zealand, and Australia.

Some fifteen years late, Vladimir "Zeev" Jabotinsky, the charismatic head of the Revisionist Zionist movement, designed a ten-year "evacuation plan" aimed at bringing 1.5 million east European Jews to Palestine.[36] The matter was "a question of life and death for Polish Jewry," he explained.[37] Meeting with heads of state in Poland, Hungary, and Romania, astonishingly Jabotinsky secured their governments' agreement to his proposal.[38] Touring eastern Europe in 1936, like a prophet he broadcast an apocalyptic vision of European Jewry's future[39] and alerted his brethren to their treacherous position on the edge of the proverbial volcano.[40]

The Jews of Europe, however, did not buy the message, though millions would soon regret it. Even when immigration numbers reached their peak, only one out of every 250 of the world's Jews came to Palestine.[41] The Polish community was particularly hostile, feeling that he was reinforcing the deep-seated distrust of Jewish national loyalty and playing into the hands of local anti-Semites. Jabotinsky clairvoyantly countered that dark clouds were gathering over the heads of the Jews in Europe.[42] Their lack of enthusiasm and complacency was ultimately moot. Not only did the British reject Jabotinsky's proposal out of hand, even Chaim Weizmann, the chairman of the World Zionist Organization, was dismissive.

These failed campaigns were early examples of the central lesson that can be gleaned from a century of Zionist efforts to "ingather" Jewish exiles. Jews have always made pilgrimages to the Holy Land and venerated Jerusalem in daily prayers. Impressive Jewish idealists, with strong philosophical convictions and utopian visions, have been moving to Israel since the end of the nineteenth century. But Zionist pleas for immigration only seem to gain traction among mainstream Jewish communities when their baseline political or economic circumstances are deteriorating and when they lack a feasible geographic alternative.

For most immigrants during the Mandate, it was not euphoria at the Balfour Declaration that brought them to Palestine. Rather it was sheer terror following the bloodstained aftermath of the Russian Revolution.[43] The Communist uprising created a power vacuum that was filled with lawlessness and cruelty, often directed at the vulnerable Jewish communities living in the east European "Pale of Settlement." By the time order was finally restored by a ruthless Bolshevik regime, an estimated one hundred thousand Jews were killed and half a million were left without homes.[44] Even Palestine's hostile Arab population did not seem frightening to immigrants after this particularly cruel round of pogroms.[45] Given the expectations created by the new British gatekeepers in Palestine, actual immigration numbers in retrospect appear surprisingly modest.

A noticeable surge in Palestine's population occurred between 1924 and 1928, when some seventy thousand largely "mercantile" Polish Jews arrived on the "Fourth Aliyah." It was not idealistic zeal but economic adversity that motivated most of them: When Polish finance minister Wladyslaw Grabski nationalized several industries in the 1920s, the results for Poland's Jewish community were disastrous. About one in three Jews ended up declaring bankruptcy. Many had little to lose by moving to Palestine.[46]

The 1931 Mandate census offers an official picture that appears reasonably accurate. The birthrate among Jewish families was considerably lower than their Muslim neighbors, but then Jews lived a lot longer: infant mortality was three times higher in Muslim than Jewish families. The likelihood of Muslim toddlers not reaching age six was 900 percent higher than for Jewish children.[47] (By way of contrast, infant mortality in Egypt during this period was far lower than among Palestinian Muslims, but still 50 percent higher than among Jewish Palestinians.)[48] By the end of the Mandate, Muslim life expectancy in Palestine increased impressively, from thirty-seven years in 1926 to forty-nine, but still remained far below local Jewish longevity.[49]

A yet-unresolved (and unceasingly acrimonious) historic debate about the period involves the number of *Arab* immigrants who arrived in Palestine during the Mandate period. In a best-selling 1984 book, *From Time Immemorial: The Origins of the Arab-Jewish Conflict over Palestine*, American journalist Joan Peters reassessed Palestine's demography during the British Mandate. Peters's central thesis was that an exceptionally high number of Palestinian Arabs immigrated (illegally) to take advantage of economic prosperity during the Mandate. (The Mandate's 1931 census acknowledged only ninety-two hundred, but that is almost certainly an understatement.)[50] Peters unearthed numerous reports by British officials (including Winston Churchill) who acknowledge the phenomenon of Arab infiltration into Palestine and the complicity of the Mandate administration in allowing it.[51]

Reviews alternatively praised the book's systematic presentation of demographic data or excoriated the work as unscholarly. Her critics, inter alia, cited the phenomenal Muslim-Israeli birthrate in subsequent years as proof of the high fertility among Arabs during the Mandate.[52] But they failed to acknowledge the pitiful life expectancy for Muslims that characterized most of the period or the fact that the British themselves reported average family sizes of only 4.5 persons.[53]

There is plenty of evidence to suggest that Peters was not exaggerating.[54] Conservative estimates counted an annual average of 2,054 Arab "infiltrators" to Palestine each year without authorization.[55] Sixty thousand Arab immigrants over thirty years is not an insignificant migration, but in retrospect, neither was

it a "game changer." Ultimately, it is an interesting historical debate but of dubious relevance to the present political and ecological challenges that Israelis and
Palestinians face.

Whatever the reason, Palestine's Arab community was surely expanding rapidly and enjoying a far higher quality of life under British rule. This did little to
quell its concerns about the conspicuous growth taking place in the Jewish
community and its ultimate intentions.[56] The resentment boiled over intermittently. Episodes of violent Arab attacks on Jews and Jewish property as well as
on British officials punctuated the Mandate years. It was only a matter of time
until this discontent would explode into a full-fledged rebellion in April 1936.
The Arab political leadership in Palestine called for cessation of Jewish land
purchase and Jewish immigration.[57] It would take three years, some twenty-five
thousand British troops and 3,000 "official" Arab casualties (along with the
deaths of 415 Jewish civilians) for the sides to decide that they had had enough.[58]

The British foreign office had always been ambivalent about whether its national interests were truly served by preferring Jewish to Arab nationalism in
Palestine. With the winds of war threatening in Europe, and Arab support holding even greater strategic significance, it capitulated to the Arab demands: a
government white paper significantly curtailing Jewish immigration was promoted by British colonial secretary Malcolm MacDonald and approved by the
House of Commons on May 23, 1939. A yearly quota of ten thousand immigrants
was imposed, allowing for an additional twenty-five thousand "refugee emergencies" to be spread out over a five-year span. The grand total of Jewish immigration during this critical period was limited to seventy-five thousand.

Four months later Hitler's armies invaded Poland. Already the Jews of Germany and Austria were desperate to flea the Nazi regime. But the world was
unaccommodating to Jewish refugees seeking safety. In July 1938 representatives
of thirty-two countries convened at the French resort of Evian to discuss the
refugee crisis. The only country willing to accept even a modest number of additional immigrants was the Dominican Republic.[59] In appeasing the Arab Revolt, the British Mandate at once rewarded violent lawlessness and implicitly
reneged on the country's commitment to the League of Nations to facilitate a
national home for the Jews. With draconian immigration restrictions in Palestine in place, the fate of millions of Jews who sought refuge during the next six
years was sealed. The British colonial officials did not even implement the full
five-year, seventy-five-thousand-person quota.[60] While Zionist mythology lion-
izes the illegal immigration (Aliyah Bet) of the period, it enabled no more than
twenty thousand Jews to come to Israel during those trying years.[61]

Due to the British restraints, only ten thousand Jewish immigrants annually were
allowed to escape the nightmare of Nazi Europe and move to Palestine—like
these lucky young European immigrants arriving by ship in Haifa in 1945.
(Lazer Dinar, KKL-JNF Photo Archives)

When World War II finally ended, hundreds of thousands of despairing
Holocaust survivors sought sanctuary in Palestine. But British policies were as
inflexible as ever. Dilapidated boats with Jewish refugees began to head to
Palestine's shores. Most were intercepted by British military warships. Thousands of the most forlorn people the world has ever known were transferred to
more years of detention in twelve concentration camps, hastily constructed in
Cyprus. Only 70,700 made it into Israel during this period, a modest number,
but nevertheless more than the mere 15,000 desperate refugees who managed
to sneak through the Mandate's naval blockade operating during the years of
World War II.[62] This chapter in British history is still remembered with indignation and continues to contribute to the axiomatic principle of unlimited Jewish immigration in modern Israeli culture.

By the time the British officially informed the newly established United Na-
tions in February 1947 that it was ready to move on, 1,970,400 people lived in
Palestine. Roughly one-third of those people were Jewish; a full 1.1 million were
Muslim, and 143,000 were Christian Arabs.[63] The Arab population of Palestine

doubled during the British Mandate. But the Jewish population had grown six-fold, enough for Zionist leaders to gamble that they had the demographic nucleus and organizational infrastructure required to survive as an independent country.

New arrivals helped provide the troops that Ben-Gurion would need to withstand the attack of five neighboring Arab armies along with the Palestinian irregulars and defend the fledgling Jewish state. After the war, the prime minister of the infant country reflected, "We might have been able to capture the Triangle, the Golan and the entire Galilee, but conquering these would not have bolstered our security to the extent that the absorption of immigrants can. . . . The fate of the State depends on immigration."[64]

A REFUGE FOR REFUGEES

Israel's 1948 War of Independence completely changed the country's demographic balance. During the course of the conflict, roughly two-thirds of the Arab population left their homes—many on their own volition and a somewhat smaller number deported by the Israeli army, which saw them as enemy forces.[65] Concomitantly, the Jewish population in Israel began to swell. When David Ben-Gurion declared Israel's independence on May 14, 1948, there were only 649,400 Jews in the country. Increasing this number was a paramount objective for Zionists, who believed that sovereignty would not be consolidated without an undisputable Jewish majority. The centrality of immigration to the country was among the key principles emphasized in the Declaration of Independence that the first prime minister read to the nation that Friday afternoon at 4:00 P.M. on Kol Yisrael, the national radio's first broadcast: "The catastrophe which recently befell the Jewish people—the massacre of millions of Jews in Europe—was another clear demonstration of the urgency of solving the problem of its homelessness by re-establishing in Eretz-Israel the Jewish state, which would open the gates of the homeland wide to every Jew and confer upon the Jewish people the status of a fully privileged member of the community of nations. . . . The State of Israel will be open for Jewish immigration and for the ingathering of the exiles."[66] Already ships with hundreds of refugees had set sail for Haifa.[67] They were the harbinger of many more to come. By 1952, fewer than four years later, the number of Jewish Israelis had more than doubled.[68]

Israeli independence also signaled a change in demographic dynamics within the Jewish world. Once a Jewish state opened its gates, globally most Jewish migrants headed for Israel. Many Jews definitely choose to live elsewhere: Between 1948 and 2008, Israel received 63 percent of Jewish migrants worldwide with the other 37 percent settling in myriad Western nations. Some 14 percent of the latter group involved Israelis who wanted to try life elsewhere.[69] Nonetheless, after 1948, the Israeli option emerged as the default destination for Jews seeking a new country.

The mad rush of desperate people who came to Israel during its first years was almost more than the country could handle. By February of 1949, the last of the 56,000 Jews imprisoned in Cyprus were liberated and sailed to the new state. From the displaced persons camps of Europe, some 130,000 Holocaust survivors joined the 25,000 that had already made their way clandestinely to Israel.[70] Many were pressed into military service during Israel's War of Independence. All told, 230,000 Holocaust survivors came to Israel in 1949.[71] By 1950 Jewish DP camps in Europe were empty.

In July 1949, Israel signed the last in a series of armistice agreements with Arab countries, bringing with it de facto recognition of Israel's borders. The newborn country could take a break from fighting to focus on its unfinished demographic agenda—absorbing the many Jews inclined to join the new state. Abominable conditions greeted most of the immigrants who reached Israeli shores during the country's initial year of independence. The best Israel could do for them upon arrival was pitch tents in crowded, fenced military camps. Historian Tom Segev describes "a confused mass of people of all ages, from all countries, bewildered, helpless, rushing about, carrying suitcases and baskets, crates, bundles and babies, with countless children who screamed in every language under the sun."[72]

After suffering the indignity of assembly-line medical examinations, chest X-rays and delousing with DDT, the new immigrants were left to a squalor that Israeli officials acknowledged was worse than that existing in the DP camps of Europe. Rations were extremely meager and crowding unimaginable. Somewhat more spacious transit camps, or *ma'abarot*, were soon set up around the country, but their conditions were also basic. By the end of 1951, 220,517 immigrants lived in these temporary transfer camps, constituting one-sixth of the overall population.[73] Several transit camps would be transformed into development towns: Khalisa on the Lebanese border became Kiryat Shmoneh; Har Tuv in the Judean foothills became Beit Shemesh.[74] And still the refugees kept on coming.

The campaigns and operations that brought massive numbers of Jewish immigrants during its first years are part of Israel's national mythology. Every Israeli has seen the remarkable photographs of the 1949 "Operation Magic Carpet," which flew 49,000 Jews from Yemen to Israel. Most of them had never before seen or even heard of an airplane. Their wide-eyed wonder suggests that the flight to redemption was truly seen as miraculous.

Transit camps (*ma'abarot*) circa 1949 in Beit Lid house the
wave of immigrants that doubled Israel's population within
a few years of its independence. (Zoltan Kluger,
KKL-JNF Photo Archives)

In 1951, the vast majority of Iraqi Jews—110,000 strong—came to Israel as
part of "Operation Ezra and Nehemiah," a reference to the biblical leaders
who returned to Israel from Babylon. The Iraqi government had already enacted
discriminatory laws placing restrictions on Jews. Now it required that Jewish immigrants sell all property, limit their luggage to sixty-six pounds, take no more
than $140, and bring no jewelry whatsoever. Undeterred, Iraqi Jews didn't think
twice. An entire community was flown to Israel within two years. By 1952 40,000
Turkish Jews, some 18,000 Iranians, more than half of the Jews in Yugoslavia,
and almost all Bulgarian Jews moved to Israel.[75] Unlike the pre-state breakdown,
where males dominated the different immigration waves, beginning in 1949
gender balance was equal.[76] The fact that slightly more females came to Israel
than males during this period reflects the transfer of entire communities.

After the country caught its breath, extensive efforts were made to move the
new arrivals out of the tents and into permanent homes and jobs. The many Arab

Iraqi immigrants arrive at the airport in Lod in 1951 as part of the
mass "Operation Ezra and Nehemiah." By the next year, the
pace of immigration had slowed considerably, and Israel only
gradually brought over Jews from Arab and European countries
during the 1950. (David Hirshfeld, KKL-JNF Photo Archives)

villages abandoned during the war provided accommodations for countless
immigrants. The quaint artist colony Ein Hod was originally Ein Hawd. Beer
Sheva was an entirely Arab town when Israel conquered it in 1948. Jews who had
just arrived from India were the first to move into the city's empty houses. Arab
neighborhoods, like Jerusalem's chic Bakka quarter, were filled with newly landed
refugees. The list goes on and on and is painstakingly documented in Palestinian
Web sites. But even this "available" housing stock was soon exhausted.

Not only did immigrants face a housing shortage; there was no work. It was
not ecological zeal but joblessness among immigrants that led to Israel's plant-
ing 56,400 dunams of land with pine trees in 1951. Thousands of immigrants
were taken in the early morning to bald rocky hillsides and given shovels and
saplings. So great was this labor supply that a single year of afforestation
exceeded the entire area of woodlands planted during three decades of work
by the Mandate's forestry department.[77] Many new farming villages were
established, even though their financial viability from the start was shaky.
Labor-intensive production became a priority for the government, which scam-
pered to establish factories to produce food, textiles, and leather goods.[78] And
still unemployment was pervasive.

Mass immigration contributed to an economic malaise, already severe given the devastation of the economy during the War of Independence. Israel was a developing country in its first years, and most of its citizens were poor. The burgeoning demand for housing, education, medical services, and consumer goods increased inflation. Shortages became extreme. Rationing basic commodities was required of all. The balance of trade suffered. With a decline in the labor-capital ratio, productivity dropped.[79] The influx of unskilled workers caused wages to fall.[80] Veteran citizens had to bankroll the new immigrants, even as they themselves were struggling through economic crises. These dynamics would be repeated, albeit more moderately, during other immigration booms.

When disillusioned refugees began to vent their frustration and stage protests, some violent, there was concern for the political stability of the country. On November 21, 1951, the daily newspaper *Haaretz* published an article that actually called on the state to finance selective *emigration*.[81] Such extreme positions were anomalous. After the trauma of the Holocaust, few had the temerity to question whether the rate of immigration should be controlled. Most politicians saw immigration as the paramount political priority for the new country.

A LAW AND AN AGENCY FOR JEWISH IMMIGRATION

It was not coincidental that the Law of Return granting Jews the right to immigrate to Israel was among the first statutes passed by Israel's parliament. Much more than symbolic legislation, its operational provisions were passionately debated. Some expressed discomfort with a law not sufficiently "inclusive," especially given the Jewish people's historic experience with discriminatory immigration laws. Accordingly, the original bill proposed by the Ministry of Justice gave no preferential treatment to Jews at all but assumed the country would naturally provide logistical support that would facilitate Jewish immigration.[82] This position gave way to a more pragmatic particularism that favored Jews.

Over the years, Israel's critics (internal and external) have vilified Israeli immigration policy as a clear manifestations of the "racist" nature of Zionism and the Jewish state. There are, however, compelling justifications for Israel's preferential treatment of Jewish immigrants. Among these are affirmative action as compensation for centuries when Jews faced discrimination, all countries' entitlement to self-definition, the right to allow unification of families and communities, and international law's clear recognition of the legitimacy of national immigration criteria along ethnic lines.[83] The probity of similar "preferential policies" for immigrants with appropriate national heritages in Germany, Finland, Greece, Hungary, Ireland, Poland, Bulgaria, Slovakia, the Czech

Republic, Slovenia, Turkey, and Croatia is rarely challenged. This cannot help but make many Israelis wonder whether the detractors' motives are disingenuous.

Calling the statute the "Law of Return" implicitly emphasized that Jews were not simply migrating to a random destination but in fact coming home: The law's opening and operational paragraph proclaims, "Every Jew has the right to immigrate to Israel."[84] The definition of a Jew, under the law, has been interpreted leniently. Despite ongoing calls by Israel's religious parties (and most recently by its present chief rabbi)[85] for more discriminating criteria, the Supreme Court of Israel has consistently ruled that non-Orthodox conversions overseas be accepted for purposes of immigration.[86] The welcoming orientation grants immigration rights to non-Jewish spouses—as well as to the non-Jewish spouses of sons and daughters or grandsons and granddaughters.[87] Given their husbands' lineages, should Chelsea Clinton or Caroline Kennedy and their children ever feel Zionist leanings, they enjoy the legal right to immigrate and receive Israeli citizenship.

Another heated argument was the debate over how selective Israel should be in processing Jewish immigrants under the Law of Return. Zionism to this day has an express preference for attracting young people, who can "build the land." But for the most part it has always taken all-comers.[88] Many legislators felt that the right of Jews to immigrate should be absolute. If a Jewish criminal or ne'er-do-well wanted to come to Israel, he could not be denied, even if it meant taking him directly from the port to prison.[89] David Ben-Gurion, saw it differently. "There is nothing better for the people of Israel than Zionism," he railed on the Knesset rostrum. "But the Zionism of fools is not good for the people of Israel. I oppose MK Gil's comments that said that if there are criminals or prostitutes or lunatics we should bring them and put them in jail or a hospital. We are not building a jail or an insane asylum. We are building a model state for the people of Israel."[90]

In 1950, Ben-Gurion usually got his way. Accordingly, the final language in the statute grants the minister of the interior authority to disqualify a Jewish immigrant if one of three conditions is met: the applicant is engaged in an activity directed against the Jewish people, is likely to endanger public health or the security of the State, or has a criminal past, likely to endanger public welfare.[91] It was pursuant to the last caveat that gangster Meyer Lansky was denied entry into Israel in 1972 due to his nefarious history.[92] In fact, this was an extremely unusual exception to an "open door" policy.

With a law firmly in place and the initial burst of immigration more or less accommodated, an administrative agency for facilitating the absorption process was required. For most of Israel's history this role has involved a partnership between the Israeli government and the Jewish Agency for Israel. Founded in 1929 as the *Jewish Agency for Palestine*, during the period of the British Mandate, "the Agency" (as it is often referred to in Hebrew) served as the de facto operational executive body for the Yishuv. Once Israel was established, the Jewish Agency was authorized to oversee aliyah promotion and facilitation of immigrant absorption. Because its budget is largely based on donations from Jews around the world, Israel could pass on the expenses associated with immigration to world Jewry, whose resources dwarfed those of the nascent state.

Twenty years later the Israeli government decided it needed to be more involved, and in 1968 it established a Ministry of Absorption, which still assumes much of the formal funding and policy making for immigration. Nonetheless, the extensive network of emissaries sent around the world to expedite the marketing and paperwork associated with immigration is largely hired and managed by the Jewish Agency. It runs absorption centers around the country offering newcomers a home for a nominal fee during their initial stay. The Agency provides Hebrew language classes, university scholarships, and field trips for immigrants to become acquainted with their new country. In short, it is a multimillion-dollar operation dedicated to expanding Israel's population.

During the very first years of the state, for international work, the Jewish Agency often relied on the Mossad LeAliyah.[93] In friendly European countries, the Mossad's role was largely that of "travel agent." But agents would also organize highly aggressive, pro-Israel propaganda urging Jews to emigrate without delay, claiming that exit permits and Zionist assistance would soon be unavailable. In countries where immigration to Israel was not permitted, particularly in Arab lands, the Mossad smuggled Jews over the borders.

In the shadow of the Holocaust, agents were particularly conscientious about their mission. They did whatever they could to facilitate aliyah, even if it meant worsening conditions for Jews. Yitzhak Ben-Menachem, an Israeli military hero, was drafted for special operations in Europe. He was almost Machiavellian about his role: "Mass immigration will pour in only as a result of distress. This is a bitter truth, whether we like it or not. We must consider the possibility of initiating the distress, of bringing it about in the Diaspora. . . . For Jews have to be made to leave their places of residence."[94]

With Israel's economy in tatters, the country's primitive absorption facilities bursting at the seams, and ubiquitous human deprivation, the pace of immigration appeared to be unsustainable. The Jewish Agency came to realize that its resources were stretched too thin. While not empowered to or interested in formally closing the country's doors, the Agency promulgated internal guidelines on November 18, 1951, to limit the number of immigrants it would assist in moving to Israel. Its "rules of selection" required that 80 percent of immigrants be under age thirty-five, show reasonable health levels, and sign commitments declaring a willingness to work in agricultural or semiskilled labor. The rules did not apply to immigrants who were skilled workers, who were supported by relatives, or who had ten thousand dollars in personal wealth.[95]

This chilled the pace of immigration, immediately creating a heated battle between advocates of continued "open immigration" and those who felt that such policies risked infiltration by hostile foreign agents and non-Jews. It would take the full weight of Ben-Gurion's political support to restore the free flow of immigration.[96] In retrospect, the pause facilitated the gradual integration of immigrants into an economy that by the mid-1950s began to stabilize and then quickly grow.

IMMIGRATION WAVES

Not only the pace but the people who were immigrating changed. By 1952, twice as many immigrants came to Israel from Asia and North Africa as from Europe. Efforts to bring over North African Jews were decidedly less frenetic than those directed at European Jews, and many claimed this was not coincidental, given their darker skins and Middle Eastern cultural proclivities. For the Jews of Morocco, the timing of the more casual policy could not have been worse. In 1952, a growing wave of North African nationalism caused a marked deterioration in local political conditions. In response to Israel's War of Independence, anti-Semitic riots in the cities of Djerada and Oujda led to the murder of forty-four Jews and the wounding of fifty-five more.[97] In light of Moroccan Jewry's growing vulnerability, the government's position seemed obtuse.

Representatives of the Moroccan Jewish community complained bitterly to the Jewish Agency in public forums about the quotas. Of the 265,000 Jews living in the country, it estimated that 100,000 were ready to leave immediately. The Agency's monthly cap for all North African Jews was 5,000.[98] After 1955, quotas were relaxed and some 25,000 Moroccan Jews immigrated that year. Yet it would take a decade until Israel brought over communities deemed less able to contribute economically to Israel. During this time 200,000 Jews came to Israel from North Africa.[99]

This is an impressive number but still lower than the 235,000 North African Jews who opted to move to France.[100] These Jews make up some 80 percent of the French Jewish community today. In other words, those North African Jews who could, largely chose France over Israel. Consequently, half of the immigrants arriving from North Africa and Asia (generically called in Hebrew: "Mizrachim"—technically "easterners") during the 1950s were categorized as "uneducated," and only about 2 percent arrived with formal higher education.[101] During Israel's early years, 3.4 percent of Mizrachi immigrants worked as scientists or in technical professions, as opposed to 8.5 percent of European immigrants.[102] France still enjoys a reputation as home to Moroccan and Tunisian Jewish elites.[103]

Moroccan Israelis faced a tougher reality than their cousins who went to Europe.[104] Upon arrival, scores of North Africans were put on trucks and taken to development towns in Israel's periphery. Often driven at night, they could not see where they were going or protest. Opportunities for gainful employment and social integration were more limited, and a social "pathology" of an Israeli underclass developed along ethnic lines.[105] Most of these immigrants did not want to come to the Negev at all. Many nevertheless remained, creating the industrial and settlement infrastructure for this arid, frontier region.[106]

All told, over 350,000 immigrants came to Israel from Morocco, Algeria, and Tunisia. This considerable human mass was soon dwarfed by 1.2 million Russian-speaking immigrants who arrived in Israel once the Soviet Union opened its doors. Until the 1970s, there was barely a trickle from these countries, as Communist regimes formally prohibited their citizens from leaving. Annual immigration was no more than a few hundred a year. An exceptionally generous year during the 1960s might see 2,000 Russian-speaking people move to Israel. Then things changed dramatically.

The critical mass of Russian-speaking Jewry arrived in two phases: before and after the collapse of the Soviet Union. The first wave began in 1971 and continued steadily until 1980, bringing 155,858 immigrants to Israel. Extensive efforts by Israel and Jewish communities worldwide to highlight the oppressed condition of Soviet Jewry began to affect world opinion, creating a public-relations fiasco for the Moscow regime. Espousing a spirit of détente, Soviet leader Leonid Brezhnev was keen to increase trade with the United States. Relaxing restrictions on would-be Jewish émigrés seemed a small price to pay for the anticipated economic return. In 1971, 12,839 Jews were allowed to leave for Israel—ten times the previous year's quota. By 1972 the numbers jumped to 31,652. This relative leniency stretched on for a decade. Once it became clear that favorable trading conditions with America were not forthcoming, the gates were shut tight. In 1982, only 782 Soviet Jews reached Israel.

Even during this period of ostensibly open immigration, Soviet Jews requesting exit visas still needed to display tremendous personal courage and faith that their sacrifice would eventually lead to departure. Demands for receiving an exit visa were exhausting, including proof that family members were waiting in Israel. Once filed, applicants were promptly demoted or lost their jobs entirely. Students were summarily dismissed from their universities. Harassment by the KGB was common. Most applications were in fact rejected. Those approved were not for top engineers and scientists from Moscow but more typically for less-skilled applicants from the Republic of Georgia.

"Soviet Jewry" was an expensive operation, and by 1974, budgeted by the Israeli government and the Jewish Agency at $250 million a year.[107] Getting immigrants to Israel was the least of the expense. By the 1970s the government was granting new immigrants an "absorption basket." Besides rent subsidies, free health care, and national insurance, they received sweeping tax exemptions. Immigrants served less time in the army and could go to the university for free. The investment reflected a recognition that times had changed. Many Soviet Jewish immigrants had skill sets enabling them to emigrate to other lands if conditions and employment opportunities were not competitive.

A decade after the first Soviet tidal wave subsided, Israel was hit by a human tsunami. Under Mikhail Gorbachev's steady liberalization and perestroika policy, Soviet emigration policy was completely reformed. During the waning days of the Communist regime, in 1990 an astonishing 185,227 Soviet Jews arrived in Israel. This signaled a torrential deluge that brought 1 million more from the former Soviet Union over the subsequent decade, until the year 2000, when numbers fell to 20,000. It was by far the largest group of immigrants Israel ever absorbed. To what can this astonishing migration be attributed?

When the shadow of subjugation and poverty characterizing Soviet Communism was lifted in the 1990s, initially the Jewish community was elated. For the first time in half a century, synagogues were open and Jewish culture could go public. Discrimination was reduced; Jews enjoyed an even playing field professionally; Israel was no longer a state enemy. But soon the Russian economy began to implode, and Jews could see the writing on the wall. Ethnic and national rumblings frequently had anti-Semitic overtones. Israel was available and a very welcoming destination.[108] More importantly—the United States was not.

During the previous Soviet migration during the 1970s, immigrants to Israel were routed via Vienna and later Ladispoli, a resort town northwest of Rome. While appreciative of Israel's extraordinary efforts to establish contact with them, fabricate relatives to justify emigration permits, and defer the cost of travel, most Russian Jews were not Zionists. Rather, they were just anxious to leave the suffocation of Communism. In 1974, 35 percent arrived in western Europe but chose not to go to Israel. By 1976 the number of "dropouts" exceeded 50 percent.[109]

As more Soviet Jews chose the United States it raised a philosophical and practical problem for Israel. Jewish federations in American cities raised funds to meet the needs of the new Soviet immigrants—money Israelis felt was needed to support its parallel absorption efforts. Seeing the immigrants as political refugees escaping Communism, the U.S. government even allocated a thousand dollars per person in financial assistance, with matching support expected of American Jewish institutions. Suddenly, Israel's claim to be a sole haven for oppressed Jewish masses seemed hollow. The American dream provided a more-compelling alternative. Tensions between Israeli and American Jewish institutions mounted. Elected in 1976, Menachem Begin was less belligerent about the issue and felt he could not deny Soviet Jews "freedom of choice." Consequently, most Soviet Jews who could, voted with their feet. Israel was seen as a smaller market with fewer opportunities.[110]

When Mikhail Gorbachev began rolling back the despotic Soviet polices a decade later, Israel was ready. Having learned the lesson of the Soviet "dropouts" in Vienna, the government moved to plug the leaks when emigration restraints were relaxed. By 1989 almost 90 percent of Soviet Jews arriving in Italy expressed a preference for resettlement in the United States rather than in Israel.[111] As many as sixty thousand were expected to leave the Soviet Union that year.[112] In February 1987 Israel's prime minister Yitzhak Shamir requested that the United States no longer consider Soviet Jewish émigrés as political refugees. This time, the American Jewish community was more inclined to accede to Israeli demands. The anticipated costs of settling enormous numbers of Jews was prohibitive. Israeli absorption was less expensive. Most American Jews paid lip service to "freedom of choice" but actually felt Israel needed the people more and was a more-appropriate place for such a large influx.

Eventually, Congress, the Bush administration, and the Jewish community reached a compromise limiting the number of refugee visas for Soviet citizens to fifty thousand, with 80 percent of these to be granted to Jews. American embassies in Europe were prohibited from processing Russian visa applications. Willing to take all-comers, Israel quickly reestablished itself as the default destination for Russian-speaking Jews. To reduce the risk of dropouts, transit sites run by the Jewish Agency were moved out of western Europe (Vienna and Rome) to Warsaw, Bucharest, and Budapest, where the direct line to Israel was more inevitable. Within four years, four hundred thousand more Soviet immigrants had landed and were scattered across Israel. In short, the reason why so many Russians moved to Israel is that quite literally they had nowhere else to go.

The Russian immigration was quantitatively and qualitatively significant enough to change the face of Israeli society. The lion's share of the arrivals had academic training. Among the immigrants were forty thousand professional musicians, twenty thousand research scientists, fifty thousand teachers, ten thousand doctors and dentists.[113] Israel scrambled to provide housing, jobs, and Hebrew schooling for the Russians. Initially, many were unable to find suitable employment. It was not unusual to see a surgeon doing janitorial work, or a symphony musician playing on a street corner, passing the hat for donations. Within a few years, however, a rapid shift from blue- to white-collar jobs took place, first among men and then among women. Some left the country to pursue better professional opportunities abroad. But roughly 88 percent of the highly skilled workers remained in Israel; less-skilled émigrés stayed as well.[114]

Israel's new Russian community was unabashedly proud of its heritage, culture, and erudition. While professionally ambitious, many Russians did not feel a particular need to integrate culturally.[115] By the mid-1990s, they supported some fifty Russian newspapers, several television and radio stations, as well as political parties with sufficient muscle to determine the balance of power in Israel's government.[116] There were innumerable talented Russian immigrants, from European champion pole-vaulter Alex Averbukh to Boris Gelfand, runner-up in world chess championships. Many link Israel's remarkable success as a "start-up nation"—with more companies listed on the NASDAQ than any country outside the United States—to the massive influx of engineering and technical competence provided by the Russian aliyah.[117]

This Russian immigration also included some three hundred thousand immigrants who technically were not Jewish, many unapologetically Christian in their religious identity.[118] Israelis from all political camps expressed resentment at overzealous emissaries who forgot that their mission was not simply to generate immigrants but to bring Jews to Israel. In practice most non-Jewish Russian immigrants had no problem succeeding in Israeli society and are largely indistinguishable from genetically Jewish immigrants. In Israel's military meritocracy, the ultimate societal "melting pot," Russian immigrants excelled. Serving in elite units with dangerous missions, casualty rates among this group were three times higher than the Israel Defense Forces (IDF) averages. One-quarter of recipients of medals for bravery were Russians. Some 15 percent of "non-Jewish" Russian-speaking soldiers asked to convert.[119]

The twin waves of Russian immigration were followed by two from Africa, smaller in dimensions but no less dramatic. It took years for the Israeli establishment to recognize the estimated twenty-eight thousand Ethiopians living in Gondar province as Jewish. Never really accepted by their neighbors, this ancient "Beta Israel" community had been cut off from the Jewish mainstream for centuries. But its Jewish identity endured. After the fall of historically sympathetic emperor Haile Selassie in 1974, the community's fate grew increasingly precarious. In the early 1980s, the Marxist Ethiopian regime outlawed Judaism, banned Hebrew teaching, and arrested many Beta Israel leaders as Zionist spies on trumped-up charges.

A bold escape choreographed by the Mossad, known as "Operation Moses," was organized. Unfazed by violent bandits, starvation, and ambushes, Ethiopian Jews defiantly walked for days until they reached Sudan, a predominantly Muslim country. By bribing the president and senior Sudanese ministers, creating a fake tourist village on the Red Sea and devising sundry subterfuges, between 1984 and 1985 Israel's navy and air force worked with Israeli secret agents to bring 10,213 Ethiopians to Israel. The operation was truncated when word got out and Arab nations protested, leaving the majority of Ethiopian Jewry stranded in Africa.[120]

Soon thereafter, Israel reestablished diplomatic relations with Ethiopia, but the Addis Ababa government was loath to anger the Arab world, and immigration was not renewed. Once the Soviet Union collapsed, it would not take long for Ethiopia's Communist government to follow. The Jewish Agency saw an opportunity and moved scores of Jews to Addis Ababa. During a gripping, thirty-six-hour span, between May 24 and 25, 1991, "Operation Solomon" (an allusion to the biblical king's wife, the Ethiopian queen of Sheba) was launched.[121] As the capital city was about to fall to the rebels, $40 million in bribes enabled thirty-three aircraft to swoop in and extricate an even larger group of immigrants.

These two dramatic quasi-military operations, in retrospect, were just a start. Many more people in Ethiopia declared themselves Jewish, but questions emerged as to whether they actually were. Methodically, bureaucrats began to filter the flood of additional applications. In the interim, Ethiopian immigration became more routine, with 91,000 Ethiopians ultimately moving to Israel.

Public opinion was never as universally enthralled with immigration as Israeli and Zionist propaganda suggests. There has always been ambivalence among Israelis regarding its immigrants. For the most part, people like the idea of their country serving as a sanctuary for Jewish refugees. But not everyone has the energy or patience for the newcomers. Surveys conducted during the 1990s suggest that as more immigrants arrived, the public's tolerance for them diminished, especially among poor populations with low education levels.[122] During the immigration surge from the former Soviet Union, Arab-Israelis were concerned that their positions in society would be further marginalized by the attention and resources required for absorption.[123]

Immigrants to Israel were often stunned at the less than enthusiastic reception they received in their promised land. Stereotypes accompanied every wave of Jewish immigration: Romanians were thieves, Americans spoiled, Kurds dim, Russians promiscuous, Moroccans uncivilized, Germans obsessive-compulsive.

While the ethnic stereotype provided plenty of material for comics and low-level humor,[124] it also reflected the labor pains associated with birthing a multicultural society.

The mechanics of absorption for the Ethiopian community were especially challenging. It required a transition from rural Africa to a postindustrial society.[125] Israel's Ethiopians are unable to change their skin color and blend in like immigrants from earlier waves. Many faced excruciating bigotry, which spawned periodic protests. Progress was slow but steady. It is reflected in the selection of Yityish "Titi" Aynaw, a native Ethiopian, as a particularly poised and intelligent Miss Israel in 2013. That same year, Aynaw's achievement arguably was surpassed by Tahounia Rube, an Ethiopian model, winning the million-shekel prize on Israel's *Big Brother* reality TV show. Ethiopian Knesset members are now commonplace.

Ethiopian Jewry's arrival in Israel may not have produced the professional dividends of the Russian immigrations, but it validated Israel's national raison d'être as a haven for Jews with nowhere else to go. The massive transfer of Ethiopian Jewry to Israel also signaled the end of an era. It will probably be the last meaningful, national Jewish community that needed or wanted to be saved.

PUSH, PULL, AND THE FUTURE

For most of Israel's history, the United States was home to more Jews than any other country. (It is telling that the massive leap in American Jewish numbers took place between the 1880s and the 1920s, when Zionism was only able to attract a trickle of immigrants to Palestine.) Today, roughly 5.3 million Jews live in the United States.[126] Over sixty-seven years of Israeli history, a mere 100,000 American Jews moved to Israel.[127] That's an average below 2,000 per year, less than a good day for the Russians in 1990! Most estimates suggest that at least half of those who come ultimately return.

For a brief period, it looked as if a North American demographic shift might be in the making. In 1967 fewer than 1,000 immigrants came to Israel from the United States. But the dramatic military victory of that year's Six-Day War created almost a mystic aura of divine destiny. Many young American Jews, influenced by the counterculture of the 1960s and disenchanted with American military involvement in Vietnam, began to see Israel as an option. In 1969 6,459 arrived; that number grew to 7,158 in 1970 and peaked at 8,122 in 1971.[128]

Arie "Lova" Eliav, a highly respected leftist Israeli politician and intellectual, waxed optimistic in his 1972 book, *The Land of the Hart*: "We shall have to institute a professional revolution in the various branches of our economy if they are to be open to hundreds of thousands of American Jews. . . . If we fulfill these expectations, then I believe that immigration from America will increase. The immigration within a single generation of hundreds of thousands of Jews from the United States may now appear to be a daydream, but I believe that it is a goal attainable by Zionism."[129]

Lova Eliav was a great visionary. But that time, he got it wrong. Eliav did not realize that the idealistic young American Jews streaming to Israel in those days, founding new kibbutzim like Ketura, Gezer, and Yahel, were in fact a small, anomalous "elite." They enjoy great respect within the American Jewish community, but are not a model for emulation. For most of the Jewish world today, no real "push" exists to leave, and Israel's "pull" has limited potency.

This became clear in June 1968, only a year after the Six-Day War, when the 27th Zionist Congress convened in Jerusalem. Representatives from Jewish communities around the world came to celebrate the historic reunification of Jerusalem. On the agenda was a new declaration elevating aliyah, making it a compulsory component of Zionist identity. Sensing a historic opportunity, Zionist leaders thought to leverage the exhilaration surrounding the great "conquest" into a new expectation that all Jews around the world move to Israel.[130] But the American delegation, by far the largest at the congress, was absolutely opposed. A compromise was reached with the new 1968 Jerusalem Program, offering a tepid acknowledgment that one of the goals of Zionism was "The ingathering of the Jewish people in the historic homeland, Eretz Israel, through aliyah from all countries."[131] And so American immigration continued its crawl at a rate of roughly two thousand Jews a year.

In 2002 a new phase in Israel's immigration experience for English speakers began. During the previous decade, Israel increasingly embraced capitalism. More and more government activities were privatized or moved to nonprofits, from water planning and police academies to mineral and gas production. (Israel's Supreme Court put the brakes on privatizing prisons.) It was hardly surprising when another area of government affairs—immigration—was delegated to a new NGO: Nefesh B'Nefesh (Soul by Soul). The idea was hatched in 2001 in Boca Raton, Florida on a Saturday "Sabbath visit," when a partnership was launched between businessman Tony Gelbart and his rabbi, Yehoshua Fass. "Rabbi Fass said, 'Can we take a Sabbath walk?' He proceeded to tell me that his young cousin, who was 14 at the time, had been murdered by an Arab terrorist at a bus stop. He felt it was important for him to move to Israel as a result, and for more people to move to Israel to fight the injustice. I said, 'I'm glad you want to make aliyah and saddened about your cousin, but how can I help?' He proceeded to tell me about some ideas he had to pursue his dream. We

Young American immigrants arrive in Israel on a flight chartered by Nefesh B'Nefesh. In 2014, 3,762 intrepid American Jews came—an impressive number, but hardly a demographic game changer. (Sasson Tiram, courtesy of Nefesh B'Nefesh)

talked about the issues of aliyah. It took twenty-four hours to start something and that's how it all began."[132]

The idea behind the initiative is simple: start treating North American and British Jews like highly prized clients, and provide them the services to ease their transition. The Nefesh B'Nefesh Web site enumerates a long list of pre-aliyah guidance and support amenities, which include assistance during pilot trips, employment webinars, and an Israeli call center, open conveniently for American time zones. Full charter flights bring the immigrants over en masse, free of charge, where they can be greeted by staged dancing and singing of awaiting Israelis.[133] Sometimes, the prime minister shows up to congratulate the immigrants. Rather than spend countless hours chasing the Israeli bureaucracy to get set up in Israel, the flights offer "one-stop shopping" for immigrants who can efficiently complete all the maddening paperwork for their health care, identification cards, and rent stipends. "Post-aliyah assistance," includes buddy programs, seminars, monthly follow-up phone calls, you name it. Last but not least, immigrants receive money. In the past, grants to new Anglo immigrants (purportedly based on need) went as high as twenty-five thousand dollars a family.[134]

Gelbart justifies the assistance because "economic concerns are the main deterrent" for American immigrants. "These young people still have student loans to pay. Mortgages weigh them down and by the time the families have stabilized economically, they have also found a place socially and professionally where they live and so aliyah loses its relevance for them."[135]

Critics counter that privatization undermines equality—always a hallmark of Israeli absorption policy. These are not services that immigrants from other countries enjoy. Presumably, that's because so much of Nefesh B'Nefesh's budget comes from private donors—presently 50 percent.[136] During its first ten years of operation, the organization received roughly $125 million in tax-exempt donations. Nefesh B'Nefesh argues that it is an excellent investment. American immigrants make a particularly meaningful contribution to Israel's economy. A study commissioned by the organization reports that as of 2012, some 1 billion shekels in benefits can be identified with immigrants it recruited.[137]

Haaretz, the daily newspaper, printed a blistering exposé about the organization in 2012, calling into question the $200,000 annual salaries for top managers, the high rent for the organization's offices, the hiring of Erez Halfon, a Ministry of Absorption director without the mandatory delay before moving to the private sector, and misappropriation of funds. The story claimed that Nefesh B'Nefesh took credit for many immigrants it had nothing to do with recruiting, such as the children of Israelis in the United States who come to serve in the army via the Friends of Israel Scouts.[138]

If Nefesh B'Nefesh had delivered on its promise to bring massive American aliyah—or even ten thousand Jews a year—critics would probably be more forgiving. English-speaking immigrants are grateful to the organization: its assistance helps many of them find their way in the new country. But after a decade of intensive work and massive investment, North American immigration to Israel remains stagnant. Total numbers are insignificant, rarely exceeding three thousand a year.[139] A proverbial red carpet was rolled out, but there was no stampede to the Promised Land.

When asked why more Americans don't come, Rabbi Fass explains, "The pool of American Jews is much smaller than the 5.5 million usually cited. Remember, aliyah is for individuals who have visited Israel once before. If you haven't dated Israel, you aren't going to marry her. Some 82% of American Jews have never visited Israel; take away senior citizens; remove the Haredi population who won't move to Israel for fear of getting drafted and who are fundamentally anti-Zionist. In the end, it's a very small percentage of potential immigrants remaining." (In fact, the comprehensive 2013 Pew Research Center study estimates that 43 percent of American Jews have visited Israel.) Nefesh B'Nefesh argues that the financial sacrifice required today is too great. "The basket of support for immigrants has not been increased in ten years," explains NBN's vice chair Erez Halfon. "Today, many American immigrants can't afford to buy an apartment in Israel and must sell their homes in the U.S. at a loss."[140]

The simplest explanation, of course, is that it is hard to leave the prosperity and security that Jews enjoy in North America. Most Jewish Americans are doing well. The percentage of Jewish households earning over seventy-five thousand dollars a year is twice the national average. The vast majority of American Jews are university graduates; they are four times more likely to have advanced degrees than the national average.[141] America offers a rich menu of meaningful alternatives to an essentially liberal Jewish community; Israel discriminates against non-Orthodox Judaism. Even if someone overcomes the transition to the new country, with its new job, new language, new house, new climate, and new culture, no one can guarantee that quality of life will be better. And it is never easy to leave family and friends behind on a different continent.

Religiosity appears to be a predictive factor regarding American immigration today. Some 62 percent of North American immigrants coming to Israel identify themselves as "modern Orthodox." This percentage is noteworthy, as only one-tenth of the affiliated American Jewish community is Orthodox. Any sizable aliyah from the United States in the future is likely to come from this populace. Among non-Orthodox immigrants, 18 percent identify themselves as "Conservative," embracing a moderate, religious tradition; only 6 percent are Reform Jews, with a decidedly progressive approach to Jewish theology.[142]

One new development in the Jewish world that might have expanded American immigration involves the remarkable number of young Jews visiting Israel in the Birthright Israel program. The brainchild of philanthropists Charles Bronfman and Michael Steinhardt, the initiative targets young Jews from around the world. Since Birthright was established in 1994, the program has covered most of the costs for more than 400,000 Jewish young adults from sixty-six countries (including 215,000 from the United States) on a ten-day intensive educational tour throughout Israel.[143] This might be considered the "date" that could lead to a more-serious geographical commitment. But Fass explains that Birthright is not designed to strengthen Israel, but rather the Jewish identity of young people, who are expected to return to their communities. Even so, several hundred "Birthright graduates" are among the Americans who move to Israel each year.

When asked whether they think their peers might come to Israel, most recent American immigrants are blunt: Michael Maze moved to Tel Aviv from

Austin, Texas, and works for PayPal, combating credit-card fraud. His own experience suggests that there are few American Jews who come to Israel, and that many leave. "I don't see a large potential for mass immigration from the states. Those of us who came here and stayed, even for a significant amount of time, are probably considered a little odd," explains the thirty-one-year-old Maze.

> We tend to be very ideological people, but we live in a post-ideological era. There are some downsides of aliyah which are simply unavoidable. Distance from family matters, even with all the new communications technology. In an age of individualism when people grow up in an individualistic country, it is legitimate to worry about moving to a country where you aren't a native speaker; where you didn't grow up; and wonder about the likelihood of finding self-fulfillment. You see aliyah is really not the goal—it's the start of the journey. The goal is to make successful aliyah. So the question becomes: "What do you do as a citizen to find personal fulfillment as an individual?" I don't know if these were questions American immigrants asked when Israel was younger and more Socialist. It was more about the collective then than it is now. I don't see the impetus for most American Jews to come to Israel today.[144]

Another country that might yield a massive aliyah is France. With a core Jewish population close to five hundred thousand, after the United States it has the largest Jewish community outside Israel. The community is largely traditional, and Jewish family size is greater than France's general fertility level of 2.08 children per family.[145] The Jewish community should be growing, but it has shrunk 10 percent since a post–World War II peak in 1970.[146]

There is no shortage of reasons for Jews to leave France. The past decade saw a precipitous rise in anti-Semitic acts, with the number of physical attacks against Jews nearly doubling in 2012.[147] Most of the attacks are associated with radical French Muslims whom local Jewish leaders liken to Nazis.[148] That year some two hundred violent anti-Semitic acts were reported, culminating in the killing of a rabbi and three Jewish children in Toulouse by a French Muslim, who trained with Islamic militants in Pakistan.[149] In 2015, a kosher delicatessen was targeted, and four Jews died.[150] Cumulatively, these create an ominous day-to-day atmosphere for the community.

Yet the number of French immigrants coming to Israel in 2012 was among the lowest of the decade. In sixty-five years, fewer than 80,000 French Jews moved to Israel, with average annual immigration below 2,000. (The year 2013 saw a surge with 3,070 moving to Israel, and in 2014, the number reached 7,000.)[151] But it is also estimated that some 20–30 percent of these immigrants soon return to France.[152] French Jews are indeed leaving France in record numbers. Only they are not moving to Israel: Montreal, Miami, even London constitute far more common destinations.[153]

Armand Sibony, a leader in the French Jewish community, believes that economic opportunities trigger emigration among French Jews today. With a stagnant French economy, young Jewish professionals with skills in high-tech and computers seek positions in Silicon Valley. The elite in finance see London as the most promising destination. Beyond the challenge of language competency, professional opportunities in Israel, for the most part, cannot compete. Israeli earning potential remains smaller than that which most Jews enjoy in France.[154]

At the same time, each year about one thousand French Jews appear to be hedging their bets by buying vacation apartments in Israel—just in case.[155] In the first five months of 2013, it was estimated that French Jews invested $103 million in residential real estate,[156] with cities like Ashdod and Netanya being particularly popular sites for second homes.[157]

The French and the American stories continue a century-long dynamic, which was summed up clearly by demographer Professor DellaPergola's overview of aliyah to Israel: "Ideologies were necessary but not sufficient to generate large-scale migration. The principal stimulus to leave came from the experience of personal insecurity and economic stress of Jews in the countries of origin. The somewhat intriguing conclusion is that migration to Israel, although supposedly motivated by the Israeli pull, was very little connected with what was actually occurring in Israeli society."[158] Natan Sharansky, the current head of the Jewish Agency, has come to adopt a similar view. He talks about a new model, which he euphemistically calls "aliyah by choice."[159]

THE END OF THE ALIYAH ERA

Immigration to Israel changed the face of the country and created a fascinating, unruly, but ultimately rich multicultural mosaic. Israel's gates remain open and Jews continue to come. But there is little to suggest that the numbers will be sufficient to meaningfully affect the overall size of Israel's population.

In their voluminous anthology about Israeli immigration, sociologists Judith Shuval and Elazar Leshem conclude, "Careful documentation shows that in fact Jews from Western, democratic countries did not 'rise up' and come. Those who came from post-war Europe were Holocaust survivors and persons prevented from entering Palestine during World War II and detained by the British in Cyprus campus. Those from Islamic countries came to escape extremist Islamic and anti-Semitic groups whose hostility increased when the state was established. Indeed, thousands did come; however motives and attributes were not very different from those of refugees in other settings."[160]

Jews living outside of Israel today are anything but refugees. Over 90 percent of Jews living outside of Israel reside in the planet's most developed countries, where they enjoy economic opportunities and human rights.[161] Learning from the past, for the foreseeable future, the millions of Jews living in the United States, France, and throughout the world will not seek a home in Israel.

Of course the age of prophesy is long over, and the history of Israel has had many unanticipated demographic developments. Nonetheless, the human reservoirs of oppressed and impoverished Jewish populations that might *drive* mass immigrations in the future are gone. The Israeli economy is rapidly approaching the per capita GDP of Europe, but the country's *pull* is not sufficient. Looking back, the percentage of total demographic growth attributable to immigration was once as high as 65 percent. Today it has inconsequential dimensions.

All told, the country's present net immigration balance is neutral. Here's how the numbers stack up: On the deficit side of the ledger, since 1990 on average 22,000 Israelis leave the country each year, even as 9,218 Israelis return home.[162] The net annual loss of citizens comes to 12,800. In addition, many Russian Jews who immigrated during the 1990s decided to move on. Between 1990 and 2010 the total number of Russian Jews leaving Israel was 129,000. (Some 26,000 of them eventually thought better of it and returned to Israel after testing foreign

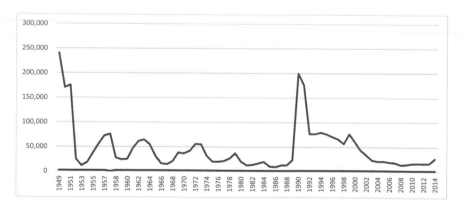

Annual immigration to Israel: This graph shows the initial surge of Holocaust refugees, the subsequent arrival of Jews from Arab countries, and the mass absorption of 1 million Russians during the 1990s. Since then, immigration appears to have tapered off for good. (Source: Israel Central Bureau of Statistics)

waters.) In other words, on average, an additional 5,000 Russian Israelis left the country each year.

On the plus side—once the extraordinary Russian aliyah subsided, during the past decade 26,000 Jews immigrated to Israel on average each year.[163] With the completion of Ethiopian immigration, this number actually dropped to 16,000–18,000 per year between 2010 and 2012. The years since then saw a modestly upward turn, with over 20,000 immigrants arriving annually, on average.[164] The immigration-emigration balance in Israel is starting to stabilize, with any gains or losses trivial in relation to overall population size.

Israel's first president, Chaim Weizmann, liked to quip, "To be a Zionist, it is not necessary to be mad, but it helps."[165] This remains largely true today. Over the years, there have been scores of Jewish idealists captivated by the "Zionist idea" who answered the call. It was not distress that brought them, but visions and dreams. These Zionists frequently were exceptional people and they made extraordinary contributions to the country. It is likely that such remarkable people will continue to percolate into Israel, fertilizing the society with new ideas, energy, and professional capacity. Collectively, their numbers have never been sufficient to constitute a mass movement, and there is little to suggest that this will change.

From the perspective of sustainability, this can be characterized as an ideal situation. Sustainable growth, after all, is an oxymoron; stability is the ideal. If Israel's paramount mission is to serve as a sanctuary for Jews around the world, present dynamics should in no way be considered a failure. The opposite is true: the present equilibrium is a triumph. For over sixty years, Israel served as a critical haven for persecuted Jews or for Jews facing economic privation. Despite occasional mistakes, the country carried out this assignment with distinction. Israel was a land of opportunity for immigrants. Veteran Israeli taxpayers (along with generous Jews from around the world) willingly footed the bill for associated absorption costs.

But this stage is now over. It is possible to move to the next phase in the Zionist evolution, which focuses on building an Israeli society that is a paragon of creativity, culture, tolerance, justice, and sustainability. It is also time to embrace a new, more-mature relationship between Israel and the Jewish world—a relationship of mutual admiration and respect.[166] Today, 85 percent of Jews in the world, more or less evenly divided, live in Israel and the United States. There is in fact a precedent for such a bifurcated demographic reality.

For over a millennium, from 600 B.C. until A.D. 600 a substantial Jewish community thrived in Babylonia. For many years there were parallel academies in Israel and Babylon. For much of the time, the latter was even considered to be the more authoritative center for the Jewish world. Looking back today at the rich variety of approaches that the geographic divide produced, the split seems fortuitous. The vast world of Talmudic literature and law was greatly enriched. Even without phone lines or Internet, the two communities remained connected and coordinated. Jewish diversity was celebrated. Great scholars spent time in the great academies of both lands. They understood that the sum was greater than the parts.

There is no reason why Israel should not embrace a more-deferential approach to North American Jews and to the other remarkable Jewish communities that flourish today around the globe. There was a time when the Jewish state zealously brought immigrants to its shores because it desperately needed more people. That is no longer the case.

5

BLESSED WITH CHILDREN: FROM DOGMA TO SUBSIDIES

> The poor laws of England tend to depress the general condition
> of the poor in these two ways. Their first obvious tendency is to
> increase population without increasing the food for its support.
> —Thomas Malthus, "An Essay on the Principle of Population," 1798.

A NEW NATION GOES NATAL

David Ben-Gurion was a very talented man. But he was never known as having a gift for small talk. For much of his public life he compensated by relying on one basic icebreaker with which he greeted the many women he met. It could be a housewife in Beer Sheva or the international president of Hadassah. After learning the woman's name, Ben-Gurion would invariably ask, "How many children do you have?" If the woman said "two," he would respond, "Why not three?" If she said "three," he'd respond "Why not four?"

Ben-Gurion saw large Jewish families as a matter of national survival. As early as 1943 he called on Jews to go far beyond 2.2 total fertility rate replacement levels. In formal settings he sermonized about parents' "demographic duties," even though he himself fathered but three children. In 1967 he wrote, "Any woman, who does not have four children, as much as it depends on her, is betraying the Jewish mission."[1] Upon retiring to Sde Boker, at kibbutz weddings, Ben-Gurion would address brides directly under the canopy and urge them to have four children.[2] Large families—or what soon became dubbed "internal aliyah"—was the only way to ensure that Israel not become "a second Cyprus."[3]

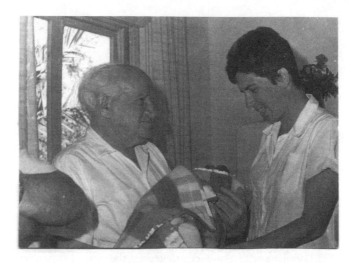

In his personal campaign to increase the birthrate, pro-natal
prime minister David Ben-Gurion never refused requests to
serve as a "godfather" for newborns during circumcision rituals
(bris). This is one of many such ceremonies at Kibbutz Sde
Boker, 1969. (Photograph courtesy of Kibbutz Sde
Boker Archives)

Numerous collective sentiments lie behind Israel's pro-natal agenda. The first
of these is Jewish nationalism. One of the legacies of the Mandate was the framing of competing national claims along demographic lines. Founders of the
nascent state felt strongly that the battle for sovereignty between Arabs and Jews
would only be resolved when Israel was predominantly Jewish. They believed,
with some justification, that Arabs would never accept the idea of a Jewish state
in Palestine until Jewish numeric superiority was absolute.

This existential concern has been a salient fear among Israeli political leaders and senior officials throughout the country's history; it constitutes the first
and arguably most powerful force behind Israel's demographic policies. Other
nations, like India and Pakistan, or Greek and Turkish Cypriots, resolved their
ethnic divisions by partition and population exchanges. Yet for most Zionist
leaders, expulsion of Arabs from Israel was either deemed immoral or detrimental to the country's international image.[4] It was clear from the start that Israel's
Arab citizens weren't willing or able to go anywhere else. Thus the demographic
battle, begun under the British, continued. Jewish family size became an issue
of security and a sacred national mission.

Natality (having large families) was tantamount to patriotism. Ben-Gurion University social scientists Jon Anson and Avinoam Meir analyzed election results from the 1984 elections and showed that fertility rates were strongly correlated with nationalist sentiments in the Israeli collective conscience. This nationalism, they argued, is heavily informed by Israel's unique and vulnerable position in the Middle East.[5]

The associated rhetoric was invariably sanctimonious and manipulative. In 1987, at a conference on Jewish population trends, Knesset member Moshe Katsav (later Israel's ninth and ultimately notorious president) labeled Israeli women who had abortions "selfish."[6] Ben-Gurion likened Jewish women with fewer than four children to draftees who evade military service.[7]

A second, related motivation for many was informed by strong emotions prevailing in the aftermath of the Holocaust.[8] After 1945 many Jews felt that replacing the 6 million lost Jewish lives with newborn Israelis was an act of defiance against Nazism as well as a moral debt and statement of solidarity with the victims. The idea of replenishing the dead lost in a national catastrophe reemerged in the aftermath of the Yom Kippur War, when 2,686 Israeli soldiers lost their lives.[9] Israeli Arabs had their own parallel ideology, which saw large families as their own defiant response to Palestinian national tragedy and exile.

The third motivation involves a religious perspective prevailing among many Jews and Muslims. The more zealous members of Israel's major religions, by and large, have always been uncomfortable with birth control[10] and abortions.[11] In 1943, the chief rabbi of Israel, Isaac Herzog, went so far as to speculate that the Holocaust might be a divinely engineered reproach against the sinful Jews of Europe, whose "modern style of living" limited family size. He foresaw a Jewish people that numbered tens of millions.[12]

Another clear force that manifests itself in pro-natal policies involves a commitment to social and economic equity.[13] Large families have always faced greater economic challenges and have been disproportionately poor. Historically, Israeli society was committed to equal opportunity and reduction of poverty. Especially during the country's early years, financial assistance to large families was considered an issue of social justice.[14] Making it materially more comfortable to raise large families meant incentivizing fertility. (In more recent years, an opposite view has emerged: it holds that while ameliorating short-term distress, over time, subsidies actually perpetuate poverty.)

Since Israel's inception there has always been a strong cultural inclination to glorify large families. Despite their country's poor showing in areas of housing or education relative to other Western countries, Israelis consistently rank high in comparative national happiness surveys.[15] One explanation is linked to the country's small dimensions, enabling continuous family interaction and maintenance of family ties; nuclear and extended families are a central part of most Israelis' social and cultural lives and a source of personal happiness, regardless of ethnicity.[16] When families aren't driving each other crazy, Israelis love spending time with their kin. So strong are these family bonds that young Israeli soldiers typically opt to go home while on leave for the weekend during compulsory military services. This habit continues through the university years; campus dormitories will empty out on Friday afternoon as Israeli students return for a traditional meal with their parents, often with laundry in tow. Extended families convene on the Sabbath, during holidays, for life-cycle events, at children's recitals and soccer games. The togetherness provides an *emotional* safety net and a *physical* energizer, which many find critical for confronting the country's tumultuous day-to-day reality.[17]

Finally there are those who believe that large families make an important contribution to Israel's economic development. For instance, during the 1960s, in light of labor shortages, Prime Minister Levi Eshkol, called for pro-natal policies to provide the workforce necessary to attain his vision of economic prosperity.[18]

Judged by any objective criterion, since the country's very first days, Israel's public orientation has encouraged fertility. Like many countries, Israel allows its prisoners to have conjugal visits. Yigael Amir, the assassin who murdered Prime Minister Yitzhak Rabin, is arguably the most vilified citizen in Israeli history. Yet when Amir filed a legal petition to enjoy conjugal visits, the Supreme Court ruled in his favor—even as it rejected his numerous requests to be released from solitary confinement. In 2007 Larisa Trembovler bore him a son.[19]

Throughout its history, Israel has been unabashedly open in proclaiming its pro-natal national ideology on the international stage. In Cairo in 1994, the United Nations convened its only serious conference focusing on overpopulation and public policy. The Israeli delegation, however, advocated an extreme pro-natal position.[20] More recently, the United Nations compared demographic agendas among the world's sixty-seven "intermediate fertility countries." All but two proclaimed their national strategic objective was reducing or maintaining present population size. Only Israel and Uruguay expressed an interest in increasing their numbers.[21]

THE ANTECEDENTS TO ISRAEL'S PRO-NATAL POLICY

The Israeli preoccupation with encouraging large families was part and parcel of the new state. Already in September 1948, while the battle for independence still raged, the minister of health appointed a committee that was to study different pro-natal alternatives that might translate Ben-Gurion's vision into public policy. Nine months later, on July 19, 1949, Israel's first cabinet approved a prize of one hundred liras (three hundred dollars, according to the existing exchange rate) to women bearing their tenth child. The government explained that the prize was intended "to encourage large families, to provide incentives to mothers in Israel to give birth, and to encourage reproduction." At the time it was projected that one hundred Jewish families qualified for the prize. Arab women citizens were eligible, too, but little data were available for any estimates.[22] The annual allocation from the prime minister's office's budget amounted to one hundred thousand dollars. Symbolically, the program might be called part of the ongoing war strategy for national independence, as the prize was approved the day before the final armistice agreement was signed with Syria. A new battleground in the struggle for Jewish sovereignty was declared.

The prize was symbolic of many of the country's pro-natal policy initiatives: the intervention successfully influenced human behavior and family decisions but did not achieve its intended purpose. Designed to encourage higher Jewish birthrates, the vast majority of recipients were Arab women. Ten years after its implementation, the award was quietly discontinued.[23] Ben-Gurion would ultimately recommend that a comparable prize be awarded by the Jewish Agency, a particularistic nongovernment agency, that legally could direct preferential assistance to Jewish families.

This episode also highlights a central irony that has characterized Israeli demographic programs from the outset. Because Israel is not only committed to being Jewish but also democratic, it is very difficult to design public policies to increase *Jewish* births that can withstand judicial review for nondiscrimination. A preferential *immigration* policy for Jews is an easier and ethically less compromising way to pad the Jewish majority.

During the country's initial decades of independence, the Knesset's only meaningful demographic legislation was the Law of Return. But Israel's parliament was not entirely complacent about fertility. Between 1954 and 1962, on twenty separate occasions, parliamentarians submitted motions urging the government to take more concerted action to increase birthrates.[24] In retrospect, policy measures were starting to coalesce. For example, in 1954, as part of the Employment of Women Law, new working mothers were guaranteed paid vacation for twelve weeks at 75 percent of their existing wages. A pregnant woman could begin maternity leave six weeks before her intended due date and take the other half of the furlough subsequent to it.[25] In 2010, the law was further amended: maternity leave was extended to twenty-six weeks: fourteen paid and twelve unpaid.[26] A new mother could delay her return for an additional twelve weeks without being fired by her employer. In 2013, new legislation guaranteeing fathers an eight-day paternity leave found surprising support in the Knesset.[27]

Another convention encouraging women to both work and have children is institutionalization of childcare. After initial hesitations, during the 1970s and 1980s working women with children increasingly came to rely on Israel's highly developed day-care centers.[28] Childcare essentially begins with a working mother's return to work after maternity leave. Most centers have no curricular or educational guidelines. Day-care subsidies are granted based on a variety of criteria, including income level, area of residence, and family size.[29] It undoubtedly made life more convenient for women in the early years of statehood and made the transition to motherhood less costly and traumatic. Experts from the time concluded that Israel's childcare system had little effect on women's decision of whether or not to have additional children. Birthrate remained relatively low during these years, especially among native-born citizens. The country's political leadership believed that this had to change.

With immigration waning at the advent of the 1960s, Prime Minister Ben-Gurion and his colleagues decided to launch a more-aggressive policy. Ben-Gurion had long since known that the best person to oversee its design was the inimitable Professor Roberto Bachi. Bachi moved to Israel from Italy in 1938 in the wake of Mussolini's anti-Semitic legislation. He was the son of a famous economist and grew up in the assimilated Jewish community of Rome. Bachi was something of a prodigy, publishing his first academic article at the age of twenty and becoming a full professor at age twenty-five.

Although Bachi had identified with Jewish nationalism since age fifteen, even visiting Palestine in 1933, he had a hard landing professionally after immigrating. The best position he could find was a job as a junior statistician at Hadassah Hospital in Jerusalem. At work, he taught himself the new language while calculating infant mortality and collecting other biostatistical data. Bachi immediately noticed that the birthrate among Jews in pre-state Palestine was low.[30]

At once he began to write formal and informal reports on topics from epidemiology to abortions. These were decidedly pessimistic demographic projections[31] that highlighted the need to promote "internal aliyah" and higher Jewish fertility.[32] The Jewish Agency, the acting Zionist government in Palestine at that time, took note. Soon Bachi was included in some of its key deliberations about the policies and institutions of the anticipated state.

On the population issue, Bachi put his money where his mouth was. When his wife went to have her fourth child delivered in Jerusalem, she was insulted when the German Jewish doctor made a disparaging remark about primitive

Professor Roberto Bachi, head of Israel's Central Bureau of
Statistics, delivers the country's second census to President
Yitzhak Ben Tzvi in 1961. The following year Bachi was
appointed chair of the committee that designed Israel's
demographic policy. (Photograph courtesy of
Margalit Bachi-Bejarano)

Italians who couldn't control their family size. (Little did he know that his primitive patient was fluent in numerous languages—including the German he spoke to the nurse!)[33]

In 1962 Ben-Gurion appointed a committee officially called the Committee for the *Problems of Natality*. Yet it was (and is still) generally referred to as the Bachi Committee, after its chair.[34] It had eight members, most of whom were senior government officials; only one was female. The formal task of the committee was to consider the general demography of Jews worldwide and to recommend ways to reconcile high fertility levels with family welfare.

It would take four years for the committee to submit its findings and recommendations, which it did in the spring of 1966.[35] Only on April 9, 1967, a year later, did the Israeli government discuss the report. The cabinet enthusiastically adopted the proposed pro-natal demographic policy for the country. Despite many vacillations along the way, it remains largely intact to this very day.[36]

The Bachi Committee report began by differentiating between distinct sectors in Israeli society. It explained that diverse policies were required to target specific groups that were in "different stages of their social and demographic" development.[37] Specifically, the committee focused on contrasting fertility levels among three groups: Jewish women of European extraction, Jewish women of Mizrachi (North African and Asian) origin, and Arab women. With an average of only 2.3–2.4 children, birthrates among European Jewish women were characterized as "extremely low"—lower than thirty-two out of thirty-three developed countries for 1963–1964. Bachi's projections showed that such modest fertility rates would only produce an 8 percent increase in population size over the course of a generation.

The committee well understood the reasons for this low birthrate: "The reduction in fertility among Jews from European backgrounds primarily is a direct result of the decision of parents to greatly reduce the number of their children and of the considerable use of birth control as well as artificial abortions."[38] By comparison, total fertility rate among Jewish families with Mizrachi origins at the time was 250 percent higher,[39] averaging 5.5 children during the 1950s.[40] The committee pointed out that the fertility gap was more related to discrepancies in educational levels than to ethnic differences per se. Only a tiny fraction of men arriving from North Africa and Asia during the 1950s had formal academic degrees, with women from these communities enjoying even lower levels of training.[41] During this period, Israeli women without any education on average had 6.8 children. When the data were controlled for education, family size in the two Jewish ethnic groups was indistinguishable.[42]

The Bachi Committee framed the disparity in terms of social equity and saw the gap as problematic. Detractors would later charge that ethnic distinctions gave the report eugenic undertones,[43] but this does not emerge from the language of the report. European families enjoyed a more privileged place in society and tended to be in higher socioeconomic brackets. The committee argued that the demographic gap perpetuated this economic advantage because children in smaller families performed far better academically and subsequently had better professional opportunities.

The committee also addressed the extraordinarily high birthrate of Israel's Arab citizens: 8.2 children on average for Muslim families, and 7.2 for Christians at the time. The report pointed out that this rate was higher than any of the ninety-one countries for which the United Nations kept reliable records. Use of birth control was extremely limited in the Arab sector then, and abortions—at least publicly—were unknown.[44]

Accordingly, the committee faced a dilemma. Everyone knew the reason the committee was formed in the first place was the asymmetrical demographic trends that so troubled Zionist political leadership. For Israel's first twenty years, despite massive Jewish immigration, the proportion of Arab citizens remained steady at around 11 percent. Yet due to the anticipated population momentum resulting from the young age of Arab Israelis, this percentage was expected to rise. Arabs eventually could overtake the Jewish majority, especially once immigration began its inevitable decline. There was also concern among the Ashkenazi power elite that Jews from the European communities, who had "founded the state," would soon be outnumbered by Mizrachi Jews. In short, Israel's population during the 1960s was humming along just fine, boasting a robust average annual increase of 3.2 percent.[45] But for the political leaders, the *wrong people* were having children. Given the country's commitment to being a democratic, nonracist society, this created considerable dissonance. Formulating nondiscriminating policies that could effectively counter these trends was a perplexing challenge.

The Bachi Committee decided to present its findings in the form of three concerns. First, in light of unprecedented demographic losses during the Holocaust, the low birthrate among Jews needed to be greater. Secondly, the concentration of large families in the low educational and economic strata exacerbated societal inequality; and, finally, the proliferation of abortions "caused health, demographic and moral damage."[46] The report called for educating the public about what it considered appropriate family size: "Only families with four children or more are contributing their full part to the demographic revival of the nation."[47] By shaming families with two or even three children and stymieing abortion, the committee was implicitly targeting the European Jewish cohort, whose birthrate it was trying to influence.

The operational implications were more complex. It was with great ambivalence that the committee decided that all interested citizens should continue to have full access to contraception. Any resulting damage to demographic objectives would need to be offset by intensifying efforts to reduce abortions.[48] This would be achieved by a system that closely regulated and limited abortions to authorized hospitals.

The real heart of the proposed strategy consisted of an array of pro-natal economic interventions. First and most influential to this day was general financial assistance to large families. The report called for income tax exemptions for children, which would increase with each additional child. For working mothers, it would take the form of day-care subsidies. The committee also recommended that employers be required to grant flexible and reduced working hours for mothers. Mortgages or grants for families who wished to expand their homes to accommodate more children were proposed.[49] In addition, the committee called for establishing a permanent government *Natality Committee*, which would monitor and address demographic challenges and associated issues involving family welfare.

The Bachi Committee's views and proposed policies have long since been criticized by a range of interest groups: from pro-choice feminists to representatives of Israel's Sephardic community. In fairness, Bachi never supported a ban on abortions or birth control. Indeed, he always held that the full gamut of family-planning options should be available to all and that no one should be forced to have children they did not want. (The dramatic increase in utilization of birth control by Mizrachi women in the late 1960s suggests that part of the country's efforts to integrate these immigrants into Israeli society was dissemination of birth control and family-planning counseling.)[50] Nor was Bachi a fan of extremely large families; he found the "ten-child award" to be a misguided enticement. His warm relationship with his Mizrachi sons-in-law suggests that he was not prejudiced toward non-European Jews. But he did feel strongly that Israeli society could and should make it easier for people to have large families.[51]

The formal government decision that operationalized the Bachi report began with a commitment: "To act in a systematic manner to implement a demographic policy designed to create an atmosphere that allows for the encouragement of natality, considering its critical role in the future of the Jewish people." In an extended sentence reflecting the demands of different lobbying agencies, the government program called for "ongoing pro-natal, promotional campaigns and the removal of economic and social barriers and to offer relief in areas of education, housing, insurance, etc., with the goal of encouraging families to increase the number of their children."[52] The decision emphasized the need to curb abortions that are "worrisome from the national-demographic perspective and from that of women's health."

All government ministries were to join the national crusade to increase the birthrate. A Center for Demographic Problems was established, overseen by a public council operating out of the prime minister's office. The center was charged with formulating associated legislation and government activities designed to implement the policy. It was also to conduct relevant research and encourage public organizations to act on behalf of a common demographic policy.[53] With a strategy formulated, the country moved forward with sweeping pro-natal programs.

In 1986, some twenty years after the Bachi Committee's recommendations, the Israeli government formally discussed "demography" for the second time in the country's history. Then Prime Minister Shimon Peres and the cabinet essentially endorsed Israel's existing program. Its declaration quoted directly the Bachi Committee–inspired decisions:

> The government decides to adopt a comprehensive and coordinated, long-term demographic policy that will inter alia lead to ensuring an appropriate level of growth among the Jewish population. . . . The policy will be built on directing, coordinating, and taking measures that are likely to influence population growth, like encouraging families and their desire for children, strengthening families and removing obstacles in their way, preventing unnecessary abortions through counseling and appropriate publicity, assistance in the area of welfare to families that have difficulties enlarging their families. . . . The government reinforces again the principles in its decision from April 9, 1967. The government will strive to ensure that its policy encouraging birth guides all government ministries and is expressed in the concrete planning and implementation of their activities.[54]

In short, the spirit of Roberto Bachi continues to inform public policy until the present. (Indeed, during the 1970s, families often called their third or fourth offspring their "Bachi child.")[55] This pro-natal strategy still provides the benefits and subsidies that make Israel an incubator for large families.

ISRAEL'S PRO-NATAL PROGRAM

It literally pays to have a large family in Israel, even as the monetary benefits have fluctuated greatly over time in response to political vicissitudes. Support begins even prior to delivery. Prenatal care in Israel is free and it is exemplary, improving the collective health of mother and child dramatically.[56] Maternity services in Israel's hospitals are also free. The money starts to flow with birth itself. Since 1954, all Israeli mothers are entitled to a grant from the National Insurance Institute. Originally, the payment was more than half an average monthly salary for each delivery. Over time, the relative amount dropped precipitously. Today, first-time mothers receive 1,751 shekels ($500); after giving birth to their second child, 788 shekels ($225); and a mere 525 shekels ($150) for every subsequent child. In cases of twins, however, the grant is 8,757 ($2,500), and for triplets, a whopping payment of 13,136 ($3,750).[57]

Like all of the related programs, the *"pro-natal"* and *"welfare"* motivations behind child support policies are intertwined and difficult to disaggregate. The Israeli government has always claimed that birth grants are first and foremost a public health intervention, encouraging Israeli women who previously avoided maternity wards to give birth in hospitals.[58] Infant mortality rates soon dropped as the health care system's clinical conditions were more hygienic than Bedouin tents and conventional homes across the country.[59] Today, infant mortality in Israel is among the lowest in the OECD.[60] In addition to the grant, working mothers receive fourteen weeks of paid maternity leave.[61]

Large families continue to enjoy a broad range of economic benefits today. Assistance starts with schooling. As of 2013, day-care centers were able to offer discounts of 100 shekels a day for families with two children, and double that— 200 shekels per child—for families with three or more.[62] There is, of course, no free lunch. The subsidy costs the government 1,723 shekels a month per child or 2,273 shekels per infant. *Haaretz* correspondent Meirav Arlosoroff recently calculated that over the course of their children's preschool career, a family of eight receives 200,000 shekels in day-care subsidies, while paying only 80,000 shekels out of pocket.[63]

Special stipends for public school children ages six to fourteen are also available for families with four or more children. Prior to the start of every school year it publicizes the amounts to which families with four or more children are entitled. Presently, disbursements are set at 1,557 shekels per year (roughly $400) for children ages six to eleven, and 865 shekels for children twelve to fourteen.[64] Children in large families can also receive special scholarships for higher education. For example, the speaker of the Knesset runs a special scholarship fund that is only available to applicants who are orphans, blind, deaf, or living on the border in tense "security" situations. Students coming from families "blessed with children" are also eligible.[65]

Another benefit granted only to large families is preferential treatment for access to public housing. These residential units are significantly cheaper than comparable housing in the private rental market. Even though there is a long waiting list and a general shortage of subsidized housing, families with five or more children are moved to the top of the list and entitled to two offers of public housing before they select one in which to live. Moreover, for the first two years of the rental period, the government will provide housing stipends, as long as the family has not bought a home or does not have a third party pay the rent.[66] This does not include remunerating part of home rental payments for large families. Although empirical analysis has not found a clear statistical correlation between housing subsidies for large families and birthrates,[67] it surely contributes to the total impact of the pro-natal program.[68] International research corroborates that fertility increases when housing assistance is part of a broader package of support.[69]

While many cities have their own policies, large families typically receive a substantial discount in their municipal taxes. In 2011, Eli Yishai, then minister of interior and chairman of the Shas party, which encourages large families, approved new criteria for granting discounts from city taxes. Large families are entitled to a 25 percent reduction. By contrast, families with someone serving in the military reserves receive only 5 percent.[70] Even Israel's military has a soft spot for large families. Married soldiers are entitled to home leave every weekend unless critical operations prevent it. And once a reserve soldier has six children, the constraints on military service are so ponderous that functionally combat duties become impossible.[71]

SUBSIDIZING BIRTH

The most persuasive and controversial component of Israel's pro-natal program is child allowances. These payments actually preceded the Bachi Committee but were trivial then, adding only 2–3 percent to average income.[72] It would not take long, however, for allowances to reach sizable dimensions. Many of these policies are implemented through the National Insurance Institute. The agency is also responsible for distributing a range of welfare benefits: from social security pensions to unemployment severance. The institute was established in 1953 with three primary departments: Aged/Holocaust Survivors, Occupational Accidents, and Motherhood.[73] In 1959, the Knesset added a new division: Child Allowances. Since then, the institute grants child allowances as nontaxable payments directly to mothers. Some social justice advocates cite this as a praiseworthy, progressive element of an anti-poverty strategy, particularly in patriarchal communities. Lessons from around the world suggest that when husbands have sole control over a family's finances, too often welfare payments go to "cigarettes and alcohol." When funds are deposited separately in a woman's bank account, the likelihood of the money reaching the children is far higher.[74]

In its official publications, the institute portrays the original motivation for the initiative solely in terms of "welfare" and social equity rather than boosting fertility per se:

The State recognized the need to assist families in the raising of their children. . . . With the establishment of the State, scores of immigrants arrived in Israel with families blessed with children. In addition to the difficulties of adjusting to the initial period of their immigration, support was needed for numerous people with minuscule income. Thus a social-economic gap was created between new immigrants, most of whom were from Mizrachi countries and the veteran Israelis that were well established economically with few children. In research conducted two years after passage of the law, it was found that child allowances were indeed reaching the societal strata that the legislator intended and its social benefit was great.[75]

Nonetheless, a related and by no means secondary goal of the subsidies was to make life more comfortable for large families in order to encourage more of them in the future. This was alluded to by Israel's minister of labor, Mordechai Namir, when he presented the objectives of the new child-allowance program to the Knesset in 1959. Namir declared that the program, inter alia, was "to arrest negative trends in demographic developments."[76] By this he meant that the allowances would be designed to encourage large *Jewish* rather than *Arab* families, even as it may not have been clear to him at the time how he would do that.

During this first iteration, child allowances were only paid to families with four or more children, with criteria for receiving child allowances dependent on the employment status and salaries of parents, making it a progressive, negative tax. (Upper-middle-class and wealthier families were not eligible.)[77] Under the initial law, allowances were exempt from income tax and paid on behalf of children until they reached age fourteen.[78] In 1965, the age was raised to eighteen. Eventually all children of salaried workers became eligible,[79] with large families granted income tax deductions for children.[80] For some time, the effect on the Arab sector was attenuated due to the inaccessibility of National Insurance offices that were not conveniently located in Arab regions. Thus many Arab citizens de facto did not receive their allowances.[81]

In 1970, the preferential treatment received by Jewish families was made even more prominent. A new program granted yet an additional allowance to families with four or more children if one of the children's parents, siblings, or grandparents had served in the military.[82] The child allowances for families with military service were considerably higher than the original, socioeconomically driven (and color-blind) allowances.

The new 1970 program meant that most Arabs (who were not drafted) and many ultra-Orthodox Jews (who chose not to serve in Israel's defense forces for theological reasons) de jure would not be eligible for the most sizable allowance payments. In practice, many ultra-Orthodox Jews managed to circumvent this constraint as criteria were bent. For instance, families with uncles or aunts who had served in the military were included. In addition, alternative payment schemes were created to pay the "veteran stipends" to citizens studying in yeshivas (Jewish religious academies).[83] Many Israelis were uncomfortable with a welfare payment that so clearly discriminated between citizens. Moreover, the system of subsidies that emerged was convoluted and complicated. The time was ripe for restructuring and simplification.

On December 15, 1974, the finance minister, Yehoshua Rabinovich, appointed Haim Ben-Shahar, a professor of economics, to head a five-man committee to consider tax reform. Of all of the committee's recommendations, the one that is most remembered was not even mentioned in the minister's authorizing letter: changing the child-allowance system.

The first recommendation of the committee was to cancel the economic criteria that previously determined whether or not families received child allowances. Child support disbursements were to become universal for all parents, not just for families with more than two children or in a low economic bracket. The effect was to make allowances less "progressive" and more pro-natal. Furthermore, until that time, children constituted a deduction for purposes of income tax. These deductions were canceled in favor of direct subsidies.[84] To be sure, the monthly grants were now subject to income tax according to recipients' family salaries, which erased any regressive aspects of the program. The amount received by wealthier families constituted an inconsequential percentage of their personal income relative to poorer families.

Ben-Shahar's committee also recommended establishment of a point system, which was soon adopted and largely survives until the present. Families were allocated points that translated into a monthly payment. Each point was valued at one hundred liras, 5 percent of the average salary at the time. This sum was linked to the cost of living index. A family's first two children were awarded 1 point each, then for the third child onward 1.25 points were awarded. The new criterion had nothing to do with economic need and everything to do with fertility promotion.[85] The bottom line was that families would be getting paid more to make babies. The Ben-Shahar committee also did not call for cancellation of the Jewish bias associated with special allowances for families who had served in the military.

The pro-natal shift was not lost on social policy observers and was summarized in a *Haaretz* op-ed essay critical of the increased allowances: "In 1960, the allowance granted a family with ten children was less than a quarter of the average salary in the economy. Ten years later, in 1970, it reached a third. In 1975, as part of the reform of the Ben-Shahar committee it jumped 2.7 times to 92%."[86] Child allowances had come of age.

THE POLITICAL POLARIZATION OF CHILD ALLOWANCES

By the 1980s the issue of pro-natal subsidies had become a divisive political issue. The primary beneficiaries of child allowances were the Arab and the Haredi ultra-Orthodox communities that often were not held in high regard by the secular Jewish mainstream. Many Israelis were increasingly resentful of ultra-Orthodox communities, which they perceived as draft dodgers and economic freeloaders. In 1977, ultra-Orthodox political bargaining led to cancellation of limitations that had been placed on military exemptions for Jews studying in religious institutions. The number of ultra-Orthodox Jewish men avoiding conscription in the Israel Defense Forces skyrocketed.[87] Most continued to study in their academies even after their draft deferral was over, exploiting sundry public stipends to support their families. (In many cases, stipends were paid to Haredim who were not studying at all after fraudulent declarations were submitted.)[88] Diverse voices among the Jewish Zionist majority felt that the country was not only rewarding parasitism but subsidizing its own demographic destruction.

Journalist Shahar Ilan captured the secular public's growing displeasure in the *Haaretz* newspaper:

> Every year about forty women in the Shaarei Tzedek hospital give birth to their sixteenth and seventeenth child and even more. (Nineteenth is already considered a rare event.) Another 180 women give birth to their twelfth to fifteenth child. . . . In a site visit that took place in the hospital at the start of the year, the Hospital Director, Dr. Yonatan Levi reported that in December '99, there were close to 800 births in Shaarei Tzedek. Eighty percent of them were by ultra-Orthodox women. Professor Juval Mayshar and Charles Manski calculated and found that the allowance for the sixth child and up is about 20 percent higher than the marginal costs of the child among families living on the poverty line. They argue that these children "constitute a net income source for parents living on the poverty line or under it. . . ."
>
> If Malthus was right in his argument that childhood allowances are a poverty trap that encourage natality and serve as a negative incentive for labor . . . it is doubtful whether there is any society where one can see the forecast of Malthus realized so fully as ultra-Orthodox society. . . . The incidence of ultra-Orthodox men that are not a part of the labor market (in other words— study in a Yeshiva rather than work) rose from 50 percent in 1980 to 67 percent by the start of the 1990s. . . . In 1981, 23 percent of families with many children were below the poverty line. Since then the percentage has increased dramatically, by 95 percent—almost double.[89]

The Jewish secular majority had even greater qualms about the Arab birthrate. The Arab minority was now well aware of child allowances and sought to take greater advantage of them. In 1992 Arab Knesset member Abdulwahab Darawshe submitted a bill to cancel special benefits granted to families whose members had completed military service. Right-wing parliamentarian Rehavam

"Gandhi" Ze'evi, was particularly crass in the ensuing Knesset debate: "The proposal is an incentive for making more Arab children. They will live off us forever. They will give birth to 70 children; they do anyway. . . . They will make 50, 60, 70 children and we will pay them discharged soldiers' grants."[90]

Given the enlightened "affirmative action" spirit of the ruling Rabin government toward Israel's Arab minority at the time, this type of rhetoric was ineffective. The clashing views over what had once been a consensus national welfare program, however, were now openly and publicly articulated. Darawshe's bill passed in 1993 and went into effect in 1994, removing a key discriminatory aspect of Israel's welfare program. But the political divides that now characterized Israel's polarized demographic dynamics were increasingly clear. In 1960 only 4,731 families had seven or more children. By 1995, the number of families with seven or more children had jumped to 18,823.[91] The vast majority of the increase was from the Arab and ultra-Orthodox communities, communities that were patently unenthusiastic about serving the Zionist state that was supporting them. These two minority sectors were well represented by sectorial parties in Israel's parliament, and their respective parliamentarians began to cooperate in promoting an even more lucrative system to fund large families.

A retrospective review of the fluctuations of child allowance shows that initially they were driven by economic conditions and the ongoing rate of immigration. But during the past several decades, ultra-Orthodox politicians had a lot to do with increasing the level of subsidies. Against this background, in November 1999, one of the most dramatic episodes in the long litany of political battles over child allowances was played out.

The Ehud Barak–led Labor government's coalition was somewhat chaotic. Shmuel Halpert, a parliamentarian from the ultra-Orthodox Torah Judaism party, saw an opportunity. He submitted a bill entitled the Assistance to Families Blessed with Children Law, soon known simply as the "Halpert Law." It pushed child allowances to unprecedented levels: a family with four children would receive an extra monthly stipend of 790 shekels for every additional child, five times the rate that the first and second child received. For Halpert's constituents, it made for a handsome bonus.

While the government opposed the law, it was outmaneuvered by the religious and the Arab parties, along with a majority of the opposition Likud party members. These strange bedfellows had no problem cooperating, and the Likud, seeking the future favor of ultra-Orthodox parties, garnered the necessary votes to pass the statute. The legislative debate was especially lively. Opponents called the bill "theft in the light of day," and sarcastically argued that secular citizens could no longer afford to have a second child as they had to work to subsidize the eighth ultra-Orthodox baby. The rebuttal defending the expanded allowances was equally fierce. David Tal of the ultra-Orthodox Shas party accused his opponents of "lacking in sensitivity and social understanding, demonstrating an inexplicable obtuseness. The law will encourage natality which will help provide a solution to the demographic problems of Israel. David Ben-Gurion will be merry and happy in his grave as a result of the law."[92]

When the Law of Families Blessed with Children ultimately passed, the minister of finance, Beiga Shochat, furiously told the press, "What happened here today is an act of villainy. It is a wanton, corrupt law, even anti-Zionist. The law was born in sin and ratified in sin. It's a disgrace to have it in Israel's lawbook."[93] As the official responsible for balancing Israel's government budget, he had reason to be concerned. The new levels of child allowances were unheard of, even in Israel. By 2001 over nine hundred thousand families representing over 2 million children were receiving child allowances, costing the public coffers 8.3 billion shekels.[94]

With such high subsidies, it made a lot of economic sense to produce a lot of children. For many citizens lacking professional skills, who could not expect attractive salaries in Israel's labor market, it simply did not pay to work. Unemployment in certain sectors, particularly among ultra-Orthodox men, swelled to even greater heights,[95] while Arab women's entry in the workforce only crawled forward. For instance, in 1979, just 20 percent of Haredi men did not work; by the year 2000 the number had climbed to 65 percent.[96] On average, 32 percent of these families' incomes came from child support.[97] It was these dynamics, rather than births among non-Zionist Israelis, that made this particular political triumph of the pro-natal alliance short-lived.

SECULAR PUSHBACK

When charting the history of child allowances, a pattern emerges that shows that subsidies tend to fall when economic conditions grow worse.[98] This was surely the case three years later when the minister of finance, Benjamin "Bibi" Netanyahu, initiated a massive reform that essentially canceled the Halpert Law.

Netanyahu was offered the position of finance minister in 2003 by the newly elected prime minister, Ariel Sharon. The offer was seen as a slight that Netanyahu was unlikely to accept. Presumably, it was insulting to offer the finance portfolio to a former prime minister when more-prestigious cabinet positions, like the foreign or the defense ministries, were available. Yet not only did Netanyahu accept the position, he embraced it with unconcealed exuberance. He set out on a quest to slash government spending as a tough but unavoidable remedy for the country's sluggish economy. Netanyahu was the first Israeli minister of finance to bring an unapologetically capitalistic orientation to social spending.[99] In a nationally televised speech, he likened the condition of Israeli taxpayers to that of a stooped, exhausted porter attempting to move forward while carrying a pile of freeloaders on his backs. Netanyahu's mission was to lighten the load.

It was neither demographics nor Zionism, but social philosophy and concern for the Israeli economy that motivated his policies to dramatically scale back child allowances. When questioned about its effect on women and children, Netanyahu justified his position as liberating them from a mentality of dependence: "The women that receive subsidies are used to not working. And their children are used to their mothers not working. It's a trap of dependence; it's a thick morass from which it's impossible to escape. In this kind of environment children learn from adults to extend their hand and ask for support. I look at them and say to myself: 'Master of the Universe, a new generation of subsidy recipients has grown up here.' I must release these children from the culture of dependence and government welfare so that they don't join the chain."

Netanyahu was and is a consummate political pragmatist. When he started applying his scissors to the national budget and the culture of child-allowance dependence, he refrained from imposing "cold turkey" withdrawal. All told, 220,000 families receiving child allowances faced meaningful reductions.[100] In the year 2000, child allowances cost Israelis 8.1 billion shekels, or 1.5 percent of the country's GDP. By 2004, after the Netanyahu reform, this amount dropped to 4.6 billion shekels, a reduction of 44 percent.[101]

After the reductions became law in 2004, the finance minister explained, "People who work quickly raise their status and lead themselves out of poverty. When two wage earners in a family work, poverty is simply erased. And therefore, regarding the argument that asserts we need to be protected or need to protect the policy of subsidies as the key to eliminating poverty—the opposite is true . . . the policy of subsidies perpetuated poverty, increased it and expanded inequality. They say that this is despite a policy of subsidies. I say it is because of the policy of subsidies."[102]

Yet this policy turnaround was only an interim round in a never-ending political struggle. In the coalition negotiations of 2006, the newly elected prime minister, Ehud Olmert, discreetly agreed to accept a demand from the ultra-Orthodox Shas political party to maintain the high, pre-2003 child allowances at their original levels in return for their support in forming a government. By 2012, the country was once again paying out 7.5 billion shekels in child allowances on an annual basis.[103]

History repeated itself a decade after Netanyahu set out to trim child allowances. In 2013, with neither ultra-Orthodox nor Arabs allowed in the ruling government coalition, the newly appointed finance minister, Yair Lapid, announced cutbacks of child allowances that would save the economy 2.5 billion shekels.[104] The 2003 "grandfathered" date was no longer considered sacrosanct: A family's first child, even if born before 2003, would only receive 159 shekels ($39 a month) as opposed to $49 dollars a month. The second child in a family would also receive only $39, about half of the $70 dollars a month they were receiving under existing rules. Subsequently the amounts increased moderately: the third fourth and fifth child would receive $48, $94, and $99 a month respectively, down from previous amounts of $82, $109, and $129.

In July, when the Knesset convened to vote on the 2013 budget, representatives of Arab and ultra-Orthodox parties were vociferous and bitter in their heckling: "A disgrace and a shame"; "You are cruel"; "Being smart at children's expense," they shouted at Lapid.[105] In the public relations campaign, protestations did not rely on "pro-natal" lines of reasoning. Unlike the nationalist arguments that had informed earlier debates, opposition to the cutbacks was based on calls for compassion and socioeconomic equity. For an Israeli public apprehensive about the steady demographic expansion of the two non-Zionist sectors of Israeli society, hungry children and poverty were deemed more politically palatable rationales for supporting large families. There was no shortage of social justice advocates available to join this fight. Most notable was Professor Shlomo Mor-Yosef, the director of the National Insurance Institute, who spoke out openly against the reductions. Mor-Yosef claimed, "More than 40,000 families will be pushed under the poverty line, and many already poor families will become poorer."[106]

Finance Minister Lapid's response was remarkably similar to that given by Netanyahu a decade earlier. In defending the policies on the Knesset rostrum, he explained that while the State of Israel wouldn't allow any child in Israel to go hungry, "I want to remind [you], the institution responsible for caring for children is called their parents. When you bring a child into this world, [you] are the primary person responsible for it. Bringing a child into the world is a heavy responsibility and so you should bring children into the world not based on the assumption that other people will care for them, but rather on the assumption that it's your obligation to take care of your own children."[107] On his Facebook page Lapid cited Margaret Thatcher: "For years upon years it has been proven that child allowances do not get people out of poverty, they only make poverty permanent. Only one thing allows families to exit the cycle of poverty—and that's working."[108]

DO CHILD ALLOWANCES REALLY INCREASE
FAMILY SIZE?

In considering the merits and shortcomings of pro-natal subsidies, it is well to ask a preliminary question: Do they actually encourage people to have more children? Haredi spokesmen are emphatic that the subsidies do not influence family size in their communities. Meir Porush is a second-generation Haredi member of Knesset, representing the ultra-Orthodox Agudath Yisrael party: "There's no doubt that the present government has decided to evade any obligations for child allowances. (Once it was considered an honor). This surely makes life harder for large families in our sector. There are those in the government who discreetly told me that we need to cancel child allowances to reduce the number of Arabs. It may mean fewer Arabs—I'm not an expert about Arabs and can't tell you if it will affect them. But I can tell you that it definitely won't change anything in the Haredi world."[109]

Traditionally, academic demographers have been divided on this issue, according to two opposing schools and competing assumptions about the actual drivers of individual fertility decisions: Backers of the *"Homo economicus"* approach believe that economic calculations determine how people choose optimal family size. The *"Homo sociologicus"* school believes that decisions are less rational and primarily influenced by religious and social norms in their community.[110] Like so many academic schisms, both sides are partially right. The general feeling among the Israeli public is that subsidies do influence fertility decisions. After all, before the age of significant child allowances, birthrates were generally low, even among ultra-Orthodox families. Empirical research validates this intuition.

Methodologically there are a variety of ways to assess the impact of incentives. One approach is to identify increases in fertility associated with an increase in allowance levels. For instance, a study published in 2000 by economist Elli Berman contrasted the growth in birthrates among ultra-Orthodox European Jews to those of North African or Asian descent. Berman showed that when subsidies for Sephardic ultra-Orthodox families increased in 1984, as a result of the new sectorial political party (Shas) that lobbied on this constituency's behalf, the birthrate of Sephardim began to rise. (Large Ashkenazi ultra-Orthodox families already received high payments.) The differential increase in child allowances within the ultra-Orthodox community was analyzed and clearly demonstrated the persuasive power of child allowances. Berman's research summarizes:

> The total fertility rate of Sephardi ultra-Orthodox women was 4.57 in the early 1980s. It rose by more than two and a half children by the mid-1990s to reach 7.24 children per woman! The velocity of this remarkable increase in

fertility is phenomenal in current demography. It dwarfs even the 0.89 child increase in total fertility experienced by the Ashkenazi ultra-Orthodox women over the same period. The difference between the Sephardi and Ashkenazi fertility increase is 1.78 children per woman and is statistically significant, indicating that fertility increases sharply with subsidies among ultra-Orthodox Jews.[111]

This conclusion was supported by Charles Manski and Juval Mayshar, American and Israeli economists, who created a model to characterize the effect of allowances. They began with the observation that in the 1950s, the birthrate among ultra-Orthodox and non-Orthodox Jewish families of European descent were essentially indistinguishable. Yet when they compared women married prior to 1955 (before the era of child allowances) with those married between 1970 and 1980 (when they were entrenched public policy), a profound shift emerged: ultra-Orthodox birthrates essentially doubled; at the same time, fertility among non-Orthodox Israeli women, especially of non-European origin, dropped.[112] The researchers "conjecture, but cannot prove," that increases in the birthrate would not have occurred among the ultra-Orthodox were it not for the financial assistance provided. They explained that economics does not tell the whole story: there are powerful social interactions and cultural forces at play as well that influence the family-planning decisions of different sectors.

Other studies verify that child allowances do not work in a vacuum but in a familial context. Hebrew University demographer Jona Schellekens assessed the effect of child allowances on the fertility of different ethnic groups, as well as for women of different educational backgrounds, during the years leading up to 1994. Focusing on individual decisions to have a third child or more, he found that the incentives had a significant effect on a family's decision to have an additional child "at every parity."[113] In other words, it affected the decision of mothers with two children, six children and twelve children. Schellekens also assumed that the marginal cost of raising a child decreases with each birth, which theoretically should encourage large families. But at the same time, the marginal benefit derived by parents from each additional child should also drop with each addition. Given these dynamics, he was not surprised to find that family allowances affect family-planning decisions heavily until the fifth birth, at which point they still matter but are less powerful.[114] One unanticipated finding from Schellekens's analysis was that child allowances appear to have a greater effect on highly educated women's decisions to have an additional child than on women with lower educational levels.

A second methodological approach is to assess the impact of allowances retrospectively. The ongoing fluctuations in child allowances enable researchers to look backward empirically and quantify their effect on fertility. In 2009 a team at the National Insurance Institute published a report on the subject,[115] with key results reprinted by the Bank of Israel. Looking at birth patterns between 1997 and 2004, the study quantified the impact of the dramatic cut in child allowances initiated by Benjamin Netanyahu in 2003.

The institute's report found that the policy shift led to a 6–7 percent drop in the likelihood that married Arab women would have an additional child, and a 3 percent drop among ultra-Orthodox women. (The reduction in allowances did not affect non-Orthodox and Druze birthrates at all.) The overall impact on Israel's total population was estimated at less than 2 percent.[116] The study was based on data collected soon after Netanyahu's policy reform, so that the post-intervention, time-series calculations involved only a brief time span. The full impact of the policy shift may well have been understated.

In another assessment, the National Insurance Institute researchers calculated that on average, an increase of $220 for the monthly child allowance raised the probability of giving birth among Jewish Israelis by between 3 and 14 percent. No effect was found among non-Jews' birthrates.[117]

The most recent and comprehensive characterization of the impact of subsidy reductions was published by a team led by Alma Cohen, a Tel Aviv University economist. Their results are also the most pronounced. The researchers found that decreases in child allowances have a large, negative and significant effect on fertility that appears to have affected all religious and ethnic backgrounds.[118] Specifically, when subsidies are reduced by thirty-four dollars a month per child (roughly 2 percent of average income and 3.3 percent of median income), there was almost a 1 percent drop in the probability of an "incremental child" being born.

There may be modest disparities in the precise results of different Israeli econometric and demographic studies conducted thus far. Yet they all point in the same direction: while not the only factor, child allowances along with other subsidies significantly affect hundreds of thousands of individual decisions to have additional children. The Israeli results are completely consistent with parallel research in Western countries.

Faced with nonreplacement levels of fertility, many European nations began subsidizing large families. A recent review by Dutch demographer Adriaan Kalwij surveying fertility and child allowances in seventeen European countries confirmed some seven previous studies.[119] For instance, in Canada, a mere

one-thousand-dollar increase in a child's first-year benefits raised the probability of having a child by 16.9 percent![120] Kalwij's comparative national analysis concluded, "the relationship between family (or child) allowances and
fertility are unambiguous, showing that transfers to families with children (cash
and tax exemption) have a positive and significant effect on fertility."[121]

Even though the OECD reports that Israeli child allowances are relatively
low,[122] they probably are *more* effective than those provided in Europe. Rather
than combating Western fertility trends, the payments target a population that
is culturally predisposed to having large families. An abundance of empirical
Israeli research proves that regardless of religion and ethnicity, money is a key
part of couples' fertility calculations. It is also important to remember that even
the most "extreme" reforms did not eliminate Israel's child allowances but only
reduced them. It takes time for an economic signal to be internalized by relatively insular populations socialized by a contradictory system of incentives.
This is particularly true because the two previous allowance decreases turned
out to be short-lived, creating a sense among many families that cutbacks invariably are temporary. Their very savvy representatives in parliament eventually find a way to bring high allowances back. If pro-natal subsidies were to be
canceled altogether, once and for all, far greater drops in local fertility rates
could be expected.

Confidence that the pendulum of child-allowance policy would swing back
was validated in 2015 after the ultra-Orthodox parties reentered the government:
not only did newly elected finance minister Moshe Kahlon agree to a 77 percent
increase in child allowances for second, third, and fourth children, but he created a special savings account that the state would set up for children from large
families and transfer to them at age eighteen.[123]

Ultimately, child allowances are just a fraction of the actual subsidies that
Israel provides for its children. Misha Shauli, one of Israel's rare sustainable-
population advocates, runs the Web site 3kids.co.il, which disseminates data
about the implications of overpopulation in Israel. Among the information provided on the site is a rough analysis of the actual amount of money paid out per
child in Israel. For instance, according to the 2009 figures of Israel's Central
Bureau of Statistics, each year a preschool child costs the government $3,998; a
year of elementary school reaches $5,202 per child; and high school, as much as
$5,842. Subsidies for health care on average cost $5,000 during a child's first
eighteen years.[124] Shauli reckons that today the total amount of money expended
on a child during her first eighteen years exceeds $100,000.[125]

Israel is justifiably proud of its love of children. Nobody in Israel proposes
libertarian policies that would stop funds for public schooling. Yet it is well to

remember the meaning of "dependency ratios" and the burden children place on an economy. When families decide to have another child, they internalize only part of the actual costs with the additional externalities born by society.

YOU GET WHAT YOU PAY FOR

Critiques of public policies that bankroll fertility are as old as Thomas Malthus, who argued that subsidizing large families would not reduce poverty in the short run and that doing so in the long run would only increase the number of poor people and future misery. Today the principal objection raised against child allowances for large families in Israel is that they create a culture of dependency and indolence, sabotaging the work ethic and locking entire sectors into cycles of poverty.

There are also those who claim that these arguments are a pretense. Behind the real opposition to pro-natal policies, they say, is a fundamental dislike of the communities that exploit the incentives as well as a discomfort with demographic trends in Israel. (This is ironic, because for many years child allowances were among Israel's most discriminatory programs, aggravating relations with Arab citizens and making a mockery of the country's commitment to equal opportunity.)

Regardless of the motivation, when distilled down to its essence, the heart of the argument against pro-natal payments is that they produce unintended, negative social consequences. Rarely does one hear opposition to these policies because they are so successful. But indeed they are. The problem is that this success is dysfunctional for Israeli society. Reassessment of pro-natal subsidies is critical for Israel's future economic and societal health.

Child allowances, housing assistance, preschool subsidies, property tax discounts to large Israeli families, grants to new mothers, and other pro-natal incentives do precisely what they are designed to do. Subsidies crafted to encourage large families in Israel have been effective. They may not be the sole factor in fueling the precipitous increase in the country's population, but they have definitely been significant, contributory drivers. There may well have been urgent security reasons for a young and sparsely populated state, concerned about preserving a Jewish majority, to invest heavily in encouraging large families. But things have changed.

Israel's new demographic dynamics, the extraordinary density and pernicious impacts of rapid demographic growth, call into question the very logic that motivated Ben-Gurion and Bachi to incentivize large families. Legitimate concerns about the cancellation of child allowances' impact on poverty, in particular on the children of poor families, can and should be addressed through a variety of alternative "in-kind" welfare measures.

Even if the early policies can be rationalized in retrospect, paying people to have children in Israel today constitutes bad public policy. That's because population growth in Israel was always an instrumental goal, a means to an end. The underlying objectives are no longer served by pro-natal interventions. Israel is already overpopulated with a growing underclass. Because child allowances exacerbate these dynamics, they have become a perverse subsidy. It is time to subsidize sustainability.

6

WOMEN'S REPRODUCTIVE RIGHTS:
ABORTION, BIRTH CONTROL, AND
FERTILITY POLICIES IN ISRAEL

Removing from women the shackles of external reproductive
control would more quickly reduce birthrates worldwide than
any other imaginable policy.
—Robert Engelman, president, Worldwatch Institute, *Life on the Brink:
Environmentalists Confront Overpopulation*

In an age of modern medicine and prolonged human longevity, societies have sustainable population dynamics when women choose to limit the number of children they have and are able to take the necessary measures to do so. This *reproductive autonomy* is increasingly recognized as a critical human right.[1] Pregnancy involves as intimate and irreversible a physical transition as a woman can experience. Having a child changes one's life forever. An unwanted pregnancy imposes profound changes in economics, relationships, and independence. That is why society should ensure that women have every opportunity to attain contraception to prevent pregnancy if that is their desire. Because reproduction occurs inside a woman's body, only she should be authorized to decide whether a baby will grow there or not. Unfortunately, Israel maintains a policy that neither provides women with easy access to birth control nor to an abortion after an unwanted pregnancy.

In pretty much every human society, the burden for child-rearing falls primarily on women. In Israel, the asymmetry in responsibility for childcare is manifested in a variety of taxation and welfare entitlements. This can be called "chauvinism" or "realism," but it does not change the fact that in the vast majority of families, women are the primary caretakers. It follows that women should be free to decide whether or not to assume this enormous responsibility.[2] There are far too many cases in Israel where they do not enjoy this freedom.

Legal scholar Gila Stopler explains, "A substantial fear exists that women's freedom of choice in Israel is compromised. A state is entitled to enact a pronatal policy by creating a supportive environment where parents can raise children in an optimal way by giving them the best possible conditions to do so while preserving the equal ability of parents to be integrated into the labor market and develop their skills. . . . From the perspective of human rights, measures to encourage birth, like prohibition on abortions or preventing access to birth-control are unacceptable, as they completely negate the ability of women to freely choose."[3]

Israel's government likes to call its pro-natal policies part of a general effort to strengthen gender equality.[4] Yet in practice they are actually part of the problem. One of the reasons why Israeli women on average are still paid 45 percent less than men,[5] constrained by the proverbial "glass ceiling" and destined for low-prestige occupations, is that society continues to expect them to spend most of their time and energies raising children.

At best, when viewed through a feminist prism, Israel's demographic strategy is markedly inconsistent. On the one hand, working mothers are given significant support—especially in the area of early childhood education. Legislation contains provisions that make it much easier than in the past for a woman to simultaneously have a career and a family. At the same time, public policies regarding abortion and contraception are decidedly patriarchal, infringing on women's basic rights to control their bodies and pregnancies. The reason for this discrepancy is actually simple. Despite occasional lip service and considerable media coverage, women's rights and gender equality remain largely irrelevant in this policy realm. The government's historical position can in fact be thus summarized: If pro-natal policies happen to empower women—then so much the better. If they happen to impinge on women's rights to reproductive autonomy, it constitutes unfortunate but acceptable collateral damage.

Jewish and Islamic law are relatively liberal on matters of contraception and abortion. Unfortunately, narrow interpretations of Jewish law among Orthodox lawmakers and overzealous pro-natal passions among Zionist politicians continue to cast a cloud over Israeli women's reproductive decisions.[6] The imperative of large families and political pressures from religious political parties trumps other ancillary issues.

To understand the dynamics of women's reproductive predicament, a few words about Israel's health system are in order. In 1994, the National Health

"To the committee": An uncomfortable corridor where Saroka
Hospital's Pregnancy Termination Committee considers
whether women's requests for abortion meet narrow
statutory criteria. (Photograph by author)

Insurance Law was enacted guaranteeing health services for all the country's
citizens.[7] Four health service organizations provide the bulk of Israelis with
their medical needs. But their coverage is limited to pharmaceuticals and procedures approved by the Ministry of Health as part of the national "basket of
medicines." Provision of free contraception is an extremely common component
of public health programs around the world,[8] a policy that has been shown to
reduce abortion rates.[9] In Israel, however, the costs of contraception are only
partially covered and only for girls until age twenty,[10] while expensive assisted
reproductive technologies (ART) are generously subsidized. If a woman wishes
to have an abortion, she must pay to submit a request[11] to a committee that may
or may not approve the procedure under very proscribed conditions.

It is difficult to estimate just how many births have taken place over the years
in Israel among mothers who would have preferred another outcome. The
actual number of unwanted pregnancies undoubtedly reaches into the hundreds
of thousands and beyond. This is a result of public policies that prefer Jewish
nationalistic, pro-natal objectives and Orthodox dogma to the human rights of
its citizens. The normative framework designed for preventing and terminating
pregnancies historically made it complicated and costly to receive birth control
or to abort. Israel's male-dominated political leadership understood that low

birthrates, particularly among Jews of European ancestry, could be countered by making it hard for sexually active women to avoid and stop pregnancy.[12]

In all fairness, politicians during the early decades of the state seemed to be aware that they were walking a fine line. As people with generally liberal attitudes and appreciation for human rights, they understood that women should not be forced to have children against their will. Thus, birth control and abortion were not entirely prohibited. But they also sensed that if they made accessibility difficult for women, they would add scores of Jewish children to Israel's population without crossing any clear moral boundaries. Since these policies were designed, "women's liberation" has swept much of the planet. Israel, presumably, has been part of the revolution. Yet these outdated laws and directives remain largely unchanged.

CONTRACEPTION

The one consistent component of Israel's health policies regarding contraception is that birth control has never been free. From the country's earliest days, theoretically, contraception was available to women in Israel, even if some forms were not easily attained. Soon after they became available in the West, oral contraceptives and intrauterine devices (IUDs) were approved for local use by Israel's medical establishment. Ironically, though, neither promotion of contraception nor systematic family-planning assistance was included in subsidized health services. Consequently, as late as 1971 less than half of Israel's urban population used birth control.[13]

Results were predictable. Researchers at the time remarked that Israel's situation was idiosyncratic: "An inverse relationship between fertility and contraceptive usage exists for most countries: if fertility is high, contraceptive usage is low; if fertility is low, contraceptive usage is high. Israel represents an exception to this relationship: fertility levels are relatively low but usage of efficient contraception is also low."[14] The unwanted pregnancies that ensued contributed to countless abortions, sought primarily by Israel's secular Jewish majority.

Why has Israel, a Western, liberal country, where women fight in the military alongside men, discouraged—at least de facto—the utilization of birth control? There may be times when historians exaggerate gender-driven forces in public policy. In the present case, a "feminist analysis" is extremely compelling: men who designed policies about reproductive technology never really conferred with Israeli women. For Israel's first forty years, the two primary forms of birth control were coitus interruptus and abortion, mechanisms that are ultimately controlled by men.[15] Under such circumstances, sexually active women did not always have a lot to say about whether or not they got pregnant.

Part of the reason why birth control usage was so low during Israel's first decades involved the economics of socialized medicine and the low salaries of medical professionals who needed to supplement their incomes. Until the late 1970s public health infirmaries did not provide family-planning services. Israeli women could only formally consult about contraception or be fitted with intra-uterine devices by physicians. Consultations about contraception as well as any prescriptions were covered out of pocket by citizens, even though most had full medical insurance coverage. Because so many doctors derived a substantial part of their income from private practice in which they issued birth control prescriptions, they had little interest in changing the status quo.[16]

Particularly during the country's early years, when the population became dominated by immigrants, cultural inclinations and historic taboos held powerful sway over a large segment of the country's population. Jews immigrating from Asian and African countries arrived largely unfamiliar with modern contraception. This steadily changed, both among women in the immigrant population and then quite dramatically among their daughters. It would take a little bit longer for Arab citizens to make this transition. Eventually, most Muslim women joined Israel's Christian Arabs as consumers of birth control, making its utilization widespread across all Israel's population groups.[17]

Some researchers reviewing Israel's policies during this period contend that there was never a deliberate and conscious governmental policy opposing provision of family-planning services. Rather, no government ministry afforded it any importance.[18] Few statistics were recorded about contraception. Its oversight was scattered among different government agencies. For instance, the Ministry of Commerce and Industry oversaw importation of condoms and diaphragms because they were classified as rubber goods. Birth control pills were considered pharmaceuticals under the Ministry of Health's authority.[19] Contraception was a bureaucratic orphan, with no government agency truly interested in its promotion. After all, the Israeli cabinet had called on ministries to do whatever they could to increase the birthrate, not suppress it.

It follows that there was precious little government funding available for the smattering of NGOs that emerged to provide the family-planning services so many citizens wanted and many more needed. This meant that in an age before the Internet, the burden of getting information about pregnancy prevention was borne by Israeli women; they also bore the financial costs of contraception.

The medical profession did little to make it easier. One survey in the 1970s indicated that 27 percent of Israeli doctors believed the government should encourage a higher birthrate. Many public clinics simply refused to prescribe oral contraceptives.[20] But that's when the attitude of the health establishment appears to have evolved. The change was in part a response to the social unrest and demand for economic improvement among the relatively indigent Mizrachi populace, exemplified by the newly formed radical "Black Panthers" organization.[21] Not only were Israeli social services asked to address the problem of the Mizrachi underclass, the country's medical system was expected to do its part.

The issue of family size emerged as one of the most important factors in predicting children's academic performance and ability to succeed professionally, especially over the long run. A Commission on Youth and Distress was established during the 1970s to review a range of issues surrounding poverty and opportunity in Israeli society. It recommended the country establish a program for coordinated family planning.[22]

The transition was swift: Israeli men historically have never felt responsible for birth control, either via vasectomies or condom use. But Israeli women among all ethnic groups began to "get with the program."[23] In one 1974 study, 81 percent of Israeli women under the age of fifty-four reported using contraception, albeit the survey considered abortion to be a form of birth control. The researchers also identified a generational component to contraception preferences. Use of birth control pills for women married prior to 1944 was only 3 percent, as compared to 66 percent among women married after 1965. At the same time, one-third of the women in the older, childbearing strata still relied on withdrawal to prevent pregnancy, while only 13 percent of the younger respondents were willing to put their faith in this historically unreliable[24] method.[25]

Everything changed when intrauterine devices became the local contraceptive of choice.[26] If the late 1960s issued in the era of "the pill" for Israelis,[27] by the 1980s, several hospitals were specializing in "family-planning centers" that essentially functioned as assembly lines for IUD insertion. Centers began to set up shop in major hospitals. Statistics from the time show that 10 percent of the women who came for counseling were prescribed oral contraception; the other 90 percent, IUDs.[28] Women happily paid $125 out of pocket for insertion and the inconvenience of a doctor's visit for removal.[29] This form of contraception is still subsidized as part of the "basket of medicines."[30] (Vasectomies remain so uncommon in Israel that top Ministry of Health officials are unable to say whether it's a subsidized medical procedure or not.)

Women often had to wait a couple of months to receive an appointment. Once they arrived at the clinic, they reportedly felt very much more like products in a mass-production factory than patients. But by the mid-1980s, Israel had essentially entered an age of universal access to contraception, with the use of withdrawal as a family-planning strategy dropping to only 11 percent among the Jewish popula-tion.[31] The challenge at this point became educational and financial.

In her book: *Fertility Policy in Israel, the Politics of Religion, Gender, and Na-tion*, Jacqueline Portugese describes the transition in less than sympathetic terms: "When the state did begin to play a greater role in the provision of plan-ning services, it did so primarily out of eugenic considerations and in order to stave off political conflict rather than to promote women's sexual freedom or re-productive health. This is evidenced by the fact that the services were aimed primarily at large families living in poverty, namely the Mizrachim. Moreover, the State's foray into family planning was rationalized along social welfare rather than feminist lines."[32]

It would seem that efforts to promote contraception were primarily part of the general effort to integrate the most recent arrivals into Israel. Hebrew Univer-sity sociologist Barbara Okun clearly identifies the Mizrachi women who began to use birth control in the 1960s and 1970s as those who were most assimilated into secular Israeli society. For example, she identified high usage among women who had served in the military. As time went on, even these ethnicity gaps in contraception usage began to disappear.[33]

Today, more than forty-five years after this transition, Israel's pro-natal orien-tation remains strongly manifested in the costs of contraception. For the past decade, birth control pills have replaced IUDs as the most popular form of con-traception in Israel.[34] In fact, they are the only form of contraception subsidized in the government's "basket of medicines"—and only partially, for females under the age of twenty-one. Birth control pill prescriptions are only given for periods of three months, imposing on women (and their doctors) the inconvenience of making appointments on a regular basis.[35] And pills are not cheap. Over the av-erage period of a woman's reproductive life, they can cost as much as six thou-sand dollars.[36]

Onlife is not an especially feminist Israeli Web site. It focuses on fashion and home economics. But in 2013 it hosted a special blog on the issue of contracep-tion pricing that cataloged and protested the present menu:

> A non-hormonal IUD costs 200 shekels and insertion another thousand. It is effective for five years. A hormonal IUD costs 1,000 shekels and another 1,000 shekels for insertion and is also effective for five years. In practice, a woman will pay between 7,200 shekels and 12,000 shekels during her fertile period. A package of 12 efficient condoms cost between 40 and 55 shekels. If we calculate

the cost for a package per month (and that's not much) it costs between 14,400 and 19,800 shekels for the period of fertility. A woman's condom is even more expensive. What I'm trying to say is that there is a lethal infringement on the rights of women to health and to equality. Women are discriminated against by the very fact that it is a special medical procedure for women, both in the case of terminating pregnancy and (insertion of contraception devices). The State has the responsibility to remedy this injustice and to include birth control medication and devices in the basket of medicines. It should also cover all forms of termination of pregnancy as part of a woman's right to national health insurance.[37]

For young Israelis, often the problem is not so much lack of funds as lack of knowledge about contraception. Not every parent feels comfortable talking to their children about birth control. That's one of the reasons why schools should teach the pros and cons of different contraceptive options to children prior to their becoming sexually active. Considering popular attitudes toward sex (which, among the country's secular majority, have always been fairly liberal) it took a long time for Israel's curriculum to include the mechanics and health implications of contraception. Sex education was only taught after the Ministry of Education adopted a 1973 educational program designed by a government commission. Presumably the motivation for establishing the committee was concern about the spread of venereal disease rather than teenage pregnancies.[38]

A step backward was taken recently when the state's religious public school system removed all references to the reproductive system from eighth-grade science books that had previously covered the topic.[39] In fact, these are the youths that most need information because of family pressures and the isolation of many religious communities from the outside world. Frequently the subject is taboo and not clearly presented, even when young Orthodox women finally receive what passes for a sexual briefing just before marriage. To go to a doctor or to a public pharmacy and request birth control constitutes a humiliating admission that a girl is sexually active in a community that strictly forbids this. (A 1997 law allows doctors to prescribe contraception to girls from age sixteen on without their parents' knowledge or consent.)[40] Many religious Israeli girls after high school, during or subsequent to completing national service, face a profound crisis. The taboo is so deep that they cannot even admit their sexuality to themselves.[41] Not that secular schools do especially well in this area, either: a recent study found that, in practice, 40 percent of Israeli elementary and junior high schools don't teach sex education at all.[42]

One might imagine that given Israeli society's general openness about sex and the ubiquitous, sexually explicit images that children encounter via the Internet and television, today's generation would be better informed about contraception. Hedva Eyal oversees medical technology issues at the Isha L'Isha feminist organization. She believes the opposite is true. "Today I see tremendous ignorance among kids. We like to think that they know more than we did. The youth surely talk about sex. But often they don't understand anything. And this constitutes a great risk, especially because so many don't use birth control. In some cases it has even become socially unacceptable. Teenage pregnancy is common. Young girls have seven weeks to gain access to a 'morning after' pill, which given the embarrassment factor is not a trivial task."[43] Hadas Tal worked as a counselor with high school youths at risk in Jerusalem's poor neighborhoods. She reports that secular adolescent girls who complete Israel's public school's sex education curriculum largely remain informed by fictions, disinformation, and myths about contraception's risks and benefits.[44]

Promotion of contraception is a sensitive issue, and it is possible to cross "red lines" that lead to prescribing birth control without consensual agreement. This is especially the case when immigrants, largely unfamiliar with contraception, are involved. Old concerns about "eugenics and birth control" resurfaced again in 2012, when Israeli television news reported that Ethiopian women had been given Depo-Provera, a long-acting contraceptive, without their consent. The women claimed that the injections had begun in refugee camps run by the Jewish Agency in Ethiopia.[45] Some of the women thought it was a vaccination against disease and were angered when they discovered that they had been deceived. (Others, in radio interviews, offered an alternative explanation, which is commonly heard in Africa: many Ethiopian women, fearing a violent response from their husbands who oppose birth control, felt a need to conceal their contraception use. Infrequent injections of Depo-Provera offer a convenient solution.) Regardless of the explanation, it seems that in addition to acculturation, aggressive provision of birth control may be one of the key factors behind the 50 percent drop in the birthrate among Israeli Ethiopians during the past decade.[46]

The experience of the Ethiopians underscores the significance of "culturally sensitive" but scientifically precise educational programs about family planning. Especially for ethnic communities where sex is unmentionable, the state plays a critical role in teaching boys and girls (and frequently their parents) about available contraception alternatives and their relative scientific, economic, and personal advantages. Just as nobody should be forced to take birth control, no woman should be denied access. Unfortunately, Israeli governments over the years, notwithstanding their political orientation, have been consistent in their policies. They are willing to spend enormous funds to help women get pregnant but are decidedly stingy in providing funds to help women avoid pregnancy.

ABORTION

In many countries the debate over the issue of abortion is combative because of the commonly held conviction that termination of pregnancy constitutes an egregious act of murder. In Israel, opponents tend to be less dogmatic. This is because Jewish law does not hold that human life begins immediately at conception. Rabbi Shlomo Yitzchaki—"Rashi," the eleventh-century scholar, considered the definitive interpreter of the Bible and Talmud—specifically endorses this view: "As long as it has not emerged into the world, it [a fetus] is not a human being and therefore, it can be killed to save its mother."[47] The Bible makes it clear that causing a woman to miscarry is a civil offense and not a capital crime. This is not to say that Israel's anti-abortion camp is complacent. There are many citizens, especially religious ones, who consider abortion to be morally wrong. Implicitly, this has been the prevailing position of the powers that be in Israel for roughly a century.

The British Mandate's 1936 Criminal Ordinance outlawed termination of pregnancy altogether,[48] but the prohibition was never really enforced. In practice throughout the period of British rule, abortions were extremely common, especially among the secular Jewish population. Lip service continued to be widespread during the first decades of the state. For those who could pay, terminating pregnancy was not only a private but essentially an "underground" medical service.[49] Formally "banning" while informally "winking" became the normative state of affairs early in the country's history. In 1952, Israel's attorney general issued a directive that participants in abortions would not be prosecuted unless they were conducted in a negligent fashion or caused the death of the woman.[50] Like the old British unenforced prohibition against homosexuality, which remained in force after the Mandate, these were the kinds of criminal offenses that nobody wanted to prosecute but that no government official wanted to pay a political price for canceling. Israel's legal system could conveniently express moral disapproval while not actually taking any concrete measures. This "mixed message" about abortion, to a large extent, continues until the present.

Government officials were well aware of the patterns of pregnancy and pregnancy termination in Israeli society. The highest rate of abortions continued to be found among women in secular European families. It was precisely this cohort's fertility that Israel's decision makers wanted to increase. When the Bachi Committee considered what national demographic policies needed to be adopted by the country in the early 1960s, it had reasonable estimates about the scope of abortion. The committee's recommendation to amend existing legislation was in no way an initiative to encourage abortion or to grant the procedure legitimacy. Rather it was a pragmatic recognition that while the Israeli public would not accept a blanket ban on terminating unwanted pregnancies, it would not oppose regulation of abortions. Procedural obstacles, like limiting abortions to licensed hospitals and creating a special committee to review requests for pregnancy termination, could be built into the process. It was hoped that when enforced, these would serve to significantly limit the phenomenon. In its recommendations, the Bachi Committee states, "It needs to be clear [to the committees] that the primary goal is to reduce drastically the number of abortions."[51]

The new policy, therefore, had *little* to do with concerns about the rights of the unborn fetus and *everything* to do with expanding Israel's Jewish population. Once the baby was born, the state was largely indifferent as to whether it would be kept by the biological mother or given up for adoption. Persuasion to forgo abortion could be achieved through manipulative education or bureaucratic impediments that created aggravation, intimidation, or contrition. For instance, in the 1980s, Israeli's minister of health, Haim Sadan, put forward the macabre proposal that all *Jewish* women considering abortion be forced to watch images of mangled and dead fetuses in addition to pictures of Jewish children murdered in the Holocaust.[52] For many women facing stigmas, bureaucracy, financial expenses, and social pressures—it just wasn't worth the fight.[53]

In 1966 the legal framework pertaining to abortion began to reflect the Bachi Committee's recommendations. Indeed, over the past fifty years, with one small but important modification, Israel's restrictions regarding pregnancy termination have been surprisingly static. While abortions are not illegal, they can only be conducted according to precise legal stipulations. A woman must submit a formal written request to abort, which must be approved by a governmentally appointed committee. A doctor, who "stops a pregnancy" and knowingly flouts these rules faces five years imprisonment,[54] even as the woman having the abortion is not to be prosecuted.[55]

As with the old attorney general's directive from 1952—it is understood that law enforcement against violators will not be vigilant or even symbolic. The Ministry of Health reports that it only initiates enforcement action when it receives information about violations: "This is a violation where there is a natural 'conspiracy of silence.' Women typically have no motivation to complain, unless damage is caused to women during the process." Certainly in the past five years, there have been no actual government interventions taken to limit unlawful abortions.[56]

Special regulations have been prepared that detail the many steps that must take place before a woman can undergo the procedure. The initial ones are prerequisites to the hearing held by a hospital's Termination of Pregnancy Committees. For many years there was a shortage of such committees,[57] but today all government hospitals with maternity wards maintain committees to review requests.[58] Private hospitals can also receive authorization from Israel's health ministry to establish such committees, and many of them do. Of the forty committees authorized to approve abortions operating throughout Israel, only three are based in Arab communities—all at medical centers in Nazareth. This apparently is a function of the preponderance of Israeli hospitals' location within Jewish cities.

Termination of Pregnancy Committees are to be comprised of the following members: an obstetrician or gynecologist with an expertise in birthing; another physician with an expertise in family medicine, internal medicine, or public health; and a social worker, as well as a committee secretary. In a rare, implicit acknowledgment of male domination in Israeli OB/GYN wards, the law requires that at least one of the committee members be female.[59]

Thus, legal abortions in Israel begin with a tedious bureaucratic excursion. A woman submitting a request must bring her identity card to the committee's offices, along with a detailed medical report describing the case-specific circumstances if she claims that the health risk justifies the procedure.[60] She is then required to fill in a questionnaire about her personal situation and the reasons for the request. Once these steps are completed, the woman must have a consultation with a doctor and/or social worker. This session can often be a very unpleasant experience. According to the official ministerial directive issued by the minister of health, the committees are expected to explain the risks of the abortion procedure and its alternatives, presumably to dissuade the applicant. The applicant is provided a list of other medical agents with whom she can consult before making a final decision. Today's law also requires committees to receive the applicant's written confirmation that all physical and emotional risks associated with pregnancy termination have been explained. (Cognizant of complicated and charged family dynamics, a minor from age sixteen onward does not need her parents' approval for the procedure.)[61] The Ministry of Health estimates that the application process takes two weeks on average, although under pressing circumstances, it is possible to expedite a committee meeting.[62]

Surprisingly, the application process itself is not free, nor is it covered by any of the health insurance packages. Nonetheless, women under twenty are exempt from the associated fees.[63] Hence, just asking for permission to abort costs a woman 400 shekels, or more than $100, today. The situation is made more difficult for the applicant because she often is alone. Women's organizations who provide counseling and moral assistance in these cases note that rarely are women applying for abortions accompanied by a man, either during the paperwork stage or in their appearances before the committee. For the most part, women face the costs (and emotional stress) by themselves.[64]

Once the application process is completed, the Termination of Pregnancy Committee convenes to discuss the request and decide whether to approve or reject. The committee must offer a written explanation for its decision. There is no formally established appeal process.

These are the procedural requirements. What are the substantive reasons why a committee might approve or disapprove a request to abort a fetus? At least in theory, women in Israel can only receive permission to have an abortion if they meet one of the four conditions stipulated by the 1977 law. These include:

1. *age:* women under eighteen or over forty automatically are entitled to abort;
2. *status:* an unmarried woman or a married woman whose pregnancy is due to a man other than her husband or the result of an illegal act (either rape or incest) is also automatically granted approval;
3. *condition of the fetus:* if the baby is likely to be physically or mentally deformed, pregnancy can be terminated; or
4. *health:* in cases where continuing the pregnancy is likely to endanger the life of the woman or to cause physical or emotional damage, committees can grant approval.[65] In emergencies, where a woman's life is in danger, abortions can be conducted without the permission of the committee.

The list of permissible conditions was once more liberal. The original legal provisions that passed the Knesset in 1977 included a fifth reason for approving abortion: a so-called "*social provision.*" It allowed women to have abortions in the event that "continuing pregnancy was likely to cause severe damage to the women or her children, due to the woman's difficult family or social conditions or her environment."[66] For instance, in cases where a pregnant woman, married or not, could show that she faced poverty or domestic violence, she was entitled to an abortion. While this provision was in effect, it provided the justification for some 40 percent of approvals by Termination of Pregnancy Committees.[67]

Unfortunately, *the social provision* was canceled in December 1979 as part of a political agreement between the Likud party and Agudath Yisrael, an

ultra-Orthodox party that was then part of the government coalition. While
Israel's national religious population never was especially comfortable with
abortion, it was never insistent on imposing its discomfort on the secular majority. Yet ultra-Orthodox political parties are far more extreme and began to adopt
heated "pro-life" rhetoric, using it as a lever for their participating in the coalition government. At the time, the Likud held a narrow majority in the Knesset
and needed the ultra-Orthodox votes to remain in power.

In a bombastic 1979 editorial appearing in its semiofficial newspaper, the
Agudath Yisrael party explained, "The Likud knew from the beginning that
this issue is closest to the heart of those who abide by religious laws. . . . The
abortion law as a whole, and the social provision in particular, allow the murder
of embryos in their mother's womb. . . . We as believers are afraid that much
of the moral decadence in our land is the result of this law which contradicts
one of the commandments which we have received at Sinai, 'Thou shalt not
kill.' "[68] Agudath Yisrael decided to play hardball, making deletion of the "social clause" a condition for its continued parliamentary support of the coalition
government.

When the issue came to a vote in the Knesset, many Likud parliamentarians
refused to back the cancellation of the "social provision." They did not feel the
existing policy to be immoral, and they well understood that the proposed
amendment was pure political blackmail. It appeared as if there would be no
majority in the parliament to pass the amendment. Facing a coalitional crisis,
Likud party leaders decided that the easiest way to ensure that the law passed
and their ruling coalition remained intact was to turn the vote about the "social
clause" into a "vote of no confidence" in the government. If the amendment was
not approved, then the country would face new elections, something that
Likud politicians, large and small, thought inadvisable. The political "brink-
manship" worked, and within a week the amendment expunging the clause
passed the first, second, and third parliamentary readings.[69] Since that time,
despite periodic attempts to revive the "social provision," it never found its
way back into Israel's law books. It should be noted that subsequent bills were
proposed that sought to ban abortion altogether, or alternatively to allow
abortion on demand. None of them were successful. Thus, the 1979 legislation constitutes a surprisingly stable equilibrium and remains the law of the
land.[70]

The removal of the justification of abortion on social grounds essentially
made abortion illegal for married women between the ages of nineteen and
forty. For many, this turned out to be a game changer. Statistics are hard to

come by, but the legislation undoubtedly had a chilling effect: many women, who are anything but happy upon learning they are pregnant, are nonetheless dissuaded from seeking an abortion. They realize that Termination of Pregnancy Committees are not empowered to approve the procedure for them, and so they carry to term. Many others simply lie to the committees.

Data presented at a 1982 meeting in the government's Jerusalem-based Demography Center showed that the actual number of women requesting abortions had dropped only moderately since the amendment had passed two years earlier. What had changed was the large number of women now justifying their abortion applications by reporting that the pregnancy was the result of extramarital sexual relations.[71] In such cases the law allows the Termination of Pregnancy Committee to grant permission. Lying about adulterous liaisons is hardly an edifying experience when women just want to avoid an unwanted pregnancy, but over the years, hundreds of thousands have done it. As the years went by, committees frequently began to interpret the fourth clause liberally, citing the potential "emotional damage" of an uninvited birth on a woman (married or otherwise) as sufficient justification under the law.

It is important to emphasize that the Termination of Pregnancy Committees are hardly neutral adjudicatory players in the process. They operate under a directive from the overseeing Ministry of Health, which imposes on them a pronatal, promotional role. The *directive*, which is legally binding for government workers, states, "We once again call members of the committees—doctors and social workers—to dedicate time to discussions with women who have turned to the committee so they will reconsider their request. We are convinced that amongst the women applying are many who are ambivalent; the intention is to married women who already have one or more children. An open ear and an explanatory discussion and persuasion will certainly be able to influence. We therefore request cooperation in the area."[72]

In most hospitals, there is no shortage of cooperation as committees subtly or not so subtly find ways to talk women out of terminating unwanted pregnancies. Ministry of Health official Yoram Lotan testified before the Knesset Committee on the Status of Women in 2005 and shared the real story behind the extremely high rate of approved abortions by Termination of Pregnancy Committees: "You need to know how to read statistics. The fact that 98% of the requests were approved simply shows clearly how the committees work. Many social workers there are doing 'holy work.' They invest hours and days in meetings with applicants so that many times, when you see the number, it actually says that a large portion of women don't even make it to the committee (that

costs money)."[73] Does Israeli society really believe that it is "holy work" to ma-
nipulate vulnerable women, who have made a decision to perform what many
consider to be a harmless medical procedure?

This was not always the case. In 1988, over 10 percent of the applications to
the Termination of Pregnancy Committee were rejected. By 2011, however, the
percentage had fallen to 0.9 percent. Figures from that year are representative
and call for interpretation: 20,596 women submitted requests for terminating
pregnancies to committees located in hospitals across the country. Of these,
20,191 received a positive answer, and 19,214 abortions were actually performed.
That means that only some 2 percent of requests were rejected. But another
5 percent of women who received approval did not continue the process, apparently dissuaded after having second thoughts. There surely were some who simply could not wait for Israel's sluggish hospitals to set a date, and they found the
funds to have a more-expeditious "illegal" abortion.

Feminist advocates explain that the higher approval rate by committees is
simply a function of women being more aware of the rigid legal criteria. Married women in Israel who wish to abort know that their request will not be
granted unless they either lie about having an extramarital affair or feign mental
duress about their psychological state. Such lies constitute public declarations
that are not only humiliating but could be used against women should their
husbands ever want to initiate divorce proceedings.[74]

The truth is that that these statistics are merely the official figures. They do
not tell "the entire story." An enormous illegal "abortion industry" continues to
exist quietly in private doctors' offices. If a hospital is needed, many doctors will
simply "ignore the heartbeat" and report a miscarriage that requires treatment.[75]
Because it is "unlawful," there is no official reporting. Still, women's organizations insist that at least half of the abortions conducted each year in Israel
are outside the confines of the law. Common estimates are that 20,000 "illegal abortions" are conducted by private physicians annually.[76] Most of the clients are married women who do not meet the criteria and do not want to lie in
front of the committee.

This is corroborated by a cursory consideration of government statistics. The
Israel Central Bureau of Statistics reports that between 1988 and 2011 there was
only a slight increase in the number of requests for abortions (from 18,015 to
18,974). Yet, during this time Israel's population increased from 4.5 million to
7.8 million. On a per capita basis, that reflects a meaningful drop in the number of applications.[77] In 1988, fifteen out of every one hundred pregnancies were
aborted.[78] By 2011—the official number had dropped to ten. The fact that the
absolute number of abortions remains steady, despite a growing population, has

something to do with increased utilization of birth control in all sectors of Israeli society. This is a phenomenon that could already be identified by demographers in the 1980s.[79] Arab women in particular have begun to adopt contraception as a normative practice. But the real reason may be the high number of unreported abortions by women who wish to avoid the indignity of lying to an unwelcoming, bureaucratic committee.

A more analytical breakdown of the numbers tells an interesting sociological story. Abortions among Arab Israelis have increased both in relative and absolute terms. In 2002, there were some 1,807 abortions among Arab women in Israel. Nine years later the number was 2,543, a jump of 40 percent. Today, the rate of requests for abortion among Muslim and Druze citizens is about half that of Jews and Christians. Teenage pregnancy, particularly among secular Jews in Israel, remains a common phenomenon: 11.7 percent of the requests for abortions involved women under the age of nineteen. Some 44.6 percent of the applicants were single, with half of the approvals made because the pregnancy was reported to be the product of extramarital relations.[80]

Most illegal abortions are conducted by doctors. But there are cases where the high costs of a private operation push women into "backroom" procedures that compromise their health. In 2013, the press widely reported the story of a woman in her twenties who chose to have an abortion in her home. Apparently, it was performed by an unskilled friend. Massive infection resulted, which spread throughout her body. She arrived in critical condition at Wolfson Hospital in Holon, and only through aggressive antibiotic treatment was her life saved.[81]

The economics of abortion in Israel tell another important story. In a country with a strong system of socialized medicine that covers most medical procedures, terminating pregnancy is anything but free. The Ministry of Health determined that when a minor under age nineteen is pregnant or when the pregnancy is a result of rape or incest, health insurance will cover the expense. This is also the case when a woman faces a life-threatening situation or if the fetus is defective. In these cases, the fee for review by the committee is reduced to 300 shekels. Women over forty, single women, or women who are carrying a child "not fathered by the husband" may be entitled to have abortions, but they are expected to pay the full expense themselves. The Israeli army, which provides a full range of health services to female soldiers,[82] commendably pays the costs for any who seek abortions.

The costs of an abortion (presently around 8,000 shekels) have been rising steadily by roughly 15 percent per year. Today, early-stage pregnancies can be terminated by chemically inducing a miscarriage. (The generic name for Israel's leading "morning after pill" is mifepristone.) By blocking the hormone progesterone, the lining of the uterus breaks down and the pregnancy ends. Another medication, misoprostol, causes contractions of the womb, resulting in the cramping and bleeding that occurs during a miscarriage. According to the Internet, this medicinal procedure costs 1,812 shekels. Early surgical termination costs roughly twice that, and there may be many additional health expenses as well as a number of lost work days.

Officially, in 2012 women in Israel paid out 50 million shekels for registered abortions in hospitals, 23 million of which was reimbursed by health insurance. In other words some 27 million shekels were spent by women on registered abortions: 8 million shekels went to cover fees for the Termination of Pregnancy Committee, 5 million was returned to the state, and the remainder stayed in the coffers of the hospitals. The cost of private abortions for women who do not qualify for or opt out of the public health system is far higher, bringing the aggregate amount to hundreds of millions of shekels.

It's not as if there have not been clear and competent voices criticizing these rules. Professor Esther Herzog, a social anthropologist and feminist activist, is one of many. She rails against Israel's current abortion policy, which to her mind is no different than Ben-Gurion's prize for mothers of ten children: "In both cases there is a perspective of the woman as an object for the purposes of multiplying the collective by increasing the Jewish population and preferring the collective interest over privacy and individual interests. Preferring the right to life of the fetus in the body of a women over the will and the needs of the woman—giving it a subjective, independent will with its own personal needs—is unacceptable in a democratic, liberal and egalitarian culture."[83]

EFRAT AND THE BATTLE TO SAVE JEWISH EMBRYOS

Efrat is an organization established during the 1950s by Herschel Feigenbaum, a Holocaust survivor. Upon reaching Israel he decided to establish an association to increase Jewish birthrates. His mission was to replace the 1.5 million children who were murdered by the Nazi regime.[84] The nonprofit group did not gain much traction until Argentinean Israeli surgeon Eli Schussheim replaced him in the 1970s and decided to dedicate his considerable talents and passion to its work, with a new focus on abortion prevention. Schussheim insists that the goal of his organization is not to ban abortion but simply to encourage the birth of those already conceived:

> As the son of Holocaust survivors I was shocked. Abortions have become an epidemic. I decided to dedicate my life to saving these lives. And I discovered this framework that was already established. Now I actually had trouble with

the idea of an organization that had adopted as its goal "encouraging the public to have children." I said: "This is the most intimate thing that a couple can do. No one should intervene." But we can encourage birth—not by telling couples what to do (where we have no right to interfere)—but by saving those lives that are already created. You have to understand, that we're talking about the greatest catastrophe the world has ever seen: more than all the natural disasters; more than all the wars. Hundreds of millions of abortions are performed.[85]

Whatever Efrat's strategy is, it appears to be highly effective. Some thirty-five years after Schussheim launched his attack on the abortion "scourge," the organization claims to have persuaded fifty-six thousand women to give birth. At present they average a success rate of about four thousand pregnant women a year. With a 13-million-shekel annual budget, their public relations efforts are ambitious: lectures are given at military bases, at universities, high schools, or wherever the organization's "thousands of volunteers" can secure a venue. There they describe how a fetus looks and try to imagine what it feels. Their Web site alternates between images of developing fetuses and testimonials of women describing how relieved they were after forgoing abortion.[86] Neutral-sounding advertisements and signs throughout the country call on women facing unwanted pregnancies to take advantage of Efrat's free counseling.

The organization also offers support to pregnant women and to families of young babies for a period of two years. This comes in the form of food for the baby and accessories for its general needs but does not include direct monetary support. The organization's expansive warehouse in Jerusalem holds every conceivable amenity for infants: milk formula, baby food, cribs, and sundry other newborn paraphernalia. These are distributed gratis to new mothers in the Efrat network during their baby's first two years.[87]

Although Efrat's leadership claims that modest resources limit its effectiveness, the organization appears to be omnipresent. This story told by Avishag Lev could be related by untold numbers of Israeli women. At the time, the twenty-four-year-old college undergraduate awoke to find that she was unexpectedly pregnant. After much agitation and ambivalence, she and her new boyfriend decided that neither of them was in a position yet to raise children and that an abortion was the most appropriate alternative under the circumstances. Sitting in the hall in the Safed Hospital, awaiting their turn to be interviewed by the Termination of Pregnancy Committee, they were accosted by an Orthodox woman who introduced herself as a representative of Efrat. Avishag was highly distraught and already in tears given the emotionally charged circumstances. Notwithstanding the extremely public conditions (or perhaps because of them)

The Efrat association: Beyond its aggressive army of volunteers working to dissuade women from having abortions, a program to provide food and accessories to mothers in need of support is run out of a Jerusalem warehouse. (Photograph courtesy of the Efrat Association)

the woman berated them: "You're irresponsible." "You're murderers." "You'll never be able to have children again." The couple begged the woman to leave them alone, but she would not relent.

After the interview, she followed them into the elevator and continued the verbal assault, forcing a booklet into Avishag's hand. The brochure explained that with conception, an embryo has a soul and abortion murders the soul. The couple threw the booklet away and went ahead with the procedure. This story has a happy ending: The couple completed their studies, years later got married, and today have two healthy and happy children. But they cannot forgive Efrat the brazen insensitivity and disrespect that turned an awkward and challenging experience into a harrowing emotional trauma. In other cases, Efrat's uninvited interventions work, bringing unwanted children into the world and ruining young lives unnecessarily.

Professionally, Avishag Lev has since worked with adolescents at risk—girls who are homeless without even minimal capabilities for responsibly raising children. She found that Efrat is relentless in targeting these despondent girls when they become pregnant, pressuring them to carry to term. In many cases, the efforts succeed, likely contributing to the next generation of single teenage

mothers. Innumerable other women reportedly choose to have an abortion performed privately (and technically break the law) rather than face the indignities
imposed by Efrat's legions.[88]

Hillary Clinton has often expressed the view that abortion should be "safe,
legal and rare."[89] Indeed, most pro-choice advocates agree that abortion is not a
conventional medical procedure and certainly should not be seen as just another
means of birth control. Terminating pregnancy has emotional and ethical ramifications that should be considered. Nonetheless, this difficult decision by women
should be made dispassionately and without the interference of ideological
advocates who are motivated by a pro-natal, nationalistic, or religious agendas.

IMPROVING FERTILITY

While Israeli public policy discourages abortion and does little to facilitate
contraception usage, it is extremely keen to promote fertility treatments, using
assisted reproductive technologies. These include sperm donation, electro-
ejaculation for men with spinal cord injuries, freezing of ova during cancer
treatment, and surrogacy. By far the most prevalent new technology adopted by
Israel's medical system is in vitro fertilization (IVF). Introduced in 1981, IVF
treatment became a central feature of Israel's pro-natal health policies, with
massive subsidies offered to cover the high associated costs.[90]

Around the world, 8–14 percent of couples have difficulty conceiving. While
women often feel responsible for these infertility problems, the causes appear
to be evenly divided between the sexes.[91] Adoption for such families in Israel is
possible but not simple. Like most Western nations, the demand for children,
especially infants, is higher than the supply. Typically, four hundred Israeli
couples are on a waiting list to receive healthy infants, when only about fifty are
available in any given year.[92] During the past decade, the average annual number of legally adopted children in Israel rarely exceeded three hundred, counting international adoptions and adoptions of older children.[93] This constitutes
an average of roughly two adoptions for every thousand births. (By contrast, the
supply of *special needs* children is so great that even noncitizens are allowed
to adopt them.)[94] With such a small reservoir of healthy babies available IVF is
a far more compelling option for many couples. The treatment can solve problems involving low sperm counts, fallopian tube imperfections, and endome-
triosis (a painful disorder in which tissue that normally lines the inside the
uterus grows outside of it.)

Robert Edwards did the pioneering scientific work in England, which led to the
1978 birth of the first in vitro, "test tube" baby. By the time Edwards was finally

awarded a Nobel Prize for his work in 2010, Israel's first in vitro baby, Romi Neu-mark, was a well-known television news reporter who was turning thirty. She publicly congratulated Edwards and thanked him for giving her the gift of life.[95]

Israel and its IVF practitioners moved quickly to eliminate any conceivable barriers to treatment. Because of the high cost, there was a deductible charge initially, with women receiving IVF treatment expected to cost-share. In a 1989 Knesset debate, the minister of health, Eliezer Shostak, was taken to task: "What does the Minister intend to change in the health care system to avoid a situation where a person may be prevented from bearing a child because of health care costs?"[96] Shostak took the criticism to heart and found the funds to make fertility treatment free. Israel soon came to lead the world in fertility treatments: Today, the country's per capita rate of IVF treatments is forty times greater than France's or Germany's and one hundred times greater than that of the United States.[97]

It is a credit to the country's medical system that there is no discernible discrimination in granting access to reproductive technologies. Widows are enti-tled to treatment using embryos fertilized by their late husbands. Single women, lesbian couples, Arabs—all are entitled to receive treatments and do.[98] If their ex does not object, divorcees can use zygotes frozen during their days together. While Muslims may be modestly underrepresented in IVF treatment rates, this can be explained both by Islamic religious constraints and geography. The higher concentration of Arab citizens in the periphery makes treatment centers less convenient for them. This is a geographic obstacle that affects all citizens who live far from the twenty-three IVF treatment centers located across the country.[99]

Fertility treatment is an expensive business. But Israel's National Health In-surance Law remains generous in coverage. Under present internal policies, a woman until age forty-five is entitled to full funding for fertility treatments for her first two children (and not just her first two pregnancies). If a woman receives eggs from an external donor, the right to treatment is extended until age fifty-one. Should a couple remarry, they get to start the count anew and are entitled to free treatments, even if they have children from a previous mar-riage. In practice this means four cycles of treatment a year for at least two years. Almost all of the hormonal treatments and drugs are covered by the of-ficial "basket of medicines." After a relatively brief period of adaptation, couples who hold a higher level of health insurance coverage are entitled to an addi-tional IVF treatment, even if they already have two children.[100]

When these services are added up, it comes to an extremely costly societal commitment. In the United States present estimates are that one IVF cycle of

Undisputed in vitro fertilization international champions: Israel's IVF laboratories
create life, Saroka Hospital, 2015. (Photograph by author)

four treatments costs $12,400.[101] Health costs in Israel tend to be lower than in
America. During the 1990s, when treatment became widespread in Israel, the
cost of IVF was $2,000 per treatment cycle in public hospitals and $3,000 in
private fertility clinics.[102]

So just how much does in vitro fertility cost the Israeli tax payer? As of 2012
some 34.5 million treatment cycles had been conducted. That means that the
country had invested hundreds of million dollars in IVF treatments. A recent
assessment by the economic daily *Globes* reported that each of the 6,752 Israeli
IVF babies produced to date cost an average of $15,000.[103] This figure is a
conservative one, as it does not include the higher levels of hospitalization,
follow-up care, and lost workdays associated with the resulting treatments and
pregnancies.

The next question naturally is: What is the return on the investment? While
the Ministry of Health does not release official figures, medical practitioners
report a 16–20 percent "take-home baby-per-treatment cycle."[104] According to
the Ministry of Health, in 2007, 26,679 treatment cycles were registered in
Israel, a 48 percent increase over the year 2000. Altogether, 3.7 percent of total

deliveries in Israel in 2007 were the result of fertilization treatments. This comes to 17 percent of the treatments resulting in births.[105] The rate is in fact far lower. In 2014, the *Yedioth Ahronot* daily newspaper ran a headline: "A Multitude of Fertility Treatments—Few Pregnancies." Dr. Shlomo Mashiach, a leading expert in the field, went public with allegations that in the previous decade, a combination of poor selectivity and old technologies produced only a 12–14 percent success rate among Israeli couples (after calculating 20–30 percent miscarriages in IVF pregnancies).[106]

Why has Israel embraced IVF and reproductive treatments with such gusto? Professor Daphna Birenbaum-Carmeli, a Haifa University health specialist who studies the political and social implications of medical technologies, argues that it goes beyond Israel's traditional pro-natal passion. To begin with, she identifies a "nationalized narrative of productive medicine as a source of international acclaim." Israel and its medical establishment are extremely proud of the country's sensational fertility programs and the steady stream of innovations developed as Israeli doctors perfected their techniques.[107]

Moreover, she recognizes a personalized narrative that considers fertility treatment an act of compassion for women who experience acute mental distress (and public indignity) due to their infertility. Would-be mothers in Israel are seen as tragic figures. Their suffering is no different than that of biblical protagonists Hannah, who silently prayed for a child in the book of Samuel, or Rachel, the matriarch, Jacob's forlorn and barren wife. There is a view, central to Jewish tradition, that everyone should be a parent.

IVF treatments were also seamlessly integrated into the national ideology that promotes "internal aliyah." Soon after completing his tenure as health minister, former general Motta Gur quipped to a woman's magazine that while fertility treatment was expensive, "it was a whole lot cheaper than bringing in new immigrants."[108]

Politically, the reason why fertility is so disproportionately well funded can be traced to the open support of Israel's religious and ultra-Orthodox parties. Unlike contraception and surrogacy, which received unfavorable welcomes from the religious establishment and its political parties,[109] assisted reproductive technologies were readily embraced by Israel's Orthodox communities.

Because IVF treatment typically involves sperm from the mother's husband, it raises few reservations about adultery among Jewish legal experts. There is, however, the matter of fertilized eggs aborted early in the pregnancy, in cases where multiple zygotes succeed in surviving. (In Israel, typically this number will not exceed four.) Since the culling process greatly increases the survival of the remaining fetuses, it has been largely deemed acceptable, as Jewish tradition is highly utilitarian about matters of life. After all, an unborn fetus is not yet considered a person with associated human rights.[110] After evaluating the physiology and ethical implications of IVF, Orthodox Jewish leaders reached a positive position that has been called "more liberal than any other religion." By way of contrast, Islam prohibits the donation or receipt of eggs.[111]

Political representatives from religious parties are not the only ones supportive of Israel's investment in IVF technology. Medical researchers, among the pioneers in the field, naturally seek opportunities to further explore innovative technologies and treatment. Doctors in the field also constitute an "interest group" that lobbies to maintain present levels of funding.[112]

Given its defense expenses, strapped social programs, poorly funded schools, and long-term debt, Israel's government budget is chronically running short. There is simply not enough blanket to cover all the feet. Many lifesaving medicines are not covered by health insurance or government subsidies. But for the sacred mission of bringing forth life and expanding Israel's population, no expense appears to be too great. When Israel's fertility treatment program is contrasted to those offered by other countries, the pro-natal magnanimity is unprecedented and needs to be reassessed.

Birenbaum-Carmeli argues:

> We view the availability and routinisation of IVF as highly value-laden. In Israel, where budgetary cuts are constantly in the news, the unlimited funding of fertility treatments sends out a strong message to women—and men—on the "infertile body" as flawed, yet reparable, with IVF its remedy. Within this climate, it is not surprising that the rate of usage of IVF in Israel far exceeds that of any other country. . . . While IVF may well be highly beneficial and effective for some women, for others, primarily those with a family history of breast cancer, those who are older, and those who have undergone numerous unproductive cycles, whose chances of conception are comparatively small—it may incur health risks.[113]

Hedva Eyal, from the Isha L'Isha feminist NGO, emphasizes that the health implications of present Israeli IVF protocols are not sufficiently considered: "The present policy doesn't set limits and leaves the number and frequency of treatments to the discretion of the physician overseeing the process. There are women who receive twenty treatments. This is crazy—truly a health risk—pushing incredible amounts of hormones on their bodies. The resulting hyperstimulation can cause death."[114] The dangers were brought home to the general Israeli public for the first time when television journalists Orli Vilnai and Guy Meroz made a highly personal film about their own experience in IVF fertility treatments. The documentary depicts how Vilnai became extreme ill due to such lack of restraint.[115]

A more nuanced and reasoned policy response should recognize that treatment results are highly dependent on the age of the recipient. For example, in the Maccabi health program, of the 3,460 treatment cycles among women over age forty-three, ninety-one babies were born, making the costs roughly $110,000 per child.[116] This is not an optimal use of public funds. Dr. Yaakov Segel, the head of gynecology for the Maccabi Health Services, told a Knesset committee, "The infinite generosity of the Israeli health basket in the area of fertility treatment has a heavy economic price. It's an astronomical expense, and I think that we need to begin to think about it. We need to ignore the economic component that exists in the treatment, but instead explain to women when their chances are minimal. A woman may want to take these resources and direct them to other things."[117]

From the perspective of public policy, Israel's commitment to IVF and fertility treatments represents an allocation of scarce societal resources for the benefit of few.[118] Other countries with efficient and compassionate public health systems, like Canada or Australia, have chosen to cap expenses for these kinds of treatments so that other lifesaving interventions can be better funded.[119] While Israel limits full IVF subsidies to two children, it in no way limits the number of treatments offered couples.

The right to have children surely is no greater than the right to receive treatment for cancer, breathe fresh air, or receive a quality education. Society is obligated to make a reasonable effort to assist couples overcome infertility problems, not a disproportionate one. Pregnancy is not an inalienable right that can be guaranteed.

At the same time, women should absolutely be given the opportunity to choose *not* to have children if that is their desire. The present asymmetry between Israeli society's commitment to fertility treatment and its unwillingness to cover full costs of contraception and abortion is bad public policy not just because it subsidizes overpopulation. It means that many women are not free to make fundamental choices about reproduction.

7

"BE FRUITFUL AND MULTIPLY": JEWISH PROCREATION AND ULTRA-ORTHODOX FERTILITY

Clearly, a Jew should not attempt to interfere in God's affairs. . . .
He is to leave the question of pregnancy to God.
—Menachem Schneerson, "the Lubavitcher Rebbe"

THE GROWING WORLD OF HAREDI JUDAISM

Birthrates among most secular Israelis—Jewish and Arab—are only modestly greater than those in many Western countries. Ultra-Orthodox Jewish Israelis (Haredim), and Israel's Bedouin citizens are the clear exceptions, and their fertility is indeed exceptional. Although the last decade has actually seen a modest reduction in their total fertility rates (TFRs), on average Haredim still have 6 children, more than twice the national average of 3.0 children per family, and many have 10 or more offspring.[1] (National religious or modern orthodox also have relatively large families, but on average 2.5 fewer children than Haredim.)[2] This means that Israel's population growth is increasingly driven by high Haredi fertility. Unless it drops significantly, the social and environmental indicators by which quality of life in Israel is measured will not improve. Most ultra-Orthodox parents have more children than they can afford and have to rely on charity and government subsidies to survive. Given the poverty into which most Haredi children are born, they do not enjoy equal opportunities for a prosperous future.

It is time to consider what lies behind the Haredi community's large families and to design policies that will facilitate greater economic self-sufficiency, integration into Israel's workforce and a more sustainable culture of family planning among the ultra-Orthodox. Haredi leaders vigorously resist these objectives. But

Israel will remain on an unsustainable trajectory until it changes the demographic dynamics in this community.

As Israel's ultra-Orthodox community grows it becomes more diverse and generalizations become less reliable. For instance the Chabad community (which includes some fifty thousand to sixty thousand spiritual followers of the Lubavitch Hasidic rabbinical line in Israel)[3] is extremely committed to employment, with religious studies seen as a supplementary activity. Other groups, especially among the Lithuanian Haredi world (comprising 22–24 percent of Israeli ultra-Orthodox), are totally committed to studying Torah and prefer not to enter the workforce. But all Haredi groups appear to share an inclination for large families. In 2010, the Central Bureau of Statistics (CBS) reported that Haredi Jews in Israel are increasing at a rate of 6 percent a year. That is more than three times the 1.8 percent general growth rate of Israeli society.

Some 22.5 percent of Haredi households have six or more children—compared to 2.5 percent of Israelis overall. That means that there are a great many Haredi families in double digits. It also explains why 60 percent of Haredim today are under the age of twenty. Only 5 percent are over age sixty-five. Such asymmetrical demographic profiles are typical of developing countries. The median age of Israel's Haredi community is sixteen, but there are ultra-Orthodox neighborhoods where it is twelve, and in Ashdod's Neighborhood C it is ten. By way of contrast, the median age is thirty-four among immigrants from the former Soviet Union![4] The immutable force of population momentum means that even if future Haredi birthrates drop precipitously, a majority of Israel's future population will still be born to their children. Stated simply, "All of tomorrow's parents are alive today."[5]

There is little doubt that the dramatic increase in family size among the Israeli ultra-Orthodox is part of a broader international phenomenon. Technion University researcher Daniel Orenstein contrasted family size in ultra-Orthodox communities living outside of Israel (which received no child allowances) with those living in Israel and found them to be comparable.[6] The comprehensive 2013 demographic survey of the American Jewish community prepared by the Pew Research Center reported that some 2 percent of Jews in the United States age sixty-five or older are ultra-Orthodox. By way of contrast, a full 10 percent of American Jews between ages thirty and forty-nine are ultra-Orthodox, and 9 percent are ultra-Orthodox in the eighteen-to-twenty-nine demographic.[7] Other sources contrast them with the more moderately religious "Modern Orthodox" American families, who have 3.3 children on average—half the present 6.6 total fertility rates among "ultra-Orthodox" families. Some Hasidic Jewish communities in the United States may average as much as 7.9 children per

family.[8] In the United Kingdom ultra-Orthodox fertility is even more pronounced: three-quarters of that country's Jewish births today are among ultra-
Orthodox families, sufficient to stem the steady drop in the size of an otherwise
declining British Jewish community.[9]

Within Israel, what was once a relatively small sector is starting to dominate
the country's demographic profile. Some 25 percent of first-graders identify
themselves as Haredim. Israel's Central Bureau of Statistics projects that by 2019
only 40 percent of Israel's elementary schoolchildren will study in the national
public school system, with the majority either in the Haredi or Arab sectors' independent systems.[10] If policies are to be designed to successfully reduce population growth in Israel, they must reflect an understanding of the cultural and
religious dynamics behind this community's exceptional propagation.

Prior to considering their idiosyncratic societal values and inclinations, it is
important to define who is a Haredi. This is not simple, because the term com-
prises an extremely diverse and fragmented cohort, divided along geographic, ethnic, and theological lines into movements, streams, courts, and communities.
These range from the virulently anti-Zionist "Neturei Karta sect" to Sephardic
Haredim, who can be difficult to distinguish from parts of the National (Zionist) religious communities. To identify a Haredi, many people do not look beyond the external dress and its emphasis on physical modesty. In fact, the
Haredi uniform is anything but *uniform*: it generally involves beards, black suits
(and "black hats") worn by Haredi men, and long sleeves, dresses, and stockings,
along with head coverings or wigs among women. But there are innumerable
variations and nuances.[11]

One definition sees Haredi Jews as people whose private and public lives are in
strict compliance with the dictates of Jewish law and tradition. Prolonged study of
the Torah among men is especially venerated and considered a "higher calling."[12]
Others highlight the complete, voluntary submission to a rabbinic authority figure, empowered to make key personal and communal decisions in all aspects of
his followers' lives.[13] Another definition characterizes Haredim as religious Jews
who prefer the more stringent rulings in Jewish law to the more lenient ones.[14]
Yet, others have pointed to their cultural seclusion, to avoid spiritual or cultural
contamination[15] or the tense relations with mainstream state institutions and
nonreligious Israelis.[16] All these definitions are correct and compatible.

Notwithstanding their diversity, there are many shared sociological traits that
characterize Israel's Haredim. Marriage constitutes a paramount value: 82 percent
of Haredi adults are married (14 percent are single; 2 percent divorced, and the
rest widowed). This contrasts dramatically to the general population, where
35 percent are single.

As numbers grew and housing prices skyrocketed in the 1990s, young Haredi families could not find housing in the traditional enclaves and began to move on. While Jerusalem and Bnei Brak remain the twin centers of Haredi life, major Haredi communities emerged throughout the center of the country in cities like Beit Shemesh, Rehovoth, Rishon LeZion, Petach Tikva, and Ashdod. Today 87 percent of the Haredi community lives in Israel's heartland center rather than the Galilee or the Negev. In the same period, new cities comprised entirely of Haredim emerged, particularly in the West Bank, where Haredim now make up one-third of Jewish settlers.[17]

Each community may have its own special character, but they all tend to be poor: the Central Bureau of Statistics reported that in 2010, 80 percent of Haredi households earned 2,000 shekels (about $515) or less per capita per month. Among the total population, only 36 percent earned so meagerly. On average, Haredi families live with 1.4 people crowded into a room. This is 75 percent higher than the national average of 0.8-person-per-room density.[18]

There are two obvious factors that drive the high rate of Haredi poverty. The first is family size itself, which divides and depletes household income. The other involves the low level of employment among Haredi men. In 1979 roughly 85 percent of Haredi men worked; in 2012 that rate had fallen to below 50 percent.[19] Strong societal norms, however, which encourage humility and nonmaterialist values, enable Haredi communities to thrive despite their economic distress. Additionally, remarkable internal networks of charity and mutual support help reduce much of the acute suffering, neediness, and general want within Haredi society.

Perhaps the single most conspicuous societal trait of the Haredi communities is their commitment to insularity. While they cannot escape some connection with the "outside world," they resist integration with mainstream Israeli society.[20] Many Haredi homes do not contain a television or have access to the Internet. But Israel will have to learn how to engage this community, with its unique values and societal norms, if it is to attain sustainable levels of fertility.

UNEASY ADVERSARIES: HAREDIM AND ZIONISTS

The Jewish world has always been divided by theological, ideological, and sociological schisms. The stereotypical joke about the lone Jew stranded on a desert island who builds two synagogues (so that there is one "that he would never set foot in") is based on a rich tradition of diversity—or alternatively of infighting. Tradition holds that the Temple was destroyed by the Romans because of the gratuitous hatred between rival Jewish groups.[21]

Historic conflict between Jewish factions was soon dwarfed when a secular Jewish identity emerged, influenced by the European Enlightenment movement of the eighteenth century. New political norms arose in much of Europe and North America. For the first time Jews were able to integrate into Western society. Many were quick to answer the call. Moses Mendelssohn, a German Jewish philosopher, championed the notion that one could be a Jew in one's house and a German in the street, and he is often associated with transforming a social opportunity into a new ethnic ideology.[22]

The Jewish religious establishment in Europe at the time was not at all enamored of the enlightened perspective. It scorned the more flexible interpretation of traditional norms as heretical.[23] Leading rabbis during the period felt particularly threatened when new Jewish denominations, like Reform and, later, Conservative Judaism, began to offer alternative ways to be Jewish. Jewish legal experts increasingly resisted modifying ancient Jewish practices, which the newer approaches often deemed to be outdated or even immoral.[24] Defenders of this new "ultra-Orthodoxy" claimed that the real motivation for these calls for change was that Jewish rituals and traditions had become inconvenient (or in some cases simply embarrassing) for enlightened Jews who were trying to impress gentiles. They claimed that Non-Orthodox Jews mimic non-Jewish institutions to assimilate into the greater, increasingly secular society.

Theologically, the existential argument over what it means to be Jewish—an unresolved argument that continues to rage today—caused many Orthodox to "dig in their heels" and opt for a more defiant, insulated, pious, and static form of Judaism.[25] Orthodox Jewish religious leaders saw profound dangers in liberal approaches, fearing that they would lead to secularism and assimilation (which they often did), and to doctrinal dilution and divine retribution. Better to simply freeze the religion and ensure the continuity of the Jewish people and its holy mission.

These theological impulses coalesced in 1912, when a conference was convened in Katovitz, Poland, which created the Agudath Israel movement and signified the *political* birth of modern Haredi Judaism. Some 230 Orthodox leaders from Europe, North America, and Palestine came together after numerous, unsuccessful attempts to unite the competing streams in the Orthodox world. Given the great disparities in geography and doctrine, this was a formidable task.[26] It took the perceived success of the early Zionist Congresses and the inroads that nationalism was making in Europe's Jewish world to galvanize rival Orthodox sects to resolve their differences and establish a united front against the growing secular movement.[27] Agudath Israel soon claimed a membership of one hundred thousand across Poland alone and, at the time, was a political force in the Jewish world second only to the Zionist movement, which quickly became anathema to these hard-line Haredi Jews.[28]

Even though the European ultra-Orthodox movement rejected "Zion" as a panacea to the Jewish problem, it surely "did not forget" Jerusalem." Indeed, these first "Haredim" soon established ties with their natural partners based in Palestine, the religious enclaves living in the "old Yishuv." These were the many Orthodox Jewish families that had never left Palestine during the time of exile. Their communities were intermittently reinforced by scattered waves of Jewish immigrants who arrived over the centuries from around the world. For example, the noted scholar Elijah Ben Solomon Zalman (reverently referred to as "The Genius—Gaon—of Vilna"), sent disciples to settle in Israel during the eighteenth century. These ultra-Orthodox communities were primarily based in Jerusalem, Safed, Tiberias, and, to a lesser extent, Hebron. In 1919, Jerusalem rabbis had already formed the "Eda Haredit" as an umbrella ultra-Orthodox community organization. It survives to this day, primarily as an anti-Zionist Haredi advocacy group that publicly shuns all connection with the State of Israel. The Eda Haredit maintains its own agencies overseeing licensing services for kosher food (through its "Badatz"—acronym for Court of Justice—network) and other aspects of its members' lives.[29]

Ultra-orthodox numbers in Israel during the first half of the twentieth century were hardly extraordinary. While there are no definitive census figures, a retrospective analysis of the results of the 1920 elections to the British Mandate's "Assembly of Representatives" infers a "Haredi" community of about fifteen thousand to twenty thousand people.[30] In 1933, the celebrated rabbi Abraham Isaiah Karlitz (commonly known as the Hazon Ish) moved to Bnei Brak, contributing to its emergence as a major new center for ultra-Orthodox Jews.

The schism between the Haredi and Zionist communities in Palestine was still bitter in 1937 when the British government's Royal Commission of Inquiry (Peel Commission) floated a "partition plan" to create two states from the British Mandate: an Arab and a Jewish one. It sought input from the two communities. David Ben-Gurion headed the Jewish Agency at the time. A consummate pragmatist, he embraced the Peel partition plan, especially given the dire conditions facing German Jewry as Hitler's persecution grew worse.[31]

But the British were well aware that Ben-Gurion did not speak for all of Palestine's Jews. The Peel Commission invited ultra-Orthodox representatives to give testimony. At the time, Haredi Jews were dominated by the vociferously anti-Zionist Agudath Israel. The organization passed a resolution emphasizing that the land of Israel belonged to the people of Israel "because the Lord of the world gave it to them as an eternal covenant." The ideology and theology as then espoused remains, at least formally, something of a mission statement for the ultra-Orthodox world and Haredi leaders to this very day:

> Because of our sins we were exiled from our land and. . . . we will be redeemed by our righteous Messiah—and this is the central principle of our holy religion that all people born to Israel believe. The existence of a Jewish state will only be possible if the constitution of the Torah will be recognized as the foundation of the land, as the rule of Torah and in the leadership of the state. A Jewish state that is not founded on the rules and ruling of the Torah is a denial of the source of eternal Israel and is lacking in the essence and character of the people of Israel and undermines the existence of people—and ceases to be a Jewish state. The Council of Torah Sages recognizes that all negotiations taking place regarding the fate of the Holy Land, without Jewish Haredi representatives have no legal basis.[32]

In the end the Peel Commission gave little weight to the ultra-Orthodox rejectionists. Haredim at the time lived almost exclusively in Jerusalem, which was to remain under British rule under the Peel partition plan. They would not have to be part of the Zionist state they so abhorred.

In 1947, the United Nations considered a modified partition proposal. Ben-Gurion saw the possibility of a Jewish sovereign state within grasp and wanted to minimize any risk of being sabotaged from within by a Jewish opposition. After a decade of violent conflict between the Yishuv and the local Arab communities, there were many among the ultra-Orthodox who began to take a more-conciliatory view toward the largely secular Zionist majority.[33] Moreover, Agudath Israel had received special status to represent the Jewish people in the newly established United Nations.[34] It could not be ignored. This prompted Ben-Gurion to "cut a deal" with the Haredi leadership, as represented by Agudath Israel. The agreement has since become known as the "status quo." Concessions on behalf of the Jewish secular majority to the sensitivities of the Haredi minority, it was hoped, would quell the internecine conflict between Orthodox and non-Orthodox Jews and strengthen unity.

Among the four points in the agreement was granting educational autonomy to the country's religious communities and to Agudath Israel in particular, to continue to teach religious subjects as they saw fit without government interference. The arrangement attained its objective, and Agudath Israel did not express objection to the creation of the state. Indeed, many ultra-Orthodox Jews assisted in the military efforts during the War of Independence.

Within the Haredi world there were groups considered more extreme (most notably the Neturei Karta and the Satmar Hasidim) that vehemently rejected any reconciliation and refused to recognize the legitimacy of the new Jewish state. Some went so far as declining to use Israeli legal tender! But once the state was established, these groups became marginalized. Israel's Haredim were modest in number and stunned by the extermination of so many millions of their brethren in Europe. The "status quo" afforded the community considerable autonomy to rebuild its lost world of Torah scholarship and replenish its numbers.

POPULATION BOMB

And replenish they did. There are many estimates, none of them precise, about the actual numbers of Haredim in Israel today. At the founding of the state there were only thirty-five thousand to forty thousand ultra-Orthodox Jews in Israel. After sixty-five years, their numbers have increased by 2,000 percent. After the Holocaust, having children took on an entirely new ideological meaning. Rabbi Menachem Schneerson, the revered spiritual leader of Chabad Hasidim, with scores of Israeli followers, emphasized this point often: "It is the obligation of our generation, we who are all 'brands saved from the fire,' to not only act on behalf of all those who died in sanctification of G-d's name, but also—and this is of primary importance—to actually replenish the [depleted] population of the Jewish people."[35]

In fact, for many years, there was a substantial gap between the preaching of rabbis and actual practices of religious Jews in Israel: Haredi birthrates during the 1950s and 1960s were not significantly higher than those of secular Jews.[36] Tamar Rotem grew up in the ultra-Orthodox town of Bnei during this period. Looking back she recalls that "after the Holocaust most of the families in Bnei Brak had few children. Only a select few had large broods and they were looked at with disdain. My mother would not allow me to connect with children from homes like these, because 'surely—their homes are not clean.'"[37]

But a radical change began to take occur, and Haredi fertility rose steeply. In addition to a solemn commitment to renew Jewish ranks after the Holocaust, several factors have coalesced to produce the phenomenal fertility levels that today leave a typical elderly Haredi couple with over one hundred progeny.

First there are the mechanics of demographic growth. The early age of marriage, for instance, contributes greatly to Haredi numbers. In Israel, the average age of marriage is twenty-seven for men and twenty-four for women. In contrast it is only twenty-one for men and twenty for women among the Haredim.[38] Despite the opposition of Haredi political parties, the minimum age of marriage was recently raised in Israel from seventeen to eighteen. In promoting the law, legislators cited a Bar Ilan University study that reported the marriage of some

Growing up in Jerusalem's ultra-Orthodox Mea Shearim
neighborhood in 1959, when Haredi families had on average
between two and three children. (Abraham Malavski,
KKL-JNF Photo Archive)

forty-five hundred minors in Israel each year (a quarter younger than sixteen
years old). Many involved girls from Haredi communities.[39] By the time most
secular Israelis complete the service in the army, take their trek around the
world, complete university, and begin to think about a family, a Haredi couple
of the same age may have five or six children.

Another reason for the Haredi community's growth is that they rarely emigrate from Israel. That's why some 82 percent of Haredim are native Israelis as
opposed to 60 percent of the general population.[40] At the same time, relatively
few immigrants join them. Of the large immigration from the former Soviet
Union, only 16,250 (or 5.5 percent) are Haredim, even though they are 20 percent
of Israeli citizens.

A parallel contributing factor involves the "role of women" in many Haredi
communities, which first and foremost involves baby production. As Dr. Rivka
Neria-Ben Shahar writes:

Haredi women experience a double jeopardy—as women and as members of
the ultra-Orthodox community, with its discriminatory norms and practices.
The essence of this derogatory attitude towards women often cited in Haredi
literature is expressed in the Hebrew saying "Kol Kvoda Bat Melekh Pnima"
(Psalms 45:14), meaning that even a king's daughter should turn her honor
inwards—be quiet, keep a low profile, occupy as little space as possible. To

After-school outing in Jerusalem for Haredi schoolchildren in
first grade, who today make up over 60 percent of the city's
Jewish first-graders. (Photograph by author)

secure this gender system, girls and young women are socialized into their
future role as mothers, wives and homemakers, responsible for the smooth
functioning of the household, while men are encouraged to pursue their advanced Torah studies, politics, and other masculine goals. . . . This level of
fertility exerts a heavy physical burden, a tremendous workload and psychological responsibility on the women and older girls in Haredi families.[41]

More recently, fertility became politicized by the ultra-Orthodox. The political astuteness of Haredi political parties made a critical contribution to today's
pro-natal reality. In 1977, as part of a coalition agreement with Agudath Yisrael,
Prime Minister Menachem Begin agreed to expand the exemption from military service for Haredi men who were yeshiva students. Later, subsequent
governments increased the stipends for studying in yeshivas indefinitely. This
meant that Haredi men could afford to marry young. As child allowances grew,
they were rewarded financially for producing larger families.

Moti Kaplan, one of Israel's leading urban planners, grew up ultra-Orthodox
and was a promising scholar before choosing to pursue a more secular path at
Hebrew University. He reflects on the current situation: "In the Haredi culture,
a lot of things changed. Today hundreds of thousands of Jews don't work. This
was never known previously in Jewish culture—indeed it is unknown in human
history. In the 1960s and 1970s this culture was not yet established. The other

thing that is completely unique about Haredi culture is the fact that the women started to enter the work force, but it in no way reduced their birth rates. You can even argue that it increased it."[42]

In short, a new Israeli-Haredi culture emerged that was different from Haredi norms outside Israel or those that had previously characterized ultra-Orthodox Jewry. The majority of men no longer sought work. Economic and social status was enhanced by having many children without being responsible for their support. In private discussions, both rank-and-file Haredim and their leaders express confidence that it will take little time to reestablish the numeric superiority of ultra-Orthodoxy within the Jewish world. For instance, Meir Porush, who has represented the Agudath Yisrael in Israel's Knesset since 1996, openly asserts that within twenty years, 40 percent of Israel's Jews will be Haredim.[43]

This confidence now has an empirical basis: between 1961 and 2006, the number of voters for Ashkenazic Haredi parties increased threefold.[44] By 1979 the number of people living in Israel who identified as Haredi was counted at 140,000. In 2003 there were an estimated 100,000–130,000 Haredi households, with 700,000–780,000 people, a full 11 percent of the population. In 2009 the CBS estimated the population to be roughly 785,000. Presently, the number exceeds 830,000 people.[45] Current Haredi fertility is not a calculated response to the Holocaust, nor is it a tactic to gain political influence. Rather, it is an expression of religious zeal, a source of community political power[46] with a modicum of economic savvy.

MARRIAGE, SEX, AND CONTRACEPTION IN THE JEWISH TRADITION

Haredim are defined by a complete commitment to implementing traditional Jewish law, which they understand to be divinely decreed. Accordingly, procreation constitutes a binding directive for Haredi men; Haredi women see themselves as partners in this divine mission. To understand Haredi birthrates, it is essential to consider the rules and values of the time-honored Jewish legal and spiritual tradition. While there are always minority views and nuances, the preponderance of Jewish doctrine facilitates a powerful pro-natal agenda. Key elements include:

- a religious obligation for men to produce children;
- the perception of sexual relations as a positive and even holy activity;
- laws of "family purity" that direct the time of sexual relations to the most fertile days in women's ovulation cycle;

- male conjugal duties, involving legal expectations for frequent lovemaking (sex needs to be regulated within a marriage, but should take place regularly);
- aversion to birth control, which is only to be approved for women under narrow conditions and only after families have at least two children;
- encouragement of early marriages.[47]

There are in fact two competing views about the purpose of marriage and sex in Judaism.[48] The first emphasizes their instrumental value: procreation constitutes the ultimate purpose for getting married and having sexual relations. The definitive catalog of Jewish law, the *Shulchan Aruch*, written in Israel in 1563, opens its volume on family life with a clear pronouncement: "Every man is required to marry a wife in order to procreate."[49] The Talmud quotes Rabbi Eliezer as saying, "He who does not engage in procreation is as if he spilled blood."[50] This expectation is based on the directive from the book of Genesis at the opening of the Bible: "Be fruitful and multiply and fill the earth." Procreation was never seen as a recommendation; it is Scripture's very first commandment.

Maimonides, the eminent twelfth-century scholar (and physician), saw the procreation imperative as applicable to males from age seventeen and up. If by age twenty a Jewish male is not married and has not begun a family: "He is considered to have transgressed and violated this positive commandment." Moreover, the expectation that men father children is ongoing, even after producing a critical mass for Jewish survival.[51]

Procreation is a commandment based on results. Simply trying to have children was not enough for the rabbis. The Mishnah, the core text around which the Talmud is based, specifically states that if a man is married to a woman for ten years and she has not yet produced children, he is "not allowed to neglect further the commandment of procreation."[52] Accordingly, after ten years of marriage, a childless husband is expected to divorce his wife (or take another one); though his wife is also entitled to marry again.[53] Rashi, the greatest interpreter of the Bible and the Talmud, explains that this can be deduced from the patriarch Abraham who had a child with Hagar, his wife's handmaiden, ten years after he and Sarai began their unsuccessful efforts. The Talmud goes on to stipulate that if a man has not yet fulfilled the commandment of being fruitful and multiplying, he cannot marry a woman he knows in advance will be barren.[54]

Yet there is a competing view that sees intrinsic value in the companionship engendered by marriage and sexual relations. Even before the Bible compels procreation, the creation story explains God's motivation in creating a woman: "It is not good for man to be alone" (Genesis 2:18). Over the years, the rabbis softened the rules, explaining that a happily married man who has no children after ten years is entitled to divorce his wife but has no obligation to do so.[55]

With the Bible so filled with love stories, many rabbis inferred that God wanted romance to be part of the connubial package. Rebecca becomes so overwrought at seeing her betrothed Isaac that she falls off of a camel (Genesis 24:62–67); the two are seen laughing and flirting (Genesis 26:8) long after years of marriage would have reduced most ordinary relationships to routine and humdrum. Jacob gladly works for Rachel's hand for fourteen years, which flew by "as if they were but a few days" (Genesis 29:20), so intoxicated was he by his beloved.

Some of the greatest fables of the rabbis in the Talmud reveal passionate and inspirational couples. Most famous of these is Rabbi Akiva, whose wife sent him away to study while she, a rich man's daughter, supported him. She worked in abject poverty for twenty-four years, and they were only reunited after he emerged as the greatest scholar of his generation. Upon meeting her, thousands of his students who joined him had no idea who she was, but Akiva explained that he (and they) were nothing without her.[56]

The empathetic observation that "man should not be alone" is more than an idle reflection about the forlorn state of the solitary Adam in the Garden of Eden. It is a pragmatic recognition of the dangers of human libido. According to this view, matrimony contains implicit expectations. More than simply bestowing the inherent benefits of companionship, marriage is seen as a normative and healthy framework for channeling the natural male and female sexual drives. The Talmud justifies marriage not just as a means for fulfilling procreation duties but a framework for avoiding lascivious thoughts and inappropriate behavior: "He who reaches the age of twenty and has not married spends his days in sin. "Sin"—really? Better to say, "all his days in the thought of sin."[57]

Matrimony's essential role in keeping young men on the straight-and-narrow path constitutes a consistent "party line" over the centuries. The position is repeated throughout the Talmud with attendant obligations. Fathers must make sure their sons are married while they are yet young.[58] Unlike in Catholicism, a "married state" is considered holier than a single status; celibacy is disdained. Only one rabbi in the Talmud openly exhibited monastic inclinations: Shimon Ben Azzai. Ben Azzai "excused himself from fulfilling the duty of procreation, but did not hesitate to urge it on others. When his colleagues chided him for preaching rather than practicing, he responded: 'What can I do? I am in love with [the study of] Torah. The world will be perpetuated through others.' "[59]

Jewish law is clear about males' duty to procreate, but the precise quantitative dimensions of the obligation are debated. Early on, the two leading academies of first-century B.C. Israel, headed by the great competing rabbis Shammai and Hillel, held opposing views. The central passage on the subject is found in the Mishnah: "A man is not exempted from being fruitful and multiplying unless he has sons. The school of Shammai says: he needs to give birth to at least two males; and the school of Hillel says: male and female as it is said [in Genesis 5:2] 'Male and female created.'"[60]

Because the disagreement over fertility levels sets the standard for minimal procreation among many religious Israelis, it is well to consider the nature of the debate between Judaism's greatest rabbinic rivals. Why did the school of Shammai insist on two sons? The Talmud explains it as emulating Moses, who had two children: Gershom and Eliezer—in other words, two boys. After having two sons, according to tradition, Moses separated himself from his wife. So Shammai argued that two males constitutes a minimum requirement for meeting the "fruitful and multiply" standard.[61] By way of contrast, the school of Hillel's explanation is based on biology and the nature of conception: having children of both genders guarantees the future of the world.

In typical fashion, the Talmud further complicates the debate. It quotes a musing of the later rabbinic authority, Rabbi Natan, who doubles these expectations to two boys and two girls. His contemporary, Rabbi Hunah explains: Adam and Eve had four children—two girls and two boys. (According to legend, Cain and Abel each had a female twin.) Finally, the Talmud offers yet another more-lenient opinion: in fact, Rabbi Natan explains, the school of Shammai was misquoted. Accordingly they too were content with a boy and a girl, while the school of Hillel's position was even more permissive: producing a single son or a single daughter is enough to fulfill the procreation commandment. "Rava, a third-century Babylonian scholar, explains: What is the reason for Rabbi Natan's view? Accordingly it is based on the book of Isaiah: 'Thus sayeth the lord—Maker of the Land'; and God didn't make the land so that it would be empty, but rather created it to be settled."[62]

So much for theory. In practice, the Halacha, or binding legal requirement, for men adopts the original ruling of Hillel: one girl and one boy.[63] Jewish law does not make it easy for men to meet even these fertility obligations. The great third-century scholar (and reformed bandit) Resh Lakish posited that a convert to Judaism who had children prior to converting still needs to have more, having not yet fulfilled the commandment. Rabbi Yochanan (his friend and intellectual rival) believed he has.[64]

In the context of family planning, the most salient feature of Jewish law is its fundamental asymmetry. The duty to be fruitful and multiply is only binding on men. This grants women considerable latitude not only to determine family size (and utilize contraception) but also to determine the frequency and nature of a couple's sexual activity.

According to the Bible (Exodus 21:10), in marrying, a Jewish man makes a commitment to his wife that contains three components: providing food, clothing, and sexual activity—or euphemistically, "conjugal duties." The Talmud specifies minimal frequencies of intimate interaction based on husbands' professions,[65] even suggesting optimal times (midnight is preferable). Sailors and traveling salesmen have lower obligations than scholars who work near home. This means that before a man can accept a job that takes him away from his family, he must consult with his wife. The Talmud grants her veto power to decline her husband's professional opportunity if she feels it will detract from her sex life excessively.[66]

Conventional wisdom as stated in the Talmud is that "a woman prefers less income and the frivolity of her husband to greater income and separation from him."[67] An entire treatise, *The Holy Letter*, attributed to the great thirteenth-century Rabbi Moshe Ben Nachman (the Ramban), offers detailed recommendations to men about how to conduct their sex life to ensure their wives' satisfaction. The motivation for the book involves reproduction, based on the assumption that when a woman has the right frame of mind, fitting children will be born.[68] While Masters and Johnson might take issue with some of the recommendations, the underlying assumptions are that women's physiology and psychology are different than men's and foreplay is critical.[69]

Women's sexual rights in marriage include the right to refrain. While they are surely encouraged to help men fulfill the commandment, they are under no obligation to do so. A woman can be called a "rebel" in marriage, denied certain civil privileges, or even divorced if she refuses to have sex with her husband.[70] But she cannot be compelled to have sex or give birth to a child. The legal code, the *Shulchan Aruch*, and Maimonides absolutely prohibit men from forcing themselves on their wives. While a man is expected to remarry if his wife is infertile, "a woman has permission to never marry or to marry a man who is infertile." Jewish sages surely encouraged women to "settle the earth" based on the book of Isaiah's expectation that "the world was created to be inhabited"(Isaiah 45:18). The operational assumption among religious Jews has always been that all things being equal, having more children is better. But for wives, sex need not have anything to do with procreation.

It is this fundamental asymmetry that created the legal basis for women's utilization of birth control over the years. Primitive forms of contraception—beyond coitus interruptus—were certainly known to the rabbis. In particular a "mokh," an early but reportedly effective form of a diaphragm, was common.[71]

Because males are not entitled to curtail their fertility, not all contraception is permissible. In light of God's terrible wrath against Onan for reneging on his duty to father a child with his widowed sister-in-law (Genesis 38:9), Jewish men are not permitted to "waste their seed." This not only has been interpreted as a ban on masturbation, but also a requirement that males complete the sexual act. Thus condoms constitute an unacceptable form of birth control. Rabbis waxed physiological about the point at which the flow of seed could be obstructed. Beginning in thirteenth-century Italy, rabbis insisted that contraception not interfere with normal intercourse or mutual sexual pleasure.[72] Intrauterine devices and other oral contraceptive methods that do not impede the delivery of sperm into fallopian tubes do not pose a problem. Postcoital contraception (for example, douching) is also allowed. As ensuring women's satisfaction is also a religious requirement, inconvenience also constitutes a factor in the ranking of different forms of birth control. This contributes to birth control pills' general popularity.[73]

Not only does Jewish law not prohibit contraception, there are even instances when contraception is compulsory. An early rabbinic discourse ("Baraita") describes three cases where birth control is mandatory. The first involves a minor; the second, a pregnant woman; and the third, a nursing woman. The passage justifies each case: For the minor, contraception is required because the girl might become pregnant and die. For a pregnant woman, unprotected sex might cause her fetus to become a *sandal* (a flattened or compressed fetus) that will need to be aborted. A nursing woman may use birth control, because otherwise she might have to wean her child prematurely, endangering its life.[74]

Despite encouraging reproduction late into life, there are cases when husbands are exempted from procreational duties due to events beyond their control. Jewish tradition recognizes circumstances when it is not only irresponsible but unlawful to produce children. The land of Israel, with its stochastic rainfall patterns, is given to episodic famine. There is nothing new about this. In the book of Genesis, Jacob and his sons are forced to leave Canaan and move to Egypt to avoid starving during a lean period. Experience suggests that drought years can come in clusters. Recognizing that prayer does not always produce precipitation, ancient Israelites undertook "adaptation" measures, which included abstention from having children during the times of famine.

This theme is taken up in a lengthy exchange in the Talmud (Taanit 11A): "Rav Yehduah said in the name of Rav: Anyone who starves himself in years of famine is saved from an unnatural death, as it is said 'In famine, he redeemed from death.' . . . Resh Lakish said it is forbidden for a man to have marital relations in years of famine. As it is said 'and to Joseph were born two sons before the year of famine came.'" Presumably, Joseph was privy to prophetic knowledge about imminent famine, so he stopped having children in order to stay within the land's carrying capacity. Jews who do not abstain from procreation during famine are thought to expel the divine presence from Israel and are seen as committing a violent act of bloodshed.

Dr. Jeremy Benstein, an expert in Judaism and the environment from the Heschel Center in Tel Aviv, points out that in contrast to his grandfather Isaac, who had two children, Joseph's father Jacob had two wives, two concubines, and at least thirteen children. Faced with a grim ecological reality in which herds only had access to shriveled and shrunken biomass, unable to feed the family, Jacob and his oversized clan were forced to leave the land of Israel.[75]

Later rulings introduce moderate leniency on this point. Notwithstanding Resh Lakish's exemption: a *Tanna* (a rabbi during the time of the Mishnah) taught, "those without children may have marital relations in a year of famine, as it is said: 'And to Joseph were born two sons before the year of famine came.'"[76] In other words, it is up to a childless couple to decide whether or not they wish to bring a child into the world, knowing that it may face starvation and exacerbate the general scarcity.

In the present context, the question arises: Should Israel's present environmental crisis be understood as the modern equivalent to "times of famine," requiring solidarity and reduced reproduction? There is certainly ample ecological justification for such a view. And there is biblical precedent: Benstein refers to the account given in Breishit Rabba (31:7), a commentary on the book of Genesis (6:18), about the great flood. Noah and his sons were told to enter the ark with "your sons, your wife and your sons' wives" (Genesis 6:18). Yet, when they left the ark, the Bible describes them coming out of the ark: "with your wife, your sons and your sons' wives." Rabbi Yehudah Ben Shimon explains that the modified order of the words reflects the separation imposed between the sexes during the time of flood and ecosystem collapse. Under such catastrophic environmental circumstances, procreation was prohibited. Benstein suggests that "given contemporary threats to biodiversity and living systems, our world is often compared to the ark, and our own mission to that of Noah."[77]

Jewish law requires men to have a minimum number of children. Barring catastrophic circumstances, Jewish culture encourages them to have many more. Nonetheless, there are circumstances in which maximum fertility is not only deemed inappropriate but is in fact unlawful. There is a legal basis in Jewish tradition for setting demographic objectives at replacement levels or even lower. Such positions have yet to resonate among Israel's Haredi leadership. Conveying this message constitutes one of Israel's paramount ecological and demographic challenges!

THE STATUS OF HAREDI WOMEN

A society's birthrate is generally thought to be directly linked to the status of women.[78] What is the status of Israel's Haredi women today, and is it changing? Women in the Haredi world surely do not have the same rights and opportunities as men. For instance, women would never be allowed to become rabbis or to assume political leadership in any of Israel's Haredi cities. At the same time, attitudes about gender roles are not monolithic.

On one end of the spectrum are Haredi sects and individuals that have grown progressively liberal about the status of women and the professional opportunities they should enjoy. Adina Bar-Shalom is the eldest daughter of the late, revered Sephardi Haredi Rabbi Ovadia Yosef. For some time she has been a passionate advocate for improved teaching of math and English in Haredi public schools.[79] In 2001 Bar-Shalom's focus moved from secondary to higher education, establishing the Haredi College in Jerusalem. The college offers women degrees in computer science, medical science, psychology, and social work.[80] Advanced education cannot help but contribute to female empowerment. By delaying marriage it may also affect fertility. But it is not at all clear that this kind of openness represents a "trend." Haredi leaders surely deny it.[81] For instance, soon after succeeding Ovadia Yosef as chairman of the Shas Council of Torah Sages, Rabbi Shalom Cohen ruled in June 2014 that it was "unthinkable for women to go and learn academic studies in any framework because this is not the way of the Torah."[82]

Once married, most Haredi couples immediately try to conceive. Some Haredi brides will even "go on the pill" in the months prior to their nuptials to control their menstrual cycle and synchronize ovulation for the wedding night. There are, however, some young women who wish to continue their studies after high school and put off marriage or delay conception. This can be a very hard decision, in light of overwhelming societal and familial pressures to find a good match and avoid an unbearable "spinster" fate. Meir Porush, Agudath Yisrael political leader, claims that everyone starts to pity a young person in the Haredi world who is not married by age twenty-one.[83]

Nonetheless, a growing number of Haredi girls are exploring the expanding menu of professional opportunities, as gender norms are showing signs of change among many younger Haredim.[84] As new models are established, some parents are beginning to believe that a better education may actually increase a women's status in the marketplace of matchmaking. Bar Ilan geography professor Yosseph Shilhav has conducted several studies about working women in Haredi society. He argues that its dynamics are unlike any other society in the world. In other societies, the entry of women into the workforce is associated with a drop in birthrates; among Haredi women, it is not. His explanation is that for these women, work is not driven by career ambitions and is not perceived as having inherent value. Rather, their work only holds instrumental value, allowing husbands to study, and enables families to support more children.

Shilhav asserts:

> The Haredi social view ascribes an essential role to a woman. This does not refer to the various epithets found in religious texts regarding her importance and the importance of treating her suitably, but to the status granted her in the community and family structure. In many Haredi communities there is a social tradition of a division of labor, based on the Midrash about Issachar and Zebulun. . . . According to this Midrash, the man, who studies Torah, could be defined as fulfilling a spiritual role, while the woman has the instrumental role of satisfying the needs of the student. Thus, the woman supplies the economic infrastructure that enables her husband to devote all his time to learning. As it is understood to be instrumental, employment of women is tolerated and not perceived as a threat to the community's values.[85]

The fact that women in many Haredi families have become the primary breadwinners has created a complicated dynamic.[86] On the one hand, Haredi women work as teachers, accountants, computer programmers, and even lawyers. Many eventually assume positions of responsibility. It is increasingly common for Haredi women to have more general education and professional qualifications than their husbands.[87] While their professional competence per se does not seem to be a source of great anxiety, many Haredi men are uneasy with their wives' exposure to unhealthy Western norms.

While some Haredim may be justifiably proud of their women's accomplishments in the workplace and their reputations as excellent employees, this is not translated into esteem among the Haredi establishment and rabbinic leadership. Indeed, Shilhav's research points to increasing tensions and perceptions of women's education as a threat to the establishment: "This is the source of the threat she presents: her skills are not hidden from the community, which is well aware of the importance and status of many Haredi women in the 'outside world.' But it raises heavy suspicions among the veteran leaders. If women pay the bills, they may also start to call the shots."[88]

These concerns strengthen reactionary voices in the ultra-Orthodox world of people who believe that Haredi women already enjoy excessive freedoms that need to be curtailed. Additional demands include more-stringent dress codes requiring utmost modesty (the traditional wig, high socks, and long-sleeved dresses are no longer enough), a strict prohibition on female singing in public places (and dinner tables), and other limitations on participation in societal life. Photographs of women, for example, are banned from the public arena—from kosher restaurant menus, billboards, and buses to photos of the Israeli cabinet.

In a recent column to the Internet newspaper *Ynet* entitled "Obsession with Modesty Is Killing Us," Esti Shoshan, a Haredi woman journalist, details this widening campaign of harassment against Haredi women: "While in Saudi Arabia women are rising to protest against the driving ban imposed on them, in the democratic Holy Land the voice of Haredi women is barely heard. . . . The phenomenon of radicalization when it comes to modesty is new, and it appears that the Haredi society doesn't really know how to deal with it. Girls dressed in shawls, women in veils, kosher buses, men spraying bleach on women and destroying their clothes. These are things which did not exist in the past, and it is getting worse and worse."[89]

These changing norms are apparent in a city like Modi'in Illit. With sixty thousand residents, the all-Haredi municipality of Modi'in Illit is Israel's fastest growing city. Numerous informal discussions with men there reveal fairly common expectations about what a normative Haredi family should look like: Single men rarely describe their "idealized" or anticipated family as having fewer than ten children. There is a widespread commitment (at least publicly) to indefinitely continue Torah study with little or no interest in conventional employment or military service. Wives are expected to financially support husbands, despite concerns that contact with the outside world might have a corrupting effect. Indeed, of the two polar perspectives toward women, the more conservative view is predominant among Modi'in Illit's male residents. The majority is uncomfortable with the notion of advanced training and higher education for women, even as they accept the economic necessity of wives working to finance husbands' Torah study. "Being able to bear children is the gift that women received. That is the task that God has assigned to them. They only need enough schooling to fulfill this role."[90] This reflects a commonly held opinion.

All Haredi men interviewed in Modi'in Illit believed that the women in their community are far better off and more protected than their secular counterparts (who are alternatively seen as "treated like dirt and humiliated" or impugned for wanton, licentious inclinations.) While no Haredi adult in Modi'in Illit openly acknowledges women's entitlement to rights equal to men (for example, the right to give evidence in religious court), certain civic prerogatives, like the right to vote in national elections, are now accepted.[91] By any objective standard, a highly chauvinistic perspective about gender roles still endures. This is also reflected in attitudes about family planning.

For decades surveys of Jews in Israel indicate that contraceptive prevalence declines with increasing religiosity.[92] Haredi husbands do not use birth control. Married Haredi women are also not expected to use protection. (Considerable effort is made to ensure that unmarried women do not come into unsupervised contact with males, so premarital contraception is unthinkable.) Haredi rabbi, politician, and father of twelve, Meir Porush proudly declares, "Don't ask me any questions about birth control. We surely don't use it in my house!"[93]

Yet because Jewish tradition does not specifically forbid birth control for females, once authorized by an ultra-Orthodox rabbi, Haredi women are permitted to utilize forms that do not compromise their husband's fulfillment of procreational duties. As mentioned, utilization of IUDs and birth control pills are common, as they do not impede the flow of semen. Because many Haredi women are uncomfortable approaching a rabbi about such intimate matters, husbands frequently will ask for permission on their wives' behalf.

While Haredi men and women like to refer to the matter as a joint decision, most concur that contraception is ultimately the wife's call. There have always been nonmedicinal strategies used to prevent pregnancies. For instance, one study confirmed that Haredi women will postpone their monthly immersion in the ritual bath (mikvah) long after menstruation is over in order to delay sexual activity to a less-fertile period in their cycles.[94] Prolonged breastfeeding has long been practiced by religious Jewish women as a child-spacing technique.

Birth control is only considered acceptable after the first or second child. After that, the conditions for approving its use are not clearly demarcated. Haredi spokesperson Shneur Rosen explains that typically, a Haredi rabbi will not grant approval to use contraception because of economic concerns associated with having a large family.[95] Mental duress or physical maladies, however, are sufficient justification. For instance, postpartum depression is a well-known phenomenon in the Haredi community and today is recognized as a legitimate reason for approving the spacing and controlling of births.[96]

If one looks for trends, contraception has made inroads among Israeli Haredim in recent years, a prerequisite for any future reduction in fertility. Recently, a Haredi resident of Bnei Brak was arrested at Ben Gurion Airport smuggling in seventy-eight hundred spermicide dispensers without paying import taxes or receiving a permit from the Ministry of Health. More important than access to contraception for controlling birth is the motivation to prevent pregnancy. In his defense, he claimed he was but a courier for sundry birth control suppliers in the Bnei Brak community.[97] A market is developing, even as many Haredi women would prefer their utilization of contraception not be public knowledge or even known to their husbands.

To what extent do Israel's Haredim see negative ramifications arising from their high birthrates? Most members of the community are totally unfamiliar with the dismal *environmental* impacts associated with Israel's exponential demographic growth. For those familiar with these concerns, gloomy forecasts are considered to be unreliable or beyond the limited, myopic capabilities of human comprehension. Like so many other unpleasant scenarios, it is easier to rely on an omnipotent deity for deliverance.

Neither do the *economic* ramifications of large families seem to faze Haredi men. When questioned about their financial situation in light of their communities' demographic growth, answers typically combine a curious combination of faith, optimism, and cognitive dissonance. Mostly, there is a dogged unwillingness to acknowledge any adverse repercussions. This is surely the singular message that comes from the most venerated rabbis. For instance, the late Lubavitcher rebbe Menachem Schneerson would invariably refuse requests by devoted adherents in Israel to limit their number of children, asking rhetorically, "Is it imaginable that the Holy One who feeds and provides will not see to the feeding of new children?"[98]

Haredim like to wax rapturous about the advantages of massive families: "I grew up in a family with seven children. My wife's had six children," Hasidic rabbi Yitzhak Neuman recalls. "I never felt that I was crowded—and I never felt that I was neglected. You know I live here in the comfortable suburb of Reut. And there are plenty of families here with 1.5 children and a dog, where the children suffer from lack of attention. There are a whole lot of variables in this equation about raising children. And there is also the question of economic comfort. We don't educate for luxuries. We believe that every child brings its own blessing and prosperity. After all: 'Who is wealthy? He who is happy with his lot.'"[99]

Invariably, when the implications of oversize families with paltry budgets are raised, faith in the Almighty is summoned. Secular Israelis, it is sometimes argued, are incapable of understanding that the Haredi community lives because of miracles. Jerusalem rabbi and Haredi community leader Dudi Zilbershlag has eleven children. He is also a founder of the green NGO Haredim for the Environment. "Jewish survival has always depended on miracles involving God's dominion over, and even suspension of natural laws," he explains. "Like when Israel left Egypt and God made the seas part, divine intervention will make everything work out."[100]

Unlike most men in Modi'in Illit, Yosef Balmas works. He cites biblical precedent for Haredi confidence about the future:

> There is evidence that the Jewish women in Egypt had between six and sixty children. Pharaoh tried to stop Jewish fertility—and look what happened to him! Today, the only thing we need is enough faith. We really don't need strength. And if we as a nation had faith, we wouldn't need an army. I mean who paid for all those children in Egypt? There were no child allowances back then, but women had children as an act of faith. It's the same for us. Who paid for my mother's children when she moved from Morocco? Secular Jews, who have made materialism a central part of their modern culture, can't understand this. But they should come inside the houses here and see what kind of poverty exists and what kind of dedication it takes to maintain a life of Torah.[101]

AN OPEN DISCUSSION ABOUT LIFE STRATEGIES WITH HAREDI WOMEN

The formality of empirical research makes it hard to assess whether signs of transition in the status of women are harbingers of reduced future birthrates. Informal discussions with Haredi women provide richer insights into present cultural norms and future trends. Beitar Illit offers an ideal setting to talk about these matters.

Beitar Illit was established in the West Bank, ten kilometers south of Jerusalem, in 1984 by a group of nationalist Zionist Jews. It did not take long for the city to be transformed into a homogeneous Haredi community. Young Haredi couples and families sought the subsidized housing that West Bank settlers enjoy and quickly built an insulated community of their own. In 2003, the population was already twenty-three thousand. Only then did a bona fide population explosion begin: By 2006 the city had grown to twenty-nine thousand; a year later, thirty-five thousand—and by 2013 Beitar Illit was home to forty-five thousand people.[102] Current projections anticipate one hundred thousand residents by 2020. Over half of the residents are school-age children.[103] Reflecting the labor patterns in the Haredi community, some 64 percent of the men and 45 percent of the women are unemployed.

On a warm July 16 morning in 2013, a leisurely, open conversation with three thoughtful and opinionated women from Beitar Illit about family life and family planning in the Haredi world considered the evolving dynamics in Israel's

Haredi community. The discussion between the author with Zissy Malovitsky, Yochi Sanders, and Bat Sheva Fried was possible because it was Tisha B'Av, a national day of mourning and fasting commemorating the destruction of the Temple. Driving into the community was allowed, but no one went to work. And no refreshments interfered with discussions.

The women's' spouses were still at their respective synagogues that morning. Their husbands are affiliated with different houses of worship, which provide them with their primary social frameworks. Women are not required to attend and typically do not. This allows Haredi women in Beitar Illit to become friendly with women from a rich variety of "ultra-Orthodox backgrounds giving them greater social diversity than their husbands. Bat Sheva explains, "Generally, when you marry a man, he has already made his decision about affiliation. The woman goes after the husband in everything—not only his family name but his rabbi."[104] While the women are proud of having friends from Hasidic and Lithuanian persuasions, there remains relatively little mixing between Haredim of Ashkenazi and Sephardic backgrounds.

All three women are married, having given birth to several children by their mid-twenties. Bat Sheva, age forty-one, has had eleven children in twenty-one years of marriage. This is by no means exceptional. She explains that a local rabbi's wife recently became distraught when she had to undergo a hysterectomy during the birth of her seventeenth child. (The rabbi's mother stays with the family to help raise the children, and the rabbi atypically "helps his wife cook for Shabbat.") Medical exigencies have temporarily forced Yochi to stop having more children; she has six. But she is proud that her sister-in-law is also expecting her seventeenth. Zissy's circumstances are somewhat anomalous. She decided to stop after four when she found she lacked the emotional strength to cope with more, and she emphasizes that her husband was supportive. Nonetheless, as she is still quite young; she may decide to have more at some point in the future.

They all refer to Beitar Illit as a "Garden of Eden for children." From playgrounds to infirmaries to synagogues, the critical infrastructure for raising Haredi kids) is very accessible. Schools offer religious education in the morning and more-secular subjects in the afternoon. Children are given a hot meal in between the two sessions, unlike in Israeli mainstream public schools, so mothers do not have to prepare lunches. There is no shortage of parks. Yochi rhetorically asks, "The Rebbe took thirty-eight kids on a bike trip around Beitar. Where would he take them in Jerusalem? It's too dangerous. No. There is no better place for children." And there are a lot of them. Typically, the city's standard sixteen-unit apartment buildings will house between fifty and one hundred children. But there is one with two hundred!

All three women work: Zissy is a medical secretary, Yochi runs her own wig business, and Bat Sheva is a full-time teacher. Yet, in the short time that has elapsed since they were eighteen and considering marriage, employment options for girls in the Haredi world expanded. Today the job market is more crowded and more "professional." Rather than going straight to work or betrothal from high school, many girls in Beitar Illit prefer to acquire proper training or even a degree. A growing number take advantage of Ono College, which has a special program for Haredim that ensures the separation of the sexes. Research confirms that a greater range of socially acceptable professional opportunities are open to their daughters than was available to themselves.[105]

In the past, few girls delayed marriage beyond age twenty. Today, even though many parents urge their daughters not to rush, there are still many girls who make marriage their top priority once they turn eighteen. Getting married so young is not so much about fulfilling divine expectations regarding procreation as it is about concern for "missing the matrimonial boat."

Zissy grew up among the Belz Hasidic sect, although she decided to marry outside it. She describes her own attitude toward marriage as typical of many girls: "When I was deciding about getting married, I wanted things to be calm and make sure I was set up. It wasn't a matter of romance or love at all. I needed to know that I would be taken care of. Later, I got to know my husband, and six months into the marriage I started to feel love. But at the time it was doing what I needed to do and making sure that I wasn't left behind."

Haredi girls are expected to adopt their husband's religious inclination and its extensive normative package in all matters—from attire to education. This makes a match, made at a very young age, a most fateful decision. While dating is out of the question, there is a selection process that offers girls the opportunity to veto potential husbands. While intuition is involved in deciding, there are also objective criteria. Yochi explains, "I was talking to a woman in Beitar Illit and she told me: 'I don't need my daughter to marry a Torah scholar. It's enough that he be a good Jew.' I told her: 'You are shooting yourself in the foot.' Parents want clear information about levels of religious scholarship and a groom's character." There are also clear red lines that should not be crossed. Yochi continues, "A boy who goes to the army—well he screws up his entire life. He won't find a match among the Haredim, not among the national religious, and not among the secular."

While the cacophony of large Haredi families living in such close quarters often appears excessive from the outside, many Haredi women say that it is really only adults who suffer from the density. Zissy clarifies, "Having a large family for a child is an adventure. I was the youngest in my family, so while growing up there was no one around. I was always going over to my neighbors and preferred to be surrounded by their ten siblings. When you are a child, you can't really relate to your parents' world. Children like having company. Now, perhaps I appreciate the quiet. But when you're a kid, you love having other children around you."

For Yochi, more than mere companionship, a large family is a source of strength. Her closest friends are her siblings and relatives: "I heard about a situation where a newspaper reporter came into a first grade class in China. He asked: 'Who has a brother or a sister?' Not a single child had one. Then he asked: 'Who would want one?' Every hand in the class shot up. And why was that? The children explained: 'So I'll have someone to talk to. My parents are old!'"

Notwithstanding their declarations of joy in producing life, the women are open about the price they pay for their astonishing fertility. Invariably, any talk about the hardships of running a household with a dozen mouths to feed, beds to make, and innumerable problems to solve comes back to an underlying sense of duty. Bat Sheva explains, "It's not easy to have so many children, but that's our mission. It makes us happy. For me—it is the only thing I want to do. It was clear to me from the start that this was the purpose of my life."

Coming from a family of nine children, her parents can be thought of as the prototypical Haredi "elders" who have over one hundred progeny. With that many birthdays and anniversaries to keep track of, they have to keep a special calendar, but they manage to call on every occasion. Yochi believes that by having large families, someone can literally see what the future world holds in one's own lifetime. "My husband's parents didn't come from a Haredi household. He only became Haredi in his teens. So my mother-in-law has one brother who completed a doctorate in law. He had degrees and everything—undoubtedly a professional success. But what did it do for him? Today he is as lonely as a dog. He lives by himself in an old age home. Compare his situation to my mother-in-law who had thirteen kids. When she died young at age 64, she told me: 'I am going to my death with happiness. I couldn't ask for more.' She already had seventy-five grandchildren."

Ultra-Orthodox life, by design, is highly regimented leading to a rather deontological ethical orientation. As Zissy explains, "When you are Haredi, being in a clearly defined group is intrinsically good. It gives you a clear framework. People need a community. How would you know where to send your children if you didn't have a well-identified brand? You see when you are Haredi, you don't do what you want. You have a mission. You are subservient to a particular Rabbi. A child won't be obedient to his father, even if his father also happens to be a rabbi. There is a clear hierarchy in our world: The children listen to their parents, who are deferential to the Rabbi. And the Rabbis bring the word of God."

This regimented hierarchy also applies to routine procedures for contraception. In a normative situation, women are expected to receive approval from a rabbi before using birth control. Such a decision is far too pedestrian to be brought to a "rebbe," the spiritual head of a Hasidic sect, who needs to be free to address weightier issues. Like other questions of Jewish law, the request is presented to the neighborhood rabbi, who is available "24/7." The neighborhood rabbi may well be from an entirely different Haredi camp. A Hasidic Jew may well go to a Lithuanian rabbi to receive permission. This is because the question involves legal rather than spiritual matters. After the second child, there is general societal recognition that slowing down by using contraception carries no stigma. Among themselves, women speak openly about birth control.

They admit that some Haredi women don't bother asking a rabbi if they can use birth control. They tell their husbands, "If you want to get permission from the rabbi—go ahead. I'll do what I need to do." There are also times when a rabbi will say, "You can space out your pregnancies by taking birth control pills for a year." But in these cases, a woman usually will use contraception as long as she wishes.

Because procreation is a commandment that only binds males, the women agree that in many cases a wife won't even tell her husband that she has begun using birth control, so that she doesn't put him in a position of knowingly failing to perform a critical commandment. Ultimately, the prevailing view is that in a Haredi family, the woman has considerable say about how many children she has.

Some women are embarrassed to ask a rabbi for permission to start using contraception, and frequently a neighborhood rabbi's wife will serve as an intermediary to make it easier. There are some basic things that a *rebbetzen* can decide based on her own experience. Even in matters of Jewish law, de facto, she can be authorized to answer a question if she has heard it asked time and again. Consent for birth control use can be such a case.

Given the standard of Hillel and Shammai, why do more Haredi women not stop at two? Many Haredi women do not feel that they are authorized to "stop souls from entering the world." For this they need a rabbi's approval. The women explain that aspiring for significant family size falls into the category of *hiddur mitzvah*, or beautifying or glorifying a commandment. Jewish tradition has always held that the *mitzvoth*—the commandments—can be embellished and upgraded through human devotion. Rather than buying an ordinary etrog (citron) fruit as required for the succoth holiday, the most perfect one possible will be sought. Going the extra distance offers the opportunity to make a personal state-ment of reverence for God. Having many children, going beyond the manda-tory number, is seen as an act of devotion to the Almighty.

It is very hard to find a Haredi—male or female—who will openly acknowl-edge that economic concerns are a factor in determining his or her family size. Yochi quotes from the Talmud that "Every baby is born with its loaf of bread" (Nidah 31:2). From this perspective, they believe that God imbues every child with its own blessing. While admitting that there may be a small percentage of Haredi women who consider financial implications in their family planning, Yochi comments wryly that Jews did not survive over the ages by conducting cost-benefit analyses before having additional children. In any case, the deci-sion to use contraception purportedly is based on psychological considerations rather than economics. At the same time, they admit that there are cases where dire economic circumstances can affect a woman's state of mind. There is a strong sense among Haredi women that one cannot predict the future finan-cially, so economics constitutes an inappropriate basis for making decisions about family planning.

Environmental considerations are also not thought to be legitimate reasons for limiting family size. Yochi interjects, "You ask is there room for all these new people? I believe that just like it says in the Talmud—at the Temple, people were crowded in so completely that there was no room to move. And yet (through a miracle) they were able to bow down inside. One-third of the world lives in China. They have a demographic problem. Israel still has plenty of room: The 'Land of the Gazelle' will open up and receive more. It's a matter of faith. We don't really talk about our faith, that things will be all right if we have more children. We just live it."

Zissy uses an environmental analogy to explain how Haredim approach carrying capacity: "There are plenty of people who never look at the big pic-ture. People won't return bottles to the recycling bins because they don't really think about why it's important to recycle garbage. They will only think about what is comfortable. 'I'll do what's convenient for me.' Rarely do they connect individual actions to a global situation. This is especially true when you accept the authority of a Rabbi. Basically, Haredim know that it is against the rules to prevent pregnancy. You have to trust that the Rabbis know what is going on in the big picture."

TOWARD A SUSTAINABLE FUTURE

To what extent is the Haredi world in Israel changing? There are surely many ultra-Orthodox individuals who are inconspicuously drifting toward more liberal world views. The women in Beitar Illit speak dismissively about "modern Haredim." They sometimes wear colored shirts. Some may shave. They don't define their lives by the rulings of a single rabbi. They tend to have fewer children. Worst of all, if their sons are inclined, the parents don't object to their joining the Israeli army. (At the end of the enlistment year 2014, 1,972 Haredi youths had joined the army—863 in combat units—compared to 1,416 in 2013 and 1,327 in 2012. At the same time, over 11,000 eighteen-year-old Haredim requested exemptions from military service.)[106]

The women in Beitar Illit see these modern Haredim as a corrupting influence and only want their children to study with "true Haredim." It is difficult to ascertain whether this newly feared flexibility is a marginal phenomenon or whether the Haredi world is in the early stages of a sea change.

The difficulty arises from the gap between public and private postures, so common in a tight-knit community that has a penchant for applying strong social pressures to enforce conformity to religious norms. There are certain "mantras" that need to be repeated. Yet, several sociological studies confirm modernization trends within Haredi society: these are manifested in adoption of new technologies, recreational patterns, professions, and even the way Haredi DJs broadcast on the growing number of Haredi radio stations.[107] But to what extent is this encounter with modernity affecting the procreational proclivities of the Haredi community?

First, the facts: between 2003 and 2009, Haredi fertility rates fell from 7.6 to 6.5 children per family.[108] This represents a statistically significant shift, which presumably continues. It can be attributed to a variety of factors. Even as they find much objectionable, there are surely Haredi communities who have made their peace with the secular Jewish state: its customs, benefits, and constraints.

Haredi patriotism is manifested in unexpected ways, such as pride in the work of the nonprofit organization "ZAKA," whose members tenderly collect the battered remains of terror victims for burial.[109] And despite the disapprobation, two thousand Haredi youth did join the army last year.[110] The Sephardic Haredi party Shas was never a fan of traditional Zionism, but in 2010, for the first time, it requested formal representation in the World Zionist Congress, which implicitly meant defining itself as a Zionist party.[111] Cynics presumed that the decision was driven by the potential funds and jobs for party activists that participation might bring. But such open identification by a Haredi political party with Zionist institutions was unimaginable in the past.

Veteran Shas politician Rabbi Eli Yishai does not hesitate to praise Haredi birthrates as playing a crucial role in the distinctly Zionist demographic struggle: "Haredi women work and they still have many children because they have awareness and understand its national importance. We need to remember that

A rapidly expanding community: over eight hundred thousand attend the funeral of revered Haredi rabbi and Shas founder Ovadia Yosef on October 7, 2013. (Yossi Zamir, KKL-JNF Photo Archive)

our demographic situation is not a simple one and that we risk becoming like Europe where families only have one or two children. If we wish to preserve the Jewish majority it is in the national interest of the State for Jews to have many children. The State should welcome the fact that Haredim have such large families. We need more children from secular families as well."[112]

If pro-natal attitudes are linked to the "national good" rather than being merely the requirements of Jewish law, then there may be more room in the future for considering societal sustainability in family-planning decisions. This is a hopeful sign.

Nechumi Yaffe, a doctoral researcher at Hebrew University and herself a proud Haredi woman, has assessed public opinion in the Haredi world on poverty and gender issues: "I think that expectations about family size are dropping. This can be seen in two main trends: a greater awareness among women about the importance of receiving more advanced education and a concern for providing more individual love and attention to children."[113]

Although neither of these aspirations appears to be directly contingent on financial resources, in fact—given the privatization of social services in Israel today—they are. Yaffe explains, "I never heard a woman say: 'I don't have enough money to bring children into the world,' even if they actually think this constitutes a reason not to have so many kids. Because of the culture, they would never say so." Yaffe's position is confirmed in a 2013 study by the Adler Institute, reporting that 60 percent of secular Israelis acknowledged that the economic situation made them consider not having another child. Among Haredim and religious parents, only 5 percent openly expressed this view.[114]

There do indeed appear to be discernible differences between generations. Yaffe identifies another, totally new influence on familial culture in Israel's Haredi world: *zugiyut*, or the nurturing of affection between a couple. In the traditional tension between the two concepts of marriage emerging from Genesis (*"be fruitful and multiply"* versus *"man should not be alone"*), a new balance is being struck. Among Yaffe's parents' generation of Israeli Haredim, it was understood that a man and a woman came together for the sole purpose of bringing children into the world. Romance was a foreign notion. Symbolically, when women gave birth, their mothers would take them to the hospital.[115]

The dynamics among the younger generation of Haredi couples are decidedly different. Selecting a bride or a groom today is not merely an exercise in status maximization or economics but also a matter of the heart. (Yaffe qualifies, *"Oy va voy*—woe to you—if the decision is *only* made according to the heart!") But increasingly, Haredi women in Israel have come to see "love" as having a place in marriage, expecting that energies be reserved for developing and maintaining passion. Yaffe insists that today, even among the most "hard-core" Haredim, couples take a weekend away together every year without the children so that they can enjoy each other's company. Husbands join their wives at the hospital for the delivery of a child (and sometimes will bring the grand-mother along). These changes are clearly the result of "culture contact" with the larger, secular society.

One sign of enhanced expectation from marriage is the increase in divorce rates among Haredim, which are now comparable to general societal rates among Jews: 1.7 cases per 1,000 people per year.[116] (This is roughly twice what it was forty years ago, but still only half that of the divorce rates in OECD coun-tries.)[117] Yaffe, whose own parents are divorced, sees this as a positive develop-ment. In the past, because of societal taboos, many incompatible couples stayed together but suffered greatly.

Other conventions central to large Haredi family dynamics are increasingly questioned. For instance the merits of "older children raising the younger ones," once a source of pride, are no longer entirely clear. Yaffe explains:

> I once asked my aunt: "How did you raise thirteen kids?" and she answered "the other twelve." She herself is one of eleven children. But I know many women who were raised in such large families who won't bring as many into the world. There is a sense that their mothers were not there enough for their children. I mean it's a nice idea to get the children involved in raising the younger children. But perhaps it has gone too far. If a girl of eleven years has to prepare sandwiches in the morning, pick up a younger sibling at the kin-dergarten and come home and diaper, she doesn't have time to be a girl her-self. I know someone whose eldest daughter literally runs the house. Some Haredi women don't work around the house at all; perhaps they weren't mature enough themselves to run a family.[118]

There are other objective consequences associated with the high birthrates of Israel's Haredi community. Some are mere inconveniences, like the disrup-tion caused by innumerable days when substitute teachers fill in so that per-manent teachers can scramble to take care of their own enormous clans.[119] Some are more disturbing. The unfortunate truth is that many Haredi parents find it impossible to effectively oversee their unruly offspring. A 2013 survey by the Joint Distribution Committee uncovered a phenomenon that the Haredi establishment would rather not publicize: Some 30 *percent* of Haredi junior-high- and high-school-age children are defined as "hidden dropouts": students who are technically registered in an educational framework but are dysfunctional students, unable to perform successfully in their schoolroom environment.[120]

In 2014, the Knesset Committee for the Status of Women convened a hearing on the state of women's health in the Haredi sector. A coalition of Haredi women's organizations—Meuravut—collected data for a year and presented a detailed report on the subject. High morbidity levels were identified in the sector—largely a result of factors such as poverty, the young age of marriage, and the number of births and children. Frequent hormonal treatments to increase fertility have a negative impact on health. High levels of anemia and even malnutrition are phenomena that reflect many families' dire economic conditions. The report cites 2009 research indicating that as the number of children in a household increases, the number of visits to doctors by the mother drops. As a result, Haredi women do not take advantage of available lifesaving, advanced, diagnostic techniques. The report claims that some 50 percent of Haredi women have never had a mammogram, which explains why death rates from breast cancer are twice as high among Haredi women as they are among women in Israel's general population. The report concludes, "The very high birth rate relative to the average, directly affects their health."[121]

Children are also affected, in particular their cognitive development. Professor Shilhav reports that a considerable percentage of Haredi children are special-needs children. They are "mentally and physically challenged due to the phenomenon of marriage within a tight-knit community with a common gene pool, as well as norms related to fertility and childbirth: multiple pregnancies, women still giving birth at a relatively late age, and the avoidance of fetal testing."[122] Research by Tel Aviv University scientists Ilana Brosch and Yochanan Peres reveals that the IQ of children in Israeli families with more than five children on average is nine points lower than those raised in smaller families.[123] These phenomena are not unknown to Haredim, especially Haredi women who are starting to consider alternative models.

Still, in most Haredi circles, birthrates remain extraordinarily high. If Israel is to attain a stable population, it is well to consider how public policies might contribute to reducing such high fertility. Like the debate over universal conscription and the imposition of penalties on Haredim who avoid military service, the question, many believe, is largely tactical. Almost every Haredi "spokesperson"—as well as the "man and woman in the street"—argues that a trend already exists in which Haredi boys increasingly volunteer to serve in the military. They insist that making military service compulsory and punishing noncompliance creates a "backlash." Haredim, who might otherwise be more moderate and complacent, "push back" and become radicalized against Zionist hegemony. Reaching consensus and using persuasion are deemed the only effective public posture. This may be true. But it is also true that positions favoring cautious incrementalism are always proposed by people resisting social reform. There are countless examples—from civil rights to smoking prohibitions—in which firm government intervention was needed to change societal norms.

What sort of interventions promoting sustainable population levels make sense given the Haredi community's unique characteristics? Typically, advocates of societal transformation need to select between two general strategies: changes that are facilitated through "top-down" or by "bottom-up" initiatives. Because Haredi society is so hierarchical, engaging the leading rabbis and Councils of Sages in the myriad Haredi communities about the issue seems to make sense. After all, Jewish law allows families to limit their size after two children—or according to Rabbi Natan of old—even one.

In time of famine and other ecological calamities, procreation can and should be limited. Moreover, beginning with the story of Noah's ark, Jewish tradition was deeply concerned about the natural world and protecting the only other known creatures with whom humans share God's creation. Even before the flood, a well-known midrash recounts how God tells Adam in the Garden of Eden to take a good look at all of creation and "make sure not to spoil and destroy my world because what you spoil no one can repair."[124] Presumably, Israel's present biodiversity crisis, along with the broader environmental impacts of the rapid population growth, would have traction with rabbis. When given the hypothetical case of ecological apocalypse, some ultra-Orthodox rabbis acknowledge that if environmental conditions became grave enough to constitute "a famine," it could trigger a two-child maximum.

At a practical level, such a 180-degree doctrinal reversal is exceedingly unlikely. For over a hundred years, ultra-Orthodox rabbis made an entire theology out of resisting change. Appealing to Haredi leaders on environmental grounds will not be an easy sell. The response is likely to resemble that of Haredi parliamentarian Meir Porush's stance, which dismisses ecological concerns out of hand: "I don't know of any limitations on childbearing. I know of God's promise to bring the Jews to the land of Israel—a land of 'milk and honey' that will provide for all—if the people will but walk in the way of the Lord."[125]

Rachel Ladani, a highly regarded environmental educator from Bnei Brak and a Haredi mother of eight, has exemplary ecological consciousness and credentials. But on procreation she is unrepentant: "God brings children into the world. He'll find a place for them." Fully conversant with the dynamics of carbon footprints, she admonishes, "My two daughters and six sons produce less carbon dioxide in one year than someone from America visiting Israel does in one flight." When asked about the implications of the anticipated doubling of Israel's population by 2050 she shrugs. "I don't have to think about it. God made the problem and He will solve it."[126] Until Israel's environmental movement makes a strong, uncompromising case for stabilizing population, with solid data demonstrating the consequences of surpassing local carrying capacity, it is unlikely that Haredi rabbis will think about it, either.

Going "bottom-up," or directing population stabilization policies at the Haredi rank-and-file level, constitutes the alternative strategy. Eilon Schwartz, a leading environmental thinker, is among those secular Israelis who earnestly seek greater engagement and common ground with the Haredi community. Schwartz questions the wisdom of policies explicitly designed to reduce Israel's birthrate or that target Haredim:

> It would seem to me that the more you go head-to-head, the more people will go into their bunkers. There is a place for questions, but this is an extremely sensitive issue. I believe you need a policy that supports existing trends, not one that bucks them. By calling for a drastic reduction in birth rates, you may be undermining the trends rather than reinforcing them. The real question regarding the Haredi community is the work force—not even the army. Ultimately, the biggest indicator of reduced fertility among the Haredi population (and Arab citizens too for that matter) is their "Israelization."[127]

Government programs prioritizing a particular population sector's high fertility can be criticized as illegitimate because they "smack of eugenics." To the extent possible, public policies should be designed so that they apply equally to everyone. If no one envisions "one-child" legislation limiting family size anytime soon, what are the associated positive trends that might be strengthened through broader policy initiatives?

For some time, scholars have identified an "Israelization" process among Haredim that flies in the face of their aspirations to remain impenetrable to external influences.[128] *Geography* should be harnessed to promote Haredi integration into mainstream Israeli society. Physical integration into Israeli society begins with geographic proximity. Some argue that the high percentage of Haredim living in the West Bank has already affected their political ideology, aligning them more closely with right-wing Zionist parties.[129] Most ultra-Orthodox Israelis still prefer to live in their own neighborhoods. But proliferation invariably leads to diffusion: In 1980, 85 percent of Israel's 150,000 ultra-Orthodox Jews lived either in Jerusalem or Bnei Brak. By 2012 the percentage was but 40 percent and it continues to drop.[130] Secular and Haredi Jewish Israelis need to learn to live together and to get to know each other. Young Haredim are "quietly" purchasing apartments throughout Israel's periphery.[131] This is a good thing. The proclivity for building new, exclusively Haredi cities, like Elad or Kasif, perpetuates separation, alienation, and ultimately promotes fertility. It constitutes bad public policy.

Encouraging employment and successfully getting Haredi men into the workforce also makes a contribution. There are signs that changes have begun on a meaningful scale. In 2015, Israel's Council for Higher Education reported that ten thousand Haredim pursued academic studies in colleges and universities around the country, up from fifty-six hundred students just two years earlier.[132]

Military participation by Haredi boys remains modest but has grown by 90 percent during the past few years.[133] New government policies should increase it much more by 2017. Most importantly, between 2002 and 2011, employment among Haredi men rose from 35 percent to 45 percent.[134] By 2015 it had increased to over 56 percent.[135]

These trends will affect Haredi birthrates: Haredi families with fathers who do not study in a yeshiva have one fewer child on average (5.5) than those whose fathers do (6.5).[136] The presumed explanations for the discrepancy are social pressures in the yeshiva or scholars' proclivities for fulfilling procreation duties. Policies that provide real incentives for men to work and serve in the military while penalizing those who do not will contribute to lower fertility.

Lowered birthrates ultimately occur because of women. This is particularly true in the Haredi world because contraception for the foreseeable future will remain entirely a female affair. While their public position is invariably dismissive, *economics* may matter more to Haredi women. Hebrew University's Nechumi Yaffe conducted surveys about perceptions of poverty within the Haredi world. She found a deep gender gap in the way Haredim apprehend poverty: women feel the effects of indigence far more than men do. Yaffe attributes this to the fact that not only do women work they usually are the ones expected to run the household. They go to the grocery store and see that that their credit line is overextended. "Women know the meaning of money" as opposed to men, who spend long hours in their academies and "do their wives a favor when they look at the bank statement."[137]

The high cost of raising children in modern Israel is becoming more onerous. Yaffe explains, "It has become impossible to be so poor and still be a good parent. Fifteen years ago you just had to put food on the table and of course you didn't ever need to buy new clothes for your kids. Now parents are expected to send their children to any number of therapies. It even costs money to have them diagnosed. You can't dress a child in clothes that have been worn nine times already. It's not materialism. We aren't talking about buying private planes! But more people in the Haredi community are starting to say: 'I can't take it anymore.' They want to live with dignity."

Yaffe's assessment finds support from Rabbi Porush: "I think that the Haredi community grew more and that's why we see more poverty now. Today, we are 17 percent of the Jews in Israel, so it has become impossible to ignore. But there was always poverty among the Haredim. People just didn't see it."[138]

Even those Haredim insouciant about providing for large families concede that housing has become a real crisis for Haredim who wish to marry. Across all Haredi divisions, a common expectation is that parents of the bride and groom provide their children with an apartment as a wedding present. By eliminating the need to pay rent, even a small dilapidated place gives newlyweds the stability they need to have a child and allows husbands to study in peace with a modest stipend. The price of housing in Israel today, however, makes it practically impossible for parents to provide such support to one or two children, much less a dozen. Yaffe recalls that two hundred thousand shekels from her parents provided her and her husband with half an apartment. Today it's hardly a down payment.

For many years, ultra-Orthodox Shas ministers ran the housing ministry and rigged criteria for mortgages to favor large young families. This often left secular couples, after their military service, unable to compete with Haredim. This bias remains a hotly contested issue. Evening the playing field for mortgage entitlements will create further incentives for financially responsible family planning.

Bottom-up policies might prove successful because there are signs that while maintaining lip service to their rabbis' authority, Israel's Haredim are growing more independent in making individual decisions. From voting patterns to military service, without leaving their communities or their faith, Haredim are making up their own minds. They may need to be pushed a little bit to see that for the good of their family, society, and land, "less can be more."

8

$\longrightarrow$ ◆ $\longleftarrow$

THE DEMOGRAPHIC TRANSITION

In little countries and big countries, capitalist countries and
communist countries, Catholic countries and Moslem countries,
Western countries and Eastern countries—exponential population
growth slows down or stops when grinding poverty disappears.
This is called demographic transition.
—Carl Sagan, *Billions and Billions: Thoughts on Life and
Death at the Brink of the Millennium*

THE FOUR STAGES

Since the early twentieth century, Jews and Arabs in Israel have chosen to reside in towns and villages that are geographically separated and socially segregated from each other. In many ways Arab Israelis live a life autonomous from Jewish society, leaving them with a distinct demographic profile. This heterogeneous community includes four significant subgroups: Muslims, Christians, Druze, and Bedouins, each with unique traditions, religious beliefs, and population patterns. Actual divisions, of course, are far more nuanced: at the end of the nineteenth century, for example, the diplomat and anthropological researcher Laurence Oliphant, studying rural villages around Haifa, identified nine distinct ethnic and religious categories.[1] Any review of this diverse cohort's demographic history, therefore, will suffer from oversimplification. Still, it is fair to generalize that during most of the twentieth century, Arab families in Israel were very large.

For much of this time, their exceptionally high birthrate was the source of considerable anxiety and even paranoia among Zionist leaders. Yet in recent decades, a detectable change in the Arab birthrate has taken place. When Arab Israeli fertility levels are considered in retrospect, the story that emerges conforms precisely to a pattern quite common around the world, known as the "demographic transition."[2]

In 1929 Dr. Warren Simpson Thompson, the leading American demographer of his era, identified this phenomenon in a groundbreaking academic article.[3] Thompson, a Columbia University sociologist, was founding director of the Scripps Foundation for Research in Population Problems. This was probably the first independent organization to focus on the implications of global demographic shifts and rapid population growth.[4] Thompson reviewed the history of human civilizations and posited that as societies advance, their populations typically go through four distinct phases:

Stage 1 characterized all of humanity from the advent of agriculture, when animal husbandry and land cultivation began ten thousand years ago, until the eighteenth century.[5] Throughout this prolonged, premodern phase, birthrates and death rates were high, with infant mortality bringing average longevity down significantly. This caused populations to largely remain in a steady state, waxing and waning according to the availability of food supplies. Although women gave birth many times, most of their children died young. During this stage, there actually was little difference between the population dynamics among humans and other animal species.

People in *Stage 1* societies reproduced enthusiastically, not only due to instinct but because additional progeny offered the possibility of "social security" in old age for an insignificant investment. Besides feeding them, raising children cost little. From a very young age, those that survived could assist their agrarian families in the fields, carrying water or helping with domestic chores. With little knowledge about disease prevention, water contamination, and public health measures, for most of human history, life expectancy at birth was very low. Accordingly, annual global population growth in *Stage 1* rarely exceeded 0.05 percent, and during many periods, the number of humans dropped.[6] At that pace, scholars estimate that it took from one thousand to five thousand years for global population to double.

Stage 2 of the transition can first be identified in Europe in the 1700s, which witnessed a gradual increase in agricultural yields along with industrialization and urbanization processes. Hitherto-unknown nutritional sources from the New World appeared. The first vaccines were developed; medicine and new medications became more effective. Much more significant to human longevity were the improvements in food and water quality, sewage infrastructure, personal hygiene, and the use of quarantines. Progress in public health translated into a decline in illness and death rates, with no corresponding reduction in births.[7] Indeed, greater affluence enabled couples to marry at a younger age, providing a head start for child-rearing.

The significant demographic expansion characteristic of *Stage* 2 dynamics was seen immediately throughout Europe and, later, with the advent of Western technology, in Asia and Africa. At the same time, the population generally became "younger," reflecting a pyramidlike demographic structure.[8] Today, many developing countries, such as Nigeria, Liberia, Burundi, Yemen, or Afghanistan, whose populations grow more than 3.0 percent a year,[9] show all the indications of a *Stage* 2 state with attendant population explosions.

During *Stage* 3 of the transition, a drop in birthrates leads to a drop in the *rate* of population growth. There are many factors that combine to expedite this change.[10] Parents, even in rural areas, realize that the precipitous decline in childhood deaths means that there will be offspring to care for them in old age, even if the nest isn't bursting with chicks. Children's ability to contribute to family income is no longer meaningful. Many societies go so far as to *prohibit* child labor, making the question of immediate economic benefit from offspring irrelevant. As pensions and social safety nets become part of modern societies, concerns about the future are further assuaged. Urbanization and a shortage of living space often lead to changes in values, along with a reconsideration of the role of women in general and fertility in particular.[11]

A critical component of this stage involves a transformation in the status of women. As females become better educated and independent, they enter the workforce. This both delays the age of marriage and gives them areas of competence beyond motherhood. The introduction of contraception surely accelerated women's ability to influence the decision of family size. But modern birth control was hardly a prerequisite. Many countries in Europe reached near-replacement fertility levels long before contraception was widely available. Of course, initially there is a delay in population stability or reduction, due to "population momentum," when a disproportionately young society passes through its childbearing years.[12] That explains why China's population still continues to grow after decades of implementing its *one-child policy*.[13]

Stage 4 presumably constitutes a final equilibrium phase in the transition cycle. Both birthrates and death rates are low. Populations begin to stabilize and in some cases contract; this is happening in countries like Japan,[14] Italy, and Greece.[15] Economists report that this last transitional stage reverses the positive correlation between income and population. In modern economies, despite reduced or even negative population growth, countries can expand per capita income and GDP.[16]

For much of Israel's history, Arab population dynamics appeared typical of *Stage 2*, with exponential growth resulting from high birthrates and increased life expectancy. In the sixty-seven years since Israel's establishment, the number of Arab Israeli citizens leaped more than tenfold: from 156,000 in 1948 to 1.7 million in 2015.[17] But profound and fundamental changes in this society were underway, producing a remarkable transition into *Stage 3*: Peak birthrates were reached in 1965 when Arab Israeli women *on average* had 9.2 children.[18] By 2015 the total fertility rate had plummeted to 3.3 children per Muslim family and 2.2 among Arab Christians and Druze.[19] Based on experience around the world, there is every reason to believe that fertility rates will continue to fall.

Despite decades of efforts by both Jewish and Arab political leaders to politicize demography, Israel's Arab citizens increasingly came to make sober and economically rational decisions about family planning rather than ideological ones.[20] While the "transition" is not yet complete, it has come far enough to consider how and why it took place.

THE POLITICS OF FERTILITY

For many years Yisrael Koenig headed the country's interior ministry in Israel's Northern District. In 1976, he wrote an internal report about prevailing demographic trends and how to counter them. The report was soon leaked to the leftist newspaper *Al HaMishmar*. Koenig warned his superiors, "The natural increase in the population of Arab Israelis is at a rate of 5.9% a year as opposed to the natural growth of the Jewish population at 1.5% per year. This problem is especially severe in the northern district, where the Arab population is large. In the middle of 1975 the Arab population in the northern district reached 250,000 people while the Jewish population in the district was 289,000. There are grounds for serious apprehensions that within the next decade, an Arab political and demographic takeover of the Acre and Nazareth areas will occur."[21]

Koenig did not limit his report to demographic forecasts. He made concrete recommendations to his superiors to reverse the trends, measures that would make Arab Israelis' lives harder and perhaps facilitate their emigration. For instance, he suggested limiting the number of Arab workers in government-supported factories to 20 percent. He proposed incentives to help Arab Israelis study abroad, in the hope that they would find foreign lands agreeable and decide to stay. As the leisure produced by Israel's progressive social conditions was "abused" for purposes of nationalistic thinking and organizing, he proposed that the government find ways to reduce it. At the time, Arabs comprised 14 percent of the country's taxpayers but contributed only 1.5 percent of the taxes. Koenig proposed special "tax collection" for Arab Israelis, who he believed were not paying their fair share. Koenig also believed that child allowances to Arabs should be canceled, by transferring responsibility for payments from the government to the Jewish Agency, a nongovernmental public organization.

The report was never adopted; nor did it ever represent Israeli government policy, which has consistently avoided blatantly undemocratic measures. Yet Koenig's perspective was hardly an aberration. For many Jewish Israelis, even liberal ones, the fear of an Arab demographic inundation colored attitudes toward Israel's minorities and led them to endorse discriminatory policies. The publication of the Koenig report caused something of a stir, as senior Israeli officials are expected to be color-blind about the ethnic identity of citizens they are serving. Such open advocacy of extreme measures favoring the Jewish majority crossed many lines. It surely did little to ameliorate the simmering tensions between the state and the Arab Israeli community, whose worst suspicions were confirmed by such an openly prejudiced program. But Koenig's sentiments surprised no one. Neither Israel's Arabs nor its Jews had ever seen demography as anything but a battlefield upon which their competing national claims might be resolved.

Such deep-seated suspicion is not an artifact of the distant past: On the morning of Israel's general elections, on March 17, 2015, Likud party's Prime Minister Netanyahu galvanized his right-wing power base by playing on fears of an Arab takeover. Posting an urgent plea on Facebook and sending innumerable text messages to Jewish voters to "Go vote,"[22] he warned, "The right-wing government is in danger. Arabs are arriving in enormous numbers en masse to the ballot boxes." Netanyahu would eventually apologize to Israel's Arab citizens for the episode,[23] but the damage was done.

Relations between Arabs and Jews in Palestine after World War I started off badly. The British government had not even begun its civilian rule in spring 1920, when Muslim rioters took to terrorizing the Jewish community of Jerusalem during the annual "Nebi Musa" celebration.[24] The toll from several days of looting and random violence included 5 dead and 216 wounded.[25] The events established a tone for almost a century of discord. Both populations saw themselves as indigenous and aspired to control the same homeland; any dialogue was given to "zero-sum game" dynamics. The British leadership realized the legitimacy of each side's claims. It made more than symbolic efforts to quell the intermittent outbreak of Arab hostilities and facilitate a compromise. But the Arabs in Palestine were not receptive, and the British lacked the stature and political will to impose an agreement.

In retrospect, given the mutually exclusive aspirations, war was probably ineluctable. The independence gained during the first half of the twentieth century in neighboring countries like Lebanon, Egypt, Syria, Iraq, and later Jordan created a false sense of confidence among Arab leaders in Palestine. They assumed their national future would be no different and were not inclined to bargain.[26] Almost from the advent of the British Mandate, it was militant voices, like that of Haj Amin al-Husseini, the Grand Mufti of Jerusalem, or Izz ad-Din al-Qassam, the Haifa-based imam, who prevailed, promoting unconditional hostility toward reconciliation and a strategy of violence to prevent Zionist settlement.[27] There were many Zionist leaders during this period who feigned optimism about resolving differences amicably with the local Arab population.[28] Even relatively militant Zionist leaders, like Ze'ev Jabotinsky, opposed expelling Arabs from Palestine.[29] But Jabotinsky also had no illusions about the inevitability of armed conflict, calling for a proverbial "Iron Wall" that would ensure a favorable outcome.[30]

The sides soon began to collect arms and establish militias in preparation for the long-awaited military confrontation. Demography was recognized as a parallel combat zone where the struggle between the two peoples would play out. Long before the State of Israel was declared, high birthrates among the Arabs of Palestine gave Zionist leaders no rest—just as Jewish immigration was the bane of Palestinian Arabs' existence. As the twentieth century and the infrastructure built during the British Mandate ushered in vastly improved economic conditions and urban development, Palestine's Muslim and Christian communities passed quickly into a new, second phase in its demographic transition. Total Muslim fertility rates during the Mandate shot up from 6.4 in 1926, when the first government census was conducted, to 9.4 in 1944–1945, when the last estimates from the period of British rule are available.[31]

When David Ben-Gurion read out the country's Declaration of Independence in 1948, he openly called on the Arab inhabitants of the State of Israel to preserve the peace and participate in the building of the new country.[32] Israel's founders implicitly accepted the presence of a significant Arab-speaking population in the Jewish state by conferring full citizenship and representation in the new state's institutions. This had been part of the Zionist vision since Herzl's original utopian novel, *Altneuland*, contained an Arab protagonist who joined Jewish immigrants in nation building.[33] In fact, even Jabotinsky's vision of a Jewish state included full Arab participation in any future government.[34] Such calls for a common future went unheeded, and the winds of war howled out of control. The country's Jewish leadership never really thought that it might be otherwise. In the face of a fierce Arab attack, their efforts, justifiably, were not focused on preventing the inevitable contest—but on winning it.

Israel's War of Independence changed demographic dynamics radically. The success of the Zionist forces on the battlefield and the associated exodus of Palestinian Arabs from their homes during the 1948 war completely reshuffled populations in the new country. The extent to which this departure was voluntary or forced, premeditated or spontaneous, is still debated.[35] The extent of the relocation is not: the official United Nations Conciliation Committee appointed to assess the Palestinian issue estimated "that the refugees from Israel-controlled territory amount to approximately 711,000. The fact that there is a higher number of relief recipients appears to be due among other things to duplication of ration cards, addition of persons who have been displaced from area other than Israel-held areas, and of persons who, although not displaced, are destitute."[36]

Israel's first census in November 1948 showed that of the 160,000 Arabs who remained, 21 percent were Christians. Christian Arabs historically were the wealthiest, most urban and urbane subgroup among Palestine's Arabs. Women in this community were always relatively independent, which explains why Israeli Christian fertility rates were the first to begin to drop. Some 9 percent of Israel's Arabs at the time were Druze. Ethnically Arab, but since the eleventh century theologically distinct from Shia Islam from which the religion emerged, its adherents traditionally were loyal to the ruling governments in their country of residence. Israel proved to be a case in point: Druze opted out of the Arab war efforts against the Jewish state in 1948 and soon thereafter requested to serve in Israel's military.[37] Not a single Druze was forced to leave the country during the demographic perturbations of the time, and their integration into Israeli life, although hardly seamless, has been substantial. The remaining 70 percent were Muslim, whose birthrates were traditionally high. Over the course of Israeli history, Muslims returned to their demographic dominance within the Arab community and make up about 90 percent of Israel's minority population today.[38]

With only 20 percent of Palestine's original Arabs remaining after the war, Jews became the majority in the new State of Israel. The Arab minority in 1949 comprised only 12.4 percent of the country's citizens. Massive immigration soon solidified this demographic turnaround, and in 1966 the percentage dropped to 10.6.[39] Those Arabs who did not leave were stunned by the magnitude of the defeat. Unwillingly, they had joined their enemy and suddenly made up less than a fifth of the country's population.[40] For Zionists, the Palestinian national disaster, "Al Nakba," was an outcome more favorable than the most optimistic Jewish nationalist scenario. Many Arabs who left—voluntarily or involuntarily—wished to go back to their homes. But Israel was disinclined to soften the demographic outcome of the war. A few exceptions were made to reunite families, but for the most part, Arab refugees were not allowed to return, and "abandoned" lands were nationalized.

Al Nakba (The Catastrophe): Arabs flea Haifa on April 22, 1948, joining the 711,000 estimated Palestinian refugees, after losing the battle for the city to the Jewish Haanah forces. (Fred Chesnick, KKL-JNF Photo Archive)

There were certainly justifications for this position. After such fierce fighting, it was not easy for the young and insecure State of Israel to embrace the Arab minority, whose leadership refused to recognize the legitimacy of a Jewish state.[41] During the war, the government empowered Israel's minister of defense to apply the British Mandate's Defense Emergency Regulations on Arab communities that were seen as immediate military threats. These "temporary" security precautions continued for a full eighteen years. Arab citizens were subject to military authority and rules that significantly limited their movement and civil rights. To this were added a range of other discriminatory policies, which were largely terminated over time.[42]

With a profoundly dispirited sense of defeat that came from being supplanted as the dominant presence in the land,[43] Israel's Arab citizens considered their political options; three different approaches presented themselves.[44] The majority adopted a pragmatic, cooperative posture with the hope of gaining political and economic favors from the ruling Jewish government. At that time there were no significant Arab political parties, so they voted for "satellite lists" of Zionist parties, largely affiliated with the ruling Mapai labor coalition and, in return, received parliamentary representation and token patronage.[45] There was also a significant group that opted for a Communist line and united with a small cohort of like-minded Jews. Preferring to present collective grievances in terms of an international class struggle, the group sought political support from the Soviet Bloc.[46] Finally, there was a more militant nationalist trajectory that did not accept the finality of the war's outcome. Inspired by Pan-Arab ideologies, this group supported continued military resistance until a united Arab victory attained its political objectives and destroyed the Jewish state.[47]

The most confrontational of this last group engaged in sabotage, blew up agricultural machinery and buildings, and supported guerrilla incursions by incipient Palestinian terrorist organizations.[48] In retrospect, it was a feeble effort by a tiny minority; Israeli counterintelligence[49] proved far too effective for these radicals to meaningfully damage the new Jewish state.[50] Yet these few disruptions caused irreparable damage to the reputation of the local Arab community, which was perceived as a fifth column that could not be trusted by the Jewish majority.

On an individual level, the vast majority of Israel's Arab population adopted an acquiescent position of resignation and reluctantly became law-abiding Israeli citizens. Demography, however, offered one arena where they could express defiance. Arab Israeli leaders and intellectuals well understood the hysteria among the Israeli leadership who feared being "outnumbered." Before the phrase "population bomb" was invoked to connote sustainability concerns,[51] Israelis spoke of a "demographic time bomb" that became part of the rhetoric of conflict.[52] Family size for Palestinian Arab nationalists became an arena in which Arabs could pursue national aspirations with impunity and even boast about it.

In his 1964 poem "Identity Card," noted Palestinian poet Mahmoud Darwish took a decidedly "in your face" position to fertility:

> Write down!
> I am an Arab
> And my identity card number is fifty thousand
> I have eight children
> And the ninth will come after a summer
> Will you be angry?
>
> Write down!
> I am an Arab[53]

Anthropologist Rhoda Ann Kanaaneh grew up in the Arab town of Arrabe in the Galilee and tackled the complex dynamics of fertility among Arab Israelis in her doctoral research during the 1990s. The resulting book, *Birthing the Nation: Strategies of Palestinian Women in Israel*, offers a thoughtful review of what she calls "Israeli political arithmetic." She describes the nationalistic ideology accompanying Arab Israeli birthrates during Israel's early years: "Some Palestinians claim they should directly defy the Israeli population control plan by having as many children as possible to fuel the revolution and to outbreed Jews, just as the Zionist planners fear—the Zionist demographic struggle in reverse. Some Palestinians have embraced the Arab 'time bomb' as a form of resistance and have called for encouraging the natural increase in the Arab population and 'Arabizing' areas where Jews are now in the majority."[54]

Kanaaneh offers several anecdotes that highlight this position. For instance, shortly following the publication of the Koenig report, former Knesset member Tawfiq Ziyad sent a card to Koenig informing him about the birth of his daughter; it was printed as a death announcement in black. Kanaaneh's father, a well-regarded Arab physician in the Galilee, told her that during this period, female patients gave up contraceptives as an act of protest against the report.[55]

Within this highly charged, adversarial climate, concern throughout the 1950s and 1960s among the Jewish majority was only natural. The majority was well aware that Muslim families had an average of 9 children. Total fertility only tapered off to 8.4 in 1974 and then in 1979 to 7.2. By projecting Muslim fertility rates forward from the 1960s, Israeli demographers forecasted that Arab Israelis would overtake Israeli Jews demographically by 1990. It left them terrified. David Ben-Gurion reportedly was traveling in the Galilee during the 1950s and exclaimed to his entourage, "Am I traveling in Syria?" Orders were given to create the new Galilee city of Carmiel, which was established a decade later and is now home to a predominantly Jewish population of close to fifty thousand.[56]

It was self-serving for politicians and extremists on both sides to fan the flames, framing Palestinian demography and family-planning decisions in the context of the national struggle. In retrospect, however, this did not reflect what was actually going on. With the wisdom of hindsight, the high birthrate among Arab Israeli citizens was primarily a manifestation of a rural population moving into *Stage 2* of the transition, albeit with a particularly tumultuous political backdrop. In fact, the Arab community's exceedingly high fertility rate during Israel's first decades was less a seditious response to the new Jewish state than a continuation of trends that began at the end of the nineteenth century and were part of a well-documented global pattern.

PALESTINE'S PATHOLOGY OF POVERTY: STAGE 1, A RETROSPECTIVE

For most of the past millennium, Palestine was a mistreated and destitute place. The population waxed and waned, but after 1291, with the end of Crusader rule, the number of residents plummeted significantly. For five centuries the population remained but a tiny fraction of the estimated 1 million residents who had lived on the same lands a thousand years earlier.[57] Demographer Justin McCarthy has arguably devoted more attention than any other scholar to the surviving demographic data. After poring over and reconstructing centuries of Ottoman censuses and internal reports, he concluded that the population of Palestine showed no net gain between 1550 and 1800. The total number of residents edged up to 340,000 by 1850, but overall annual population increase over these years was a mere 0.011 percent.[58]

Of the 300,000 people living in Palestine prior to the Ottoman period, more than 85 percent were Muslim. During the nineteenth century, four-fifths of the local population lived at subsistence levels in some eight hundred to nine hundred rural villages. These were typically set on the top of hillsides, whose location allowed access to fertile lands in the valleys,[59] along with a small measure of natural defense against marauding bands and armies.[60] The landscape and its denizens were indeed neglected by the ruling Ottomans. In 1881 Bertha Spafford Vester described her impressions after moving to Palestine: "the utter desolation of the country . . . arid from the long, dry months of summer and the choking reddish dust coating the road and hills" was of a degraded state "that would bring famine to another land."[61]

As the nineteenth century unfolded, Christian Arabs emerged as a merchant class, living in the "larger" towns, which were still minuscule. (Even the population of Holy Jerusalem did not exceed 9,000 people in 1800, increasing to 22,000 by 1870, largely due to Jewish immigration.)[62] For the predominant population of Muslim peasants (fellahin) life was dominated by the extended clan (*hamula*) into which they were born. For the most part, theirs was a short and unforgiving life.

McCarthy sees 1870 as the watershed date for demographic expansion in Palestine, with the Muslim population doubling to 602,000 by 1914 due to immigration and increased life expectancy. The Christian and Jewish communities (all told, 120,000 people) grew even faster.[63] The transition from *Stage 1* and *Stage 2* had begun and would continue into the 1970s. What conditions changed to precipitate such a dramatic increase in population? There were four major factors that historically kept Palestine's population so modest: poverty, poor health, lack of infrastructure, and the relentless drafting of young males. All of these improved by the advent of World War I.

One major reason why the indigenous Arabs were so poor was that their landholdings were small. The constant division of property into smaller parcels left sons of farmers with steadily reduced holdings. (In 1900 farm size averaged only

The demographic transition: With a life expectancy of thirty-seven years at the advent of the British Mandate in 1920, the Arab peasants of Palestine had high fertility and high mortality levels. (Yosef Shweig, KKL-JNF Photo Archive)

12.5 acres per family.) Ottoman land legislation was designed to favor the moneyed class, leaving fellahin to lease their modest parcels from "effendis." These absentee landowners held the titles to sizable tracts and did not hesitate to charge the sharecroppers as much as they could bear.[64] Many in this peasant population lived out their brief days essentially as serfs.

It is little wonder that infant mortality was extremely high. There were no doctors to speak of, no medical schools. Debilitating malaria was an integral part of life in Palestine. The incidence in some areas was as high as 90 percent, causing 7 percent of the annual death tolls at the end of World War I. There were villages where one of every six children succumbed to the illness within their first few months.[65] For Palestinian Muslims, approximately half of all deaths in the land involved infants under age one.[66] (Christian and Jewish newborns fared somewhat better.) There was practically no access to the vaccines and medicines that were already starting to cure people in Europe. Public health policies simply did not exist. Plagues were common, especially during periods of drought. And until 1848 there was no quarantine system to contain contagions.[67] Sewage management was essentially nonexistent. When Herzl visited Jerusalem in 1899, he was revolted by the heavy, inescapable stench.[68] (A sanitation commission was only established during the late 1800s in Jerusalem to address the problem of sewage "treatment," but meaningful investment was nonexistent.)

The economy for centuries relied on minimal, antiquated infrastructure. Although the population was dispersed throughout the country, few byways existed to connect the villages. Along the coast, the aquifer is extremely shallow, yet no village had more than one well, and many did not even have that. Water was scarce and almost exclusively used for drinking by humans and their animals. Irrigation was virtually unknown. Most houses were made of mud. During the rainy season, the dusty trails that passed for roads became impassable even for camels.[69] In the rare event that weather and individual proficiency combined to produce a bumper crop, there was no way to transport the surplus, as no shipping was available. Export of agricultural produce was trivial: in 1873 the cotton and other foodstuffs reaching the Jaffa port were only valued at 137,000 pounds sterling for the entire country.[70] Life was a constant struggle for survival, with little possibility of generating the profits that might enable purchasing draft animals or the additional agricultural inputs required to get ahead and escape poverty.[71]

A less-familiar reason why Palestine's population did not increase until the nineteenth century involved the considerable cohort of males drafted into the Turkish military before they could settle down and have families. It was not a consensual process. "Drafting raids" were staged at night, and boys were carried away, many never to see their families and homeland again. A series of military campaigns—from the Crimean War to the Balkan War—led to establishment of a conscription system that only targeted Muslims.[72] This is one explanation for Christian and Jewish communities' faster growth rates during this period than in Muslim towns.

When Mark Twain visited Palestine in 1867, his inimitable, politically incorrect accounts of the local residents depict the miserable conditions that kept the *Stage 1* local population so small. Entering the Galilee village of Magdala he describes the people who greeted him:

> The old men and old women, boys and girls, the blind, the crazy and the crippled, all in ragged soiled and scanty raiment and all abject beggars by nature, instinct and education. How the vermin-tortured vagabonds did swim. How they showed their scars and sores and piteously pointed to their maimed and crooked limbs and begged with their pleading eyes for charity! They hung to the horses' tails, clung to their manes and the stirrups, closed in on every side in scorn of dangerous hoofs—and out of their infidel throats with one accord burst an agonizing and most infernal chorus: "Howajji baksheesh." . . . I never was in a storm like that before.[73]

But just as Twain was recording his impressions, things changed rather suddenly and population began to grow.

STAGE 2: PALESTINE'S POPULATION EXPLOSION

Toward the end of Ottoman rule, modest progress occurred under the Turks that would soon be translated into incrementally higher standards of living and life expectancy. One of the first changes involved transportation infrastructure. In 1869, the Jaffa–Jerusalem pathway was fitted for wheeled vehicles so that the Austrian emperor Franz Joseph could have a dignified ascent to the Holy City. In 1881 it was actually paved as part of a modest road-development initiative. German Christian Templers began to establish colonies in Palestine in 1869 and quickly initiated a wagon service to link Haifa and Nazareth and later from Jaffa to Jerusalem.[74] Even though there were sections of the track where a good runner reportedly could outpace the locomotive, in 1892 a train from Jaffa began to chug up to Jerusalem. The economy in Palestine also began to crawl forward, strengthened by very basic but essential roads and railways.

Life in Palestine's cities under the Ottomans at the turn of the twentieth century was still plenty austere but definitely getting better. In 1882 the Turkish government began repairing Jerusalem's streets and improving the sanitation.[75] Anticipating the visit of the German emperor Wilhelm II in 1898, the Turkish administration in Jerusalem finally started to close the open sewage canals in the city.[76] In the middle of the nineteenth century, British missionaries arrived in Palestine and established the first hospital in Jerusalem, and another one later in Safed.[77] Jewish agricultural settlements struggled but managed to introduce irrigation and more-modern cultivation techniques. Still, Palestine was decidedly backward when General Allenby's army and its Australian cavalry conquered Gaza, Beer Sheva, and Jerusalem in quick succession.

Looking back, the British Mandate government deserves considerable credit for the powerful combination of accelerated fertility and greater longevity that fueled the rapid growth of Palestine's Arab population. People began to live much longer, thanks to the medical system the British introduced. Beyond hospitals and clinics, the British Mandate's Department of Health established eighteen subdistricts that took responsibility for local medical services as well as outpatient clinics. In 1926, a Palestinian Muslim born under the Ottomans had an average life expectancy of thirty-seven; by the 1940s it was close to fifty.[78] At the start of the twentieth century, one of every two hospital beds in the country had a patient suffering from malaria.[79] Within fifty years, following a series of interventions culminating in the introduction of DDT, the disease was eradicated.[80] It was during the Mandate that birthrates really began to climb. Modern birth control was unknown. Fertility rates among the Palestinian Arabs in 1930 averaged 5.5 children per family.[81] As a result, the Arab population doubled

With the best health system in the Middle East in place, on
average these Palestinian Arab children photographed in 1926
would come to live beyond fifty. (Yosef Shweig, KKL-JNF
Photo Archive)

in the quarter century between the first British census of 1922, when 660,661
individuals were counted, until 1947, when best projections estimated that numbers reached 1,323,800.[82]

Notwithstanding the ethnic and cultural diversity in Arab communities, a
"big picture" emerges from a demographic snapshot during the middle of the
British mandate. It shows an indigent, predominantly Muslim population that
was 70 percent rural and still relied on subsistence agriculture to survive. With
no social safety net to speak of and without a well-organized educational system, children remained critical to a family's short-term and long-term economic
calculus. They were put to work at a very young age and married young. As of
1931, only 20 percent of Arab children attended schools.[83]

During the first half of the twentieth century, fertility among Israel's Christian and Muslim Arabs was largely indistinguishable. In fact the 1931 Mandate
census reported that the average number of children below age ten living with
Christian mothers in Palestine was higher than among Jews or Muslims.[84] Muslim women had slightly more births than Christian women but suffered far
greater infant mortality.[85] (Because of polygamy, more children were born to
Muslim men than to their Christian peers.)

Following the British decision to terminate the Mandate and the subsequent
warfare, the number of Arabs in Palestine dropped precipitously. Many Arab

villages like Saffuriyya and Lubya were abandoned and soon obliterated.[86] The internal demographic breakdown only became more pronounced as a result of the relocations: Of the 160,000 Arabs that remained after the war, 90 percent lived in exclusively Arab rural communities, mostly in the Galilee. Only 10 percent lived in cities like Haifa, Ramla, Lod, Acre, and Jaffa. With the exception of Nazareth, all these traditionally Arab municipalities became predominantly Jewish.

A disproportionately high number of families from the Palestinian urban upper and middle class, who provided Arab leadership during the Mandate, preferred the safer alternative of clearing out until the hostilities were over. Most never returned. They left behind a population that was largely uneducated, landless peasants: the "poorest of the poor."[87] This meant that more than 97 percent of Arab women who became Israeli citizens after the war (and almost three-quarters of the men) were illiterate.[88] With little or no employment opportunities, it made sense for the women to dedicate their energies to maternal matters.

The nascent Israeli health system, with its expanded menu of socialized medical services, sent Arab demography into overdrive. Arab Israeli death rates became the lowest in the Middle East and North Africa, less than half the mortality of Egypt, Jordan, and Syria during this period.[89] As women became less religious, they were less likely to conform to the Koran's recommendation that breastfeeding continue for two years. Consequently, spacing between births grew significantly shorter.[90] Because the Arab population was so young, the crude death rates per thousand soon dropped far below the Jewish and Christian levels, and they remain so to this day. With birthrates ever higher and death rates ever lower, a population explosion ensued, with Arab Israeli numbers doubling roughly every twenty years.

STAGE 3: NATIONAL CALAMITY AND THE NEW DEMOGRAPHY

Following its War of Independence, the new state set about translating its unexpected military success into the consolidation of its national landholdings. After learning of the devastating Holocaust in Europe, Palestine's Jewish community threw itself into a War of Independence that was very much a war for survival. Losing was not an option. After prevailing against all odds, the national leadership and most of the Jewish majority felt morally justified in utilizing the "abandoned" real estate so urgently needed to house the refugees streaming in from around the world. In March 1950 Israel's Knesset formalized expropriation of land formerly owned by Palestinian refugees who departed during the war by passing the Absentee Property Law. Some ten thousand shops and twenty-five thousand buildings legally became public property. An additional 400,000 hectares of land that contained some 60 percent of cultivatable land in the country was also nationalized. Ownership of much of the country's olive orchards, half the citrus groves, and a considerable portion of the fruit trees was transferred to the government.[91]

This was only the first stage in the nationalization of Arabs lands. In 1953 a Land Acquisition Law established procedures for procuring property from Arab citizens, who were to receive monetary compensation or comparable plots.[92] This led to an additional 120,000 hectares appropriated from the Arab community. Some of the lands were sold by the Israeli government to the Jewish National Fund, and some remained in the reservoir of public lands.[93]

There is surely a basis for criticizing the morality and legitimacy of the land and housing expropriation that took place in Israel during its initial years.[94] Legal battles challenging the lawfulness of specific expropriations continue over sixty years later. Yet nobody today really challenges the finality of the aggregate sociological impact: the agrarian life that had characterized Palestinian Arab reality for centuries came to an abrupt end. The majority of those remaining in Israel woke to find themselves a working-class community within a middle-class society and subject to the laws of the new state. With few marketable skills, they took whatever jobs were available. It did not take long for the Hebrew expression "Arab labor" to become synonymous with the menial work that Jews were disinclined to pursue. For Arab day laborers, a large brood no longer offered a critical workforce for cultivating fields and orchards. Living on very modest salaries, their children were not even allowed to work but, rather, required to attend school. More births meant more mouths to feed.

A key turning point in the economic and employment profile of Israel's Arab citizens occurred in the late 1960s following the 1967 Israeli occupation of the West Bank and Gaza Strip.[95] Despite their position on the bottom rung of Israel's socioeconomic ladder, Israeli Arabs were much better off than their counterparts in Jordan and Egypt. Arab men were disproportionately represented in the local construction industry. Many began to move beyond the confines of unskilled, hired hands to the more profitable station of self-employed subcontractors and business owners, utilizing inexpensive laborers from the newly occupied West Bank and Gaza.[96]

Notwithstanding the improvement in economic conditions, it would still take decades for the cultural transition to be manifested in family planning. *Stage 2*, rapid growth dynamics prevailed among a generation that was born into the "peasant" and highly patriarchal Palestinian heritage. Most Muslim members of this generation had little formal education;[97] wives stayed home and raised the children. Those women who worked had few professional opportunities beyond teaching or low-prestige and low-paying factory work.[98] Throughout the 1970s, the average Arab Israeli family still had over seven children.[99]

The many years as a disadvantaged minority in a modern society produced a powerful educational ethos and impressive academic gains. Starting slowly, a revolution in the status of women picked up considerable steam. Given the baseline economic conditions of Arabs who stayed after 1948, the prosperity attained in subsequent years is extraordinary. While still far below Jewish socioeconomic levels, Arab Israeli incomes today exceed average earnings in neighboring Arab countries by an order of magnitude.[100] With universal access to high quality health care, life expectancy shows a similar pattern: Arab Israelis live three years fewer than Jewish Israelis on average. But Jewish Israelis are among the longest living people on the planet. Arab women in Israel today on average live to be over eighty-one,[101] a longevity higher than any country in the Middle East and higher than many in Europe.[102] With social security benefits and a relatively dense Israeli social safety net to catch them if they fall before retiring, parents no longer feared that children would not survive or that they would be destitute in old age. As a result Arab Israeli familial norms began to change beyond recognition.

By the 1990s, family size had already fallen from an average of more than 7 to 4.7 children. It continued to drop to 4.0 in 2005, and in 2013 was at an estimated level of 3.3.[103] Such *Stage* 3 dynamics were not anomalous in the Middle East at this time. Phenomenal drops to replacement or below-replacement fertility levels were reported in Tunisia, Morocco, Qatar, Saudi Arabia, and Lebanon.[104]

Another way to see the shift is in normative family size: In 1970, 40 percent of Muslim families in Israel had six or more children. In 2013 that percentage dropped to 10. In 1970 only 29 percent of Muslim Israeli families had one or two children; in 2013 that proportion had jumped to 50 percent.[105] Present trends suggest a full convergence with Jewish birthrates occurring within a decade.[106]

Within these dramatic statistics are buried many nuances. After the establishment of the state, it became impossible to refer to Arab Israelis demographically as a monolithic unit. Fertility in different Arab communities shifted dramatically after Israel's establishment, and the transition to *Stage* 3 was by no means uniform. One indication of differential fertility rates among Arab Israelis can be seen in the expansion of the Druze population. In 1931 there were ten times more Christians in Palestine than the 9,148 residents of Druze villages.[107] With birthrates comparable to Israel's Muslims for much of the country's history, by 2010 Israel's Druze community came to number over

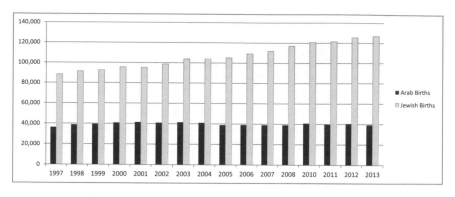

Stable Arab versus rising Jewish births in Israel, 1997–2013.
(Source: Israel Central Bureau of Statistics)

115,000,[108] roughly 70 percent of the number of Christian Arabs. Then, quite suddenly, Druze fertility levels tumbled, to a TFR of only 2.2. Family sizes are now comparable to Israel's Christian community and far lower than Jewish or Muslim birthrates.[109]

As the 1990s drew to a close, the revolution in population dynamics was undeniable. At that time, Dr. Onn Winckler, an expert on Arab demography, identified four objective factors to which he attributed the drop in fertility: *a prolonged reduction of mortality rates, the establishment of an Israeli social security system, the transition from an agricultural to an industrial and services economy, and the improvement in women's education.*[110] Now, more than a decade later, these and other factors have solidified the transformation in the culture and reproductive norms of Arab Israelis.

The politicization of demography and veneration of fertility that constituted a proud *public* posture for many Arab Israelis gave way to a new existential reality. *Lowering* fertility levels was seen as a preferable route for improving quality of life for themselves, their children, and their cause. Rhoda Ann Kanaaneh explains that this view was initially articulated among secular Arab Israelis with leftist political leanings. According to this perspective, a smaller number of well-educated, professional Palestinians poses a greater challenge to Israeli domination than a larger, poorer, and less-educated community.[111] The second and third generation of Israel's Arab minority—a cohort that anthropologist Dan Rabinowitz calls the "stand tall" generation—is recognized as more militant than their parents in demanding political rights. But this greater confidence is also reflected in an independent and individualistic approach to family planning. The number of children in a family is seen as a decidedly personal decision.

Given the objective (and subjective) obstacles to succeeding in a Jewish state, Arab parents came to believe that smaller families would allow them to better educate their children and modernize their society. Kanaaneh quotes a typical view from the Galilee in the 1990s that explains why the pro-natal ideology of nationalistic Palestinian leaders lost traction: "If we just sit back and enjoy the fact that one day we may number more than the Israelis, we'll sink under our own weight."[112] Even religious Muslims were told by their imams that there was nothing in Islam that proscribed contraception or that required high birthrates. Indeed, among Arab Israelis, there is little correlation between religiosity and fertility rates.

Rinal Shalabana-B'hote is a young attorney working in Beer Sheva. She explains prevailing attitudes among today's young Arab couples regarding family planning:

> First and foremost, it's an economic decision. If you have ten children, the chances are you'll only be able to send one child to university. And it's not only about a better life for the children: With ten kids, you simply don't have a life. All you do is raise children. Don't forget: today children don't contribute to the family's budget. In Arab society, to get ahead especially in the north of Israel, it's very accepted to send children to private schools, even a Christian school. To get ahead, you want to give them more than the public schools can give them. To raise children correctly, it costs money.[113]

Today's generation does not hesitate to blame underprivileged conditions and deficient investment in the Arab Israeli sector on historically biased Israeli policies and prejudices. Nonetheless, a common assumption is that socioeconomic gaps are exacerbated by high fertility. Arab Israelis have come to accept the simple truth that having smaller families is one of the keys to future prosperity.[114]

THE CULTURAL TRANSITION — ISRAELIZATION

There are those who believe that the shift into a *Stage 3* demographic mode is simply a result of integration into Israeli society. Arab citizens follow Israeli politics, have overdrafts in Israeli bank accounts, wait in lines at Israeli health clinics, and study an Israeli government-approved curriculum (in Arabic). Arab Israelis also began to consume imported products, travel abroad, and watch American television shows and Hollywood movies. Gradually, they came to adopt many of the cultural norms, heroes, and aspirations of Western civilization. In so doing, wittingly or unwittingly, they distanced themselves from traditional, agrarian Palestinian ways and drew closer to an increasingly homogenized, urbanized, Western, Israeli lifestyle.

For the past thirty years, Haifa University sociologist Sammy Smooha has followed the *"Israelization"* process among local Arabs[115] as they grew closer to the state and to Jewish norms in many spheres of life.[116] Other experts challenge this view.[117] There is no arguing that Israel's Arab communities still remain distinct from the Jewish sector, both geographically and sociologically. On average, Arab Israelis are younger, less educated, and poorer than Jewish citizens. Most Israelis are unaware of just how much poorer Arab citizens are: In 2004 poverty incidence among Arab Israelis was 6.7 times higher than it was for non-Orthodox Jewish Israelis.[118] Almost ten years later, in 2013, the gap had narrowed but was still substantial: 53.5 percent of Arab households were classified as "poor" by Israel's Ministry of Welfare, as opposed to 19.9 percent in the Jewish sector.[119]

Younger Arab citizens have become *very* Israeli in their *unwillingness* to passively accept second-class status, as their parents did during the country's earlier years. This was driven home to Israel's somewhat complacent Jewish majority during the widespread demonstrations and rioting of 2000. The ensuing deaths of twelve Arab Israeli citizens led to the appointment of the Or Commission to investigate the police response and consider the discrimination that was at the heart of Arab frustration.[120] Justice Or and his committee were surprisingly candid about the discrimination faced by Arab citizens and its role in fomenting the exasperation and despondency that fueled the unrest.

Arab citizens' idiosyncratic *Israeli* identity became even more salient after Israel signed peace agreements in the 1990s with representatives from the Palestinian population in Gaza and the West Bank. The vast majority of Arab Israelis, while very supportive of the peace process, preferred not to adopt this officially recognized Palestinian national identity.[121] According to a December 2014 comprehensive survey, 77 percent of Israeli Arabs said that they preferred leaving under an Israeli government than a Palestinian government.[122] More than two-thirds of Arab respondents see themselves as Israelis, and 70 percent support Israel's right to exist as a Jewish and democratic state where Arabs and Jews live together.[123] This percentage has decreased somewhat from previous periods, but is still the view of the vast majority of Arab Israelis.

It is interesting to consider the shifts reflected in Sammy Smooha's annual seven-hundred-person opinion surveys. Between 2003 and 2012, results revealed a steady "hardening" of attitudes among Arab Israelis toward the country and a reduced desire to integrate into society. The new generation of Arabs, apparently, was less forgiving about what many saw as "second-class citizenship" in a Jewish state and the associated discrimination. But this trend made a pronounced reversal in 2012, with a significantly higher percentage of conciliatory positions expressed. Smooha attributes the turnaround to disappointment with the results of the Arab Spring in the Middle East along with a growing appreciation for the economic and civic benefits associated with living in a stable society.

Israel's slow but steady efforts to reduce discrimination and boost the well-being of Israel's Arab communities may also contribute. Smooha also believes that the highly publicized position of Israel's previous foreign minister Avigdor Lieberman, advocating exchange of major Arab cities in Israel for Jewish settlements located in a future Palestinian state, constituted a wake-up call for Arab society. It suddenly had to confront the meaning of a divorce from a country with which it may not always be thrilled but that provides a reasonably high quality of life.[124] Indeed, periodic calls by Israeli politicians for transferring jurisdiction in certain Arab towns to a new state of Palestine are invariably met by angry objections by Arab residents. Apparently, they find life under Israeli rule a far more appealing prospect for them and their families' futures.

Food is another example in which Western and Israeli norms have gradually taken hold. Because of the robust Israeli dairy industry and historic subsidies, milk products have become a staple in the Arab diet. In her study of Arab Israeli culinary inclinations, sociologist Liora Givon reports that Arab Israelis typically seek a more "modern cuisine." One respondent told Givon that her family's shift to yogurt and chocolate milk was because it gave them "enough calcium to keep our back straight, not like the old people you see in Arab villages."[125] When the Israeli public launched a successful boycott of packaged cottage cheese, which forced steep prices down in 2011, Arab households were active participants.[126] Cooking provided another opportunity to see Israeli society's slow but steady progress in embracing the Arab minority. When Nof Atamna-Ismaeel, an Arab woman with three children and a Ph.D. in microbiology, won the much-watched reality show *Master Chef Israel* in 2014, she was hailed by Arabs and Jews alike. She pledged to use the prize money to open an Arab-Jewish cooking school.[127]

There are many other such breakthroughs: In 1999, Rana Raslan, a twenty-two-year-old woman from Haifa, became the first (and thus far still the only) Miss Israel from the country's Arab community.[128] Singer Mira Awad became a national celebrity when she was selected to represent Israel at the 2009 Eurovision song contest in a duet with vocalist Ahinoam Nini.[129] By then Awad was already a familiar figure on Israeli television, starring in *Arab Labor*, a hugely successful sitcom. Written by *Haaretz* journalist Sayed Kashua, the loosely autobiographical episodes highlight an Arab family and their hilarious interactions with their Jewish neighbors and colleagues, while showcasing the subtle and not so subtle indignities and prejudice faced by the protagonists. Many Israelis cheered when the B'nei Sakhnin professional soccer team from a modest

twenty-five-thousand-person Arab town, and overwhelming underdog, won the
Israel State Cup in 2004. For Arab Israelis it was a particularly sweet victory.[130]
While it is easy to dismiss these examples as "tokenism," over time the cumulative impact of so many accomplishments on Jewish (and Arab) Israeli precon-
ceptions adds up. While not erasing significant cultural differences, they surely
strengthen a sense of common interests and a collective Israeli identity among
all citizens.

By one objective measure, Arab Israeli society is looking extremely Israeli:
increased population density is suffocating the country's 108 Arab cities and
towns. Due to discriminatory land policies, beginning in 1949 no new Arab settlements were established and expansion of existing Arab villages has been limited.[131] Quickly these communities became extremely crowded, four times more
so on average than Jewish municipalities.[132] With no new residential land available, children make their homes in apartments built above the roofs of their
parents' houses. Traffic jams are increasingly common in town thoroughfares
that have no space to expand to four lanes. Infrastructure for collecting trash is
often inadequate, in part a result of low revenues from city taxes. With practically no parks and relatively few trees in the public domain, residents complain
about congestion and lack of air.

Unfortunately, crowded conditions can breed aggressive behavior. Even traditional Arab weddings, for which streets were always closed for communal celebrations, have become so cacophonous that neighbors began to file complaints
with the police. Many couples opt for smaller private affairs[133] that can look very
similar to the weddings of their Jewish neighbors. It should not be surprising
that an increasing number of Arab Israelis are interested in leaving their homogeneous but overcrowded communities. According to Tel Aviv University researcher Jamila Elnashef, a majority of Arab Israelis openly express a desire to
move to less crowded Jewish neighborhoods.[134]

EMPOWERING WOMEN

When Basel Ghattas was elected to Israel's Knesset, he brought with him
thirty years of experience as a leader in civil society who sought social and environmental justice for Israel's Arab citizens. As head of the Galilee Society for
Health Research and Services, he navigated the arcane local administrative
constraints and Arab sociological dynamics to establish innovative health-
delivery projects and economic enterprises. He managed to overcome the excruciating complex bureaucracy and regulations to facilitate sewage treatment in
Arab communities. By comparison, the question of fertility does not seem to

him to be that complicated: "Education, Education, Education. The second that women have education they want to participate in the work force and prefer smaller families. They are looking for opportunities. At present, a typical Arab, middle class family wants 3 to 4 children. I'm not sure that the birthrate will be lower than 2.6 for Muslim families. But already Christian families are below that. (They are our Ashkenazim—so to speak.) You might find that religious families have more children, but that isn't the real story: it has much more to do with the educational status of women."[135]

Empowerment of women has always been the single greatest factor in reducing fertility. This has been confirmed in empirical research in countries from Turkey[136] to India[137] to China[138] and throughout Sub-Saharan Africa.[139] To grasp the nature of the Arab demographic transition in Israel, more important than analyzing the shift in culinary inclinations or recreational culture, one must understand the evolving status of Arab women. Here, the influence of Israeli culture has been profound and the changes extraordinary. All indicators reflect tremendous progress during the past decades.[140]

In 1954, 79 percent of non-Jewish, Israeli women had never attended school; only 0.2 had any higher education to speak of.[141] That's when Israel's compulsory education law went into force. Today, almost all Arab girls attend primary and secondary school. There they consistently outperform boys: more than half the Arab student population in Israeli universities today is female. Since 1975, the percentage of Arab women with undergraduate or graduate training increased from 4 to 24 percent.[142] It is not just pursuit of knowledge that motivates young women to attend university. For many Arab Israeli women, higher education holds the sole route to a brief period of freedom and respite from the relentless supervision they face growing up and the subsequent constraints of married life. Many young women seek to prolong this period and live independently in society.

The average age of first-time mothers among Muslim Israelis is twenty-three. This is far higher than it used to be and it continues to rise.[143] The acceptable age range for getting married now reaches into the late twenties.[144] Consequently, women are getting pregnant later, after they have had opportunities to learn about reproduction and think about family planning.

Many of the traditional factors in Arab societies that hold women back still persist to some degree in Israel but appear to be improving. After marrying, women still are expected to join their husbands' households.[145] Men typically are not as involved in raising children and, as breadwinners, many feel absolved from the direct responsibility of caregiving or housekeeping.[146] (This is not unusual: there is in fact no known culture where men participate equally with women in the raising of children.)[147] Being a patriarchal society, producing sons still remains a preference for many husbands and wives. But for most Arab Israelis today, boys no longer hold the "nationalistic" meaning of the past, when mothers were expected to be part of a national struggle and deliver the males required to carry on the fight for national liberation.[148]

While there has been undeniable progress, Muslim women in Israel do not enjoy the same level of domestic safety as their Jewish counterparts (who by no means are free of violence.)[149] Many Arab women find themselves trapped in abusive relationships, unable to overcome the extreme pressure exerted by their families and society not to "rock the boat" and to accept their domestic lot, whatever that might be.[150] Those emphasizing the "half empty glass" can point to the alarming level of domestic violence that especially in Bedouin communities, is still normative.[151] (In 2012, for example, 50 percent of the women murdered in Israel were Arabs—two and a half times more than their share in society.)[152] Women do not enjoy the same leisure options. It is understood that females should stay out of coffee shops in Arab towns, with their hookah pipes and smoke-filled ambience. Rather, they usually socialize with other women at home.[153]

Ultimately, it is not socializing but working that affects fertility decisions. "A woman who is employed has fewer children," summarizes Khawla Rihani, the director of the Economic Empowerment for Women Association. Rihani heads a Haifa-based organization that helps women break out of the vicious circle that leaves so many "structurally unemployed." The association facilitates their finding challenging and reasonably paying jobs. Most of her clients are Arab and Haredi women who can't find work even though many are extremely qualified and capable. Her experience suggests that if reasonable jobs were available, many more Arab women would be employed today.[154]

This may be improving. Data indicate that since 1970 employment among Arab Israeli women increased by 300 percent. Tel Aviv University professor Eran Yashiv's research found empirical support for the notion that Arab women's employment rates are linked to education, having fewer children, and living in households that rely on more than a single wage earner.[155] Despite Naftali Bennett's persona as a right-wing politician, with little empathy for Palestinian national aspirations, as minister of economics between 2013 and 2015, he made professional opportunities and employment centers for Arab women a priority.[156] The Israeli government intends to spend $1.2 billion to improve integration of Arabs into the job market.[157]

Trends are encouraging, yet present conditions still ensure that many Arab women remain unemployed. Some argue that the glass is actually *three-quarters empty*: 73 percent of Arab women remain without work. Those women seeking to break into the Israeli job market face objective difficulties: they cannot find good day care; they rely on very inadequate public transportation to employment centers;[158] and many find it hard to get a "fair shake" from Jewish employers.[159] Many Arab women with excellent qualifications find it difficult to land an appropriate position. Research by Technion planning expert Yosef Jabareen found that *lack of jobs* was the single greatest problem facing Arab women, with other restraining effects, like traditional values or inappropriate human capital, being only secondary contributors.[160] Many women also feel that language constitutes a barrier, as many postings require high levels of Hebrew proficiency.[161] In short, increasingly independent, Arab women with professional capabilities and ambitions are an undeniable phenomenon. But there is still a long way to go.

The last holdout of conservative traditional patriarchal values affecting the status of young Arab women is sexual mores. Here too Western culture is making inroads. In 2010 Manal Shalabi, a feminist leader from Haifa, conducted one of the first systematic studies about Arab Israeli women's sexuality and practices. She reports that while Arab Israeli society is still highly patriarchal, it is not homogeneous. Arab women increasingly find ways to circumvent strict controls and taboos that Arab society places on them. To be sure, virginity remains a critical value for Arab men, and pre-marital sex a "red line" that the vast majority of Arab women in Israel are unwilling to cross.[162] But much as girls did during more-puritanical periods in the West, many Arab women find ways to express affection and address sexual desire short of full sexual relations. Here, Palestinian women appear similar to their sisters in more liberal Arab societies, such as Morocco and Tunisia.[163]

Shalabi concludes her findings by explaining, "Most of the efforts of Arab feminists in Israel today are directed at exposing political subjugation and in working on domestic and sexual violence. . . . Though the issues of equality with Jews and of violence are undoubtedly important, sexual discourse is absented from the political and social agenda. The subject is taboo such that political activists are afraid to touch or deal with it. Yet if the issue of sexuality is not integrated into agendas of political change, no real transformation in social and gender relationships will occur."[164]

When one examines sexuality in the conjugal context, contraception is just another Western technology that was initially common among Jews and that was later embraced by Israel's Arab citizens. Many Arab Israelis today are actually disdainful of large families, considering them "primitive." By the 1990s, Israel's Ministry of Health was issuing promotional materials appealing to the growing aspiration for "modernity" and middle-class status. Arabic language family-planning pamphlets featured a photo of a single male child with a Westernized young mother and father huddling over a book.[165]

Just like for Jewish women in Israel, for Arab women IUDs (*il-wasta*—"the method") are the most popular form of birth control; condoms less so.[166] Typically, an Arab woman will have an IUD inserted after giving birth to a second child, leaving it in for many years. As a sign of their growing independence, Arab women frequently make this important reproductive decision without consulting their husbands.[167]

Unlike the Haredi population, there is no blind faith among Muslims or Christians that the Almighty will "provide" and intervene to ensure the quality of life of an additional child. When faced with the prospect of unregulated reproduction, the vast majority of Arab Israelis prefer birth control. In cases where unwanted pregnancies occur, abortions, once entirely unknown, have become somewhat more acceptable.[168] For many families, recognition of the additional financial burden proves more powerful than any moral or cultural misgivings.

An interesting question involves the implications of the growing "Islamic" identity in the Middle East. Many Israeli Arabs vote regularly for the Islamic party in local and national elections. Nevertheless, it turns out that Arab Israelis are not exceptionally devout. In a 2005 survey, only 11 percent of Muslims define themselves as very religious; 63 percent define themselves as traditional.[169] Still, the very desire of so many Arab citizens to classify themselves as traditional suggests that Islam continues to have a cultural (as well as political) influence.

The Koran encourages procreation and considers children to be a "gift of God"—the "decoration of life." Muhammad also openly encouraged his followers to multiply. At the same time, Muslims do not believe that God wishes to burden believers, and Islam has long held that the well-being of children trumps the value of large families. Utilization of birth control was well known, and herbal remedies from Islamic medical books were widely read throughout medieval Europe. Muhammad himself was familiar with the practice of *al'azl* (coitus interruptus) and did not prohibit it.[170] Typically, modern contraception is allowed by Muslim authorities if it does not endanger a woman's health. There is, however, a much greater reluctance to allow irreversible practices such as tubal ligation and vasectomies.[171]

Local Muslim leaders do not believe that religiosity affects the family-size decisions of Arab Israelis. Imams in the same city can be found with two children and ten children.[172] The city of Umm al-Fahm, one of the most pious Muslim cities in Israel, has one of the lowest birthrates.[173] This pragmatic Muslim attitude toward sustainable populations and family planning can be seen in Iran's remarkable success at reducing fertility to below replacement levels, with the active promotion of the Islamic government.[174]

TOWARD A STAGE-4 EQUILIBRIUM

When Israel was established, the Zionist leadership was terrified lest the Arab minority remaining in the country simply outreproduce the country's Jewish citizens. Given Palestinian nationalism's historic "zero tolerance" for a Jewish state, the demographic surge among Arab citizens was seen as a subterfuge for undermining Israel's hard-fought accomplishments and Jewish sovereignty. Whether these concerns were justified during the country's early days or not can be argued. But the position is misplaced today. Indeed its perpetuation is destructive. For most Arab citizens, resisting Israeli domination is no longer a reason for having more children.

It was not Zionism that overcame Palestinian "resolve" in the area of fertility but simply common sense among Arab families who preferred to make rational decisions about their futures. They were undoubtedly influenced by global consumer culture, which informs the lives of Jewish and Arab citizens alike. The list of perceived "necessities" for all Israeli families continues to grow: from cars and televisions to international vacations and smart phones. Children are born into a long shopping list of expenses: from personal computers and vitamin supplements to swimming lessons, after-school clubs, and orthodontics. Then there are the educational amenities: tutoring, books, and ultimately university tuition.

Most important of all, Arab women finally have a say about their family size. They (and their husbands) are not interested in going back to the days when sprawling families crowded out their children's opportunities. Some may criticize present trends as materialism. Yet it is wrong to disparage efforts to enhance quality of life in a historically underprivileged minority group as self-indulgence. Why should they have to have large families, live in crowded homes, and be denied opportunities for greater comfort, better health, travel destinations, and enriching cultural endeavors? While Israeli society may be imperfect, opportunities for a better life do exist.

Israel's Christian Arabs have begun to embrace the benefits of reduced fertility. On average, Christians marry relatively late (age twenty-four for women and age twenty-eight for men); their families for several years now hover around replacement levels of 2.1 children.[175] This translates into remarkable academic achievements. On average, Israel's Christian Arabs perform significantly better on Israel's national high school matriculation examinations than Jewish youth do.[176] Christian Arabs are already highly integrated into Israeli society,[177] and if they start to join the army or national service, their assimilation into the economy will make a further quantum leap forward. The community serves as a model for potential integration and reconciliation.

The narrative for Arab citizens in Israel today is increasingly the story of an ethnic minority demanding its civil rights and seeking an authentic role in a Jewish state. Only a decade ago, during an acrimonious Palestinian intifada, 66 percent of Israel's Arabs still supported Israel's right to exist as a Jewish and democratic state. Traditionally, Israel's Arab parties have never been considered potential partners in government coalitions, but this may change. Currently, 80 percent of Arab Israelis support the idea of Arab parties taking a place at the cabinet table.[178] Unfortunately, intemperate politicians on both sides lapse into the narrative of demographic conflict; a high collective price is paid for such tired and outmoded rhetoric.

The most common commandment in the Bible is the requirement that Israelites deal fairly with the disempowered: the widow, the orphan, the non-Jew.[179] A key litmus test for any society is its relationship to its weakest minority.[180] If social equity and demographic stability are to be attained, affirmative action makes sense. Government efforts must start by strengthening Arab women. Public policies that make Israel's Arab citizens feel that the State of Israel offers a true home with meaningful personal and professional opportunities will do more to stabilize population rates than any nationalistically motivated, discriminatory programs.[181]

Despite a tortured geopolitical history, the demographic transition has unfolded in Israel much as it has around the planet. For those concerned about overpopulation, this should be a source of relief. Given political sensitivities, *Stage 4* equilibrium will probably not be sustained in a toxic atmosphere of ethnic conflict, but only when minorities feel they enjoy equal opportunities. If the State of Israel wishes to enjoy demographic stability, it has to do a better job of minding the gaps.[182]

GROWING PAINS: THE POLITICS OF BEDOUIN AND PALESTINIAN POPULATIONS

> If we can't defeat them in war, let's outbreed them.
> —Yasser Arafat

The remarkable drop in fertility among Israel's Druze, Christian, and Muslim Arab citizens should soon diffuse the demographic hysteria that so traumatized Israel and disfigured domestic policy throughout its history. Nonetheless, high birthrates among Israel's Bedouin citizens in the Negev, and Palestinian Arabs in Gaza and West Bank remain a source of considerable anxiety for Israel's Jewish majority. The CIA's *World Factbook* is probably as reliable and updated a census as can be publicly accessed. Its 2014 assessment reports that the average Palestinian family in the West Bank has 2.83 children,[1] while families in the Gaza Strip average 4.24.[2] Israel's Central Bureau of Statistics estimates that average Bedouin families in the Negev have a fertility rate of 6 children per family.[3]

These high birthrates inform both Israeli diplomatic and domestic policy thinking, but in different ways. The common denominator is that Israeli governments closely follow demographic developments and think, albeit not very profoundly, about ways to retain a clear Jewish majority. But there is no consensus about what the future will or should hold. There are those who believe that present Palestinian and Bedouin demographic trends no longer threaten Jewish supremacy. Much like the pattern emerging among the majority of Israel's Arab citizens, they are convinced that it is only a matter of time until fertility drops in these two communities as well. If there is a problem that needs to be remedied, they believe it is inadequate efforts to bolster continued Jewish immigration and fertility.

Others see Palestinian and even Bedouin birthrates as threats to long-held Zionist axioms of a "Jewish and democratic state"—threats that require dispassionate and decisive interventions. They are joined by sustainability advocates who seek to stabilize population levels in all ethnic communities within Israel. They believe that government intervention to this end through territorial concessions or through implementation of sustainable population policies is long overdue. Understanding the idiosyncratic nature of the two populations' demographic trends is critical for picking sides and deciding which position is correct.

Israel's Arab community has always been heterogeneous. Nomadic populations have been wandering throughout the Middle East from time immemorial. Their attitude toward land was more casual and dispersed than that of Palestine's sedentary peasant fellahin, who were more meticulous in retaining their legal and emotional connection to a specific village or parcel of land.

Most Bedouins living in Israel today belong to tribes that migrated to Ottoman Palestine during the eighteenth and nineteenth century from the Arabian Peninsula and surrounding deserts. These nomads of old made a very conscious choice *not* to settle down.[4] They brought with them a unique and ancient culture: special poetry, embroidery, legends, laws, and an extraordinary ability to live sustainably in a punishing, arid environment.[5] Part of this heritage involved an emphasis on procreation. A large family was a statement of strength that guaranteed protection in the anarchy of the region's isolated deserts. The Bedouin expression "Count your men and go to the well" was a recognition that in order to compete for scarce resources, numbers mattered.[6]

THE BEDOUIN ANOMALY

After 1948, Israel's Bedouin community split into two groups geographically: the northern contingent today includes some sixty thousand Bedouins living in villages and towns in the Galilee. Their demographic dynamics are roughly comparable to other Muslim Arabs, albeit there are conspicuous cultural disparities, among which is their historic willingness to serve in Israel's military. The two hundred thousand Bedouins of the Negev in the south, however, represent a different story. While they express a nominal sense of identification and solidarity with other Arab Israelis, Negev Bedouins are insular and protective of their unique tribal heritage. Even today, Bedouin men prohibit their daughters (and sisters) from marrying outside the Bedouin community and, frequently, beyond their specific tribe.

Heirs to a nomadic tradition of pastoralism, Bedouins are undoubtedly in the midst of a profound cultural transition. However, this is not yet manifested in

birthrates, which remain among the highest in the country despite a modest recent decline. Not very long ago, during the 1980s, fertility among Israeli Bedouins
was considered to be the highest in the world.[7] Throughout the early years of the
state, population growth among Negev Bedouins was consistently higher than
5 percent annually—150 percent more than the average national demographic
increase. For example, a retrospective analysis by Ben-Gurion University professor Avinoam Meir assessed demographic trends in 1981 and concluded that
the 1970 growth rate of 5.5 percent was a peak, after which a steady decline was
starting to occur, that he predicted would quickly accelerate.[8] But he got it wrong.

The demographic transition had not yet reached Israel's southlands. In 2005
an official report estimated that the Bedouin population was still growing at a
rate of 5.5 percent.[9] While Arab communities in Israel were converging to Western levels of fertility, the Bedouin population was doubling every thirteen years.
Bedouins have always been a special case.

The city of Beer Sheva was established in 1900; it was the only new city ever
established by the Ottomans in their expansive empire outside of Turkey. The
city's ostensible mission was to control the nomadic tribes in the Negev region
who did not abide by the usual standards nor adopt the trappings of the colonial
regime. The new outpost did little to rein them in. Bedouins continued to follow their seasonal routes, make their own rules, and control their own lives (and
frequently those of other residents and visitors to Palestine).[10] Attempts to have
them register land and pay taxes like other "civilized" communities of Ottoman
Palestine were singularly unsuccessful.

Neither were Bedouins keen about following British regulations or even participating in British census taking. As a "moving target," they constituted a considerable challenge to the Mandate's statisticians.[11] Even today, Israel's Central
Bureau of Statistics acknowledges enormous underestimation in measuring a
population that does not always live in a recognized town and is not always
interested in being counted. For instance, there was a gap of 50 percent between the fertility rates of Bedouin families formally registered in the 1990s (6.7
children per family) and what Israel's census bureau believed to be plausible
estimates of 10.1 children per family. Presently, there is a 40 percent gap: with
5.5 children reported per family and a more-likely projection of 7.7.[12]

While data are not particularly reliable, rough estimates emerging from
the Mandate period suggest that 65,000 Bedouins lived in the Negev at the approach of the mid-twentieth century,[13] divided into seven confederations and
one hundred tribes.[14] During the War of Independence many were allied with
the invading Arab armies and fought against the newly declared state. It was apparent in the aftermath that they had picked the wrong side. Rather than see

what Israel's response would be, many simply headed to Jordan, the West Bank, and the Sinai—places on their historic migration routes. Others were expelled by the nascent Israeli Defense Forces.[15]

The 1954 Israeli census reported only 11,000 Bedouins living in the Negev.[16] That was the year Israel granted them citizenship. But by then their numbers were rapidly rebounding. The Negev Bedouin population levels more than doubled during the next fifteen years, with 25,320 citizens counted in the 1969 census. Estimates of the size of Israel's southern Bedouin population in 1991 were 91,000, and by 2002 it had increased to 130,000.[17] In 2015 there were thought to be some 227,000 Bedouins in the south of Israel, divided between seven towns and thirty-five unrecognized communities scattered throughout the Negev desert.[18] Official accounts report that 65 percent live in these cities while 35 percent are in the unregistered sector,[19] but there are ample reasons to believe that the unrecognized sector is somewhat larger.

Two related questions immediately emerge from this demographic snapshot: Why are the fertility levels of Israel's Bedouin citizens so different from that of the general Arab population? And is a demographic transition within this community only a matter of time?

There are elements of Bedouin heritage and culture that distinguish the community from the other Arab citizens in Israel. Three factors in particular inform Bedouin life that strongly influence fertility. These are *the prevalence of poverty, oppression of women,* and *polygamy.* They have combined to prolong the *Stage* 2–associated population expansion by many years. Today fertility among Negev Bedouins is starting to drop, but due to these three factors remains high, with the TFR estimated at 6.9.[20]

The extreme poverty found among Israel's Bedouin citizens can in part be attributed to the way the country approached a community that was uneducated and disconnected from Western culture prior to 1948. Because they were considered a "security threat," until martial law was canceled in 1966 the southern Bedouins were confined to a narrow area of the Negev desert called the "Sayag." With little or no infrastructure, conditions were extremely primitive and educational opportunities minimal.[21] While they continued to wander, their historic nomadic proclivities began to dissipate.

Soon thereafter, the Israeli government launched a settlement policy, based on the establishment of new villages for the Bedouins, that provide them with permanent homes. Seven Bedouin townships were established across the Negev between the years 1968 and 1989.[22]

Despite the urgings of the government and objectively favorable economic conditions offered, only about half the Bedouin population chose to avail them-

Nomadic no more: Tel Sheva, Israel's recognized first
Bedouin city. (Photograph by author)

selves of the newly constructed communities.[23] Many of the Bedouins who rejected this option touted historic land claims and stayed in their traditional
tents. Over the years these were "upgraded" to the unsightly corrugated tin
shacks that have become today's *unrecognized* villages.

The future of unrecognized communities is presently the focus of acrimonious conflict. The government denies Bedouin demands for land ownership,
given the casual documentation provided and absence of clear titles. Acutely
aware of and extremely unhappy with Bedouin geographic proliferation and the
implications for the environment, poverty, and of course Jewish sovereignty, the
state seeks to complete the process of sedentarization by establishing new towns
that encompass some of the unrecognized villages. The upshot of the proposal
is that forty thousand Bedouins would need to move to new villages.[24] Needless
to say, most are not inclined.

Recognized Bedouin towns have hardly been a paragon of socioeconomic
progress. From the outset they were the poorest municipalities in Israel. But conditions in unrecognized villages are even worse. According to Israel's National
Insurance Institute, the incidence of poverty in recognized Bedouin cities is
about 70 percent. In nonrecognized villages it is even more ubiquitous: around
79.2 percent.[25] Worse yet, trends show clearly that the severity of poverty in the
Bedouin sector has actually gotten worse over the years.

An unrecognized Bedouin village, containing Israel's poorest population and Israel's highest fertility rates. (Photograph courtesy of Dani Machlis, Ben-Gurion University)

The conventional indicators of social well-being tell a discouraging story. While the housing constructed in the new Bedouin towns was reasonable and the size of the lots large by Israeli standards, no manufacturing areas or industries were established and little designated rangeland was zoned for livestock. Public transportation was essentially inaccessible to facilitate commutes to potential employment centers. (Indeed, Rahat, the largest Bedouin city in Israel, had to reach a population of fifty thousand people before even minimal bus service became available.) Those without cars had to make the long hike to a Beer Sheva–bound highway to intercept a bus serving Jewish cities. Unrecognized villages frequently are even more isolated. Getting to school is not easy. In Bedouin cities, the overall dropout rate *before* high school is roughly 32 percent. In unrecognized villages it exceeds 50 percent.[26]

Bedouins always had a hard time finding employment. Various public projects were initiated to this end, but often the effort didn't seem justified. Those jobs that were available to an uneducated population with nonmarketable skills paid very poorly. (Some of the well-intentioned development projects, such as growing flowers in greenhouses for export, turned out to be culturally incompatible with Bedouin ideas of what farming should be). Other social indicators confirm the pervasive poverty. For instance, Israel's infant mortality rate is 3.9 per 1,000 births. At 10.6, Bedouin levels are almost three times higher.[27] In 2010, the last count, only 29 percent of Bedouins had a private e-mail address, far behind the 49 percent rate among the broader cohort of Arab Israelis.[28]

The few jobs that were historically available to Bedouin women and that were socially acceptable involved early childhood education or teaching.[29] As of the last census, even the most advanced Bedouin communities had fewer than 20 percent of the local women in the workforce.[30] Under such deprived conditions and the pressure of tradition, it is little wonder that Bedouin girls marry young, sometimes before age sixteen, and begin having children without delay. With no attractive employment opportunities and continued education not an option for most, what else is there for them to do? In most cases, even if a young Bedouin woman wishes to seek a profession or strike out on her own, it is not her decision to make.

Accordingly, the second factor driving the high Bedouin birthrate is the oppressed status of women. Many traditional societies are patriarchal, but Bedouin society has always constituted an extreme case. Customary Bedouin tribal law (in contrast to Islamic principles) holds that women have no rights to their own children, cannot inherit, cannot file legal actions if they feel they are treated unfairly, cannot expose any of their skin in public, and can be beaten (on the back side only) by their husbands with impunity.[31] Distilled to its essence, Bedouin tradition determines that when girls are born they are the property of their fathers; when they marry, ownership is transferred to their husbands. Even if these laws run contrary to Israeli civil rights legislation today, the norms are still very much in force.

The vast majority of the Bedouin women's lives in the Negev are controlled by males: some 79 percent of the Bedouin women who agreed to participate in a recent survey confirmed that they had not been included in the decision about whom they married and when that would happen. Except for a tiny minority of women who have rebelled and joined secular society, they are expected to cover their bodies in dark dresses and cover their heads in a hijab. There are some tribes that still only allow a woman to have a mere slit open for her eyes when she goes out in public.

A full 80 percent of Bedouin women interviewed said that they were required to receive permission from their husbands (or fathers if they are not married) in order to travel outside the immediate surroundings of their homes. For the majority, this is only allowed when accompanied by a male. Some 79 percent reported that they were completely dependent on men financially and had no independent access to money or bank accounts.[32] Some apologists theorize that women only lost their traditional source of power in the Bedouin family when the economy went from subsistence agriculture and animal husbandry to settled semiurban lifestyles.[33] Yet that does not explain why all indicators (including polygamy rates)[34] suggest that women in recognized towns are better off than those who remain in the more traditional, unrecognized communities. The age-old Bedouin culture, with female circumcision, honor killings, and obsessive standards for subservience never accorded women any freedom.

Progress is slow. There have been meaningful advances in the education offered to young Bedouin girls: the construction of elementary schools near unrecognized communities led to a tremendous increase in overall literacy among Bedouin youth, especially among females, who for decades were largely illiterate. One recent survey claims that 99.6 percent of Bedouin girls between the ages of fifteen and nineteen can read, in stark contrast to 18.6 percent of women over sixty.[35] Another report suggests that 88 percent completed elementary school. Yet 11.2 percent of Bedouin women polled had never attended school at all.[36] For many girls, high schools are not easily accessible, making secondary education the exception, as it requires traveling outside the confines of the community. Only 36 percent of Bedouin girls in unrecognized villages complete high school; the situation in cities is markedly better.[37] When Ben-Gurion University established more flexible entrance requirements, the number of Bedouin women students attending the university doubled between 2000 and 2010. The 472 students enrolled there today is still a modest number, but it represents a strong start.[38]

Dr. Sarab Abu-Rabia-Queder, an anthropologist on the Ben-Gurion University faculty, wrote her doctoral dissertation about the pioneering generation of Bedouin women who, like herself, attended university and what became of them. Published as *Excluded and Loved: Educated Bedouin Women's Life Stories,* the ethnography serves as a platform for these remarkable people to tell heroic stories in their own words. The personal price has been enormous for the Bedouins' first female academics, all of whom endured varying degrees of loneliness and alienation. Many had to give up any hopes of a family of their own.[39] And yet they broke barriers and shattered glass ceilings.

Bedouin mayors estimate today that 80 percent of the university students from their towns are female.[40] Some argue that today, higher education actually offers a premium for a Bedouin girl when marriages are arranged because of the economic contribution graduates can make to a household's economy.[41] (Others claim that Bedouin women who wish to pursue careers are better off staying single.) But for many Bedouin girls who might have the credentials to get accepted, receiving permission from their fathers to study in an unsupervised university or college atmosphere is unthinkable. Subservience is imposed on Bedouin women and enforced by a culture where violence is normative.

On June 12, 2013, a conference was convened by feminist organizations in the Negev about the problem of domestic violence in the Bedouin community. They called it Breaking the Conspiracy of Silence: We Are Fighting for Our Right to Security. The audience was filled with Bedouin women. The center-piece of the gathering was the presentation of a recent survey of Bedouin women overseen by attorney Insaf Abu Shareb. Abu Shareb succeeded in leaving the confines of traditional Bedouin society but remains committed to assisting women from her community.

As a child in an unrecognized village in the 1980s, she would walk an hour on foot to attend elementary classes in the town of Arara. All around her girls were put down, facing a relentless regimen of corporal and other punishments. Abu Shareb developed a strategy by which she would remain silent in the face of abuse in order to reduce the level of beating. After third grade she could stand it no longer and refused to attend school. A year passed before she was convinced to return, skipped a grade, and realized that if she persisted, she could eventually use her education to empower other Bedouin women. It was not easy to convince her father to allow her to discreetly attend law school in Netanya. (She reckons that her studying law at the other end of the country was so unimaginable that neighbors assumed her frequent travel was because she was receiving experi-mental cancer treatment.) In law school she came to dress and act with greater independence and had little difficulty handling the tough curriculum in He-brew, her second language. Returning home afterward to traditional clothing and constraints, though, was not as easy. Primitive and extremely crowded conditions in her house made it almost impossible to study for Israel's grueling bar examination. But Insaf, a very determined person, prevailed.

If overcoming the constraints of Bedouin society was not enough, she still had to deal with prejudices in Israel. When she went about seeking a position for the mandatory clerking period, the stereotype created by her traditional dress undermined her prospects. (One judge at an interview did not even wait for her to be out of earshot to tell his secretary, "Don't send me any more Taliban girls.") So she defied her family and removed her head covering for good, eventually clerking for another Beer Sheva judge. She soon found work in a legal NGO, Itach (With You), which represents Bedouin women and helps them pursue their social and economic rights.[42] Today, married with her own children, Abu Shareb finds that the city of Beer Sheva offers a safer place to pursue graduate studies and raise her own sons and daughter. On the whole she seems indiffer-ent to the litany of threats that she and her organization constantly receive.[43]

The survey Insaf Abu Shareb presented was based on responses from some of the two thousand Bedouin women who received assistance from her organization over a six-year period. While it is hardly a scientifically representative sample, the alarming picture of violence and brutality it paints is so extreme that precise statistical analysis is unnecessary to convey a clear message of crisis. The Israeli media paid it no attention.

An astonishingly high percentage of Bedouin women are abused. A full 85 percent of respondents reported physical abuse that required some medical treatment; 90 percent reported psychological damage. Some 24 percent reported sexual assaults, but this is considered to be an understatement due to the associated "shame" or the fear of consequences were a public grievance to ensue. The report explains that once a Bedouin husband has taken a second wife, he frequently will appear at his first wife's home and impose nonconsensual sex. Bedouin women are terrorized into submission, so complaining to the authorities is exceedingly rare. Indeed, in the entire cohort, only one woman had ever filed a complaint with the police. For many, this is no easy task: First they face a language barrier, as many barely speak Hebrew. Then there is geography: with travel fully restricted, they cannot find a way to discreetly reach a police station. Were they to be discovered, many feared that they would lose their children or face unbearable violence.

The intolerable status of so many Bedouin women became national news yet again after the events surrounding Abir Dandis. Dandis lived with her husband's family in the village of al-Furah but had the "audacity" to pay her mother in East Jerusalem a visit with her four daughters without receiving her husband's permission. In retaliation, the suspicious husband killed their two eldest girls. The case elicited particular public outrage because the victims were but five and two years old. Worse yet, it turned out that not long before the murders, Dandis had actually come to the nearest police station in Arad. When she told the Jewish policemen of her husband's violence and fears for her children's lives, they ignored her pleas for help.[44] Although the officers involved were expelled and her husband was arrested and indicted, nobody ever suggested that these dynamics might change anytime soon. In 2012 Abu Shareb and her colleagues decided that things had gone far enough and launched a campaign to stop the violence against women:

> Look—years ago, following every incident against a woman, even murder, there would be silence. Even activist women were silent. This has changed. Every time a shocking case of murder happens we raise our voice. I believe that our protest will penetrate public consciousness. I have seen how women

sat silent when their neighbors were murdered, even when they drowned that poor girl in the well. Everyone shuts up. The girl's teacher in the Bedouin school was also silent. I asked her: "Did you conduct a discussion in class about the event and what it means?" The principal had told me: "We should just deal with it as a simple drowning." This time, however, the teacher said: "I'm going to tell the true story." When we don't speak out, violence becomes a norm. If we speak out, maybe we can change the payoff.

That's our job—and we organized a demonstration two days after the murder. We drafted our colleagues to come help from organizations up north. They said: "You are crazy. You are irresponsible. You're endangering yourselves and your clients." I didn't listen to them. Yes—the El Asam families in Tel Sheva can be dangerous. To stand at the main junction to the entrance of the town, well it had never been done. People were nervous. They were actually trembling. We knew it was dangerous, but we also got a lot of positive responses.[45]

Notwithstanding considerable personal risks, Bedouin women are beginning to organize conferences and openly protest domestic violence. Increasingly, they are speaking at demonstrations and at tribal functions, with a new generation of leaders challenging the old Bedouin elite, calling for a liberal space in the Negev. Their representatives call for a transformation from victimhood to political assertiveness, from patriarchy to egalitarianism.[46]

These shifts may represent a turning point. But it will be a long struggle before most Bedouin women have freedom to make basic decisions about their lives—decisions that affect their fertility. For instance, Abu Shareb argues that it is not access to contraception but permission from husbands that constitutes the major barrier to women's reproductive autonomy. Using an IUD without permission is tantamount to infidelity and could be grounds for divorce or worse. (Her own mother wanted to use birth control but was not allowed to by her father. So she ended up having seventeen children.) For the vast majority of uneducated Bedouin women, the only real way to improve their status is to have many children—preferably boys.[47]

The final factor associated with these problems is polygamy. It is the main cause for today's high birthrate among Bedouin Israelis. This is hardly a dying remnant of an ancient custom in its final, waning phase. Because an Israeli statute assigns polygamy a potential sentence of five years' imprisonment,[48] additional wives are often added surreptitiously and not legally registered, making precise statistics impossible. In fact, this particular law was never enforced at all. Still, the sense among most Bedouins interviewed is that polygamy is on the rise. A 2006 report by Knesset researchers estimated that 20–36 percent of

Some 40 percent of these Bedouin elementary schoolchildren grow up in
polygamous families. (Photograph by author)

Bedouin families were polygamous.[49] This official figure is low compared to
other anecdotal estimates. The *Yedioth Ahronot* newspaper reports that in villages like Said or Karinat, figures reach 56 percent. In the largest Bedouin
city, Rahat, some 40 percent of the children born in 1986 have siblings from a
different mother.[50]

The phenomenon is not limited to the "lower class" of Bedouin society. For
instance, Faiz Abu Sahiban, a past mayor of Rahat, acknowledged that every
single public school principal in his town had taken at least one additional
wife. He openly disapproved a recent union, as it involved a principal marrying
a subordinate, one of the school's teachers. As an imam he cautions that an additional wife is only permitted if it can be done with fairness and if support can
be provided to the existing spouse.[51] Indeed, Islam does not prohibit polygamy
and allows men to have as many as four wives simultaneously. But it also requires that husbands act responsibly.[52]

The first wife in Bedouin families typically comes from the Bedouin community. The second spouse is often "purchased" from the West Bank, Gaza, or
Jordan. The cost for the additional wife is reportedly two thousand dollars there

because they are considered less "genetically authentic," while the price is five thousand dollars for "racially pure" Bedouin women.[53] Palestinian wives are totally unfamiliar with Israel. In most cases, technically they are illegal aliens subject to deportation, who are hidden away and even further relegated to the home or immediate vicinity.

Dr. Mohammed Alnabari is the mayor of Hura, arguably the most prosperous of the Negev's Bedouin communities but still an indigent town. He explains polygamy's continued appeal for Bedouin males in the following way: Young people traditionally marry very young, with neither the groom nor the bride sufficiently mature to make judicious decisions. In some cases, an additional wife reflects an attempt to correct an underlying incompatibility, not unlike the high rate of divorce in Western countries. In other cases, a man will simply want more children for any number of reasons. Alnabari does not mention economic motives. But retrospective evaluations of reductions in child allowances showed that financial incentives have a powerful influence on many Bedouin families.

Like other Bedouin mayors, Alnabari's concern is primarily with polygamous families where the father is unable—or unwilling—to support the large number of children. Islam, he clarifies, calls for spacing children. While sympathetic with feminist opposition to the practice, he argues that it might be a mistake for Israel's Jewish majority to push this issue from the outside lest they create a backlash in which men take a second wife as an act of political defiance.[54]

Despite such tactical recommendations, it is difficult to remain apathetic: a series of empirical studies confirm that polygamy has profoundly negative results on Bedouin women. First wives in polygamous families are left feeling rejected, suffering from phobias and depression. Low self-esteem and loneliness are common.[55] In one study, medical examinations revealed significantly higher incidence of adverse physical symptoms among wives in polygamous families relative to Bedouin women in monogamous relationships. These include somatization, nervousness, poor appetite, and memory disorders.[56] Findings also showed that when polygamous wives had numerous female children, their self-image suffered.

The damage is not just *physical* or *psychological*. A 2011 study of polygamous families by Ma'an, the Forum for Arab Women's Organizations in the Negev, showed that *economic* circumstances are significantly worsened for first Bedouin wives with the addition of a rival who competes for the husband's limited income. Men are more prone to abuse a first wife once they have an alternative. The study reported that there was strong "anti-polygamy sentiment" among Bedouin women, even as there was little way to express it in a heavily patriarchal society.[57]

A demonstration organized by Insaf Abu Shareb, public interest attorney and
advocate against polygamy, protests domestic violence in the Bedouin sector.
(Photograph courtesy of Eliahu Hershkovitz—ZOOM 77)

When Ma'an launched a "No Excuse for Polygamy" campaign, the response
of the Islamic clergy was swift. They called the feminists "infidels" in editorials
and accused them of serving a Zionist agenda by limiting Arab birthrates.
An advertisement in a Rahat paper encouraged women who were not married
by age thirty to find a husband to share. It read, "What is the solution for 7,513
unmarried women in the Negev over the age of 30? Polygamy: a sharia-sanctioned
solution!"[58]

Like the incipient movement to enjoin domestic violence, a growing number
of feminists in the Bedouin community are speaking out against polygamy. Abu
Shareb says that it is high time that the police get involved. If they would arrest
even a handful of husbands at openly polygamous weddings, it would transform
present dynamics.[59] Dr. Sarab Abu-Rabia-Queder is among the more-vociferous
advocates fighting the practice within the Bedouin community:

> A friend of my husband's got married to a second wife yesterday. I refused to
> go. I don't go to events associated with bigamy and neither do my children.
> He already has seven children. His second wife is 24. It's not like she's edu-
> cated or anything. He works and makes a good living. Why doesn't he invest

in the children he has? Then I was interviewed yesterday on the radio and I was particularly harsh. I said that the second wife in the Bedouin sector has become a man's plaything. Instead of going to a prostitute, a man takes a second wife. In a sense, he turns all the second and subsequent wives into whores. I once was at a conference with a Bedouin professor. He turned to the Jewish men attending and said: "Look, when you all grow tired of your wives in the Jewish sector you can go to strip teases or to escort services. We don't have that option. So we have a second wife." I thought that I was going to scream.[60]

Bedouin political leaders openly acknowledge a vicious cycle in which poverty creates large families that perpetuate privation. They also see empowerment of women as a key to development. In Rahat, Faiz Abu Sahiban believes that establishing cottage industries for Bedouin women constitutes the most promising way to lead his community out of poverty. "If Bedouin women today are becoming better educated than the men—maybe they can pull the men up!"[61]

"Bedouin women always worked," explains the Hura mayor Alnabari. "When they aren't productive and just consume they suffer from obesity and high blood pressure. Men today are frustrated that they have to work so hard to make all the family's income. But if you want to expand economic development in Bedouin communities: Don't talk to 'Muhammad' talk to 'Moses.'"[62]

Omar Abu Muamar, the Bedouin mayor of Segev Shalom, shares Alnabari's view. "More than Bedouin need contraception—they need jobs. I managed to bring a factory to our town that created 1,200 jobs. There are 400 women working in that factory. I am a citizen of Israel. I don't have any other country and I am not looking for one. But I expect there to be a much more significant investment in the Bedouin sector. The social services we can provide are very minimal. When I say I want to promote women's status it's because I believe in it. But I don't have the resources to do it. I expect Israel to invest more."

OF PALESTINIAN WOMBS AND DEMOGRAPHIC WEAPONS

Members of Israel's Jewish majority concerned about Arab fertility today have ample reasons to relax in the historic demographic "competition" with Israel's minority Arab citizens. The growing population of Palestinians living in the West Bank and the Gaza Strip, however, continues to worry many citizens. Given the area's profound religious meaning, many Zionists naturally were tempted to annex the West Bank after conquering it in the 1967 Six-Day War.[63] Yet they also realized that demographically it would create an existential problem. Annexation without granting civil rights to the 600,000 Palestinian residents would make a mockery out of Israel's democratic principles. At the same time, to extend civil rights to local residents would create a situation where 40 percent of Israel's citizens were a minority.[64] Given Palestinian birthrates at the time, this percentage was likely to increase. With much encouragement from political leaders for Palestinian motherhood and its contribution to the national struggle, it did.

Recently, the Palestinian Central Bureau of Statistics reported estimates that the number of Jews and Palestinians living between the Jordan River and the Mediterranean would be equal by 2016. According to this demographic projection, from that year on, Palestinians would outnumber Jews. (They also reported 11.6 million Palestinians worldwide, a biologically remarkable, and highly improbable, tenfold increase since 1948.)[65] There is a group of Israeli commentators associated with Israel's political right wing who challenge the veracity of these numbers. But Palestinian fertility by all objective standards has been extraordinary.

Over the years, Haifa University geography professor Arnon Soffer has spoken plainly about local demography, gaining him opprobrium and censure from left- and right-wing political advocates alike. Soffer was always candid about the problematic implications of absorbing sizable Palestinian populations if Israel wished to remain a Jewish and democratic state.[66]

As a long-time lecturer in Israel's security college, Soffer became a respected, no-nonsense advisor to top military brass, including General Ariel Sharon. Sharon was then elected prime minister as a tough, security-minded leader who had initiated the construction of dozens of settlements in the occupied territories. But Soffer knew that Sharon was a pragmatist and did not hesitate to share his demographic projections with him. Soffer would drive to Jerusalem for late-night intimate meetings at the prime minister's office and speak openly about the folly of annexation:

> I said to him: 'Arik—what are you doing in Gaza? Every three weeks they give birth to a Gush Katif (the string of Jewish settlements on the Gaza Coast). What are you doing in northern Samaria in places like Kedumim?' I guess Sharon listened to me. I'm on my way home from our meeting and I get a phone call. The Prime Minister is wondering whether Kedumim—should be included as part of a unilateral withdrawal?[67]

Sharon understood well that Gaza's 1,300,000 Palestinians had one of the highest birthrates and in the world and already then made up 99.4 percent of the Strip's population. In, 2005 Sharon announced Israel's unilateral withdrawal from Gaza. In August that year, the Israeli military began to forcibly evacuate the 1,700 families living in *Jewish* settlements there.[68] It was a controversial move that fueled a fierce national protest. But the Gaza debate is tame compared to the dispute over population dynamics in the West Bank.

Yoram Ettinger was an accountant, recruited by Prime Minister Yitzhak Shamir in the 1980s to serve as consul to Houston, Texas, and later head of the government press office. Retiring in 1992, like many Israelis with right-wing political orientations he wished to promote annexation of the West Bank. After considering the basis for official statistics, he decided it was time to turn the "demographic time bomb" on its head.[69]

In 2002 Ettinger wrote an article for the daily *Yedioth Ahronot*, in which he criticized the accuracy of the population estimates produced by the Palestinian Authority. He found the 2.7 million figure to be inflated. Bennett Zimmerman, a data analyst from the United States, heard about Ettinger's arguments and was intrigued. Zimmerman was a frequent visitor to the West Bank. After driving through Palestinian towns, he felt that they were not as crowded as he had been led to believe. He also intuitively sensed that the population numbers were grossly overestimated.

Zimmerman proposed a partnership. With the help of colleagues they established the American-Israel Demographic Research Group. The group began to systematically review the data that had accrued over the years, especially from the twelve locations from which it was legally permitted to exit Israel: from the Haifa port to Ben Gurion Airport, and from the Allenby Bridge to the Arava Crossings into Jordan.[70] They published a detailed report entitled "The Million Person Gap: The Arab Population in the West Bank and Gaza."[71] Zimmerman and his team of skeptics claimed three fundamental flaws with the prevailing population estimates for the West Bank. The first involved Jerusalem residents. After Israel annexed Jerusalem in 1967 it began to relate to Palestinian residents there as Israeli citizens. Their numbers were added to Arab Israeli figures when calculating the size of ethnic minorities. But the Palestinian Authority never recognized this annexation and continued to count the 210,000 citizens of East Jerusalem in its own census. Essentially Jerusalem's Arabs were counted twice.

The second point involved the baseline numbers and sampling procedures used by the Palestinian Central Bureau of Statistics when it conducted its 1997 census. The bureau estimated the Arab population of the West Banka and Gaza in 1997 to be 2.7 million. The report argued that the Palestinians had strayed from standard procedures in census taking. When counting heads, individuals who have not lived in a country for more than a year typically are no longer considered as belonging to the local population. The report claimed that the official Palestinian population records did just that, including 325,000 former residents who had long since left the West Bank and Gaza.

Finally, they challenged the formula for growth projections, arguing that extrapolating from other more-reliable data bases (for example, school registration or electoral registers) yielded a much lower number. The report estimated that the difference came to 648,000 persons fewer than the official Palestinian figure. In an April 2013 op-ed for the daily *Israel Today*, Ettinger brought these points to bear in challenging the message of demographic realism that U.S. President Obama put to the Israeli people during his visit to the country:

> In 1898, the leading Jewish demographer/historian, Simon Dubnov, projected a meager 500,000 Jews in the Land of Israel by the year 2000. In 1944, the founder of Israel's Central Bureau of Statistics and the guru of contemporary Israeli demographers and statisticians, Professor Roberto Bacchi, projected only 2.3 million Jews in Israel by 2001, a 34% minority. On October 23, 1987, Hebrew University's demographer Professor Sergio Della Pergola, told Yedioth Ahronoth that no substantial immigration was expected from the USSR, but one million Olim arrived. In a September 2006 article, Professor Soffer projected that by 2011 there would be 4.5 million Arabs in Judea and Samaria, double the number published in 2011 by the Palestinian Central Bureau of Statistics—2.6 million. And, in fact, the Palestinian number was inflated by one million Arabs: 400,000 overseas residents; a double count of 300,000 Jerusalem Arabs, who are counted as Arab Israelis and as West Bankers. . . . In defiance of the demographic profession, the annual number of Israel's Jewish births has surged by 62.5% from 1995 (80,400) to 2012 (130,000), while the annual number of Arab Israeli births has been stable at around 40,000 annually. . . . Anyone suggesting that Jews are doomed to become a minority west of the Jordan River is either dramatically mistaken or outrageously misleading.[72]

Not surprisingly, the revised estimates were immediately embraced by Israeli right-wing politicians, journalists, and West Bank settlers[73] while scorned by Palestinian supporters.[74] Likud parliamentarian and West Bank resident Tzipi Hotovely declared that naturalization of West Bank Palestinians would not affect Israel's Jewish majority. Naftali Bennett, chair of Israel's religious party The Jewish Home happily adopted the lower figures, pronouncing, "There are 1.5 million Palestinians in the West Bank and 400,000 settlers and nobody's going anywhere."[75]

The Palestinian Central Bureau of Statistics was quick to dismiss the critique. There have been two official Palestinian censuses to date, in 1997 and 2007, both supervised by the Norwegian government.[76] The bureau's press release explained that Ettinger's claims were simply untrue: in fact it always excluded Palestinians living abroad, even when they carried Palestinian identity cards.[77]

Israel's leading demographers acknowledge the "double counting" of Jerusalem's Palestinians to be a fair point, but they generally reject Ettinger's estimates as unreliable and simplistic.[78] They are quick to point out that no trained demographer with an expertise in the region supports the alternative numbers[79] and that Palestinian birthrates remain 10 percent higher than Israeli birthrates. Israeli estimates in fact are made independent of Palestinian sources and rely on a 1997 baseline derived from Israeli sources of 2.6 million people living in the West Bank and Gaza.[80] Professor DellaPergola wonders why the detractors' calculations do not include 180,000 foreign workers and more than 300,000 non-Jewish immigrants who continue to make up a significant percentage of the people utilizing the Law of Return. At most, he reckons that any overcounting due to Palestinian foreign residency comes to 100,000 people, hardly a game changer.[81]

The revised projections of the American-Israel Demographic Research Group also tend to underestimate the effect of "population momentum" among Palestinians whose population is so much younger than Israel's (56 percent under age twenty-four). They also conveniently overestimate future Jewish immigration to Israel. Arab birthrates are not as high as in the past, but the low death rate means that the population continues to grow significantly. While Ettinger and his colleagues highlight gaps between registered voters in the West Bank and projected adult population, it is estimated that only 72 percent of Palestinians are registered to vote in the first place.[82] Moreover, their critique conveniently ignores Gaza, with its 1.7 million Palestinians and 3 percent annual growth rate. Boasting a robust fertility rate of 4.4 children in 2014, birthrates may be dropping. But 43.5 percent of Gazans are still under the age of fourteen![83]

While there is much disagreement, it would seem that all sides might agree on the following synopsis of Israeli/Palestinian demographic dynamics: Palestinian birthrates are slowing, but its population will continue to expand for years to come. At the same time, unless Israel's own population suddenly stops growing, with Gaza now out of the Israeli demographic equation, it is unlikely that Palestinians will come to "outnumber" Israelis any time soon. Yet, when Israel's Arab citizens are added to the Palestinian side of the ledger, the numbers grow closer. For the foreseeable future, between the Jordan River and the Mediterranean Sea, Jewish Israelis should retain a slim numeric majority.

SUSTAINABILITY VERSUS CONFLICT

Israel's Bedouin community has not only grown in its demographic dimensions during the past half century. Forced to leave a nomadic and subsistence economy that changed little over the millennia, its traditional norms and lifestyle were pushed beyond anything previously imaginable. Bedouin Israelis continue to scramble to find a satisfactory place in their high-paced, competitive, postindustrial country. Ready or not for modernity—here it comes. When viewed in this context, the collective achievements of the community and those of thousands of individual Bedouins are truly exceptional.

Nonetheless, societal indicators suggest that progress in Israel's Bedouin community has fallen short and that their present reality is unacceptable. Israel became much more prosperous; most Bedouins did not. They remain the poorest and least educated sector in Israel. In a sense, they have been left behind. One of the most incomplete parts of their societal transition involves the status of Bedouin women. More than a symptom of the community's deprived social circumstances, it is the cause as well as the primary driver behind high fertility rates.

Of course there has been progress, but it remains woefully inadequate. Tens of thousands of Israeli females in the peripheral Negev region find themselves citizens in a country that expects them to take part fully in the twenty-first century but does not provide them with the protection, training, or support to do so. Bedouin women face the combined burden of minority status within Israeli society, and subjugation inside their own community.

It is time for the Israeli government to launch a serious intervention to change this.[84] Any real improvement needs to start with enhancing economic opportunities for Bedouin citizens in Israel. At the same time, Israel needs to temper its historic regard for cultural sensitivities that de facto grant a carte blanche to ethnic customs that discriminate so severely on the basis of gender. It is time to prioritize the human rights of Israel's most oppressed people.

The growing number of Bedouin women now in universities suggests that when given equal opportunities a transformation will not take long. A key part of bringing progress to the community involves giving women a real say in when and whom they marry, the number of wives their husbands wed, and the number of children they bear. There is not a Bedouin mayor in the country who does not openly declare that an a priori condition for moving beyond today's crippling poverty levels is reduced fertility. Managing family size is a prerequisite for a sustainable and healthy Bedouin society.

Parliamentarian Basel Ghattas has great familiarity with the Bedouin community, having overseen mobile health units in the Negev in unrecognized villages for over fifteen years. "I can tell you that Bedouin are also starting to demand education. Although they presently have a very high birthrate, in a matter of a decade they will start to look like the general Arab population. The reduction of child subsidies may even affect the birthrates among Bedouin who are polygamous."[85]

Family planning has already begun to change Palestinian-Israeli dynamics. The politics of population historically was a central tenet of Palestinian national ideology. Yasser Arafat's frequently quoted reference to his secret weapon being the "Palestinian mother's womb" came to epitomize the significance ascribed to the demographic battle.[86] Palestinians called for *sumud* (steadfastness)—a code word that came to mean a commitment to stay put and not emigrate, notwithstanding the strains of living under Israeli occupation.[87] But like Arab Israelis, the Palestinian people are no longer buying this rhetoric. Revisionist demographers like Yoram Ettinger are correct in highlighting a dramatic drop in the Palestinian birthrate. He is wrong, however, regarding its implications.

The ongoing politicization of demography will only hurt the prospects for conflict resolution in the region. Urging Jews to take advantage of the lull in Arab fertility by boosting their own birthrates creates a race to the bottom that will exacerbate tensions as well as social and environmental impacts caused by excess population density. Whether or not Jews can succeed in retaining a slim numeric majority over Arabs offers little ethical basis for justifying Israeli control over the lives of millions of Palestinians. Furthermore, the tragic divisions and unspeakable violence that has been the fate of Lebanon and Syria suggests that large ethnic minorities are not a formula for stability in the Middle East.

The recent drop in Palestinian birthrates is excellent news, but not because it allows Israel to cement its domination. Rather, it disabuses the minority of belligerent Palestinians of any delusions about demographic ascendency. It offers the possibility of a stabilized region and reconciliation. After a century of strife, common visions of sustainability need to inform the stormy relations between these neighbors, replacing any dreams of a future human deluge that will lead to national triumph. Neither side will be better off with more people.

—◆◆—

CARRYING CAPACITY—PAST AND PRESENT

Now Lot, who was moving about with Abram, also had flocks and
herds and tents. But the land could not support them while they
stayed together, for their possessions were so great that they were
not able to remain together.
—Genesis 13:5

CARRYING CAPACITY 101

How many people *can* live in the land of Israel? How many people *should*
live in the land of Israel? The first question is the focus of the present chapter,
while the subsequent chapter considers the second question. In both cases, the
answer depends on criteria and values. There are, of course, objective measures
to help answer such subjective and ultimately ideologically laden queries. No
matter the criterion preferred, there is a limit.

The book of Genesis (1:28) commands humans to be fruitful, multiply, and
fill up the land. The phrasing *milu et haaretz* (fill up the earth) implies that the
land can be full and maximum capacity eventually reached. In theory, there
comes a time when the mission is accomplished and human population should
stop growing. But no clear biblical standard exists for explaining what this carrying capacity is or how it might be measured.[1]

Ecology was the first discipline that translated the general notion of carrying
capacity from theory into quantifiable calculations. Ecologists define carrying
capacity as the largest number of organisms a particular environment can support without reducing its ability to support the same population size of that same
species in the future.[2] Usually, a species will increase its numbers, following a
logistic growth curve, until available resources dwindle, when the upper bounds
of food supply are reached and population levels off. At this point birthrates and

death rates equalize. In equations that represent this interaction, "carrying capacity" is denoted as the variable "K."[3]

People utilize resources in very different ways. Whether or not a society is living within its means depends on whether it is rich or poor, ostentatious or modest, profligate or thrifty, technologically efficient or wasteful, and how aware it is of ecological limits.[4] For instance, in a country like Bangladesh, where the local diet is primarily rice, beans, vegetables, and fruit, a family can live on less than half a hectare of land (1.25 acres). An American family that on average eats 123 kilograms of meat each year will need an area twenty times larger.[5] Societies sensitive to environmental quality or that seek to preserve biological diversity will face entirely different constraints than those that have no compunction about sacrificing species or pristine places to maintain or improve their standard of living. E. O. Wilson, the eminent ecologist, calculated that the present arable lands on the planet could produce enough wheat to feed 10 billion people indefinitely. But that number of humans would have to limit themselves to a vegetarian regime. If they opt for a meat-rich diet, Wilson reckons the earth can only support 2.5 billion people[6]—about one-third of present numbers.

There are, of course, those who mistakenly argue that "carrying capacity" is not relevant for modern civilization, given human beings' astonishing ability to adapt and innovate.[7] This is particularly common among economists, whose entire discipline is predicated on an assumption of never-ending growth.[8] Among the most outspoken of these "cornucopian" advocates was the late Julian Simon, who championed humans' unlimited potential for growth. Simon once claimed that existing technology was sufficient to feed, clothe, and supply energy to a growing population for the next 7 billion years. When informed that a 1 percent growth rate would produce a population of 9.99×10^{99}, an unimaginably large number, he sheepishly acknowledged that he had meant 7 million years. But at a 1 percent growth rate, in only 17,000 years, the world's population would be larger than the number of atoms in the universe![9] Any rational person intuitively understands that biological systems cannot grow forever. There are thresholds that should not be crossed.

In the past it was not only such "technological optimists" who eschewed notions of limits but also "theological optimists." Judaism historically contained a school of thought that found questions of carrying capacity immaterial, especially in the land of Israel, based on a blind faith that the good Lord would provide. This perspective remains a powerful force today in the thinking of many Israelis, particularly the Orthodox and ultra-Orthodox Jewish sectors.

The Talmud contains a heated argument about the number of people who can live inside the country's borders: "Said Rabbi Judah in the name of Rabbi

Assi: 'King Yanai had sixty times ten thousand townships on HaMelech Mountain; each of them was as numerous as those who had come out of Egypt. . . .' Said Ula: 'I have seen that place and it cannot contain even sixty times ten thousand reeds.' Said a Zadoki to Rabbi Hanina: 'You lie!' Said Rabbi Hanina: 'It is called the 'Land of the Gazelle. Just as the skin of the gazelle does not confine its flesh, so is the Land of Israel: when it is inhabited—it has ample space. And when it is not inhabited, it contracts.'"[10] The exchange led to the "land of the gazelle" becoming an epithet for the land of Israel.

Another passage in the Talmud offers a similar message of unlimited horizons, describing the miraculous ability of the Holy Temple to expand and accommodate whatever number of people came to pray: "Rabbi Yehudah taught in the name of Rav that in the days when the Jewish people came on pilgrimages to Jerusalem during the three festivals, even though. . . . they would stand (in the Temple courtyard) crowded in, when it came time to bow down there was space between them. This is one of the ten miracles that took place in the Temple."[11]

Like many topics considered by Jewish sages, an opposite position was not only tolerated but advocated. When descending from the ethereal, spiritual realm to the practical challenges facing agrarian societies, issues of carrying capacity were highly germane, especially given pervasive water scarcity. Solutions were often pragmatic. The religious prohibition on marital relations during famine was precisely the remedy for overpopulation repeated by Thomas Malthus centuries later.[12] The ancient rabbis were quite cognizant of the terrible price paid by unsustainable population growth. Perhaps the first passage in Scripture that makes it clear that the environment's physical limits need to be respected involves the biblical patriarch Abraham—or "Abram" (as he was known in his early days), who dispassionately faced classic carrying capacity dynamics. In Genesis 13:5, Abram takes preemptive measures to prevent the kind of overgrazing and ecological collapse that wiped out other myopic ancient civilizations and their herders.[13] "And quarreling arose between Abram's herders and Lot's. . . . So Abram said to Lot, 'Let's not have any quarreling between you and me, or between your herders and mine, for we are close relatives. Is not the whole land before you? Let's part company.'"

Over the centuries, assessments about carrying capacity and appropriate constraints for human population began to diverge, with two fundamentally different approaches emerging: The first sees carrying capacity as linked to local sustainability and agricultural subsistence. The second views geopolitical boundaries as irrelevant, evaluating carrying capacity within a global context. This chapter considers the former, local perspective.

In a sense, a "closed system" analysis imagines a given place or jurisdiction as separated from the rest of the planet, like an area suddenly encased by an enormous bubble. It then considers what would happen if this country or city were completely shut off from material flows: How many people could live there? What would life be like? This *closed* paradigm defines carrying capacity according to the quantity (and quality) of available natural resources. It can also assess whether sufficient energy is available to support the prevailing economy and lifestyle, so that internal order can be maintained in the face of entropic decay.[14] These kinds of assessments typically ask whether adequate environmental "sinks" are available within the system to absorb all discharged wastes. Most importantly, it evaluates whether there is ample land and water for producing the food, fiber, and materials needed for local human consumption. Under such restricted conditions, cities could not function and residents would not survive for very long.

The alternative view does not attribute significance to the actual borders of a given community or state when considering carrying capacity. In a global economy, importing locally unavailable resources or technologies is manifest. Places like Singapore, Hong Kong, and most European nations have robust economies by importing "surplus" biocapacity from other lands. They acquire food, fuel, and raw materials in return for cash. These societies depend on the "global hinterland" of ecologically productive landscapes. It is in fact ironic that practically all economies that rely solely on their own food production are in developing countries.

Before pondering the implication of the present food supply on potential population levels, it is well to consider the past. This chapter opens by considering the question: How many people lived in Israel during its different historic periods before the advent of global trade that allowed for the meaningful importation of calories? It then reviews the initial deliberations about the land's potential absorptive capacity. Self-sufficiency was the starting point for traditional discussions about carrying capacity levels. A society's ability to provide itself with energy and food was deemed fundamental to its long-term survival. For a brief period during the first half of the twentieth century, whether the land of Israel could provide food and a decent living for a rapidly growing population was the subject of fierce debate. The argument still casts a shadow on present discussions of carrying capacity.

ISRAEL'S DEMOGRAPHY THROUGHOUT THE AGES

The actual number of people who lived in Palestine in days gone by is not entirely clear. What is clear, however, is that population fluctuations were frequent and substantial. Until recently the historical record was relatively silent, although occasional clues can be gleaned from ancient sources that contribute to seemingly "objective" estimates. Josephus, the Jewish general who chronicled the Romans' "Jewish War" cited an earlier estimate of 120,000 men who lived in Jerusalem during the fourth century B.C.[15] Four hundred years later, he reported 2.7 million contemporaries residing within the confines of Jerusalem in 70 A.D. during the Roman siege.[16] Most historians find this figure to be highly unlikely. The first century Roman senator and historian Tacitus wrote about the same Jerusalem population as comprising but 600,000.[17] Military intelligence shared by Josephus telling of 60,000 Jewish warriors massing in the north may be more reliable, leading some scholars to extrapolate a Galilee population of 750,000. Other experts believe that numbers might have swelled further still, reaching 2.5 million people during Roman rule of Palestine (circa 100 A.D.) before the unceremonious exile of the rebellious Jewish natives.[18]

The first serious archaeologist to consider the issue systematically was Johns Hopkins University professor William Albright. After an exhaustive examination of sources and excavation sites, he calculated that in the Roman-Byzantine period, during the first centuries A.D., Palestine's population may have reached 4 million.[19] Roberto Bachi, Israel's first academic demographer, was more conservative. Bachi only felt comfortable quoting estimates approximating 1.8 million people in the land of Israel during the time of King David (960 B.C.).

Other scholars, like Magen Broshi, a curator at Jerusalem's Shrine of the Book, and archaeologist Yigal Shiloh find the demographic estimates appearing in *all* the ancient literary sources (including the Bible) to be "invariably untrustworthy" and inflated. Based on archaeological findings and sundry estimates of carrying capacity, such as wheat consumption and water resources, Broshi argues that the population could never have exceeded 1 million, even during the relatively prosperous Byzantine period (600 A.D.).[20]

Initial population size in ancient agrarian Canaan was far more modest. Demographic appraisals from the Chalcolithic period to the end of the Middle Bronze Age (4,000–1,600 B.C.) estimate that as larger hamlets began to be settled, population grew from 14,000 to 37,000, mostly concentrating on the coastal plains.[21] Tel Aviv University historian Oded Lipschits meticulously reviewed the evidence for the subsequent period and reached the conclusion that at the end of the Iron Age (around 700 B.C.) there were only 108,000 people in Palestine. The noted Duke University archaeologist Eric Meyers also considered the size of Palestine's population from the Hellenistic to the Roman periods. He confirms that until the end of the first century A.D., there could only have been between 750,000 and 1 million residents in Palestine.[22]

Whatever the actual peak numbers were, they were surely ephemeral. Population size waxed and waned, reflecting the vicissitudes of a life in a harsh and unstable *physical* environment. The intermittently volatile *political* environment undoubtedly influenced population density even more over the centuries, with conquerors alternately slaughtering locals or leading them away as slaves. Hebrew University archaeologist Michael Avi-Yonah wrote about the demographic aftermath of one such revolt against the Romans that ended in A.D. 136: "In comparing the rates of density of settlement in the various parts of the country, we arrive at an estimate of the total Jewish Population of Palestine before the war of Bar Kochba as 1,300,000. After the fall of Beth-Ter there were left only between seven and eight hundred thousand, of which three and four hundred thousand were concentrated in the Galilee. These rough estimates indicate the full extent of the disaster which befell Jewry in the Bar Kokhba war."[23]

No matter how ruthless the generals were, invading armies ultimately were *less* deadly than germs. For instance, the great 1515 plague that hit Palestine left only 150,000 surviving residents. It was a shrunken and feeble Palestinian population that the Ottoman Empire encountered a year later after defeating the armies of the Mamluk Sultanate. Local communities slowly rebounded, but two hundred years later disease struck again. This time 225,000 made it through the Black Death's bubonic pandemic.[24] The population remained depleted well into the nineteenth century, when it finally reached 350,000.[25] (This modest number is comparable to immigration during Israel's first two years.)

The number of inhabitants living in Israel over the ages may never be known with certainty. It apparently ranged from a low of 30,000 to a peak that never exceeded 2.5 million. One million is a likely maximum population size in Palestine before the modern era. As the volatile twentieth century launched a new era of national competition, the salient focus moved from the past to the future and became "How many people *could* live in this challenging land?" Typically the question was interpreted more narrowly: How many people could the land of Israel feed? Diplomatic circumstances following the advent of the British Mandate transformed the issue from an esoteric discourse among historians and agronomists to a central controversy in the period's raging political conflict.

THE POLITICS OF "ABSORPTIVE CAPACITY"

By 1922 Great Britain was facing pressure from Arab leaders in Palestine to limit Jewish immigration.[26] The Mandate's colonial officials, responsible for maintaining order, were caught between Foreign Secretary Lord Balfour's public political commitment "to view with favour the establishment in Palestine of a national home for the Jewish People" and the volatile Arab majority that found such prospects intolerable. Confronted with a possible flood of eastern European Jews wishing to exchange poverty and anti-Semitism for their ancestral homeland, the number of immigrants allowed into Palestine became the operational mechanism for supporting one side's national claim or the other's. British officials sought an objective formula to demonstrate neutrality and defuse the explosive dynamics. Making the country's "absorptive capacity" the basis for immigration quotas offered a dispassionate, technocratic way out. After all, it was only logical that Palestine shouldn't accept more immigrants than the land could absorb.[27]

Palestinian environmental studies scholar Samer Alatout wryly notes that by adopting a "scientific, technical determinant for allowing or preventing immigration, the British rendered insignificant Arab Palestinian objections based on moral-historic logic."[28] The Jewish leadership in Palestine at the time, however, found the orientation to be refreshing, providing an opportunity to establish an objective basis for increasing immigration quotas. Carrying capacity was an issue that Zionists had already started thinking about. They harbored ambitious visions about bringing scores of Jews to the land and "making the wastelands bloom." Privately, they were also uncertain themselves whether mass migration was viable. By the second half of the nineteenth century, a variety of experts (or would-be experts) were offering estimates of how many people Palestine could absorb. The numbers ranged dramatically from 1 to 15 million.[29]

Ironically, the Zionists could rely on an iconic report by *British* experts for optimistic projections. At the end of the nineteenth century, no one knew Palestine better than Charles Warren and Claude Conder, British officers, cartographers, and amateur archaeologists. The duo mapped and surveyed the length and breadth of the Holy Land between 1875 and 1878 on behalf of the London-based Palestine Exploration Fund. The experience left them with unparalleled familiarity with the country's topography, geology, water resources, and agricultural productivity. Despite the destitute conditions, they were decidedly optimistic. Warren would eventually attain the military rank of general in the Second Boer War and is mostly remembered as London's hapless chief of police in the unsuccessful hunt for the elusive "Jack the Ripper." Long before these milestones, in 1875 he published a pamphlet, *The Land of Promise,* in which he ruminated, "Give Palestine a good government and increase the commercial life of the people, and they may increase tenfold and yet there is room. Its productiveness will increase in proportion to labour bestowed on the soil until a population of 15 million may be accommodated there."[30]

Zionist advocates seized on this number. Forty years later, in 1915, after being summarily banished from the Ottoman Empire during World War I, David Ben-Gurion and Israel's second president, Yitzhak Ben-Zvi, hunkered down in the New York Public Library to address the issue. In a rambling Yiddish tome, based on Warren's observations, the two argued that Palestine could easily support 10 million people.[31] (Arab leaders preferred Yale geography professor Ellsworth Huntington's 1911 monograph, which posited that climatic conditions made for extremely modest, local carrying capacity levels.)[32]

Even within the upbeat Zionist camp, there were plenty of prudent planners who sensed that a 15-million-person objective was an emotional and intuitive "guesstimate" lacking empirical rigor. They worried that without industrial infrastructure and job opportunities, such numbers were unthinkable for the foreseeable future.[33] Food security was the primary concern, with agronomic projections relying on the quantity of land available and potential economic yields.[34]

Looking beyond Palestine's borders offered helpful examples for crafting arguments favoring higher populations, densities, and carrying capacities. Sicily was considered an excellent model. At twenty-nine thousand square kilometers, it was only slightly smaller than the British Mandate's territories (thirty thousand square kilometers) and climatically had comparable Mediterranean conditions. At the advent of the twentieth century it was home to 3.7 million people. (Today Sicily is holding stable at 5 million.) Neighboring Lebanon was also a source of encouragement. Its 133-people-per-kilometer density in the early 1900s was more than five times higher than Palestine's, while its climate and countryside were comparable.[35]

One methodology for generating absorptive capacity estimates involves extrapolation. Looking backward, archaeologists were justifiably confident that many more people had inhabited the land in days of old than were living in early-twentieth-century Palestine. While naturally given to higher projections, there were still limits. Trained as a botanist, World Zionist Organization chairman Otto Warburg was literate in agricultural minutiae. He accepted the appraisal of German scholars who saw 3 million as an absolute upper boundary for any retrospective census. This offered a sound basis for a tenfold increase in population size.

Naturally, official experts working for the Mandate were more downbeat. British colonial secretary Sydney Webb's oft-quoted 1929 declaration that there was "no room to swing a cat in Palestine"[36] belied the government's aversion to Jewish demographic objectives. The British government's Hope-Simpson Commission went through the motions of hearing the different parties' capacity estimates. But its report ridicules Jabotinsky's claim that 16,000 square kilometers of farmland could be cultivated, as "guesswork." (Zionist settlement maven Arthur Ruppin's 12,500-square-kilometer figure was given slightly more serious credence.) Ultimately the commission reached its own conclusions. Hoping to avoid expanded immigration quotas, it held that only 6,544 square kilometers was available. This constituted roughly 20 percent of the total lands in the Mandate.[37]

As for the quality of agricultural production, it was recognized that in this dryland environment, irrigation would be crucial for expanding "absorptive capacity." U.S. Supreme Court justice Louis Brandeis helped recruit H. T. Cory, among his country's most reputable water engineers, to consider the matter. Cory calculated how Palestine's carrying capacity might benefit from massive hydro-initiatives, like the Colorado River and Imperial Valley projects he had designed in the American West.[38] Given the state-of-the-art farming and irrigation practices of the time, Zionist planners argued that 112,000 economically viable family homesteads could be established immediately. The British scoffed at such estimates. Yet the high yields produced in the Zionist settlements, especially along the coastal plain, offered empirical evidence that such visions were not entirely exaggerated. The refashioned Jewish farmers in Palestine brought new ideas and technologies, replacing the age-old (but less efficient) agricultural practices that endured from pre-Ottoman times.

During a 1938 fact-finding visit to Palestine, William Lowdermilk, a renowned soil scientist from the U.S. Department of Agriculture, reported:

> We were astonished to find about three hundred colonies defying great hardships and applying the principles of co-operation and soil conservation to the old Land of Israel. This effort is the most remarkable we have seen while studying land use in twenty-four countries. It is being made by Jewish settlers who fled to Palestine. . . . The country is emerging from a backward low-yield agricultural economy, dependent chiefly on grains and olives, and is evolving towards a modern, scientifically directed and richly diversified economy with fruits, vegetables, poultry and dairy products playing an ever greater role.[39]

Lowdermilk concluded that with ambitious water management, Palestine could support 4 million people.

The 1931 government census of Palestine acknowledged that "the annual increase of subsistence" was rising rapidly due to the novel technologies adopted in the Zionist settlements. But this sort of technocratic assessment was not in line with a tight-fisted immigration policy. A year earlier, the Hope-Simpson Commission's assessment was less complimentary about the viability of Jewish agriculture, holding that "there are few if any of the settlements which are truly self-supporting."[40] British bottom-line capacity calculations continued to err on the side of caution. Undoubtedly, the low figures helped rationalize the sealing of Palestine's gates to the millions of European refugees who were then desperately seeking asylum.

The gloomy British projections enjoyed "philosophical" validation in the writings of Thomas Malthus. The English minister and economist had been dead for almost a century, but his views about human misery caused by excessive population growth informed the thinking of the elite who ran the country. Major E. Mills was the British statistician who oversaw the Mandate's census that so informed demographic policy. Mills was keenly aware of Malthus's theories and cited them as a basis for policy prescriptions. The Palestinian census "did not dispute" the Malthusian principle that arithmetic increases in subsistence alongside geometric population increases would lead to disastrous results.[41]

Once the implications of such stingy evaluations on immigration quotas became clear, Zionists, for tactical reasons, found it unwise to get caught on the "slippery slope" of absorptive capacity estimates based solely on agricultural constraints. By the 1930s they preferred to characterize "absorptive capacity" as a constantly evolving concept, increasingly dominated by nonagrarian, economic ventures. Unlike in historic Palestine, most of the residents in the Palestine of the future would not make their living directly from the land, but from industry. It was already clear that to support a large population, the anticipated Jewish state would need to be part of a global economy, relying on imported natural resources and exported products. Accordingly, it was ill-advised to assign clear ceilings on the number of possible residents.

Arthur Ruppin, who oversaw Zionist settlement in pre-state Palestine for much of this critical period, liked to use a transportation metaphor: "A land is not a steamship or railway car that has a place for so many people. The absorptive capacity of land changes with the productive conditions of each era. In theory, one could describe a hypothetical situation when optimal productivity conditions in Palestine would obtain so that the land could absorb all 15,000,000 Jews living throughout the world. But this theoretical possibility has no bearing on the present."[42] Ruppin was a "realist." Pessimistic about absorptive capacity, he actually lobbied for the Jews of Germany to find homes in the United States and Latin America rather than in Palestine. But his was a minority stance.

With all due respect to Ruppin's integrity, his calculations did not generate the answers the Zionist movement wanted to hear. By the late 1930s, with the Holocaust unfolding and Europe "burning," Zionist leaders realized that there was no time for development to make incremental increases in the country's absorptive capacity. David Ben-Gurion, by then the most formidable Jewish politician in Palestine, set 5 million residents in Palestine as the new party line.[43] Economists, like Alfred Bonne, were hired as consultants, positing that it was "far easier for the new immigrant to obtain a decent livelihood in congenial surroundings in urban occupations than in agriculture."[44] Although it fought alongside Nazi Germany, Japan was deemed a worthy model for emulation, having made a swift transition from an agrarian economy to an industrial one. Zionists began to reframe their estimates in "maximal" rather than "optimal" terms.

Ben-Gurion had not yet conceded his vision of an agricultural nation that could feed itself. In presenting his views to the British government's Peel Commission in 1936, he conveyed the utmost urgency about the measures that had to be taken to increase the country's "absorptive capacity":

> No square inch of land shall we neglect; not one source of water shall we fail to tap; not a swamp that we shall not drain; not a sand dune that we shall not fructify; not a barren hill that we shall not cover with trees; nothing shall we leave untouched. Set free from the Mandate which enchains our trade, under a Jewish Government whose first consideration will be the increase of the absorptive capacity of the country, assisted by its position of vantage at the cor-

Soon to be Israel's first prime minister, David Ben-Gurion in 1946 presents his ambitious calculations regarding Palestine's carrying capacity at the hearings of the Anglo-American Committee of Inquiry in Jerusalem. (David B. Keidan Collection of Digital Images, Central Zionist Archives)

nerstone of three continents and on the sea coast, there will develop a Jewish industry to whose growth we can set no limits.[45]

In retrospect, all of these early calculations were flawed; neither the definitions nor the estimates for "absorptive capacity" during the Mandate period considered long-term sustainability. For instance, the first British High Commissioner to Palestine, Herbert Samuel, established an array of criteria for determining the Mandate's practical interim capacity. It included demand for labor, unemployment levels, foreseeable projects, and so on. Environmental impacts were not part of the evaluation. No one at that time imagined that overzealous pumping of groundwater from an aquifer vulnerable to seawater intrusion might cause massive contamination or that human settlement could fragment habitat sufficiently to threaten dozens of local species with extinction. A crisis in Europe and a bona fide Arab revolt in Palestine were far too distracting for anyone to pay notice to such possible abuse.[46]

Ultimately, the British decision to limit immigration quotas to twelve thousand people per year in the 1930s and 1940s had *nothing* to do with available places of employment or potential yields and *everything* to do with calming the clash of competing national aspirations.[47] The entire episode and cynicism it represented did little to enhance British credibility or demographic limits in general.

In retrospect, carrying capacity is still seen by many Zionists as a ruse—a disingenuous subterfuge that eighty years ago allowed the Mandate to stonewall Jewish national efforts. According to this view, much of the Holocaust could have been averted but for trumped-up British limits on Jewish growth and settlement in Palestine. Memories from the period and its politicized absorptive capacity debate do not make dispassionate efforts to evaluate Israel's carrying capacity easier today.

BEYOND LIMITS

David Ben-Gurion, a confirmed atheist, once jested, "Our sages warned us not to rely on miracles. It is especially forbidden to rely on miracles in this age when they take place before our very eyes almost on a daily basis."[48] Such ebullient optimism signaled that the age of "absorptive capacity" as a basis for demographic policies was over. Israeli planners during the 1950s adopted the prime minister's blind faith in the new nation's wondrous, expanding economy: no longer bound by the prudence of rational capacity calculations, Israel's development ethos was touted in newspapers, on the floor of the Knesset, and in classrooms of the first generation of Israeli schoolchildren.[49]

Well aware of Malthus's gloomy predictions, the ruling Labor Zionist ideology during Israel's first decades summarily rejected demographic pessimism as archaic in light of the stunning technological advances of the twentieth century. Chief among these was the ability to generate food at levels previously unimaginable. Israel's leaders waxed enthusiastic about the country's newfound ability to cultivate what was hitherto considered marginal and unproductive land.[50]

According to Zionist dogma of the time, if population levels appeared high, the problem was not exceeding capacity but social organization. Millions of people on the planet suffered even as they were surrounded by plentiful natural resources.[51] The Labor Zionist dismissal of Malthusian theory was consistent with general Marxist views on the subject. It held that when societies are designed equitably, technology can produce demographic expansion with no detrimental side effects.[52] Once again, Zionists looked to other nations for successful models that justified unlimited growth. The economies of Holland and Denmark produced a high standard of living despite a dearth of natural resources. Maximum utilization of land for cultivation combined with fair allocation of resources offered a sure formula for abundance.[53]

Israel's economic development policies during the first decades of independence reflected this can-do optimism.[54] A new conceptual master plan published in 1951 envisioned hundreds of new agricultural settlements scattered across the country, which would be home for 16 percent of a 2.6-million-person populace.[55] It would only take fifteen years for the vision to become a reality.[56] Due to collective sacrifice, despite a doubling of population during Israel's first decade, no one was starving. Before long, innovations in fertilizer application, pest control, and even nascent bioengineering produced a surplus.

It was a time of unusual common purpose and austere economic socialism. The cooperative effort produced remarkable results.[57] Within ten years of its establishment, the number of farming communities (*moshavim*) increased from 58 to 264; the number of kibbutzim almost doubled.[58] By 1960, Israel had become self-sufficient in food production. The country was still home to only 2 million people, and most everyone was poor, with an average annual per capita income of roughly thirteen hundred dollars.[59] Israel's status was very much that of a developing nation; lifestyles ranged between modest and spartan. Eggs, milk, and other staples were rationed by the state during its early years;[60] the amount of meat consumed was minimal. With the engine of immigration humming, it only took another twenty years for the country's population to double again. By 1980, the GNP had increased fourfold, easily outstripping demographic growth.

Water management and agriculture offered proof of concept for the "technological optimism" that was so central to Zionist identity.[61] Israel's first natural resource managers believed that hydrologically it was both efficient and equitable to take from the "rich" in the rainy north to help the "poor" lands of the arid south. Water from the Jordan River watershed was piped the length of the country for irrigation. For almost a decade, Israel invested some 80 percent of its infrastructure budget in a national water carrier which went on line in 1964.[62] Water delivery, the primary "bottleneck" in earlier rural development schemes, was suddenly reliable, with 500 billion liters pumped each year from the Sea of Galilee to irrigate degraded soils.[63] Agricultural users everywhere enjoyed water at subsidized rates. Sewage was treated in ever greater quantities and recycled by agricultural operations across the country, eventually adding 400 billion liters of water a year—an additional 33 percent—to the naturally available water resources.[64]

Israeli farmers became increasingly good at getting the maximum "crop for the drop." Bolstered by the astonishing efficacy of locally developed drip irrigation systems[65] and new plant strains, yields rapidly increased,[66] with agricultural production growing sixteenfold in sixty years.[67] Israel now produces twenty times more fruit *per person* than it did in its early years, and three times more vegetables.

Even in the twenty-first century, as climate change reduced Israel's annual precipitation,[68] water paradoxically became more abundant than ever. A 2002 government decision embraced desalination as the centerpiece of its new water management strategy. Impressive membrane technologies for filtering out salts, and efficiency innovations that capture released energy cut the associated expenses in half: a thousand liters of water now cost only fifty-five cents to produce.[69] Within a decade, the use of Mediterranean Sea water allowed the country to expand total water production by 50 percent for a price that was palatable for municipal and even some agricultural consumers. The country seemed to have beaten Malthusian limits through diligence, ingenuity, planning, technology, and imports.[70] The sky really seemed to be the limit.

The first sixty-eight years of Israeli history ostensibly vindicated Zionist leaders' insistence that the land of Israel was capable of supporting a population several times larger than conventional forecasts allowed. The country was transformed from an indigent agrarian backwater to a "postindustrial," start-up nation, with flourishing high-tech, bio-tech and clean-tech sectors. Its export economy is increasingly a function of human capital: a handful of smart people in the Tel Aviv suburb Ra'ananah think of a clever way to improve GPS navigation systems and then sell "Waze" to Google for a billion dollars.[71]

And yet, all is not well in the Promised Land. Policies so enthusiastically promoted by Ben-Gurion and his contemporaries produced loss as well as abundance. Population pressures, coupled with increasing consumption levels took their toll on Israel's resources. The natural capital that maintains life took eons to accrue but is quickly spent. The streams, groundwater, air, soil, ecosystems, and living space—by any objective standard—are worse off.[72] The law of unexpected consequences invariably raises its unsettling head. For instance, the miracle of wastewater reuse is creating a soil salinization disaster, with sodium concentrations in orchards doubling in less than a decade.[73] Some effluents eventually reach groundwater, causing contamination and potential health impacts.[74]

When the environment degrades, carrying capacity shrinks. At some point, physical constraints come into play and the land is unable to sustain a growing population. As the number of inhabitants reached new, unprecedented levels, the State of Israel woke to find it could no longer feed itself.

THE LOST IDEAL OF CALORIC SELF-SUFFICIENCY

Few people have studied human carrying capacity as thoroughly as American demographer Joel Cohen. In his fascinating book *How Many People Can the Earth Support?*[75] Cohen details methodologies for assessing global carrying capacity and disparate "maximum population estimates" proposed over the years. For instance, one popular approach assumes maximum densities based on the geographic properties of different global regions. Then it aggregates the total potential number of people from each region.[76]

The methodological menu he describes provides several possible ways to calculate Israel's carrying capacity.[77] Among these is the notion that a single constraint will eventually limit maximal population numbers. According to this approach, the most appropriate way for computing national carrying capacities in a small country like Israel involves calculating maximum population based on a single constraining parameter.[78] Generally, this involves food.

The idea surely is not new. In the nineteenth century, German chemist Justus Freiherr von Liebig proposed a "law of the minimum." The law holds that the population size of a species is limited by the resource in shortest supply.[79] Originally the concept was used to consider the nutrient constraints that restrict agriculture production. But the concept makes perfect sense as a paradigm for estimating the upper bounds of human population.

Traditional assessments of carrying capacity had a geographically finite perspective: a place was overpopulated if it was unable to support the people living there with the resources available within its boundaries. While technology, industriousness, and infrastructure investment could dramatically increase carrying capacity, there was still a bottom line: a country (or a community) unable to supply its own calories had too many people living there.

For many years, Israel's farm lobby and its patrons at the agricultural ministry espoused this time-honored perspective. In Israel's first decades, agricultural production truly outpaced population, and fruits and vegetables were a major export.[80] When farmers' decisions became driven by maximum profits rather than maximum calories, the pendulum began to swing the other way. There were soon many more mouths to feed. Nonetheless the farming establishment continued to perpetuate disinformation about agricultural self-sufficiency.[81] Even today, one can visit Web sites run by Israel's Ministry of Foreign Affairs and find patently misleading propaganda claiming that Israel produces most of its own food.[82]

The "myth" of Israeli nutritional self-sufficiency was challenged long ago. In 2003 Hebrew University water expert Professor Hillel Shuval argued that the "emperor had no clothes." According to his calculations, only 20 percent of Israel's caloric intake was produced locally.[83] During the 1980s, Shuval had initiated a public campaign attacking government policies that ignored hydrological constraints: Israel was pumping groundwater at rates that rainfall could not replenish. This created a perilous "overdraft" along the coastal aquifer that exacerbated seawater intrusion and salinization.[84] Eventually his views were validated by government hydrologists. With the new millennium approaching, Shuval took on the agricultural establishment's claims about food security.

Shuval believed that farmers were wasting subsidized water on flowers and cotton exports, while the country was forced to import basic foodstuffs: "This includes almost 100 percent of the wheat, grain, rice, animal feed, edible oils, soybeans, fish, and sugar. This means that the caloric content of almost all of the so-called local products are imported calories not grown by Israeli agriculture."[85]

Eventually, the discrepancy became impossible to deny: a 2010 report by Israel's Central Bureau of Statistics confirmed Shuval's claims. Some 99 percent of grains consumed in Israel are imported; 86 percent of the fish are *not* caught or grown locally; and 29 percent of vegetables, fruits, and potatoes are imported. But the government still proudly proclaims that Israel produces 100 percent of the local poultry and 94 percent of its dairy products.[86] It chooses not to ask where the chickens' and the cows' feed comes from. Agricultural economist Shaul Zaban clarifies that of 4 million tons per year of grains that Israeli farm animals eat, 3.8 million come from abroad.[87] Today, 80 percent of the seeds in the country are imported.[88]

The United Nations Food and Agriculture Organization identifies wheat as Israel's number-one foodstuff import, with 1,550,260 tons imported annually at

Food independent? Israel's vaunted dairy industry, including
these Holstein cows from Kibbutz Lotan, rely primarily
on imported feed for calories. (Photograph courtesy
of Alex Cicelsky)

a cost of $497 million. Beef and veal imports are next at $444,602 million; over
1 million tons of maize (corn) imports are purchased from abroad.[89] All told,
food imports come to $3.1 billion. By way of comparison, this is still less than
the $4.7 billion in foreign currency profits generated by Israel's tourist industry.[90]
For now, Israelis can afford to import their calories.

In internal discussions, the Ministry of Agriculture quietly began to admit
that Israel could no longer feed its citizens: a 2013, internal presentation by Israel's Ministry of Agriculture states, "Israel, like most of the developed countries in
the world, does not rely on food independence. Only 45 percent of the calories
in Israel are produced in Israel. The source of most of the calories consumed is
from direct import."[91]

This dynamic, of course, has been known to decision makers for decades and
was even the subject of a well-known anecdote about Levi Eshkol, Israel's good
humored prime minister during the late 1960s. When informed that meteorolo-
gists were projecting a very bad drought year, a concerned Eshkol purportedly
asked, "Where?" Upon receiving the answer he quipped, "Oh, you mean here?
Well that's a relief. I thought you were talking about the United States!" From a
food security perspective, Israel's weather was only of secondary concern.

The gap between the country's caloric demands and food production is now
undisputed. But should Israel, essentially a dryland nation, even try to produce

all of its own food? There are many reasons why a modern country may wish to be self-sufficient in terms of its food supply. Reducing unemployment, however, is not one of them. Some 64,000 people today in Israel are directly employed in farming ventures: 24,600 of them are foreign agricultural workers, mostly from Thailand.[92] The number of migrant laborers is actually greater today than the Israelis working as self-employed farmers. All told, agriculture accounts for roughly 2 percent of the country's labor force. They are doing a remarkable job: in the 1950s, 1 full-time worker in agriculture provided food for 17 people. By 2010, the number had risen to 113. Agriculture today accounts for 1.9 percent of the total GDP. The $3.1 billion paid overseas for Israeli agricultural commodities amounts to 4.2 percent of total exports.[93] Ongoing mechanization makes farming increasingly efficient and less labor intensive.

In the unlikely event that international dynamics or global food shortages prevent food imports, it is prudent to ask, How much land in an emergency would Israel need to feed its 8-million-strong population? What would it take to provide all of Israelis' caloric needs today? A back-of-the-envelope calculation assumes a per capita daily consumption level of 2800 kilocalories, or 8 trillion kilocalories annually, to feed all its citizens.[94] Based on present rates of production, hypothetically, 15.4 trillion kilocalories could be produced if all of Israel's arable land was converted to potato farms—twice as much as the 2,800-kilocalorie daily requirement.

But there is a problem. Israelis surely love their "chips" (French fries) and baked potatoes. And due to the high vitamin C content, people would not die of scurvy. But eventually even the most keen "tater" enthusiasts would grow weary of such a monotonous diet. A more acceptable dietary breakdown during an emergency might involve a mixture of corn, beans, and squash, with minimal poultry and eggs. This provides most of the population's nutritional needs and a modicum of culinary diversity. But it only yields 15 million calories per hectare per year, a third of potatoes'. In other words, some 600,000 hectares of land would be required for domestic "subsistence" cultivation. This is far more land than has ever been farmed. Much of Israel is either hyperarid or arid deserts that requires massive inputs for farming. Lands are increasingly compromised by urban development. In other words, if all of Israel's lands presently zoned for agriculture were reformatted for a diverse vegetarian diet with minimal meat, only 5 trillion kilocalories a year would be yielded, half the amount needed to feed a nation of 9 million people.

To better understand the prospects for food security in 2050, Israel's Ministry of Agriculture convened two independent panels—one comprised of academic experts and one of farmers and practitioners. They agreed that feeding a population of 15 million would require 594,000 hectares of land and 1,890

million cubic meters of water a year. Such requirements were deemed absolutely "unachievable." The teams reached the same conclusion: better start
improving long-term storage technologies for imports.[95] According to traditional
definitions of carrying capacity based on nutritional self-sufficiency, even Israel's
talented farmers cannot provide the food required for a country of 8 million.

Supplying its own food was a Zionist ideal that held great emotional and ideological appeal. Cynics can look back at the great debate over the land of Israel's
absorptive capacity and write it off as a charade. The sides well understood that
the real, unspoken debate was about demographic control and future national
domination. But modern Israel's founding generation was genuinely concerned
about agricultural self-sufficiency. Zionism was a rejoinder to the years of exile
when, in many countries, Jews were not allowed to farm. Taking responsibility
for the Jewish people's security and its food supply was axiomatic.

With the wisdom of hindsight it can also be said that both sides in the absorptive capacity argument were right. The land of Israel was surely capable of
feeding many more people than lived in Palestine during the first half of the
twentieth century. But even the most innovative and accomplished farmers on
earth will eventually come up against real biological and technological constraints if population size is not controlled.

Israel's population raced forward so quickly that most of the country hardly
noticed that the dream of agricultural self-sufficiency had been left behind in
the dust. By the time demographic levels made it impossible for local farmers to
meet domestic caloric needs, cognitive dissonance set in among many decision
makers. Importing food was no longer deemed problematic, and the country
embraced its new status as a successful member of the global village, venerat-
ing commerce and economic specialization. Nonetheless, for romantics at least,
something was lost when the State of Israel conceded historic aspirations for
nutritional independence.

It is more than legitimate to challenge caloric self-sufficiency as a criterion
for carrying capacity in a modern economy. Living sustainably does not necessarily mean growing all of one's own food, especially in a dryland environment.
But Israel does need to consider what an alternative definition for its carrying
capacity should be as it takes its place as an importing and exporting member of
the international community. It is well, therefore, to remember that the state of
the planet's resources has not changed. They remain finite and increasingly exploited. Linking one's food supply to global markets creates uncertainty, which is
likely to grow over time. It also brings with it a new global level of accountability.

11

◆━◆

TOWARD AN OPTIMAL POPULATION SIZE

> A population may be too crowded, though all be amply supplied
> with food and raiment. It is not good for man to be kept perforce
> at all times in the presence of his species.
> —John Stuart Mill, *Principles of Political Economy*

BEYOND THE BORDERS

For those who define sustainability in terms of limits, local is increasingly giving way to global. In a 1995 article published in *Science*, the eminent demographer Joel Cohen rejected the notion that for countries to be "sustainable," they need to grow their own food: "Human carrying capacity cannot be defined for a nation independently of other regions, if that nation trades with others and shares the global resources of the atmosphere, oceans, climate and biodiversity,"[1] he argued. The implication of this "global" perspective is that humanity shares a single planet, the proverbial "space ship earth."[2] When countries think about carrying capacity today, it should be within a transboundary context.

This chapter revisits the issue of Israel's carrying capacity, free of the narrow, nutrition-driven criteria that dominated historic assessments. Nonetheless, just because the "artificial" constraints of geopolitical borders are removed from the analysis does not mean that a responsible country needn't consider whether it is living within its "means" ecologically. Global sustainability and quality of life should constitute the salient criteria for indicating how many people a country should contain.

Unfortunately, decision makers rarely assess how much nature can actually supply and for how long they can continue to rely on its services. This is especially true when the "nature" they rely on lies thousands of miles away. As population and consumption rise, even renewable resources like crops and wood can easily be consumed faster than they can be replenished. Much as the doomed last survivors on Easter Island came to realize, irreversible ecological collapse can occur without a clear warning.

As do almost all economies in developed countries, Israel in fact "appropriates carrying capacity" from other places on the planet. An implicit assumption of present strategies holds that there will always be *sources* "out there" able to send Israel raw materials and food, along with *sinks* for absorbing its wastes. In the long run, this is a dangerous assumption.

Limiting calculations to the physical dimensions of carrying capacity is a highly superficial exercise. Societies typically not only seek to increase "quantity" of life, but also "quality" of life. There comes a time when these two objectives are at odds. As anyone who uses public transportation knows, more people can usually be stuffed onto a bus or a train. But when all seats are taken and the aisles are full, additional passengers may have an adverse effect on everyone aboard. At some point, the doors will have to close. More is not always better. Everyone may arrive safely at their destinations, but what could have been an enjoyable ride becomes unpleasant.

Israel must begin to consider what its "optimal population levels" should be as opposed to what its "maximum population levels" might be. The future will be more agreeable and healthier for forthcoming generations if they are bequeathed the best possible life rather than the maximum number of countrymen with whom to compete for finite space and resources. Israel is already a very crowded place. Is there a point at which additional people cease to improve the aggregate quality of life and begin to make it disagreeable?

ENERGY CONSTRAINTS AND NATIONAL CARRYING CAPACITY

According to the logic of the "law of the minimum" there are several ways, beyond food and nutrition, to compute national carrying capacity in Israel. The question is: What is the single parameter (for example, energy) or factor (land or water) that is likely to constrain population size?[3] Israeli planner Moti Kaplan, for example, argues that sinks, the capacity to absorb Israel's pollution—the emissions, radiation, effluent discharges, garbage, and hazardous wastes produced by human activities—constitute the salient parameter in shortest supply.[4] More common are concerns about limited energy and land.

Harvard University professor and sustainability sage John Holdren serves as President Obama's science advisor. Twenty-five years ago, while a young professor at the University of California, Berkeley, Holdren considered the matter of global carrying capacity. He argued that *energy* should serve as the *constraining parameter* for estimating a sustainable global population. He also assumed that even though energy efficiency would improve, an ever larger population and higher per capita demand for energy in developing countries meant that aggregate energy use would grow, thereby making it costlier in both economic and environmental terms. All the same, Holdren was willing to assume that improved technology in the future would allow the world to live well, with a high standard of living that consumes only a quarter of the demand for energy in the United States at the time. This meant that the world would have to move to an annual per capita level of 3 kilowatts.

Under such conditions Holdren assumed that a world population that stabilized at 10 billion people would annually use a total of 30 terawatts of energy, which he believed to be within the realm of possibility. (A population of 14 billion people implied a 42-terawatt demand, a level Holdren found inadvisable environmentally.)[5] Holdren's 30-terrawatt ceiling is precisely twice as much as the 15 million terawatts consumed today. Coincidentally, other recent projections expect this to be the amount of energy powering the globe in 2050.[6] It is possible that some future technological breakthrough in electricity production might produce sufficient energy to go beyond 10 billion people. Holdren rhetorically asks, "Why try to find out?"[7]

Other energy-driven estimates during the period, like that of ecologists at Stanford[8] and Cornell[9] Universities, were far more parsimonious. Gretchen Daily along with Paul and Anne Ehrlich were less optimistic, preferring *not* to preach a gospel of "carrying capacity for saints." At the same time, they were willing to assume that technological innovation would enable energy consumption to drop to two-thirds of the average 1992 American level. This would allow 2 billion people to sustainably consume energy, less than one-third of the present numbers on earth.[10] The drop in population required to meet energy constraints envisioned by the Cornell team (civil war, 100-million-person levels) was far more draconian.

If Israel were to plan its population levels by global "energy constraints," how might it calculate an appropriate population size for the future? The more lenient numbers proposed by Holdren would certainly be more palatable to the country's decision makers, who continue to operate on assumptions of unlimited growth. With 8 million people, Israel is home to 0.114 percent of the global population (slightly more than one-thousandth). But as of 2012, Israelis consumed 47.1 million megawatt hours of energy each year. This comes to 0. 244 percent of the global energy consumed today,[11] more than twice their relative share. If Israel were to try to consume energy commensurate with globally sustainable limits, it would not be able to increase population size unless it increased energy efficiency. At the same time, there is considerable room for improvements in energy conservation.[12]

It can be argued that by converting to fully renewable or, alternatively, nuclear-powered sources, Israel could pursue an energy policy that would not exceed local capacity or rely on imported resources at all. For the foreseeable future this is unlikely. Although Israel's official policy envisions 10 percent of electricity coming from renewable sources by 2020, over the past decade, the country has consistently missed its own targets for solar-power generation.[13] At this writing, less than 2 percent of Israel's electricity is renewable energy.[14] After Japan's Fukushima nuclear disaster, Prime Minister Netanyahu wisely called for a reconsideration of government plans for a nuclear-powered electricity plant.[15] Not only does Israel have plenty of seismic instability, it also suffers from political instability. It cannot ignore the zeal among terrorist organizations and hostile neighbors for sabotaging any future Israeli nuclear facility.

A far more likely scenario is that Israel's energy policies will take little notice of "global constraints." Rather, its economy will probably be powered by natural gas, available in bounteous quantities in Israel's Mediterranean fields.[16] At present, Israel's known gas reserves are 30 trillion cubic feet, with an additional 1.7 billion barrels of oil to boot, providing Israel with much of its anticipated energy needs for more than fifty years. The United States Geological Survey holds that present reserves represent only half the existing potential lying within Israel's exclusive economic zone.[17] The newly found (622 billion cubic meters) Leviathan field alone is reportedly more than enough to supply all of *Europe* with energy for over a year.[18]

But natural gas is not a "free lunch." It is still a fossil fuel, and the electricity it powers at best has about half the carbon footprint of coal-fired power.[19] As Israel's population is set to double, the greenhouse-gas reductions gained by a full shift to natural gas would be neutralized within a few decades. And per capita electricity consumption is growing even faster than demographic growth. There so are many potential sources of methane leaks during the process of exploiting natural gas that some studies suggest that it may do relatively little to reduce global warming during the coming decades.[20]

Whether or not Israel ignores its international responsibilities to mitigate greenhouse gases, it will not be long before the country can claim energy self-sufficiency, especially if it decides to scale back gas exports.[21] Surely this does not answer the question of the vulnerability of a gas pipeline to sabotage or the question of energy sources in the long term. With the precipitous drop in the price of solar electricity, surely the time has come for Israel to prioritize expansion of its renewable energy infrastructure. Nonetheless, for many years to come, it will be difficult to argue that Israel's population needs to be controlled because the country is running out of energy. That day may come, but it is not in the foreseeable future. A deficit of lands and the *biocapacity* they provide, however, poses a more serious constraint that sustainability advocates may wish to consider.

LAND CONSTRAINTS AND ISRAEL'S
ECOLOGICAL FOOTPRINT

Humans continue to draw most of their needs from lands that offer the only meaningful source of energy, materials, and food. Land also serves as a sink that absorbs the pollution produced by modern industrial society. Urban residents often are blissfully unaware of where the resources that support them come from. As a net importer of carrying capacity, Israel is no different from any of the world's cities. They too rely on the world's "hinterlands" for natural resources, nutrition, and fiber. These hinterlands are limited. Even if humans become better at substituting synthetic fibers for plant fibers, or manufactured inorganic fertilizers for soil nutrients, land is still required to sequester the carbon emissions created during production.[22] When considering the carrying capacity for an individual, city, region, or country, available land is a good place to start.

Not all lands are created equal in their ability to support life. They are home to profoundly different kinds of soils, evapotranspiration rates, and ecosystem services. At the local level, moderately accurate calculations can be made. Global averages are less precise, but still can provide a reasonable basis for making decisions. The world's lands are not a stable stock. Humans have become increasingly clever at exploiting them and frequently they push too hard. The countryside has been transformed by pavement and construction, soils eroded and contaminated by wastes, forests clear-cut, wetlands dried, and habitat extirpated.[23]

Hundreds of scientists convened to consider the state of the planet as part of the 2005 Millennium Ecosystem Assessment. It was then estimated that 60 percent of the earth's ecosystem services were damaged; 42 percent of the world's poor were forced to eke out a living on despoiled lands.[24] About 40 percent of agricultural lands on earth were strongly or very strongly degraded during the half century prior to the analysis.[25] In more and more places, there simply is not enough space to support the number of people living there. Unlike water, which frequently can be desalinized in the face of shortages, making new land or artificial islands for anything but high-density urban housing or a critical metropolitan airport remains prohibitively expensive. It is much easier to "appropriate" space from elsewhere on the planet. People never thought very

Carrying capacity accountants: Ecological-footprint pioneers
William Rees and Mathis Wackernagel. (Photograph courtesy
of Mathis Wackernagel)

much about what this meant. But a new measurement of sustainability, the "eco-logical footprint," began to change that.

Ecological-footprint analysis is a methodological tool designed to allow an increasingly interdependent planet do the bookkeeping. It can help people and societies sort out what global carrying capacity is available and who is utilizing it. First conceptualized by Professor William Rees at the University of British Columbia,[26] the methodology was then developed and applied by Mathis Wackernagel, a Swiss-born sustainability advocate who came to study with Rees in the early 1990s. Wackernagel went on to establish the "Global Footprint Network," a nonprofit organization that continues to expand the scientific basis for calculating carrying capacity and human impacts on the planet.

How does "ecological accounting" assess the effect of humans within and beyond the borders of a given country? Methodologically, an ecological footprint totals the sum of all croplands, rangelands, and fishing grounds required to produce the food, fiber, and timber that people consume. It also includes the land used to absorb wastes discharged, along with the space taken up by infrastructure.[27] Over the years, methods improved the computation of total land area necessary for maintaining the economy, including energy consumption. The resulting ecological footprints are based on units called "global hectares."[28] They indicate the *demand*, or how much land is being utilized to support a given society.

The *supply* side of the equation is called "biocapacity." The earth has surely taken a hit from relentless human abuse but remains remarkably resilient, with renewable resources and natural capital continuing to nourish humanity. The Global Footprint Network defines biocapacity as "the capacity of ecosystems to produce useful biological materials and to absorb waste materials generated by humans, using current management schemes and extraction technologies." Such capacity depends on innumerable factors, like soil qualities, topography, and precipitation. Technologies like irrigation or crop development also fluctuate, influencing fertility and yields. Nonetheless, a reasonable average can be utilized for calculations. Biocapacity is also measured according to global hectares. This creates a common *unit* for relatively simple computation of a country's ecological balance.[29]

Proponents of footprint accounting like to divide the world into two categories. Some countries are "ecological creditors." They consume fewer resources, on average, than local ecosystems can regenerate. Often they are net exporters of biocapacity. Then there are "ecological debtors," which run a biocapacity deficit. Footprint jargon says they suffer from "overshoot," using *more* resources than their countries' ecosystems can replace. These countries are net importers, receiving resources they lack from the so-called global hinterlands. At least temporarily, some may be able to exploit their own "natural capital," mining aquifers or overgrazing rangelands. Eventually, however, they will end up liquidating these finite ecological assets. Today, 83 percent of the world's people live in countries that run an ecological deficit. Already in 2008, when the total footprint of humanity was totaled up, the demands exceeded the planet's supply by over 50 percent. In simple terms this means that it took a year and six months to regenerate what the people on the planet used that year.[30] The methods that led to this conclusion are surprisingly simple: by dividing the planet's total biocapacity (in global hectares) by the total number of people on the planet, a sustainable individual footprint can be calculated. At present this comes to 1.7 global hectares per person. The trouble is that the world's average ecological footprint *already* is 2.6 global hectares.[31] And it continues to grow.

A footprint-accounting system allows countries (and individuals) to figure out how large their ecological footprints are and whether they live at a globally sustainable level. If the per capita footprint in a country is higher than the 1.7 global-hectare level, it consumes more than its share. Footprint accountants often measure performance according to "planet equivalents." This indicates the number of "earths" required to support humanity's footprint if everyone lived like an average citizen of a given country. The United States is an extreme case: If everyone in the world lived an American lifestyle, consuming resources at American levels, more than five planets would be needed to supply the attendant natural capital. When aggregate global overreach was calculated, it turned out that present total consumption levels on earth comes to 1.48 planet equivalents.

How is Israel doing according to this ecological accounting system? Unfortunately, not so well. Wackernagel actually visited Israel and even met with President Shimon Peres, to whom he presented his disconcerting calculations.[32] In the asset column, Israel's biocapacity has increased dramatically over recent decades, and the amount of arable land expanded far beyond that previously thought possible. But progress was offset by increases in per capita and aggregate consumption. In addition, the country's resource base suffered. For instance, fisheries are less plentiful,[33] groundwater is depleted,[34] and soils are more salinized.[35] Most of all, the number of people consuming local resources has climbed higher and higher. For some time now, Israel has been relying on imports, "appropriating" biocapacity from around the world to support its addiction to growth.

As part of an assessment of sustainability in the Mediterranean basin, the Global Footprint Network conducted an ecological accounting of each country. Israelis have a per capita ecological footprint of 3.96 of global hectares, more than twice the 1.7 global benchmark.[36] In a 2015 article in *Environmental Science and Policy*, the team ranked the Mediterranean countries according to "Biocapacity per Capita" and "External Resource Dependence." Along with Cyprus and Palestine, Israel ranked lowest in each category, showing an 88 percent dependence on external resources.[37] The country is importing from an "imaginary" second planet and mining resources that will eventually run out.

Israel is lucky to have its own expert in the new discipline of ecological-footprint accounting. For over a decade, Dr. Meidad Kissinger from Ben-Gurion University has researched Israel's biocapacity and its ecological footprint. Kissinger conducted the country's first footprint accounting in 2003, as a graduate student assessing the performance of Ra'anana, an affluent Tel Aviv suburb. Even then, Kissinger found that residents consumed 4.0 global hectares of land on average.[38] The "global hinterland" required to provide the town's natural capital was twice the per capita land available worldwide, and 180 times larger than its municipal borders.

Kissinger's recent efforts involve translating the amorphous global-hinterlands concept into tangible impacts so that people can better consider associated consequences. In one study he showed that the biocapacity consumed to provide Israel's grain historically came from North America. Lately, supply shifted to imports from the Black Sea region (Ukraine and Russia), where the energy footprint from transport is smaller.[39] To consider how Israel might reduce its footprint, it is important to look at Kissinger's consumption profiles.

When he considered the prototypic Israeli urban ecological footprint, Kissinger found that food, electricity, transportation, and waste disposal were the four predominant components.[40] There are concrete things that can be done to reduce Israel's domestic footprint, from decreased consumption of meat and fuel to increased public transportation and recycling. Greater conservation and generation of clean energy is imperative. As Israelis seek ever higher standards of living, this constitutes a significant cultural challenge. The analysis also highlights how important demography is in any sustainability equation. As Israel tries to do better, it is essentially playing "catch-up."

Footprint theory is not perfect. It does not include factors like susceptibility to epidemics or long-term loss in ecosystem services like pollination or pest control. But this kind of analysis does offer a global context for considering whether a country is on a sustainable track. Israel's environmental organizations and the local media pay only scant attention to the implications of Israel's biocapacity deficit.[41] They need to make a much stronger case to the public and to decision makers that Israel has a moral obligation to live within its means ecologically. This not only makes sense economically, it is the ethical thing to do in a world where natural capital and biocapacity are increasingly in short supply.

Even if decision makers come to see the light and commit to reducing ecological overshoot, their efforts would probably focus on making electricity infrastructure more sustainable and energy more renewable. In the short term, this makes sense. Had Israel's electricity demand not doubled every twenty years,[42] or were its renewable energy generation comparable to Denmark's 50 percent,[43] it would be much closer to the 1.8 per capita global hectare standard.

Transitioning into an era of fully renewable energy might make room for modest demographic growth without incurring a biocapacity deficit. But would that be wise? Does Israel want to ask How many people *can* it support? or How many *should* it support? *Optimal* rather than *maximum* carrying capacity needs to drive planning decisions about the future.

CROWDING AND CAPACITY

Ironically, it was *rodents* who first got *people* to consider the implications of living on a crowded planet. In 1958 John Calhoun, a behavioral ecologist working at the Laboratory of Psychology of the National Institute of Mental Health, took over a cowshed in the suburbs of Washington, D.C.[44] Calhoun did not fill the barn with the cows and horses. Instead he brought in five pregnant Norway rats.[45] He was curious to see how the rat population would respond to conditions of extreme crowding. In earlier experiments he had observed that rat populations seemed to naturally control themselves, never exceeding certain densities. Calhoun decided to see what would happen when they did.

In his most famous experiment, he converted the barn into what he called a "rat paradise," a veritable utopia for rodents. The animals were given all the food and water they could possibly consume. They were completely free of predation and were maintained disease free. And they had all the sex they wanted. Delighted with the physical conditions, the rats didn't hesitate and pursued their new life of debauchery with gusto. The population grew rapidly, doubling every fifty-five days.

Calhoun did set one constraint for the animals: *space.* The size of the pens where the rats lived was kept constant. Population density began to increase and, with it, dissatisfaction among the rodents. Involuntary social interactions became unavoidable, creating considerable stress. In normal environments rats can choose between "fight or flight" options and distance themselves from the group.[46] When this was no longer possible, the rodents began to go crazy.

In a well-publicized article, Calhoun reported that aggressive behavior became much more conspicuous, especially among dominant males. Packs formed that attacked young pups and females. Mating patterns grew violent, and many animals became homosexual or pansexual. Some males were classified as "hypersexual," trying to mount any rat they possibly could. Instinctual nurturing was abandoned. In little time, mothers stopped building nests properly, neglecting and eventually deserting their young. Some even attacked them. Infant mortality reached astonishing levels of 96 percent. Cannibalization grew common, and dead pups were ferociously devoured, even though there was no shortage of conventional food. Calhoun named the bizarre behavior "a behavioral sink."

It did not take long for population levels in rat paradise to crash. Notwithstanding the abundance of food and water, females stopped giving birth. Many animals withdrew into a passive mode, manifesting extreme mental distress. When the experiment was officially called off, the few surviving rats were repatriated to normal rodent communities. They were described as "utterly withdrawn" and asexual, remaining "socially autistic" and dysfunctional until they died.[47]

Many of Calhoun's rats' adverse responses to crowding have been replicated with other animals. For instance, several species of primates show similar signs of density-related discomfort, exhibiting mild and severe forms of aggression as their environment becomes crowded.[48] Others withdraw and avoid social encounters when living space becomes confined.[49] It is highly unlikely that such experiments could be replicated today. Research steering committees and advocacy groups would intervene, arguing with some justification that living with such high population densities constitutes unacceptable cruelty to animals.

The dairy industry also provides an interesting example of the interface between density, quality of life, and the physical manifestations of stress. When cows become crowded, their productivity drops. An optimal space for a dairy cow is probably forty square meters; twenty square meters per animal is probably the lowest possible density. (In terms of animal welfare, clearly this would be unacceptable.) Basically, the more space a cow enjoys—the more milk it makes. When cows have little room to move about, wallowing in their own manure, milk quantity and quality will drop.

Bill Slott, a veteran dairy farmer from Israel's southlands, explains:

> Having more space is better for the cow in every way, but usually providing more space costs money. If it were only a question of the quantity of milk, one could simply do a cost-benefit analysis of square meters per cow versus quantity of milk per cow to maximize profits. But a dairy farmer is also paid for milk quality. One wants to maximize fat and protein content while minimizing bacteria count. The more room you give a cow, the better the results will be. Beyond that, crowded cows will be less fertile and more susceptible to udder infections, both of which are crucial factors. In short, like with people—space is better, but space is expensive.[50]

For population control advocates, Calhoun's chilling findings and the results of other animal experiments came to serve as a metaphor for the human condition. Others were less inclined to draw human inferences. Certain psychologists argued that human adaptive capacity is so much greater than rodents', that there was little to be learned from the rat experiment.[51] When critically evaluating evidence from experiments involving human crowding and behavior, data can be confounded by factors like malnutrition, disease, alienation, racial origin, and nationality. Norms for personal space vary greatly between cultures.[52] And there is always the critical question of context: Is the interaction taking place in a public or private space? For how long? Were the crowded conditions entered into voluntarily?

These are legitimate caveats. Yet humans are profoundly affected by the number and proximity of people surrounding them. Associations between population density and infectious diseases like tuberculosis are well established in the public health literature, even in cities today.[53] Psychological impacts have taken longer to document. But anyone involuntarily caught in a throng trying to force its way through a poorly managed stadium entrance, or stuffed into a rush-hour subway train knows that crowding among humans can be a formula for distress.[54] It is impossible to mention the issue in Israel without eliciting memories of the Arad Music Festival in 1995, when unregulated crowds led to a crush of people who fatally trampled two young concertgoers.[55] Even in less extreme settings, density matters a great deal.

Density's negative effect on human well-being is sufficiently well characterized that environmental psychology textbooks contain special sections on the phenomenon.[56] People, like animals, need personal space.[57] Territoriality is defined as "the distance between members of the same species."[58] Despite civilization's progress, humans remain territorial animals, although there are distinct cultural, personality, and age differences. Men in particular feel more comfortable when they enjoy control over a good-size area. When density rises, it becomes harder to regulate social interactions, and the likelihood that privacy and personal space will be violated increases. When their space is invaded, people begin to feel agitated, sensing that they or their territory are threatened. If chances for winning are reasonable, they will tend to fight to defend it.[59] High densities make people more defensive of the limited space that they do have.

Cornell University professor Gary Evans conducted numerous experiments to better understand this phenomenon. Under controlled laboratory conditions he demonstrated how crowding elevates physiological stress. When deprived of personal space, people show external indications of anxiety. It takes the form of tension, apprehension, and nonverbal signs of nervousness, like fidgeting or playing with objects repetitively.[60] There are plenty of verbal signs as well. Physical manifestations include changes in skin conductance and elevated blood-pressure and stress-hormone levels.[61] Duration matters: the longer people are forced into crowded situations, the higher stress levels becomes.[62]

Women are typically better at tolerating crowding than men are,[63] suggesting that females' "personal space zones" may be smaller than males'; their tendencies to affiliate may naturally be greater. But women have their limits, too. Ensuring sufficient personal space not only protects a sense of belonging in a social group, it enhances performance in the workplace and reduces turnover.[64] In a controlled study, people in crowded rooms performed *complex* tasks more poorly than people who enjoyed more personal space.[65] More common than aggressive behavior is "withdrawal," as humans try to cope with the unpleasant dynamics of crowding. They avert eye contact, distance themselves from interpersonal encounters, and stop initiating conversations.

People are able to adapt to crowded situations, but society may pay a price in the quality of human relationships.[66] Cultures and individuals surely differ, but one meta-analysis found that residents of crowded cities have a 21 percent higher risk of developing anxiety disorders, and a 40 percent higher risk of mood disorders. The risk of schizophrenia is doubled in crowded urban environments, with a clear "dose-response" showing a correlation between crowded conditions and this debilitating mental illness.[67] Research published in the prestigious journal *Nature* used magnetic resonance imaging of the brain to highlight the neural processes of city dwellers caused by higher stress levels.[68]

Even as they sit inside the privacy of their cars, people suffer from crowding. This is important in Israel, where it is not uncommon for commuters to spend more time stuck in automobiles each year than on vacation! As traffic congestion grows, so do drivers' physiological stress. A high-density commute frequently spills over into personal life.[69] One study showed an association between difficult commuting and destructive impacts on family relations: the more demanding and harried the commute, the more social interactions within families are negatively affected.[70] Present predictions by the Israeli government suggest that during the years before 2030, Israelis will spend an additional sixty minutes a day in their cars due to increasingly congested roads. It projects an aggregate time loss of 850 million hours a year, costing the Israeli economy 25 billion shekels—up from present annual losses of 15 billion shekels.[71] No one really thinks about the cost in terms of human happiness.

It should not be surprising that density also affects educational performance. One study took advantage of contrasting conditions among children in the same New York City elementary school located on different sides of a school building. One cohort sat in a classroom contiguous to a train track and the busy outside world, while the other was relatively quiet and isolated. The reading ability of children on the noisy side of the building was significantly lower than those who enjoyed a classroom environment insulated from the crowding of society.[72] Jam-packed classrooms, of course, pose even greater obstacles to learning.[73]

What does this branch of environmental psychology have to teach Israelis about their country's carrying capacity? As annoyances and "daily inconveniences" associated with overburdened infrastructure and services pile up, it is hard to escape the sense that a threshold has been crossed. Average Israelis increasingly feel the impact of crowding; for many it is not a pleasant feeling. It might be queuing up for an hour at a post office unable to accommodate the lines of customers. It might be a visit to the beach, which can be anything but relaxing, among noisy throngs who have no other outlet to escape sweltering cities. (Tel Aviv's fourteen kilometers of beach, for instance, are overwhelmed by the deluge of 8.5 million visits a year.)[74] It could be missing a movie or important meeting because traffic came to a standstill due to suffocating congestion. These frustrations take a toll. And each year they get a little worse: *1.8 percent worse.*[75]

Israeli geographer Arnon Soffer is more candid. "A crowded country is a violent country that will steadily deteriorate, drifting towards the Third World. . . . And when it becomes crowded, people push, litter, act rudely and aggressively."[76] Soffer argues that because increased population will largely take place in the poorest sectors, poverty and social inequality in Israel will grow worse with higher density.

There are those who do not worry about Israel's increasing density, but actually see it as a virtue. Hebrew University political philosopher Avner de-Shalit has for many years been among the more thoughtful opponents of Malthusian thinking in Israel. Not only does he believe that Israel's environmental problems are primarily a function of high standards of living and consumption, he actually sees extreme density as a good thing:

> Ask most people where the "coolest" places in the world to live are and they'll tell you. It's not only a major city—but the most crowded major city. Why does everyone want to live in Manhattan? Or London? Or Paris? People like to live within walking distance of a grocery, a book store, or their favorite coffee shop. They don't see crowds as a threat but as an attraction. Indeed they want to live even more densely. For the most part, crowds don't scare people. They like the anonymity of the city. You know, there is a lot of leisure today. And people have more to do with their free time in places where there are a lot people. Most tourists are city dwellers. And where do they travel on vacation? They go to other cities. They don't go to open spaces.[77]

Professor de-Shalit identifies with the worldview of Harvard University urban economist Edward Glaeser. His best-selling tome *Triumph of the City* is a paean to high-density, urban environments. Glaeser writes, "Cities are the absence of physical space between people and companies. They are proximity, density, closeness. They enable us to work and play together, and their success depends on the demand for physical connection."[78]

Glaeser acknowledges that being crowded may have downsides: ("The same density that spreads ideas can spread disease.") Yet he argues that intervention by a competent public sector can neutralize them.[79] Ultimately, Glaeser believes that dense cities are the formula for a good life:

> There is a myth that even if cities enhance prosperity, they still make people miserable. But people report being happier in those countries that are more urban. In those countries where more than half of the population is urban, 30 percent of people say they are very happy and 17 percent say that they are not very or not at all happy. In nations where more than half of the population is rural, 25 percent of people report being very happy and 22 percent

report unhappiness. Across countries, reported life satisfaction rises with the share of the population that lives in cities, even when controlling for the countries' income and education.[80]

Cities have always been venerated by environmentalists as offering a more ecologically friendly lifestyle than suburban living does. Their success in housing the vast majority of humanity will indeed be crucial for the planet's environmental health and the future of countless habitats and landscapes. But this does not mean that there aren't limits. When cities grow too crowded, they become unpleasant. The younger generation is more prone to enjoying crowded bars and dance floors. But they still need a safety valve and secluded space to which they can escape at day's end.

It is much easier to enjoy forays into the "bustle" of Manhattan from the comfort of a sprawling penthouse. The rosy, Pollyannaish picture portrayed by Glaeser is rather selective. Glaeser acknowledges, sheepishly, that despite his love of cities, he elected to raise his children in the Boston suburbs (much as de-Shalit did in the Jerusalem suburbs). And the question he chooses not to answer is whether residents of Mumbai would be happier in a city of 3 million than today's 12 million people.

Density in a person's primary environment is more important psychologically than outdoor ambient density. Research in Chicago found the effect of indoor crowdedness to be greater than that caused by high-density external environments. For instance, persons per room accounted for most of the variance in juvenile delinquency and admissions to mental hospitals.[81] As population spirals upward, Israelis will find themselves in crowded situations with increasing frequency; high-density environments will become ubiquitous. Finding a modicum of privacy grows increasingly difficult as population climbs.

When faced with crowds and crowdedness, rather than resorting to aggression, many people lapse into pessimism and passivity.[82] Essentially they opt for a mental flight when physical escape is not deemed possible. Surrounded by neighbors, these masses increasingly live lives of silent desperation behind padlocked doors, paralyzed by anxiety and alienation. The depressing influence of high-density life is particularly apparent among senior citizens. In a national sample of British men and women over seventy-five, researchers were surprised to find that living in high-density areas was significantly associated with depression. The plausible explanation for the results was that "People are less likely to know their neighbors (i.e., the anonymity of city living) which might in turn lead to social isolation and loneliness in later life, increasing the risk of depression and anxiety."[83] This can explain why high-density housing is closely associated with inflated rates of suicide and self-injury.[84]

There are undoubtedly people with the money to purchase sufficient personal space and security to enjoy posh neighborhoods in Manhattan and Tel Aviv. But most city dwellers live far from the exciting center of town or the commercial areas where they work. They suffer long commutes into work along gridlocked roads in jam-packed buses and trains. As Israel grows more congested, society will need to find ways to better acknowledge and protect privacy to prevent psychological damage.[85] Without personal space Israelis will tend to feel out of control, ever more competitive, with a tendency to react negatively to minor annoyances.

The possible tripling of population density by 2059[86] suggests that things are going to get a lot worse. Arnon Soffer, ever apocalyptic on the topic of Israel's population, explains, "In a crowded land people fight over every tiny piece of land—and the price of lands continues to skyrocket."[87]

Presumably, Israel's parks can offer some psychological relief when locals want to decompress during leisure hours or on the weekend. Unfortunately, there is already a shortage of places to go. C. T. De Wit made one of the uppermost, high-density predictions for world carrying capacity ever published: he argued that theoretically at least, the planet earth could feed over 100 billion people. Yet, even in De Wit's "feedlot" future, the minimum space envisioned for recreational and urban needs was 750 square meters per person.[88]

In 2005 Israel's government adopted a recommended standard for minimum open spaces in the country's cities: 500 square meters for a kindergarten, 500 square meters per *classroom*, at least 4,000 for an entire institution.[89] Many Israeli schools fall short. The standard only calls for 5 meters of open space per person at the neighborhood level and an additional 5 meters scattered throughout the city, for a total recreational space of 10 meters per person.[90] This is a small fraction of De Wit's paltry benchmark. Sadly, the actual amount of parkland and open spaces in Israel's towns and cities does not even reach this modest level. For example, nestled alongside Tel Aviv, Givatayim is one of Israel's more prosperous communities. Present zoning of open spaces for the public reaches 5.4 meters per person, only half the recommended standard. Even so, only 70 percent of land zoned as parks in Givatayim in practice serves the public. Actual available space for the cities' central and northern neighborhoods is a scant 2 square meters per person.[91] Few cities are doing much better. Yet their populations continue to grow.

Daniel Orenstein is one of the first Israeli academics to write and teach about the issue of population and the environment. Based at Technion's Faculty of

Architecture and Town Planning, Orenstein sees many signs that the country is already too crowded. Open space is among the most prominent:

> A problem with Israel is that we didn't plan our open spaces like the electric company plans its national capacity. The managers there know that electricity demand goes up and down so they plan for "peak load" which is usually the hottest days in the summer when everyone is using an air conditioner. We didn't plan for open spaces based on peak loads. What happens on holidays in Israel when demand for recreational venues is highest? By mid-morning the radio announcers inform the public to stay away from the most popular parks: "Don't come to Ein Gedi. Don't come to the Hula. Don't come to the Ben Shemen Forest. There is no room.[92]

Passover 2014 in the Galilee became a nightmare for countless families, who, after waiting hours in traffic jams, were turned away from their vacation destinations.[93]

Those who do succeed in carving out a corner for themselves at popular recreational sites may find that that the experience is not as pleasing as they had envisioned. Moti Kaplan remembers the preparations for the National Coastal Masterplan during the 1970s. A plane was utilized for aerial photography, and students were hired to literally count heads and make reasonable estimates. At that time planners estimated that during the bathing season, four hundred thousand people would frequent Israel's 18.8 kilometers of public beaches simultaneously.[94] The number of beachgoers appears to have dropped over the past thirty years. Wall-to-wall, shoulder-to-shoulder dynamics make many beaches disagreeable places to be during vacation and weekend hours.

University of California psychologist Jim Moore explains that although modern urban and ecological problems cannot be fully solved by merely reducing population density, this does not mean that it does not need to be addressed.[95] One way of considering carrying capacity is turning the discourse on its head. What if "optimal population size" in Israel was not set according to the maximum number of houses that could be built, but rather based on acceptable levels of open space?

In a country where the vast majority of open space is within a five-kilometer radius of an urban community, critical land resources are always getting whittled away. Orenstein explains:

> I looked at rates of land conversion relative to population demand. The most persuasive argument about limiting population growth to me involves the building of 40,000 to 80,000 new housing units a year . . . every year. That

An aerial photograph of Rishon LeZion in 1917 bears no resemblance to the crowded Tel Aviv suburb of today as shown in a recent photograph. The elevenfold population increase during the past century has undoubtedly transformed Israeli countryside and society. It is time to stop and consider whether more people will make life in Israel better. (1917 photograph courtesy of Yehuda Salomon; 2015 photo courtesy of Rami Kopelman, AirView Aerial Photography)

figure alone is more compelling than the actual numbers of people when you consider how contentious it is to build anywhere today. There is a problem whenever a kibbutz wants to build new quarters and lease them; or if Haifa wants to destroy a pristine wadi with a new neighborhood; or even when people want to build an eco-village in the Negev desert. We'll have to build at this level every year as long as population continues growing. Of course, we can internalize the principle that Israel will be an urban landscape, but there are still ecological resources worthy of protection, or some would say, crucial to protect. The very term *sustainable* suggests some kind of balance. But 40,000 to 80,000 new housing units a year does not suggest balance or a steady state. And that's before considering the infrastructure needed for the said population growth. You should see the Jezreel Valley [the Israeli equivalent of the Napa Valley]: between the new sections of the trans-Israel highway, the trans-Emek railway, and other new roads, the valley is being transformed into a checkerboard of transportation arteries.[96]

Many people like seeing other visitors when they frequent parks or other recreational areas. It makes them feel safer. But when they feel congested in the very parks, reserves, and beaches designed to relieve their stress, they stop coming and no longer feel a connection with their environment. This is when alienation begins. If carrying capacity is seen through the prism of density, Israel has already exceeded its limits. Adding more people will not make the country a better place to be. The land is full.

TOWARD OPTIMAL POPULATION SIZE

When Paul Ehrlich and Gretchen Daily set out to consider global carrying capacity, they began by assuming that it would not be anywhere close to biophysical carrying capacity. The very notion of calculating the greatest number of people that might be sustained in a "factory-farm lifestyle" of maximal occupancy seemed nonsensical. Ehrlich and Daily proposed that society think in terms of an "optimal population size" that would be set according to social carrying capacity. This involved maxima that could be comfortably sustained under healthy social systems. A series of criteria for setting this "optimal size" was proposed. Population size should

- be small enough to guarantee the minimal ingredients of a decent life to everyone on the planet;
- ensure that basic human rights are secured, avoiding problems generated by excess numbers of people;

- be large enough to sustain viable populations in geographically dispersed parts of the world that foster cultural diversity;
- be small enough to allow other species to survive while allowing "hermits and hikers" to enjoy nature as well.[97]

They were not the first to dismiss the notion of maximizing population density. John Stuart Mill, the great nineteenth-century British political philosopher, foresaw the modern population densities when he posited:

> Nor is there much satisfaction in contemplating the world with nothing left to the spontaneous activity of nature . . . with every rood of land brought into cultivation, which is capable of growing land for human beings, every flowery waste or natural pasture ploughed up, all quadrupeds or birds which are not domesticated for man's use exterminated as his rivals for food, every hedgerow or superfluous tree rooted out, and scarcely a place left where a wild shrub or flower could grow without being eradicated as a weed in the name of improved agriculture.[98]

As Israel contemplates the future, it should rethink its historic trajectory toward maximum numbers or whether it makes more sense to pursue demographic stability. A move from maximal to optimal population objectives seeks to provide the highest possible quality of life for future generations while preserving some semblance of the country's remarkable natural heritage.

Israel is one of the most crowded countries on earth. Without the Negev desert, where only 7 percent of people live, there are already eight hundred people per square kilometer, more than twice the density of the Netherlands, Japan, or Denmark.[99] Israel could move in the direction of "city-states," like Singapore, Malta, Monaco, or Macau. These are not woebegone places. But few Israelis aspire to this model. Indeed the 2005 National Masterplan 35 clearly demarcates boundaries for existing cities and surrounds them with "green-belts," preserving the length of streams while protecting natural assets, agriculture and heritage landscapes.[100] The plan seeks to prevent a hyper-urban, sprawled existence.

Israel's population cannot grow forever; it certainly cannot continue to expand at the rates that it has during its first sixty-seven years. Even if the most frugal lifestyles are imposed, based on all-grain diets and superascetic regimens, there remains an upper limit to the number of people who can survive together on earth. This is also true of the land of Israel. Many Israelis do not feel comfortable talking about limits on population. But this is a profoundly irrational and irresponsible position. For most of the country's citizens, the idea of 100 million people stuffed into the country's present borders presumably would be unimaginable. So then the questions become What about 50 million? 25 million? 15 million? Regardless of one's vision of Israel's future, it is time to talk about carrying capacity.

Traditional Judaism is decidedly pro-natal in its views. But the ancients also recognized that geographic carrying capacity constitutes a very real constraint that cannot be ignored. If the deterioration in ecological conditions were to become unbearably acute, religious Israelis believe that their rabbis would be able to determine whether the traditional male conjugal duties were still mandatory.[101]

Dr. Jeremy Benstein, an expert on Judaism and sustainability, wonders if this makes sense: "If we take the possibility of a land filling to capacity seriously, then there will be a time when we will have fulfilled that commandment and we can stop. The question then becomes: 'When?' 'Have we gotten there yet?' And rabbis can't answer the question about what it means for the Earth to be full. That's a question for ecologists."[102]

It would seem that there is no point in putting this question off any longer. Surely there is room for research in Israel to help inform the conversation. Many more studies need to be conducted about the influence of overcrowding on Israelis' psychological well-being and how planning can reduce anticipated violations of personal space. The relationship between daily inconveniences and actual densities needs to be better characterized. But already, certain conclusions are clear:

Israel is already very crowded. Psychological and sociological research suggests that making it more so will not make life better. As Israel becomes more congested it will become more disagreeable and harried, burdened by anxiety and alienation. The anticipated problems associated with Israel's high population density need to be "brought closer" to the public. Israelis need to be confronted and asked whether their lives will improve if there are more cars on the roads, more people on the sidewalks, more crowded recreational sites, fuller classrooms, higher noise levels, more expensive real estate, and greater societal poverty.[103] Ultimately, these are rhetorical questions. Negative scenarios need to be simulated and sketched so that concrete images of the overcrowded future awaiting can be presented, visualized, and internalized.

People are only motivated to act when they feel their fundamental interests are being threatened. Whether it be rabbis or ecologists or politicians who participate in the discourse about optimal carrying capacity, what matters is that the people of Israel come to understand that their country's demographic reality must change. It is up to them to better plan their families and translate visions of an *optimal* future into new societal norms.

Today's intermittent shortages in open recreational spaces will soon become an acute scarcity. Habitat preservation for Israel's unique biodiversity will become impossible. For many, daily density will become intolerable. At the end of the day, Israelis are not Calhoun's Norway rats but a free people. When things get too crowded and unpleasant, many can leave—and they will.

Today, in the shadow of the Holocaust, it is still difficult for many Israelis to speak objectively about overpopulation. Some seventy years ago, approximately 36 percent of the Jewish people were slaughtered. Many survivors are still alive and stand as a constant reminder of the enormity of the loss. It is hard to imagine that in such a short period of time, the country is crossing demographic thresholds.

In fact there is an interesting historical parallel between Israel's present situation and that which existed in 700 B.C., after the Assyrian king Sennacherib conquered Samaria and destroyed the kingdom of Israel along with dozens of communities in Judah. It was a time of dramatic demographic descent and despair. The prophet Isaiah offered consolation to the people of Israel and predicted a spectacular turnaround: "The children of your bereavement will yet say in your ears: 'The place is too cramped for me; Make room for me that I may live here'" (Isaiah 39:20). It would seem that within the span of two generations, the State of Israel has come to realize Isaiah's vision and promise of redemption. This is a reason for joy and national validation. But it also comes with responsibilities and a need for new paradigms.

To prevent a future of 30 million people where conditions become impenetrable and there really is no room for living, it is important that Israeli society set demographic targets today. Population policies take decades to make a difference: The time for considering policy changes is at hand. If the land is full now, with twice as many people it will be intolerable.

◆━◆

We Can Do It—An Agenda for Stabilizing Israel's Population

> This will appear a dream to many—but less than any other
> country should Israel be afraid of dreams.
> —David Ben-Gurion, *Southbound*, 1956

TWO TYPES OF COUNTRIES

For global advocates of zero population growth, the past decade has been the worst of times and the best of times. On the one hand, numbers continue to increase, albeit at a reduced rate, on the inexorable march to 10 billion—and probably beyond. Present projections by the United Nations suggest that many poor developing countries will soon have to address staggeringly high populations, twice to three times their present size. By 2050 the number of countries with populations of 100 million people or more will double. There will be 398 million people in Nigeria, 137 million people in Tanzania; Uganda will have 101 million, and 309 million people will fill up Pakistan. Over 1.7 billion people will live in India, roughly the number of people who lived on the entire planet at the turn of the twentieth century![1] Life in these countries will be very crowded and, for most residents, unpleasant.

But many other societies have shown that demographic policies make a difference and as a result witnessed a rapid transition to replacement or even below-replacement levels. There are dozens of countries throughout Europe and Asia where population is essentially stable or even contracting. For example, in 1970, the total fertility rate in South Korea was 4.3; by 2000, it was down to 1.5. The average family in Iran had 6.5 children in 1980 but by 2000 only 1.96. Ireland's total fertility was 3.83 in 1970 and by 1991 was at 1.9. Thailand had a birthrate of

5.99 children per family at the end of the 1960s, but by the 1990s it was 1.99. At the end of the 1970s, Bangladesh still had fertility rates of 6.6, but today it's 2.4. And China went from 5.7 in 1970 to 1.6 at present.[2]

Two different kinds of countries are emerging on the planet. Within thirty years, the distinction will be even more marked: There will be lands where timid, myopic, or misguided leaders took a path of least resistance and let demographic inertia continue unrestrained. Life for the majority of people there will increasingly become a jam-packed, congested tangle where privacy, quiet, and natural vistas grow chronically scarcer. In the poorer of these nations, acute food and water shortages will define people's existence.

In other lands, a combination of foresight, political will, and cultural evolution will combine to produce the regulation and self-restraint required for stabilizing population. Life there will be totally different. Growing prosperity and per capita comfort will continue to spawn diverse, creative civilizations with the potential for equitable, poverty-free societies. Residents in steady-state societies will enjoy the underlying calm associated with stability. People will be able to savor the preservation of beautiful landscapes and biodiversity in open spaces, along with sanity and room for living characterizing urban centers.

Demographic decisions have a long latency period. It literally takes decades for strategies adopted today to produce demographic stability. Hence, Israel needs to decide *now* which of these paths it wishes to choose. As a society it must make the hard decisions necessary to reach a lower population and a common higher ground.

There are many fortunate places around the world where population stability evolved as a function of cultural transitions. But the demographic equilibrium and the precipitous drop in birthrates that took place in the aforementioned countries for the most part did not happen because of an invisible hand or the intoxicating influence of Western civilization.[3] Enlightened public policies catalyzed these changes in attitudes and familial norms.

For some time, population has been recognized as a problem of "unmanaged commons." It is the most natural thing in the world to let other people worry about these areas that belong to everyone and to no one in particular. In today's world, demographic growth is the result of millions of individual decisions that do not internalize the harm caused to society at large. As personal responsibility becomes diluted, collective disaster becomes inevitable.[4]

Garret Hardin's famous 1968 essay *The Tragedy of the Commons* explained it this way: "The most important aspect of necessity that we must now recognize is the necessity of abandoning the commons in breeding. No technical solution can rescue us from the misery of overpopulation. Freedom to breed will bring ruin to all. At the moment, to avoid hard decisions many of us are tempted to propagandize for conscience and responsible parenthood. The temptation must be resisted because an appeal to independently acting consciences selects for the disappearance of all conscience in the long run, and an increase in anxiety in the short."[5]

When such dynamics prevail, only government intervention can produce socially optimal results. The world is full of examples in which legislation and regulatory programs enacted for the common good curbed behavior that damages natural resources or erased age-old destructive norms and prejudices. Many of the countries that have stable populations today are the direct beneficiary of such farsighted policies. Assuming that the State of Israel prefers to take a sustainable route, it is time to consider the measures that it must adopt to stabilize population. In some areas there is a need for legislative reform and new initiatives. There is much that can be learned from the experience of other nations. In other areas, Israel simply needs to do a better job of enforcing existing laws. In either case, there is no need to reinvent the wheel. From a public policy perspective, it is quite clear what must be done and how to do it. What is less clear is how to sell this "package" to the politicians who must enact these measures and see to their implementation.

"NO REGRETS": REFRAMING OVERPOPULATION

For more than twenty years Adam Werbach has been among the world's more creative environmental thinkers and sustainability advocates. At age twenty-three he was the youngest president in Sierra Club history. He then went on to launch innumerable public-interest and sustainable-business ventures, helping to reform the environmental practices of corporations like Walmart, Procter & Gamble, and Frito-Lay. Werbach has come to understand a bit about marketing and why the general public does or doesn't buy into environmental messages.[6] He is extremely uncomfortable with the way overpopulation has been framed over the past fifty years:

> "Population control" frames the problem as too many people, and even worse, as too many poor people. Within this framework, one set of issues counts (including immigration, contraception, and abortion), while another set of key issues (the North American Free Trade Agreement, economic development, the rights of women, and poverty) remains outside. In the population-control frame, the number of people and their placement on the planet is the root problem that needs to be solved. But is that really the problem? Family planning has succeeded only where economic security has been improved for

women, including access to food and shelter, health care, and education. With this as background, the real population problem may be the treatment of women on the planet. If we reject the population-control frame in favor of the goals of women's emancipation and sustainable development, we may achieve a healthier and more stable population without inviting the unwelcome embrace of ugly exclusionists.[7]

While there is strong ethical impulse behind this view, ultimately Werbach's concern is about tactics. Sustainability advocates need to be thoughtful about how they present population policies lest they get derailed, defamed, and driven into a defensive mode. At the same time, there should be no confusion about the need to alter present global demographic trends as well as the direction in which Israel is headed.

Few thinking people would contest the notion that local carrying capacities must be respected and that the planet's population growth needs to taper off. Some methods that further these ends are more objectionable to the public than others. Coercive policies in the past have been extremely harmful to international efforts to promote a sustainable global population. They created a "straw man"— a caricature of pitiless, patronizing, social engineers—that is vulnerable to attack from a peculiar coalition of the Vatican, feminists, and developing countries.[8]

In Israel, the occasional intrepid voices that dared to point out the implications of existing demographic dynamics in the past have been ridiculed and distorted. This is unlikely to change. Those who raise the flag of sustainability and population stabilization will invariably be branded alarmists, anti-Zionists, anti-Arab, anti-Jewish, anti-Orthodox, elitists, heartless, or eugenicists. Faced with such a predictable backlash, few choose to speak openly about the disaster that Israel's pursuit of perpetual growth is creating. There are plenty of other worthy causes without such toxic fallout. And yet more and more Israelis have quietly come to realize that if demographic pressures are not addressed, efforts to improve the country will be fruitless. This silent majority can be galvanized. But when the problem of population in Israel is finally tackled, it will not be enough simply to be "right." Given what's at stake, it is critical to be "smart."

There is much that Israel can learn from regulatory experience around the world. In some areas environmentalism has been highly successful, while in others significant effort resulted in abject failure. Ozone depletion has been ameliorated[9] and whale extinctions averted.[10] Overpopulation, however, is another story. When Paul Ehrlich wrote *The Population Bomb* in 1968, there were 3.5 billion people on the planet. In the forty-seven years that have transpired, the number has more than doubled. Notwithstanding many remarkable local transitions, at a global level the outcome of decades of pronouncements and warnings about overpopulation has been most disappointing. To change direction, strategies that perform poorly need to be identified and avoided while success stories need to be evaluated and emulated so that the lessons can be translated into sustainable domestic policies.

There is indeed much to be learned from considering failures. Another global challenge where efforts have been less than satisfactory is climate change. As the debate about the science of global warming dragged on, environmental advocates realized that they needed a "new angle." Many began to frame their proposals as "no regrets options." *No regrets options* are policies that are worth pursuing regardless of whether or not climate change poses an existential threat to life on the planet. In either case, the direct and indirect benefits of many projects more than offset the costs of implementation.[11] Even climate-change skeptics agree that society benefits when more trees are planted and automobile fleets are more efficient. It makes sense for homeowners to install double-glazed windows, insulate or shift to energy saving lightbulbs.[12] Focusing on the long suite of "no regrets" endeavors engenders less resistance from the public and politicians, while producing the desired outcome of greenhouse gas reductions.

Those who wish to stabilize population in Israel need to adopt a similar perspective. It may take more than a generation until the country's pro-natal inclinations in disparate camps give way to the sustainability ethic that informs most of the developed world today. That doesn't mean that the problem of overpopulation should not be raised openly and a new, sustainable perspective promoted. In the interim, while the internal debate rages, there are any number of interventions that directly or indirectly can contribute to reduced fertility, even though they are not designed to promote that goal per se. Free contraception, abortion on demand, inexpensive day care for working mothers, enjoining polygamy, scholarships for minorities and women—all are part of an economic and social-justice package that can also help stabilize population in Israel. These policies may contribute to healthier demographic dynamics but need not be framed as population initiatives.

If Israel wishes to change demographic trends and slow population growth, it must substitute existing programs and policies with others that stabilize population. Such an agenda for sustainability will need to

- empower Israeli women and integrate them in the workplace;
- ensure greater access to contraception and abortion;
- eliminate government incentives that encourage high fertility; and
- change public norms about marriage, fertility, and family.

Programs that pursue these goals will contribute to a reduction in birthrates and help transform societal attitudes that affect population size. Yet they all have an inherently sound, parallel rationale as key components toward a better society that makes them worth pursuing, regardless of Israel's demographic circumstances.

EMPOWERING WOMEN

"Empowering women" is a slogan that has reached consensus levels of support even in multicultural, politically divided societies, like Israel. Most demographers, environmentalists, and even economists agree that independent, educated, and gainfully employed females hold the key to stabilizing population size. There is certainly a link between the two phenomena: it turns out that no society on the planet with high fertility rates also has objectively low levels of gender inequality.[13] The status of women, in particular their capacity to attain profitable and fulfilling employment, is good for any economy.

Japan offers an excellent case in point: After many years of lackluster performances, the Japanese economy finally began to turn around in 2013. The stock market increased by 65 percent in six months and attained the highest GNP growth among advanced economies.[14] One of the central reasons for the boom was the expanded participation of women in the workplace. Even though Japan is aging rapidly, women have been poorly integrated into the workforce, and the country has had one of the worst gender gaps in the world.[15] The government set a 30 percent target for female participation in the civil service, and the prime minister asked every Japanese corporation to appoint at least one woman to its board of directors.[16] Empowering women and ensuring their place in the labor force is starting to do wonders for prosperity.

Guaranteeing women equal access to education and the job market is surely good for women. During World War II, Rosie the Riveter was the illustrated poster icon who promoted the slogan "We Can Do It!" and encouraged American housewives to take manufacturing jobs during the war while their husbands were off fighting. The pitch was "If you can use an electric mixer you can use a drill." After initial hesitations women answered the call, with female employment up 50 percent by 1944. Retrospective studies show that salaries provided the initial attraction, but women soon came to appreciate the independence, the mastery of new skills, and being out of the house as part of the war effort.[17] There was considerable unhappiness when many were relegated back to their domestic lives after the war.[18]

Empowered women tend to have fewer children. Accepted economic theory holds that as the status of women improves, family size decreases. Because policy makers hold them in such esteem, it is particularly interesting to understand the logic behind economists' perspective on this inverse relationship. University of Chicago professor Gary Becker won the Nobel Prize for Economics in 1992. Becker's work on the economics of family dynamics and fertility remains particularly influential. In 1960 he published "An Economic Analysis of Fertility," an essay that considered the unanticipated *negative* relationship between income and fertility.[19]

Two centuries earlier in England, Thomas Malthus was writing the essay that established very different assumptions. Writing in 1798, Malthus argued that wealthier families are better able to pay for health care so that their children have a higher probability of surviving.[20] Moreover, wealthier families can allow their children, especially their daughters, to marry and start their "childbearing years" at an earlier age.[21]

Becker realized that Malthus's famous observation about income and family size empirically was no longer valid. He tried to understand why. Becker identified several basic changes in modern living that altered earlier dynamics and hence the role of women. Two factors emerged: First, the advent of inexpensive contraception allowed families to choose whether or not to have children, making the age of marriage or a couple's sexual activities of secondary importance to fertility. One reason why wealthier families in many societies have fewer children than do poorer ones involves greater familiarity with and access to contraception. Secondly, childhood mortality in most of the world has dropped among all classes; today it is only a minor factor in population dynamics.[22]

The real change that Becker identified in the household economics of modern "postagrarian" societies involved the *costs of raising children*. Every child brings direct costs. Children have long since ceased to be assets that produce family income. Due to their extended period of dependence in modern societies, children use up family income. A child needs to be fed, clothed, sheltered, and provided with basic goods, all of which can be very expensive. It turns out that these costs are just a fraction of the full price in many societies. Societal expectations for investment in children consistently go up as families grow richer: from preschool to university education, from summer camps to therapies, from fashionable consumer goods to entertainment—raising children and ensuring their success is costly. More children are even costlier. Becker called this phenomenon the "quality" of children. Affluent families may not buy more cars than poor families, but the cars they do buy will typically be more expensive or of "higher quality." Similarly, wealthier families will make a larger investment per child as they acquire greater disposable income. When families grow richer, they have fewer children of "higher quality" in lieu of more children of "lower quality."

Becker then went a step further. He argued that the most important change in the cost of raising children in modern societies involves indirect expenses, or "opportunity costs." This corresponds to the value of the time that is spent with "the kids" rather than at work. In his 1981 book, *A Treatise on the Family*, Becker showed that as women move up professionally, the value of their time increases. Promotions raise the effective opportunity costs of having a child. A fulfilling career also portends that meaning in life is not only derived from child-rearing.[23]

Becker summarizes, "The economic approach suggests that the negative relation between income and fertility is an indication that the effective price of children increases with income, perhaps because the wives of men with higher incomes tend to have greater earnings from market activity or higher values of their time. I believe that the interaction between quantity and quality of children is the most important reason why the effective price of children rises with income."[24]

Empirically, Becker's model appears to be validated by experience across developed societies. This was not always the case. As late as the 1970s, data from OECD countries indicated that total fertility rate was positively associated with the participation rate of women in the workforce, just as it was in Malthus's day. In other words, women who worked had a higher likelihood of having more children. But this relationship soon changed 180 degrees. By the 1980s the trend was entirely reversed. Women in the labor force were having fewer children than those who were not working. Explanations for the turnaround involve inflexible working hours, which created obstacles to raising children and greater associated stress. Higher wages surely contributed to the change. Because child-rearing is considered to be a time-intensive task, many women felt that additional children would force them to settle for less-lucrative employment. Interestingly, when unemployment surged, women did not go back to having more children. On the contrary, fertility dropped even further.[25] According to economic logic, therefore, the single most important thing that can be done to reduce fertility is to increase female participation rates in the workforce and ensure that no unfair impediments block their professional advancement.

Does empowering women need to be a social policy objective in Israel? Secular Jewish Israeli women over twenty-four already show impressive labor participation rates: 83 percent of women from this sector work,[26] far higher than the OECD average of 66.2 percent. (Only Sweden, Iceland, and Norway are higher.)[27] Some 66 percent of Haredi women work, precisely the overall average of the OECD. This is a reasonable rate but could be far higher. Those working part-time could expand their hours. The reason why the national average for women is only 75 percent involves the low participation rate of Arab women ages twenty-five to sixty-four, only 35 percent of whom are employed.[28]

An agenda with the potential to empower Israeli women must be clearly defined. The list, at a minimum needs to

- ensure access to affordable higher education and scholarships for women of limited means;
- make childcare and public transport easily available and inexpensive; and
- enforce existing legislation that prohibits differential salaries based on gender or race and laws that forbid polygamy.

EDUCATION

Education plays a central role in determining children's—especially girls'— roles and identity. It is not just about providing skill sets for an increasingly demanding job market. (Nor is it a particularly difficult pedagogical challenge to teach adolescents the mechanics of avoiding pregnancies.) Through its schools, society can impart values and aspirations that facilitate independent familial and nonfamilial roles.[29] Central to any strategy seeking to empower women is the provision of an identity and the confidence that will enable girls to lead fulfilling and challenging lives.

When given opportunities for a productive and satisfying life beyond the confines of the family, the vast majority of women opt to work. As any teenager who has taken her first job knows, a positive sense of pride, freedom, and self-sufficiency usually follows. Around the world, education, especially for women, has been highly associated with low fertility.[30] The correlation in dozens of studies in disparate countries is unmistakable. Surveys in nine Latin America countries showed that women who had little or no education had average family sizes ranging between six and seven children; those with a higher level of education had between two and three.[31]

Given the interplay between education, employment, and fertility, a new Israeli demographic policy needs to prioritize empowering women in Israel's Arab sector (especially Bedouin women) as well as among Haredim. The centerpiece of such a strategy involves higher education and training for entering an increasingly competitive job market.

Haredi Empowerment: For Israel's Haredi community, the education-fertility connection appears to be true not only for women but for men as well. Haredim who did not pursue formal education but studied religious texts in yeshivas on average have 6.5 children as opposed to those with academic degrees with 5.5 children. While this level of fertility is still prodigious, it is 15 percent lower.

To understand the magnitude of the challenge in Haredi communities, a few descriptive statistics are instructive. A recent study shows that between ages twenty five and forty-four, only 12.8 percent of Haredi women have college degrees; women between ages forty-five and sixty four are only a little higher: 17.6 percent. In terms of formal education, Haredi females are more accomplished than males: the percentage of men with degrees is only 7.5 percent and 15.1 percent, respectively. In comparison, 30 percent of non-Haredi Jewish women in all age categories hold academic degrees. This educational shortfall has enormous implications for economic well-being and employment opportunities. Half of Haredi women without academic degrees are unemployed. Among Haredi women who complete formal training after high school, the figure is only 24 percent. The figures are even more striking for Haredi men: 34 percent of those without a formal degree are employed as opposed to 71 percent of college graduates.[32]

There are some signs that change is in the wind: the number of Haredim pursuing higher education has begun to increase. In the six years between 2006 and 2012, the number of ultra-Orthodox students in post–high school academic institutions doubled. Of the 7,350 students most recently enrolled in college programs, 3,500—roughly half—are female.[33] At the same time, the number of Haredi boys completing academic high schools where "secular" subjects are taught is actually plummeting. Between 2002 and 2010, the rate of Haredi men completing formal secondary education dropped from 26 to 12 percent; the vast majority of boys opt for religious studies.

When the Ministry of Industry, Trade and Labor surveyed the Haredi community, most female respondents were willing to consider nonreligious programs, citing "general studies" as an option for future instruction. Only 30 percent of the males were open to the idea.[34] Nonetheless, Haredi women are severely limited in the workplace due to religious constraints. Basic activities frequently are not allowed, such as unsupervised contact with males; unrestricted access to the Internet, or even unregulated e-mail. At the conclusion of a recent job-training program, two Haredi women were outstanding participants and slated to speak at the closing ceremony. When permission from their rabbi to appear in a public did not arrive in time, they felt compelled to disqualify themselves from the proceedings.[35]

Israelis are starting to see the dangers associated with this phenomenon. Haredi unemployment and dependency on public welfare funds was one of the central issues in the 2013 elections, which for the first time in decades left ultra-

Haredi women study at the Ono Academic College. Although the number has
doubled in recent years, less than 15 percent of ultra-Orthodox women between
ages twenty-five and forty-four have college degrees. (Photograph courtesy
of Ono Academic College)

Orthodox parties out of the government.[36] But entrenched policies and legislation perpetuate the education gap. In 2011 Israel's Supreme Court rejected a suit
by a pair of law professors calling for religious academies to teach children "core
studies" in English, math, science, and computers. The petitioners argued that
the children's right to a basic education was being violated by a curriculum entirely based on religious subjects. The court held that it lacked the authority to
overturn existing policy, even if the judges well understood that this was a central reason why ultra-Orthodox are so underrepresented in the job market.[37]

Higher education is immediately reflected in higher incomes and escape
from the poverty trap that so burdens the ultra-Orthodox community. There are
relative few Haredi families in which both the father and mother have academic
degrees—only 5.2 percent of Haredi households, to be precise. But when both
parents have studied and work, average family income is $5,100 per month. For
the 80 percent of Haredi families in which neither parent has advanced degrees,
average income is below $2,000.[38]

Many proposals involving advanced training centers and subsidies for higher
education have been floated.[39] A "second chance" program for completion of

high school and college was proposed. Coordinated with the needs of the private sector, it includes job placement with incentives based on worker success. Helping the products of Israel's broken educational system to enter the labor force is important but ultimately only addresses symptoms of a larger problem that starts in elementary school. As long as the government continues to fund schools with curricula that fail to provide basic knowledge and skills for Haredi boys and girls, progress will be limited. To transform present dynamics, extended school days and subsidized afternoon youth enrichment programs are required. High quality afterschool programs can free up both parents to work and give the children the "head start" they need.[40]

ARAB EMPOWERMENT

The most conspicuous aspect of Israeli Arab economic conditions is the low employment rate among women. Wages of Israeli Arabs also tend to be lower than those of Jews. (Arab men earn on average 43 percent less than Jewish men do. For Arab women the gap is only 21 percent). Their presence in industries and professions where salaries are modest is part of the dynamic. Working Arab women actually earn hourly wages that are higher on average than Arab men's due to their superior education.[41]

It would be wrong not to acknowledge some good news: participation in the workforce has in fact already gone up fourfold: in 1970, only 8 percent of Arab women worked; by 2010 the percentage had risen to 22 percent. In 2015 it reached 35 percent. During the same period, in absolute terms, the number of Jewish women in the force increased even more—going from 32 percent to 60 percent. More and more young Arab women seek to enter Israel's labor force. When present figures are stratified by age, it turns out that in 1980 only 18 percent of women ages twenty-five to twenty-nine worked; by 2010, the figure was 38 percent.[42] Over 90 percent of the women in older age brackets do not work and probably never have, bringing down overall average employment rates. Still, employment levels remain very low. Furthermore, the range of employment pursued by Arab women is relatively narrow: 36.6 percent work in education; 11.6 percent work in sales; 18.2 percent in health-related professions; about 9 percent continue to work in agriculture.

Israel's high-tech sector reflects the limited access to lucrative professions among Israeli Arabs in general and Arab women in particular. The best estimates in 2013 suggest that 1,200 Arabs work in Israeli high-tech companies, only 1.5 percent of the workforce in the field. This is up from 350 people, or 0.5 percent, five years previous. Nazareth, the largest Arab city in Israel, has emerged as the center of high-tech jobs in the Arab sector: between 2008 and 2013, the number of high-tech firms in the city jumped from one to twelve; from 30 to 400 employees. Two-thirds of the workers there, however, are non-Arab and one-third are women.[43] This is hardly noteworthy, but at least it's a start. For now, in Israel's most profitable economic sector, Arabs are almost invisible.

Eran Yashiv and Nitsa Kasir of Tel Aviv University have taken a closer look at the situation. In surveys of 7,647 Arab citizens, they considered women's participation in Israel's labor market and how to increase it. Not surprisingly, education emerged as the key. The researchers considered which factors motivate Arab women to work and which encumber them. They found that those living in cities have higher employment rates, a function of transportation and accessibility. *Ultimately, the best predictor of whether an Arab woman is working or not is higher education:* the economists' regression analysis shows a notable divide in attaining employment between women with sixteen or more years of formal education and those having only thirteen to fifteen years of schooling.[44] Trends are encouraging: the percentage of Arab women studying in undergraduate programs increased from 2 percent to 12 percent during the past thirty-five years, and those pursuing graduate degrees has gone up from 1 percent to 10 percent.[45]

Yashiv and Kasir recommend seven different policies and programs to increase the participation of Arab women in the workforce. Many of these have been recommended in earlier reports.[46] The policies and programs include local occupational guidance centers, professional training courses to upgrade marketable skill sets among women, subsidies for day care to reduce the costs of going to work, and expanded transportation infrastructure and services. The researchers also suggest that more attention be paid to career tracks and job skills as part of the high school curriculum. Subsidies for higher education and greater investment in the Arab educational system remain essential. Finally, the researchers also recommend stronger legislation and enforcement against discrimination.[47]

The importance of fast, inexpensive, and readily available public transportation cannot be overstated. Most Arab women do not have access to a private car. Present transportation service to dozens of Arab communities in the Galilee and the Negev is minimal. Subsidies for taxis and ad hoc shuttles can help, but a reliable network of bus routes is better.

An interesting statistic appearing in a 2009 report prepared for Israel's Knesset states that only 22 percent of Arab women applying to employment programs had a driver's license.[48] The rate presumably will improve over time. But subsidizing driving lessons or making them part of their high school curriculum could make an important contribution to mobility among Arab women.

The new faces of empowerment: Bedouin nursing students at Ben-Gurion University. (Photograph courtesy of Dani Machlis, Ben-Gurion University)

There will be enormous "no regrets" benefits to the Israeli economy from boosting employment among Arab women. One analysis projects a 50-billion-shekel benefit to the economy from increasing the number of Arab women in the workforce from the present 100,000 to 315,000. Arab women increasingly want to go to work. Expediting this process, especially in the Bedouin sector, will contribute to social equity and demographic stability.

CHILDCARE

To integrate women into the workplace it is critical to provide a reliable framework to care for their children during the day. German mothers who utilize childcare are about 35 percent more likely to work than those who do not avail themselves of it.[49] Israeli mothers are no different. Neither are the Japanese: In 2012, Japan's prime minister, Shinzo Abe, realized that the key to fixing his economy's sluggish performance was increasing the number of women in the workforce. To do this, childcare needed to be more accessible. After giving birth, 70 percent of Japanese women stopped working and found it difficult to return. Only one-third of Japanese women with young children had jobs compared with three-quarters in Sweden. Part of the reason women's employment was so low involved the "Catch 22" they faced in day-care enrollment. Without a job, they were ineligible to send children to day care. But without a framework to take care of their children, they could not commit to a job. The new government decided to end day-care waiting lists by 2015 and established two hundred thousand new day-care openings in government monitored centers; another two hundred thousand will open by 2017.[50] Faced with a low birthrate, France instituted a policy of highly subsidized municipal day care, offering tax breaks for families employing in-home childcare workers, and universal free nursery school.[51] This may not have raised local birthrates as much as the government hoped. Yet, it led to an impressive 80 percent participation of women in the workplace compared to 60 percent in the United States.[52]

Japanese and French policy makers see day care as a way of encouraging women to have children. But the opposite is true in Israel, where feminist leaders view day care as a critical way to *reduce* birthrates by enabling women to enter the labor force.[53] This is especially germane for increasingly well-educated Arab women in Israel who are keen to work. Beyond the inadequate transportation infrastructure and bias among many Jewish employers, absence of childcare facilities in Arab towns constitutes the most significant obstacle to their employment. They simply have no place to leave their children.[54] Across Israel's diverse social spectrum, most women are willing to leave children at day care within their community and depart for work. But they won't if the service is too distant, too incompetent, or too expensive.

Haifa University's Amalia Sa'ar is an expert in the problem of employment and business among Arab women. Her research shows that poverty and lack of support makes it hard for Arab women to take initiative.[55] Frequently it simply makes no economic sense for an Arab woman to work. If she lives in Arabeh and finds a job in Haifa, employment may turn out to be an economically losing proposition by the time she pays for a car to get to work and a caretaker to watch her young children. The government has begun to provide free day care from age three. But childcare until then averages over twenty thousand dollars.[56] For working mothers of lower socioeconomic levels with modest salaries, this price is a nonstarter. Government subsidies should be expanded to help *working* parents cover the infants' first years in day care.

Of course there are enormous intrinsic benefits associated with placement of even very young children in day care. Empirical studies around the world clearly show that toddlers in well-designed early childhood day-care frameworks truly have a head start.[57] Statistically significant advantages were found among children in cognitively oriented childcare programs. These include higher cognitive, IQ, and school achievement test scores; lower rates of special education; better grades; fewer grade repetitions; and higher rates of graduation from high school: the earlier and more intense the educational intervention, the better the results. Data in Israel show similar advantages: new subsidies for childcare increased the percentage of children attending preschools as well as employment rates among their mothers, especially those with academic degrees.[58]

In response to demands from the 2011 "social protest movement," the Israeli government expanded day care with the express purpose of "encouraging the integration of mothers into the labor market." Initially, this appeared to be lip service, as there was no formal preference for working parents. Directives from the Ministry of Economy specifically allowed Haredi men who weren't working or studying a trade to enjoy free childcare. The government pays 1,730 shekels a month for every child in preschool, and 2,273 shekels when the child is an infant. No expectations were stipulated for parental entry into the labor force in return. In fact, the subsidy just made it easier to have more children and stay out of the workforce![59] Like all social policies, "the devil is in the details"; linking subsidies to employment is a critical detail.

OVERCOMING BIAS AND DISCRIMINATION

Another obstacle difficult to overcome involves discrimination. Amal Ayoub could be a poster girl for professional competence among women in Israel's Arab sector. Growing up in Nazareth, she was recognized as academically gifted at a young age. But upon completing her undergraduate degree in physics from the prestigious Technion university, she was rejected by dozens of potential Israeli employers for being underqualified.[60] So Ayoub went on to complete a doctorate as well as a postdoctoral program at Ben-Gurion University in biotechnology. This time when she came looking for work, she was told she was overqualified. Eventually Dr. Ayoub established her own company, Metallo Therapy, which develops techniques for focusing radiation on tumor cells with gold nanoparticles.[61] She acknowledges that there is prejudice in the Israeli workplace, but claims that other obstacles, such as transportation and childcare, may pose more fundamental impediments to Arab women's integration in the workplace.

One undeniable reason why many women in Israel do not work is the pathetic remuneration: it simply does not pay. Women's salaries in skilled and unskilled positions have always been lower than men's. Deliberately or unconsciously, they are passed over in promotions to senior positions. The numbers speak for themselves: Females working in Israel earn 66 percent of the salaries that males receive for commensurate work. Israel's Central Bureau of Statistics in 2014 reported that on average, Israeli men earned 10,953 shekels a month; women, only 7,244. Women are particularly underrepresented in the high-tech sector, where only 35.6 percent of the workforce is female;[62] only 20 percent of top management jobs at companies traded at the Tel Aviv Stock Exchange were held by women in 2013; only 7.9 percent of CEOs in the hundred largest Israeli companies were women. (This was up from 4.5 percent only a few years earlier.)[63] The gender gap calls into question certain axioms about equal opportunity in Israeli society and weakens the economy. It discourages women from working and surely does not help reduce fertility.

Israel's Arab women face a "double whammy" of prejudice based on gender and ethnicity. The trouble is that it is extremely difficult to prove discrimination in the workplace. Dr. Ayoub may or may not have been "under-" or "over-qualified" in the eyes of a given employer. Objective statistics suggest that it happens all the time.

Israel has begun to address the problem of the underrepresentation of Arab women in the labor market. The Or Commission, appointed by the government to consider the clashes between police and Arab demonstrators in October 2000, openly acknowledged that the Arab sector suffered from historic discrimination and neglect. Its report called for funding to close gaps in education, industrial development, employment, and other social services.[64] In 2008, the Israeli government set a goal that 10 percent of civil servants come from Arab communities by 2010. This is 50 percent lower than Arabs' percentage in the country's population, but better than the 6 percent that existed at the time. Even so, as of 2015 the target has not been met.[65]

Haredim also complain they face prejudice and discrimination when looking for work. For example, there is a substantial salary differential between Haredi and non-Haredi employees. In addition, Haredi women in Israel earn less than Haredi men (5,620 shekels per month versus 8,950 per month). They also receive less than secular Jewish women with comparable education, who earn 8,000 shekels a month.[66] Equal pay for equal work may be the law, but it is a very tough law to enforce

The creation of the Equal Employment Opportunities Commission in 2008 was an important step in confronting this phenomenon. Based in the Ministry of Economy, the commission addresses discrimination in the workplace on fourteen grounds of prejudicial treatment, including nationality, race, ethnic origin, age, gender, and sexual orientation.[67] Tziona Koenig-Yair has overseen the commission's work since its inception. A former prosecutor in the district attorney's office and later executive director of the Israel Women's Network, she brings the right combination of legal competence and ideological commitment. But hers is a particularly trying task. Koenig-Yair believes that Israel actually has excellent laws requiring equal pay for men and women, prohibiting sexual harassment and other occupational hazards, while ensuring vacation days, reasonable hours, and other social benefits. These statutes are not well enforced. "Many employers don't realize that they can't discriminate based on people's gender, race or ethnic identity," she explains.[68]

Koenig is well aware of the low percentage of Arabs working in Israel's high-tech industries (2.4 percent overall—but only 1.3 percent working as professionals). She cites the usual obstacles: distances between Arab communities and potential employers; poor public transportation; inappropriate skill sets and corporate recruitment policies. Koenig does not deny that part of the explanation involves overt or unintentional discrimination. When given the opportunity, her agency takes legal action against violators. Notwithstanding the hundreds of phone calls that bombard her hotline, illegal discrimination remains a very hard thing to prove. Proactive efforts constitute a far more promising strategy.

Israel allocated 200 million shekels for establishing *employment centers* opening around major Arab population centers, designed to help match workers with potential employers. (Pilot programs were launched preparing Arab citizens with appropriate backgrounds for work in the high-tech industry.) For instance, one initiative provides 30 million shekels in wage subsidies for employers in high-tech who hire qualified Arabs. Special industrial areas were set up to encourage start-ups near Arab communities, and Arab students are subsidized in related fields.[69] But funding levels for these programs is modest when one considers the enormous gaps that exist and the potential economic benefits to be derived from expanding Arab participation in the workforce.

The elephant in the room of course is military service. The vast majority of Arabs and Haredim, both men and women, do not join the Israel Defense Forces. Nor do they do alternative, national service, available for religious girls, pacifists, or eighteen-year-olds with health problems. Efforts to make conscription compulsory for many years became an extremely controversial political matter. In 2014 legislation was finally passed to that end, but its implementation remains a huge unknown after a newly elected government quickly agreed to Haredi demands to eliminate any associated criminal sanctions.[70]

Serving in the army may take young Israelis out of the general workforce and delay their professional training for several years. But the leadership experience and, for many soldiers, the technical skills attained are valuable assets in the job market. (It is harder still to quantify the benefit that service in elite units provides for future professional networking, but it is substantial.)[71] Moreover, numerous Israeli industries cater to the defense establishment. Without military experience candidates will not pass security clearance. Many Arab Israelis acknowledge the academic advantage accruing to Jewish students who arrive at a university as veterans—more mature and focused on their studies. They believe that national service is in the interest of Israeli Arabs because it will produce a more-seasoned student who can better compete in the classroom and the job market.[72] But few pursue it, and Arab political leaders are vociferous opponents of its expansion. This does not change the fact that a period of military or national service for Arab and Haredi youth would significantly contribute to reducing the gaps in professional opportunities, creating a more-harmonious society.

In short, a critical part of the package of social policies required to stabilize Israel's population is eliminating the obstacles facing female citizens—and Haredim—from achieving a suitable education and finding appropriate work. To the extent that it does, Israel will be a more egalitarian country. This in no way means that educated *working* women coming from cultures that idealize large families will abandon their aspirations for a bevy of children. But economic theory and empirical sociological data suggest that empowering women is a critical first step, without which fertility will not come down.

ENSURING REPRODUCTIVE AUTONOMY

It is a common myth that ignorance about contraception is limited to women in developing countries. While the percentage of women using contraception globally has increased since 1960, the absolute number of married women and men who do not use birth control has actually gone up. Of the 2.3 billion people of reproductive age worldwide, some 44 percent—or about 1 billion people—do not use contraception.[73]

Birth control may be more available in developed countries, but that does not necessarily mean it is utilized. A 2014 study published in the *American Journal of Public Health* reports that in the United States over half of pregnancies are unintentional. Some 40 percent of these are aborted.[74] Surveys around the world tell a similar story: all told, only 53 percent of pregnant women in *developed* countries indicated that their pregnancies were planned.[75] For some it is just a case of inconvenient timing, with a baby coming earlier than would have been preferred. But in other cases, there are ample personal, professional, or economic reasons why a mother or father prefers the birth not to take place at all. When miscarriages and abortions are subtracted, about one of five children in *developed* countries involve unwanted pregnancies.[76]

As women across Israeli society become independent, they need to have the final word in decisions about their bodies. Reproductive autonomy needs to be afforded legal recognition as a human right. This should not just be a high-minded declaration. Israel needs to make it as easy as possible for women who do not want to have a child to avoid pregnancy. This means that the country's vaunted public health system should provide safe and effective contraception *free* to all citizens. It also needs to remove any barriers that create discomfort, embarrassment, and inconvenience in dispensing the birth control of choice.

Beyond the many men and women who forget or can't be bothered to use birth control, many Israeli women are either embarrassed to purchase contraceptives or are afraid their husbands will disapprove. Adolescents are frightened of what parents will say. And there are some who cannot afford the expense.

Contraception policy reform is not just a matter for women. Men share equal responsibility. Notwithstanding the recent increases in the price of latex,[77] condoms remain an inexpensive method of birth control. Manufacturing costs are only about 0.04 cents per unit.[78] Their free distribution should be a priority, with dispensers in bathrooms of high schools, universities, army bases, factories, and restaurants. This approach would also reduce teenage and unmarried pregnancies and sexually transmitted diseases. Free vasectomies should also be available without deductible health-care fees.

Birth control makes some people feel uncomfortable, especially in Israel, where large elements of society do not discuss sex openly and where modesty can be taken to an extreme. These customs should be respected. There is no reason why sharing information and making contraception available need to undermine values in traditional communities. Culturally sensitive sex education packets and programs can be prepared in coordination with relevant authorities. At the same time, Israeli society should not let prudish, self-conscious, or outdated norms define its population policies. Sensitivities in Israel have evolved a great deal, and the country is fundamentally liberal on matters of sexual conduct. In the public domain (and in many families), however, there is still a way to go. Contraception needs to move from the realm of unmentionable taboo to the matter-of-fact world of familiar pharmaceuticals.

In efforts to expand the utilization of birth control, it is well to remember that NGOs matter. And yet there is no active NGO in Israel with the resources to really influence contraception accessibility and dissemination. The Israel Family Planning Association's "Open Door" network is the Israeli branch of Planned Parenthood. Its many volunteers do excellent counseling,[79] but it remain a relatively low-profile organization with modest resources. This should change.

When, in 1993, the number of HIV cases in Thailand reached 1 million—an increase of 1,000 percent in just three years—an emergency initiative was launched. The Thai government moved the "battlefield" into the classroom.

The Population and Community Development Association was pressed into service to train over three hundred thousand teachers to educate students about family planning.[80] These classes raised public health awareness and succeeded in transforming national perceptions about contraception. While some of the organization's PR antics might rankle some demure Israelis, they proved highly effective for Thailand. Distribution of condoms became a national pastime, removing any remaining stigmas and the associated embarrassment: school children blew them up as balloons, contraception festivals were held, and restaurants used them as a decorative theme. Lawmakers decided to distribute condoms free of charge and required their utilization by men in brothels.

The new distribution initiative was so successful that it led to a 50 percent drop in fertility rates, pushing the country below replacement levels. It also produced incalculable public health benefits. The incidence of sexually transmitted infections among sex workers in one province fell from 13 percent to less than 1 percent in two months.[81] Because the sex industry in Thailand is not just for tourists, with many Thai men availing themselves of local "services," the United Nations estimated that the policy prevented HIV infection among 7.7 million citizens.[82] Given the growing prevalence of sundry sexually transmitted diseases,[83] Israel would gain a "no regrets" public health dividend if it showed the same kind of perspicacity and introduced a program consistent with Israel's somewhat more staid norms.

To transform "reproductive autonomy" from an ideal to a reality, Israel's abortion policies need to change. When a woman becomes pregnant and wishes to terminate pregnancy, she should be able to do so expeditiously and safely. It is wrong to allow pro-life advocates to take a moral "high ground" and talk about "coercion" in the area of abortion. The only coercion taking place in Israel today involves citizens who cannot have a legal abortion or who do not feel free to have one because their husband or society disapproves. Despite modest modifications in recent abortion policy, an entire system designed to make abortion inconvenient and disagreeable remains largely in place. Unmarried women must face a committee of strangers and plead their case before receiving permission. This creates unnecessary delays and anxiety. For a married woman, the situation is far worse: technically it is still illegal for most married women to abort a pregnancy. She must either lie to a committee or undertake an uninsured "illegal abortion." A change in this statute may or may not have demographic implications. But it is time to put an end to this blatant infringement on women's right to decide what to do with their bodies.

Robert Engelman, director of the think tank Worldwatch Institute, writes, "Removing from women the shackles of external reproductive control would more quickly reduce birthrates worldwide than any other imaginable policy.

Imagine this world: children are born only when both partners, but especially women, are freed from the pressure of others to give birth and want to raise a child to adulthood, and women have real autonomy in the productive as well as the reproductive sphere of their lives." With a few legislative amendments and modest adjustments in the budget of the Ministry of Health, Israel could be part of that world.

AN END TO PERVERSE INCENTIVES

Good public policy rewards desirable behavior and outcomes while taxing undesirable behavior and outcomes. When governments pay people to do things that ultimately have negative consequences, it is called a "perverse incentive." In fact, it is a startlingly common phenomenon.

Here are but a few interesting and instructive examples: In old Hanoi the colonial French government placed a "bounty" on rats in order to control a growing pest problem, only to find that a small cottage industry had emerged in which locals raised rodents in return for payment by the colonial regime.[84] The U.S. Endangered Species Act's ban on development of lands with rare creatures led to extermination of animals by landowners who feared crippling economic constraints.[85] In Israel, farmers' rights to subsidized water were renewed annually on the basis of usage during the previous year. This induced some farmers to wastefully irrigate fallow fields at minimal expense, in order not to lose subsequent years' rights. The list goes on and on.

Population policy in Israel constitutes a classic case of perverse incentives. Child allowances and other benefits for large families might be justifiable in European countries that seek to maintain shrinking populations.[86] In fact, hysteria over low birthrates is misplaced. Countries like Japan are proving that modest population decline can actually lead to better paying jobs, greater social equity, quality of life, and higher per capita affluence.[87]

Child allowances in Israel don't make sense precisely because its pro-natal policy measures work so well. Much as Nobel Prize Laureate Professor Becker hypothesized, paying families to have more children reduces the opportunity costs of additional children in the short run. This changes the perceived economic calculus for child-rearing. Child allowances are not nearly enough to cover the full expenses of raising a child in Israel. But they appear to encourage poor families to have more children by creating an illusion that they will be taken care of.

Tel Aviv University economist Alma Cohen assessed the application of Becker's theories to Israel's policies. Not surprisingly, the effect of allowances on fertility is weak among richer families, where the subsidy constitutes a trivial percentage of overall earnings. Yet it has a significant impact among poorer couples, where subsidies make up a considerable sum relative to disposable income.[88] In other words, inadvertently, the policy influences the very people who are least able to support large families.

As detailed in chapter 5, when the government reduced child allowances even modestly in 2003, it immediately affected Israel's birthrate.[89] The reduction greatly affected women between the ages of thirty-five and forty-five. By this stage, the drop in fertility levels cannot be interpreted as merely a delay in having the *next* child, as women are starting to reach the end of their childbearing years.[90] The impact of canceling allowances altogether would be far greater.

Subsidies were not just designed to encourage large families but also to aid poor households, offering them a better life and equal opportunity. Over the years, the policy has had the opposite effect. Israel's child allowances discourage work while encouraging unnaturally large families. Another unintended consequence is de facto state support of polygamy. The bottom line is that subsidizing large families exacerbates the country's poverty gap. Between 1970 and 2010, welfare payments per capita in Israel grew by over 400 percent. During this time the economy doubled.[91] Yet income inequality, as measured by the Gini coefficient (which calculates the relative income distribution of the poorest segments in a society) and the percentage of families living below the poverty line, grew significantly worse.[92]

Rewarding births with welfare payments has led to unfortunate results for centuries. Malthus's 1798 "An Essay on the Principle of Population" was originally written in response to a bill submitted by politician William Pitt to "allow a shilling a week to every labourer for every child he has above three." Malthus writes of his initial affinity for child allowances, which intuitively seemed like a fine humanitarian proposal, and his subsequent change of heart:

> I confess that before the bill was brought into Parliament, and for some time thereafter I thought that such a regulation would be highly beneficial; but further reflection on the subject has convinced me that if the object be to better the condition of the poor, it is calculated to defeat the very purpose it has in view. It has no tendency that I can discover to increase the produce of the country and if it tend to increase the population without increasing the produce, the necessary and inevitable consequences appear to be that the same produce must be divided among a greater number . . . and that the poor in general must be more distressed.[93]

Phasing out pro-natal incentives is a critical *first step* that Israel must take to stabilize population. But if the country should decide to get serious about cutting its fertility rate, it must go much further. Israel can learn from countries that facilitated profound shifts in fertility and public attitudes about responsible parenting *without coercion*, through taxation and incentives.

No country has taken its demographic dynamics more seriously and achieved more remarkable results than Singapore. Upon receiving independence from the United Kingdom in 1963, the tiny 710-square-kilometer island was already very crowded. Quality of life and economic development suffered as a result. In 1966 the minister of health launched a new policy initiative, explaining, "Singapore as we all know is a very overcrowded little island of nearly 2 million people living in an area of just over two hundred square miles or a density of population around 8,000 people per square mile. Family planning is therefore a matter of national importance and indeed one of urgency for us. Our best chance for survival in an independent Singapore involves a stress on quality and not quantity."[94]

The social programs introduced reflected this pragmatic perspective: For starters, all barriers to reproductive decisions of couples were removed, and the state funded medical expenses associated with contraception. In 1969 a law was passed covering the full cost of vasectomies and tubal ligation. In 1974, free abortion on demand was allowed. The minimum age for marriage was raised to eighteen, and women were encouraged to enter the workforce. Today 42 percent of Singapore's workers are women.

Singapore's program was unique because of the comprehensive use of incentives and disincentives to encourage smaller family size. In August 1972 the country took a series of steps:

1. Income tax reductions for families with three children *or fewer*
2. Lower priority for receiving admissions to elite elementary schools for children who are the fourth, fifth, or sixth in their families
3. Higher hospital fees for delivering babies with each successive child
4. Loss of access to state-subsidized housing for large families
5. Paid maternity leave limited to two children[95]

These policies did not *punish* large families in Singapore but simply *rewarded* smaller families for doing the right thing. In the same way that society might provide incentives for installing home solar systems, public transportation subsidies, or special highway lanes for carpooling, Singapore made it easier to embrace fertility decisions that were in the public interest. Society is entitled, if not obligated, to provide remuneration for socially beneficial behavior.

In retrospect, Singapore's policies greatly accelerated a preexisting population transition. The results were unusually swift: The annual population growth in 1957 was 4.5 percent. By 1980 it was down to 1.5 percent, with the increase merely a function of age-related momentum. Total fertility in 1955 was over 6 children per family; by 1980 it was down to 1.74.[96] Abortion rates soared, up sevenfold at first, as not all citizens had mastered their contraception routines.[97] Eventually, however, the number of abortions dropped to extremely low levels.

Refuting the notion that population growth is a prerequisite for economic growth, the precipitous drop in fertility was soon reflected in the country's extraordinary economic performance. In 1960, the annual GDP per capita was roughly $2,200 dollars. With an expanding economy and a stabilized population, by 2014 the average adult in Singapore was earning $62,400—higher income than in Norway and Switzerland.[98]

Such policies are not unique to Singapore. Iran's astonishing demographic transition was not just about education and awareness. In 1993 the Iranian parliament passed legislation that canceled food coupons, paid maternity leave, and social welfare subsidies after the third child. Birth control classes were required before couples could marry. Nobody in these countries was penalized or punished for having three or more children. But the country prioritized its resources and helped those who limited family size for the benefit of all.[99]

Israel needs to formulate and implement comparable policies: it should cancel tax breaks and direct payments to families after they give birth to two children. Other financial advantages provided to large families should also be discontinued:

1. Mothers should not receive additional government birth grants after delivering their third child.
2. Youth should be given scholarships and special stipends on the basis of merit and socioeconomic conditions rather than their being born into large families.
3. If there is to be prioritization of scarce public housing, space should first be available for the smaller families that society wishes to encourage.
4. Discounts on city taxes shouldn't automatically be made to households because they have many children.
5. Childcare should be free for a family's first child, subsidized generously for the second, and only modestly covered for subsequent children.

Regarding the final point, the area of early childhood education subsidies needs to be reconsidered. Hypothetically day-care subsidies enable both parents in a family to work. But for years it has actually been part of a broader package that encourages many Israeli women to stay out of the labor force.[100] Day-care policy needs to reflect new sustainable demographic objectives. If a parent chooses not to work and does not contribute to the economy, why should society cover childcare costs?[101]

Learning from places like Singapore, which prioritized public assistance for first and second children, will undoubtedly produce howls of protest. Such reforms are invariably attacked as callous, odious, and coldhearted, throwing thousands of children below the poverty line. These critiques suffers from acute myopia. Changing pro-natal incentives can help prevent hundreds of thousands of births into underprivileged large families that cannot provide financially for them. A longer time horizon reveals that forcing families to be responsible for their children is a far more compassionate approach than providing present incentives that broaden the circle of debilitating poverty among Israel's Bedouin and Haredi underclass.

In retrospect, hard-nosed policies that rewarded small families in Singapore eliminated poverty there. Israeli society needs to send a message that while it shuns imposition of legal limits on family size, it also does not encourage people to have children if they cannot support them. For the first time, such messages are starting to appear. For instance, in defining its economic and social objectives for 2010, the city of Beer Sheva set a goal of reducing the number of families with four or more children by 50 percent by 2020—as an antipoverty measure.[102]

Clearly, a decent society will not let children go hungry. The government needs to provide necessities without positively reinforcing behavior that dooms scores of youngsters to poverty. The child of a poor family that does not have enough to eat should be able to attend preschool and after-school programs that offer a solid educational curriculum. There, the child can receive two hot meals and a full day's worth of calories. For the most basic needs, family size is irrelevant: a child should not be blamed for his or her parents' decisions. At the same time, parents who beget children they cannot support should not be rewarded.

Cutting entitlements is strong medicine, and decent, compassionate people will feel sympathy for the large families whose poverty will be temporarily aggravated. This empathy is natural and very human. But when individual behavior contributes to negative societal impacts, sympathy should be tempered by the recognition that unbecoming behaviors have social consequences. Public policy must make people responsible for their decisions. It is possible to feel badly and even lend a hand in treating symptoms without giving smokers subsidized cigarettes or providing liquor to recovering alcoholics. Granting child allowances to large families with low incomes encourages even larger families. The ultimate objective of welfare policies should be to end the cycle of poverty and dependence—not deepen it.

It is legitimate for societies to recognize parenthood as a fundamental right. That doesn't mean that countries suffering from overpopulation are obliged to pay families to reproduce beyond replacement levels of fertility. On the contrary, sound policies, based on intergenerational justice, subsidize sustainable and stable birthrates.

SOCIAL DIFFUSION

Changing social norms is a slow process that will not take place overnight. It also requires full recognition of the power that peer behavior exerts and the social pressures driving many reproductive decisions. Landmark methodological research in modern demography focusing on these phenomena was conducted by Norwegian politician and demographer Gudmund Hernes. The study analyzed why and when people get married. Hernes designed a model that characterizes the process of entry into "a cohort's first marriage." The Hernes model identified two forces that affect individual decisions to "settle down." The first involves the *social pressure* to marry, which is proportional to the number of peers already married. The second is a person's *"marriageability,"* which presumably declines with age. Before mathematically demonstrating the phenomenon, he explained:

> Single people experience the social pressure to marry in various ways as the percentage already married increases. Much social interaction is age-graded. As a larger percent of the cohort marries, single people will have reduced interaction with old friends. They will be invited less to parties, dinners or trips, partly because of the awkwardness of diverting interests, partly because of the threats to the established couples. When singles are invited, hosts often play the role of matchmakers. . . . With increasing age, the psychological experience of being unmarried as a kind of deviance is heightened by popular culture. For example, as a woman remains in the pool of the not yet married, her social definition changes from maiden to spinster or even rejected.[103]

Hernes characterized marriage as a contagion that affects those around it. His quantitative model predicts the likelihood of marriage based on "social diffusion" and increased influence of an individual's peers.[104] Fertility also is a social contagion.[105] When fertility patterns were examined in countries where family size fell below replacement levels, demographers found that the most common characteristic was the substantial increase in the age of first birth. Socioeconomic incentives alone could not explain the phenomenon. Rather, social interactions most significantly affected individual fertility.[106] In short, the decision to have children often depends less on family background or career decisions and more on the behavior of friends as transmitted through social networks. When demographers model the probability of an individual having a child, the key coefficient is determined by what peers and compatriots are doing at that time.

Demographers have applied the Hernes model to conduct probabilistic forecasting of fertility by age.[107] The calibrated models mathematically reflect the potency of these social forces, forces that are well known in most societies, especially in Israel.[108] For many years, having children is not a salient consideration in people's lives. Then, rather suddenly, there is enormous pressure on couples (and today on many singles) to have children. One sociological study describes a "syndrome of encirclement-by-pregnancies," which leaves people "feeling compelled to do what everybody else does" as the main reason for having children.[109] In Israel, the amount of pressure applied by Jewish and Muslim families on young couples can be massive.

There are many ways to integrate this insight into policy making. The most obvious involves supporting frameworks and opportunities that postpone marriage and the age when childbearing becomes normative in a certain cohort. Accordingly, higher education provides a "double demographic dividend" for population stability: it not only raises the opportunity cost of additional children for parents, it contributes to delays in marriage and fertility decisions.

In Israel there are signs that higher education and changing expectations for women defer the age of marriage and childbearing. Women in all sectors of Israeli society marry later today than in the past. In 1980, the average age of marriage was 22.4; by 1995 it increased to 23.4; in the year 2015 it is around 26.[110] Not surprisingly the average age when women first give birth has also gone up. For instance, in 2003 it was 26.3; a decade later it was 27.3.

In a multicultural country such as Israel, the value of generalizing about fertility is limited. Averages mask profound internal contrasts and opposing trends. A higher-resolution look at the country reveals that by 2009 in the secular Jewish majority, only 2 percent of secular women gave birth before reaching age 25. Today, most births in secular families are concentrated between 30 and 34. Indeed, 38 percent of secular Jewish women in Israel still have not given birth by then. This represents a profound shift in social patterns.

The picture in the religious world is completely different: Among Orthodox Israelis, 28 percent have their firstborn before age 24. Among the ultra-Orthodox, the figure is 32 percent. Israeli Muslim women's primary childbearing period is still between ages 15 and 24.[111] These figures make sense when differential fertility rates in Israeli communities are considered. Without an early "head start," many large families would not reach such prodigious sizes. To stabilize society, it is important to encourage delays in marriage and births across all sectors of Israeli society.

Just because couples may start their families later does not mean that their *desired* family size will change. But families have all sorts of aspirations and ambitions that are not always attained. People often settle for less than their ultimate house, perfect yacht, or ideal private schooling for their kids and still lead wonderful lives. Starting later means that many thousands of families may fall a little short of reaching their demographic dream.

It is important to maintain perspective about the contribution of postponement. Ultimately, delay is not a game changer. Deferring marriage and first children will only modestly put off the inevitable exceedance of local carrying capacities. But it can be part of a larger package that taken together can transform present dynamics.

Many family-planning advocates around the world share a common misconception that assumes that inadequate access to contraception is the reason why people have large families. In fact, World Bank research shows that 85–90 percent of actual family size is explained by parents' family-size targets. When motivation to limit family size is lacking, providing contraception can be largely irrelevant.[112] Many Israeli parents, especially religious Jews and Bedouins, still want to have an extraordinary number of children. Most of them will.

Cultural proclivities and sixty-five years of pro-natal policies can be seen in the mentality of mainstream Israeli society. It is reflected in demographically ambitious aspirations and enthusiasm for childbearing. Living in a country with ongoing security threats affects secular citizens' sense of family; people need something to hug in trying times. The more family members to hug, they believe, the better. For some, subconsciously at least, having more sons is an insurance policy against possible loss in the country's never-ending wars.

Furthermore, a distinctly Jewish outlook endures, one that sees family as a statement of permanence: the ultimate personal—and biological—raison d'être. The Hebrew phrase *b'karov etzlech* (May it soon happen to you) has become synonymous with cliché greetings to singles at weddings or births. Seemingly well-meaning, the patronizing implication is that young peoples' unfulfilled lives will get better once they find a spouse and have children of their own.

Hence, the second insight from social-diffusion theories of fertility is that if population is to be stabilized, existing perceptions and norms about optimal family size need to change and become more uniform across Israeli society. A fundamental shift in societal attitudes will not be easy. For the country's Orthodox Jewish and Bedouin publics, it will require nothing less than a sea change.

While the task is daunting, it is well to remember that the high percentage of staggeringly large families in Haredi and Bedouin communities is a relatively new cultural phenomenon. Fifty years ago, it was impossible to distinguish between birthrates of secular and Haredi Jewish families. The pendulum can swing back. A demographic "transition" among Israeli Arabs is occurring much faster than anyone imagined. Average family sizes fell even without the progress that might have been hoped for in the status of women and their full integration into the labor force. This is consistent with the pattern of societies around the world that have witnessed dramatic demographic shifts once modernization took hold.

There are signs that such a generational shift is taking place in Israel. Sociologist Evgenia Bystrov has identified numerous characteristics among Israel's secular public, comparable to what demographers in other countries are calling the "second demographic transition." They include a rise in the valuing of individual autonomy, postponement of family formation and childbearing, as well as an affinity for alternative lifestyles. These social phenomena combine and contribute to low or below-replacement fertility levels.[113] Bystrov found that young Israelis today, especially in the secular world, think differently than their parents do. In national surveys, a significant percentage of older, secular Israelis agree with statements such as "People without children lead empty lives"; "Households satisfy as much as paid jobs"; and "What women really want is a home and children." Younger Israelis are less inclined to agree.

The structures and dimensions of families also are evolving.[114] Israel's younger generation is more "lifestyle tolerant," showing open-mindedness about same-sex marriages, cohabitation, and single parenting. The hit U.S. television show *Modern Family*, with its assorted, socially acceptable familial units, is also popular in Israel. Many educated Israeli women decide to have a child long after choosing a career over marriage, without looking for a partner. Between 2000 and 2010 the number of unwed mothers almost doubled in Israel; 6 percent of births are presently registered with single women—precisely the same rate as in Italy and Spain.[115] There are new norms among Israel's lesbian and gay community, who are increasingly coming to see children as central to a fulfilling life.

In all the new family structures of the secular world, a common denominator is a general trend toward replacement fertility levels rather than large families. Secular women of European origin and immigrants from the former Soviet Union actually have come to average below-replacement fertility levels.[116]

The "bottom-line" question for those wondering whether Israel's population can move toward stabilization is whether religious and traditional communities will ever change their visions of what constitutes desirable family size. The age of prophecy has long since passed, making it difficult to predict the future. Looking back, there are cases of sudden and unexpected revolutions in pro-natal biases and fertility levels that took place among religious communities and countries. They suggest that Israel should not assume that what "has been" is necessarily "what will be." Given present animosities, it is hard to imagine that Israel might learn anything from Iran. Yet population policy and individual behavior in the Islamic Republic of Iran offer an unlikely story that suggests that religious Israelis could also change.

Iran's battle with Iraq raged on for eight years, from 1980 to 1988, with the last prisoners of war released only in 2003. The war was probably the longest military conflict of the twentieth century.[117] It was also one of the deadliest. The number of casualties by some estimates exceeded 1 million Iranians dead.[118] Iraq was better armed than the Iranians, but the population of Iran was more than twice that of Iraq. Iran brought its demographic advantage to the battlefield, launching "human waves" that overwhelmed Iraqi positions with numerical supremacy.

In order to resupply soldiers for the struggle, the country's spiritual leader, Ayatollah Khomeini, called on Iranian mothers to have as many children as was biologically possible and to create a "20-million-man army." The legal age for marriage was lowered to nine, family-planning offices were closed, and rationing was designed to provide larger families with economic advantages. The Iranian people responded, with annual demographic increases at a dumbfounding rate of 4.2 percent.[119] Iran's birthrate was already soaring before the war, but with the religious call to arms, the population more than doubled in just twenty years, and in 1988, reached 55 million. By then the war had stalemated to a halt, and in 1989 the ayatollah passed away. He was replaced by Ali Khamenei and a more moderate president, Akbar Rafsanjani. It became clear to Iranian economic planners that if the high fertility continued, there would be an acute employment crisis in no time; socioeconomic gaps would become unbearable. Iran's supreme leader decided to put on the brakes.

To affect this change some twenty-three thousand male and female *behavarez* (health workers) were trained, with an expertise in "family planning." Hundreds of mobile teams set off to remote regions of the country, often on horseback, where they offered a full array of conventional birth control as well as injectables and implants.[120] Even though some Muslim sects initially frowned on the program, when the economic and ecological implications of unrestricted demographic growth were explained, local Shiite clerics proved to be open-minded. They not only approved but encouraged parents to take advantage of free vasectomies and tubal ligations.[121] One hundred thousand women were sterilized during the 1990s, completely voluntarily. More surprisingly, a full 220,000 men agreed to undergo vasectomies. Use of contraceptives rose from 37 percent in 1976 to 72 percent in 2000.[122] In rural areas the increase was even more remarkable: from 20 percent to 67 percent in the same period.[123]

The program had other benefits: women began to perceive their roles in society very differently. Minimum marrying age was increased to twenty-one, and education was officially promoted. In rural regions, where females traditionally married young, some 70 percent of mothers preferred that their daughters continue their education after high school.[124] In 1975, only one-third of Iranian females were literate; by 2012, 60 percent of university students were women. As female gynecologists began to appear on Iranian television, public perceptions underwent radical change. The country was already exhausted from the war, and desired family size plummeted. The fertility rate was down to 2.1 by the year 2000 and kept on dropping. By 2014 it had reached 1.84.[125]

After falling to below-replacement levels, Iran's Islamic leaders subsequently had second thoughts and even tried to dismantle some of the contraception services. But Iranian women do not want to go back to the days of 4 percent annual growth in population. A similar story took place in Islamic Bangladesh, a land were 184 million people live in an area no bigger than Wisconsin. Radio and billboards echoed Prime Minister Sheikh Hasina's 2010 proclamation: "Not more than two children; *one is better.*" And like Iran, 35,000 women were drafted to spread the gospel of contraception throughout the country's rural hinterlands.[126] Publicly, Bangladesh officials have expressed admiration for China's "one-child policy," with the intention of introducing it as a voluntary program.[127]

These successful cases show that when religious leadership partners with government health agencies, the results can be breathtaking. For Israel to successfully change present demographic dynamics, it must engage religious leaders and confront them with the negative social and environmental implications of high birthrates. The Orthodox and ultra-Orthodox communities are not nearly as homogeneous as is commonly imagined. They have always been splintered politically and theologically. There are Orthodox rabbis and lay leaders with sincere ecological sensitivities. Others are starting to show openness to improving the status of women. While "top-down" models of change are most common in the religious world, there are signs that "bottom-up" dynamics also exist and may be even more important. Many members in these communities are already making up their own minds. Over time new norms can influence the thinking of the establishment. Still, many commentators believe that reduction in ultra-Orthodox fertility will only happen after "liberation from religious authorities" takes place[128] and the issue becomes less politicized.

To be successful, Israel does not need to launch a campaign that sends paramedics on horseback into the hills. Yet if the goal is to facilitate real change in demographics, it is time to think beyond conventional educational frameworks in spreading the message about population stabilization and reproductive autonomy. The creativity exhibited in demographic programs' interface with the media around the globe is instructive.

In some countries, popular, commercially successful television programs have done more than anything else to change societal attitudes toward contraception, women's reproductive decisions, and perceptions of optimal family size. For instance, in India, a year-long miniseries "Come Along with Me" became the country's most popular television show in 1992. Over 100 million people watched each week as the tragedy of a fourteen-year-old mother's life with her unwanted child unfolded. Follow-up surveys with 3,000 viewers revealed significant changes in attitudes toward reproductive norms, particularly among adult males.[129]

In Mexico a telenovela with an underlying message of family planning and women's rights was even more influential, reflected in ratings ranging between 60 percent and 90 percent of the television audience. Follow-up surveys showed that 70 percent of viewers felt the program affected their opinions, favoring independence for women; an impressive 71 percent reported learning "that family size should be limited." The TV network received four hundred thousand letters from the public. Radio shows in Tanzania and Kenya produced similar results.[130]

In the past, media campaigns have been highly effective in transforming the Israeli public's attitudes by promoting environmental values, from wildflower protection to water conservation.[131] On other issues as well, popular television shows have surely helped to change public perceptions of Arab Israelis, homosexuals, and the Orthodox community. Fertility experts have called entertainment broadcasting and mass-media communications the best donor investments in terms of "birth averted per dollar spent" that can be made.[132] Even if the Israeli government is slow to embrace the imperative of family planning and population stabilization, with a very free media, Israel's philanthropies can be drafted to underwrite the costs of commercials or motivational programs about the status of women and the perils of present population trends. Not all sectors of Israeli society watch television or have free access to the Internet. To reach the Bedouin and the Haredi communities, new forms of communication will need to be found. But the message must be delivered.

GROWTH VERSUS THE ART OF LIVING

As Israel muddles forward in search of some semblance of sustainability, it must realize that any true long-term strategy requires an enduring equilibrium. A balance must be struck between the number of people living in the land and the resources that support life. Israelis also need to remember that mere survival was never the vision that motivated the founders of the Jewish state. The country's progress should be measured in terms of spiritual and cultural advancement, justice and equity, aesthetics and beauty, health and happiness—rather than perpetual economic or demographic expansion whose value is only instrumental. Today, population density negatively affects all criteria that really matter. The simple truth is Israel will not realize its potential in the future if it must constantly meet the needs of millions more people. Regardless of where its borders ultimately lie, Palestine will not benefit from higher population densities, either.

Demographically, Zionism has been a sensational success. Multitudes of Jews facing oppression or economic hardship found a haven in the land of Israel. Immigration is never easy, and mistakes were surely made in official efforts to absorb so many people from such diverse cultural realities. Nonetheless, the Law of Return, along with an enormous investment in immigrant absorption, translated the Zionist dream into a national transformation. Those Jews who wish to avail themselves of the opportunity to settle in their homeland should be able to do so. But empirical historic experience suggests that relatively few will. The era of mass immigration is over.

It is time for Israel to move on to the next stage of sustainability. It is time to listen to the pragmatic voices in Jewish and Muslim traditions and salute the common-sense logic that motivates Israelis of all ethnic backgrounds to plan smaller families. Of course, setting a clear limit for the number of people who live in a particular area is never simple. But if everyone agrees that some limit exists, it is better to discuss what it is and plan accordingly than to one fine day awake and discover that it has been exceeded.

The number of people in Israel is not the only limit that needs to be considered. The amount of products and energy that Israelis consume in their increasingly consumerist lifestyles also challenge any future equilibrium. But to argue that profligate consumption means that population growth doesn't matter is as foolish and simplistic as saying that because cancer needs to be treated, heart disease can be ignored. Both need to be confronted; society is capable of addressing two existential challenges simultaneously.[133]

The time for change is now, while being proactive can still avert unnecessary human hardship and irreversible ecological damage. Decision makers need to recognize that population growth during their tenure may only have modest impacts on present quality of life or availability of resources. The cumulative impact of demographic increases, however, will be felt long after today's leaders have left the stage, even after population stabilizes, as it eventually must.[134] It is high time that Israel starts planning the best steady state possible for future citizens to pursue the art of living.

For the people of Israel, life has always been dynamic. As more humans filled the land, reality changed. The biblical commandment to "Be fruitful and multiply and fill the land" appears twice in the Bible. Initially it was part of Adam and Eve's welcome to the Garden of Eden. Years later, after the cataclysmic deluge almost wiped out humanity, Noah is again told to "be fruitful and multiply."

The Bible is never presumed to be redundant, so the sages sought an explanation for the repetition. They reached the conclusion that in the initial passage, to "Be fruitful and multiply" was simply a blessing. But then, following the dire conditions created by the flood, the status of the adage was elevated to that of commandment. Today, circumstances have changed yet again. The land of Israel is teeming with people. It still offers its residents a good life. International surveys consistently indicate that the State of Israel is a relatively joyful place to be. Yet as present densities increase, this blessed state is threatened. There is no commandment that requires cramming more people into a holy land that is already full.

In the not-too-distant yesteryear, infant and childhood mortality was high everywhere in the world, especially in the land of Israel. The physical security of Jews and the other people living there was perennially precarious. In those days, "being fruitful" was a sound individual and national strategy. But those days belong to a past that will not return. Offering Israel's offspring a chance to live well and not merely survive tomorrow means stabilizing population today. It also means recognizing that the greatest blessing of the modern age is the opportunity to celebrate the quality rather than the quantity of life.

NOTES

CHAPTER 1. INTRODUCTION

1. Alon Tal, *Pollution in a Promised Land: An Environmental History of Israel* (Berkeley: University of California Press, 2002), 181, 184.
2. Dan Perry, "Denying the Main Point," *Teva V'Aretz*, January 1995.
3. Yitzhak Bar-Yosef, "Should We Decrease Reproduction to Protect Nature?" *Yedioth Ahronot*, January 1995, copy with author.
4. Yehoshua Shkedi, personal communication, March 9, 2015.
5. Dan Perry, interview with author, July 15, 2013.
6. "Notice of Appointment of Director of the Nature Reserve Authority," *Yalkut Pirsumim* (official Israel government gazette), Jerusalem, Israel Ministry of Interior, 4334, September 21, 1995.
7. Israel Central Bureau of Statistics (CBS), "Fertility Rates, by Age and Religion" (Jerusalem, 2014), http://147.237.248.50/shnaton65/st03_13.pdf.
8. Alma Cohen, Rajeev Dehejia, and Dmitri Romanov, "Financial Incentives and Fertility," *Review of Economics and Statistics* 95 (1) (2013): 4.
9. University of Auckland, *The New Zealand Attitudes and Values Study* (Auckland, NZ: Department of Psychology, University of Auckland, 2013), http://www.psych.auckland.ac.nz/en/about/our-research/research-groups/new-zealand-attitudes-and-values-study.html.
10. Israel CBS, "Population Density per Square Kilometer of Land," *Statistical Abstract of Israel* (Jerusalem, 2012), 130, http://www.cbs.gov.il/shnaton63/st02_14.pdf.
11. Iris Hann, "Open Space in an Urban Society," in *Between Ruin and Restoration: An Environmental History of Israel*, ed. Daniel Orenstein, Alon Tal, and Char Miller (Pittsburgh: University of Pittsburgh Press, 2013), 146–167.
12. Michael Gold, *And Hannah Wept: Infertility, Adoption, and the Jewish Couple* (Philadelphia: Jewish Publication Society, 1988).
13. Vered Levi, "Secular, Affluent Families, with Many Children," *Haaretz*, December 26, 2012.

14. Sergio DellaPergola, "Demography in Israel/Palestine: Trends, Prospects, Policy Implications," (International Union for the Scientific Study of Population [IUSSP] XXIV General Population Conference, Salvador de Bahia, August 2001), http://212.95.240.146 /Brazil2001/s60/S64_02_dellapergola.pdf.

15. Fred M. Gottheil, "The Smoking Gun: Arab Immigration into Palestine, 1922–1931," *Middle East Quarterly* 10 (1) (2003): 53–64.

16. *Palestine Royal Commission Report* (Peel Commission), Cmd. 5479 (London: Her Majesty's Stationery Office [HMSO], July 1937), 331, http://unispal.un.org/UNISPAL .NSF/o/88A6BF6F1BD82405852574CD006C457F.

17. Israel CBS, *The Arab Population in Israel* (November 2002), 6, http://www.cbs.gov.il /statistical/arabju.pdf.

18. Daphna Birenbaum-Carmeli, "'Cheaper Than a Newcomer': On the Social Production of IVF Policy in Israel," *Sociology of Health and Illness* 26 (7) (2004): 902.

19. Rutti Gur, interview with author, June 26, 2013.

20. "Minister of Justice: Families with Many Children Are a Burden on Society," *Nana*, April 9, 2000, http://news.nana10.co.il/Article/?ArticleID=8144.

21. Matti Siber, "To Address Fertility among the Bedouins," *Yedioth Ahronot*, September 29, 2014, 10.

22. Arnon Soffer, interview with author, June 3, 2013.

23. The Jewish People Policy Institute (JPPI), "Jewish People Demography, 2015" Annual Assessment 2014–2015, 5775 (Jerusalem, 2015): 116–117. Also, Anshel Pfeffer, "Beating Hitler by Numbers," *Haaretz*, July 2, 2015, http://www.haaretz.com/blogs/jerusalem -babylon/.premium-1.664171.

24. Sergio DellaPergola, *Jewish Demographic Policies: Population Trends and Options in Israel and in the Diaspora* (Jerusalem: Jewish People Policy Institute, 2011), 21, 56.

25. Nigel Savage, director of Hazon, personal communication, April 9, 2009.

26. Daniel Orenstein, "Population Growth and Environmental Impact: Ideology and Academic Discourse in Israel," *Population and Environment* 26 (1) (2004): 53.

27. Avner de-Shalit, "Sustainability and Population Policies: Myths, Truths and Half-Baked Ideas," in *Global Sustainable Development in the Twenty-first Century*, ed. Keekok Lee, Desmond McNeill, and Alan Holland (Edinburgh: Edinburgh University Press, 2000), 188–199, quote at 189.

28. Ibid., 195.

29. Yaakov Garb, "Population Dynamics and Sustainability in the Israeli Context: Navigating between Demographic Warfare and Malthusianism," in *Paths to Sustainability: Shadow Report to the Government of Israel's Assessment of Progress in Implementing Agenda 21* (Tel Aviv: Heschel Center, 2002), 201–222.

30. Eilon Schwartz, interview with author, June 2, 2013.

31. Garb, "Population Dynamics," 222.

32. Israel Ministry of Agriculture and Rural Development, "National Plan for Agriculture and Rural Development" (PowerPoint presentation, June 2013), slide 17, http://www .moag.gov.il/agri/Files/tochnit_leumit_lahaklaut.pdf.

33. Eran Feitelson, "Malicious Siting or Unrecognized Processes? A Spatio-Temporal Analysis of Environmental Conflicts in Tel Aviv," *Urban Studies* 38 (2001): 1143–1159.

34. Avi Bar-Eli, "Traffic Jams Cost Israel NIS 20 Billion a Year," *Haaretz*, October 7, 2010.

35. Walter Youngquist, "An Obituary of Albert A. Bartlett 1923–2013," *Population Matters* 24 (February 2014), 16, http://populationmatters.org/magazine/0214.pdf

36. Professor Bartlett's lecture is available on YouTube, http://www.youtube.com/watch?v =2BXiy7M7Vr8.

37. Sergio DellaPergola, interview with author, July 3, 2013.

38. Sergio DellaPergola, "Demographic Trends in Israel and Palestine: Prospects and Policy Implications," *American Jewish Yearbook* 103 (2003): 3–68, especially 37.

CHAPTER 2. OF POLLUTION, PAUCITY,
AND POPULATION PRESSURES

1. Yaniv Kobovich, "One Quarter Million Complaints Submitted in 2012 about Noise Disturbance," *Haaretz*, August 1, 2013, http://www.haaretz.co.il/news/law/.premium-1 .2086487.

2. Alon Tal, *The Environment in Israel: Natural Resources, Crises, Campaigns and Policy from the Advent of Zionism until Twenty-first Century* (B'nei Brak: HaKibbutz HaMeuhad Press, 2006), 517–520.

3. Avi Gottlieb, "Noise as an Environmental Hazard: The Responses of Adolescents to Noise Nuisances," *Green Blue and White*, August–September 1997.

4. Gary Greenberg, "The Effects of Ambient Temperature and Population Density on Aggression in Two Inbred Strains of Mice, *Mus musculu*," *Behavior* 42 (1972): 119–130; G. L. Gregor, R. Smith, L. Simons, and H. Parker, "Behavioral Consequences of Crowding in the Deermouse (*Permyscus maniculatus*)," *Journal of Comparative and Physiological Psychology* 79 (1972): 488–493; or in primates: Robert H. Elton and Brian V. Anderson, "The Social Behavior of a Group of Baboons (*Papio anubis*) under Artificial Crowding," *Primates* 18 (1977): 225–234.

5. Chalsa Loo and Paul Ong, "Crowding Perceptions, Attitudes, and Consequences among the Chinese," *Environment and Behavior* 16 (1984): 55–87.

6. Alan Booth, *Urban Crowding and Its Consequences* (New York: Praeger, 1976); Alan Booth, Susan Welch, and David R. Johnson, "Crowding and Urban Crime Rates," *Urban Affairs Quarterly* 11 (1976): 291–307.

7. Wendy C. Regoeczi, "Crowding in Context: An Examination of the Differential Responses of Men and Women to High-Density Living Environments," *Journal of Health and Social Behavior* 49 (2008): 254.

8. Paul Paulus, Verne Cox, Garvin McCain, and Jane Chandler, "Some Effects of Crowding in a Prison Environment," *Journal of Applied Social Psychology* 5 (1) (1975): 86–91; also, David A. D'Atri and Adrian M. Ostfeld, "Crowding: Its Effects on the Elevation of Blood Pressure in a Prison Setting," *Preventive Medicine* 4 (4) (1975): 550–566.

9. Walter R. Gove, Michael Hughes, and Omer R. Galle, "Overcrowding in the Home: An Empirical Investigation of Its Possible Pathological Consequences," *American Sociological Review* 44 (1) (1979): 59–80.

10. Gitit Ginat, "Can Israel Become Garbage-Free?" *Haaretz*, February 9, 2012, http:// www.haaretz.com/weekend/magazine/can-israel-become-garbage-free-1.411944.

11. Liat Collins, "Aviation Authorities: Close Hiriya Dump," *Jerusalem Post*, November 14, 1997.
12. Alon Tal, *Pollution in a Promised Land: An Environmental History of Israel* (Berkeley: University of California Press, 2002), 314–315.
13. Zafrir Rinat, "Israel Ramps Up Efforts to Block Illegal Smuggling of Waste into the West Bank," *Haaretz*, July 29, 2013.
14. The Law for Collecting and Transporting Garbage for Recycling, *Sefer HaChokim*, no. 1422, June 11, 1993, 116.
15. Israel Ministry of Environmental Protection, "Waste and Recycling," (Jerusalem, October 18, 2015), http://kids.gov.il/sababa/sababa_pool/pages/4041.
16. Israel Ministry of Environmental Quality, *Solid Waste Treatment Policy* (Jerusalem, 2002).
17. Organisation for Economic Co-operation and Development (OECD), *Environmental Performance Reviews: Israel* (Paris, 2011), 190, http://www.oecd-ilibrary.org/environment/oecd-environmental-performance-reviews-israel-2011_9789264117563-en.
18. Tai Trilnick and Alon Tal, "Should We Blame the Rich for Clogging Our Landfills?" *Waste Management and Research* 32 (2) (2014): 91–96.
19. Ginat, "Can Israel Become Garbage-Free?"
20. Israel Ministry of Environmental Protection, "Solid Waste," accessed October 18, 2015, http://www.sviva.gov.il/subjectsEnv/Waste/MixedWaste/wase-site-rehabilitation/Pages/NonRegulatedLandfill.aspx.
21. Tristram's many books include *The Land of Israel: A Journal of Travels with Reference to Its Physical History* (1865), *The Mammals of Palestine* (1866), *The Natural History of the Bible* (1867), *Pathways of Palestine* (1882), and the definitive *The Survey of Western Palestine: Fauna and Flora of Palestine* (1884); Fritz S. Bodenheimer, "H. B. Tristram's Collections in Natural History, Especially of Palestine," *Annals of Science* 12 (4) (1956): 278–287.
22. Norman Myers, Russell A. Mittermeier, Cristina G. Mittermeier, Gustavo A. B. da Fonseca, and Jennifer Kent, "Biodiversity Hotspots for Conservation Priorities," *Nature* 403 (2000): 853–858.
23. Yoram Yom-Tov, "Human Impact on Wildlife in Israel since the Nineteenth Century," in *Between Ruin and Restoration: An Environmental History of Israel*, ed. Daniel Orenstein, Alon Tal, and Char Miller (Pittsburgh: University of Pittsburgh Press, 2013), 53–81.
24. Israel National Planning and Building Law, National Master Plan No. 8, National Parks, Nature Reserves and Landscape Reserves (1981), http://www.mmi.gov.il/iturTabot/tochMitarArzi.asp; Iris Hann, "Open Space in an Urban Society," in *Between Ruin and Restoration*, 146–167; Lenore Fahrig, "Effects of Habitat Fragmentation on Biodiversity," *Annual Review of Ecological Evolutionary Systems* 34 (2003): 487–515.
25. OECD, *Environmental Performance Reviews*, 131.
26. Orit Skutelski and Moshe Pearlmutter, *Reviving Streams and Wetlands in Israel: The SPNI's Vision and Major Guidelines for Eco-Hydrological Restoration* (Tel Aviv: Society for the Protection of Nature in Israel [SPNI], 2012), http://www.teva.org.il/_Uploads/dbsAttachedFiles/nechalim12.pdf.

27. Uriel Safriel, ed., *Israel's National Biodiversity Plan* (Jerusalem: Israel Ministry of Environmental Protection, 2010), https://www.cbd.int/iyb/doc/celebrations/iyb-israel-sviva-plan-en.pdf; Rachelle Adam, "Going beyond Israel: Epistemic Communities, Global Interests, and International Environmental Agreements," in *Between Ruin and Restoration*, 262–284.

28. OECD, *Environmental Performance Reviews*, 129.

29. Iris Bernstein, "Ecological Corridors: The Case of the Modi'in Forest" (PowerPoint presentation, Conference of the Israel Ecological and Environmental Science Association, September 16, 2014).

30. Haim Bibas, personal communication, Modi'in City Hall, December 15, 2014.

31. Itamar Ben David and Nofar Avni, *Threats, 2013: Report Number 6* (Tel Aviv: SPNI, 2013), http://www.teva.org.il/_Uploads/dbsAttachedFiles/Threats13.pdf.

32. Tamar Ahiron-Frumkin and Ron Frumkin, "The Environmental Price of Exploiting Natural Resources on Humans," *Eureka* (2004), http://www.matar.ac.il/eureka/newspaper18/article3.asp.

33. Yaniv Kubovich, Shirly Seidler, Eli Ashkenazi, and Zafrir Rinat, "Tourist Sites Overflow as Holiday Visitors Turned Away from Kinerret," *Haaretz*, April 17, 2014, http://www.haaretz.com/news/national/.premium-1.585923.

34. Ultimately a nonbinding "Copenhagen Accord" was cobbled together: United Nations Framework Convention on Climate Change (UNFCCC), *Copenhagen Accord* FCCC/CP/2009/L.7 (December 18, 2009), http://unfccc.int/resource/docs/2009/cop15/eng/l07.pdf.

35. Peres's speech can be found at http://www.youtube.com/watch?v=fovO22FSNq4.

36. Lucy Michaels and Alon Tal, "Convergence and Conflict with the 'National Interest': Why Israel Abandoned Its Climate Policy," *Energy Policy* (forthcoming, 2015).

37. Lucy Michaels and Pinhas Alpert, "Anthropogenic Climate Change in Israel," in *Between Ruin and Restoration*, 309–333.

38. McKinsey & Company, *Greenhouse Gas Abatement Potential in Israel: Israel's GHG Abatement Cost Curve, Executive Summary* (November 2009), 3.

39. Ministry of National Infrastructures, Energy and Water Resources, "Electricity Demand Projections for Planning the Electricity Sector," last accessed October 18, 2015, http://energy.gov.il/Subjects/Electricity/Pages/GxmsMniAboutElectricity.aspx.

40. David Wainerand Anna Hirtenstein, "Israel's 300 Days of Sun No Help as Offshore Gas Eclipses Solar," *BloombergBusiness*, September 10, 2015, http://www.bloomberg.com/news/articles/2015-09-10/israel-s-300-days-of-sun-no-help-as-offshore-gas-eclipses-solar.

41. Avner de-Shalit, "Sustainability and Population Policies: Myths, Truths and Half-Baked Ideas," in *Global Sustainable Development in the Twenty-First Century*, ed. Keekok Lee, Desmond McNeill, and Alan Holland (Edinburgh: Edinburgh University Press, 2000), 195.

42. Yaakov Garb, "Population Dynamics and Sustainability in the Israeli Context: Navigating between Demographic Warfare and Malthusianism," in *Paths to Sustainability: Shadow Report to the Government of Israel's Assessment of Progress in Implementing Agenda 21* (Tel Aviv: Heschel Center, 2002), 201–222.

43. Alon Tal, "Two Sides of the Rectangle: The Environmental Movement and Overpopulation," *Ecology and Environment* 3 (3) (2013): 271–273.

44. Israel Central Bureau of Statistics (CBS), "Emissions of Greenhouse Gases by Source," *Statistical Abstract of Israel, 2012* (Jerusalem, 2012), http://www1.cbs.gov.il/shnaton63 /st27_06.pdf.

45. OECD, *Environmental Performance Reviews.*

46. Israel Ministry of Environmental Protection, "Israel Commits to Reducing GHG Emissions 26% by 2030," October 7, 2015, http://www.sviva.gov.il/English/Resourcesand Services/NewsAndEvents/NewsAndMessageDover/Pages/2015/Oct-10/Israel-Commits -to-Reducing-GHG-Emissions-26-percent-by-2030.aspx.

47. Timothy J. Skone, *Life Cycle Greenhouse Gas Analysis of Natural Gas Extraction and Delivery in the United States* (Washington, DC: U.S. Department of Energy, 2011), http://www.netl.doe.gov/File%20Library/Research/Energy%20Analysis/Life%20 Cycle%20Analysis/NG_LC_GHG_PRES_12MAY11.pdf.

48. Noam Segal, of the Israel Energy Forum, personal communication, August 11, 2013.

49. Malin Falkenmark and G. Lindh, *Water for a Starving World* (Boulder, CO: Westview Press, 1976); also, Malin Falkenmark, "Water and Sustainability: A Reappraisal," *Environment* 50 (2) (2008): 5–16.

50. Flavius Josephus, "The War of the Jews," bk. 1 in *The Complete Works of Josephus*, trans. William Whiston (Grand Rapids, MI: Kregel Publications, 1981).

51. Sharon Udasin, "Dead Sea Not Chosen as One of New 7 Wonders," *Jerusalem Post*, November 11, 2011.

52. Friends of the Earth Middle East, *Let the Dead Sea Live* (Amman, Jordan: Friends of the Earth Middle East (FOEME) 1999), http://foeme.org/uploads/publications_publ25_1.pdf.

53. Alon Tal, "The Dead Sea," *Lonely Planet Jordan* (Sydney: Lonely Planet, 2008).

54. Tal, *Pollution in a Promised Land*, 207–209.

55. Population Division of the Department of Economic and Social Affairs of the United Nations Secretariat, *World Population Prospects: The 2015 Revision*, last accessed November 16, 2015, http://esa.un.org/unpd/wpp/.

56. Jeffrey Sosland, *Cooperating Rivals: The Riparian Politics of the Jordan River Basin* (Albany: SUNY Press, 2008), 32; Joseph Marks, "Israel's Dead Sea Sinkholes Swallow the Unwary—and Tourism," Associated Press, June 24, 2009, http://seattletimes.com /html/travel/2009379731_webdeadsea24.html.

57. Israel Water Authority, *The Dead Sea* (2013), accessed March 30, 2015, http://www.water .gov.il/Hebrew/Water-Environment/Dead-Sea/Pages/default.aspx.

58. "Sinkhole Swallows Hiker," *National Geographic*, June 29, 2009, http://news.national geographic.com/news/2009/06/090629-deadsea-sinkholes-video-ap.html.

59. Boris Shirman and Michael Rybakov, "Sinkholes along the Dead Sea Coast and Their Development" (paper presented at Surveyors Key Role in Accelerated Development Conference, Eilat, Israel, May 3–8, 2009).

60. Marks, "Israel's Dead Sea Sinkholes."

61. Bellier Coyne-Et, *Red Sea—Dead Sea Water Conveyance Study Program*, Draft Final Feasibility Study Report, July 2012, http://siteresources.worldbank.org /INTREDSEADEADSEA/Resources/Feasibility_Study_Report_Summary_EN.pdf.

62. Ora Cohen, "Israel, Jordan Sign Red–Dead Canal Agreement Project," *Haaretz*, February 27, 2015, http://www.haaretz.com/business/.premium-1.644601.

63. Alexander Kushnir, director, Israel Water Authority (oral presentation at International Conference for Rehabilitating the Jordan River, Kibbutz Nir David, October 21, 2014).

64. Alon Tal, "Management of Transboundary Wastewater Discharges," in *Shared Borders, Shared Waters*, ed. S. B. Megdal, R. G. Varady, and S. Eden (Leiden: CRC Press, 2013), 221–232.

65. Alon Tal, "Seeking Sustainability: Israel's Evolving Water Management Strategy," *Science* 313 (2006): 1081–1084.

66. Karen Asaf, "Shared Groundwater Resources, and Environmental Hazards and Technical Solutions in Palestine," and Dror Avisar, "The Mountain Aquifer: Shared Groundwater Resources, Environmental Hazards and Technical Solutions," both in *Water Wisdom: A New Menu for Palestinian and Israeli Cooperation in Water Management*, ed. Alon Tal and Alfred Abed-Rabbo (New Brunswick, NJ: Rutgers University Press, 2010), 103–121.

67. Luay Froukh, "The Impact and Management of Recent Drought on the West Bank Groundwater Aquifer System," in *Economics of Drought and Drought Preparedness in a Climate Change Context*, ed. A. López-Francos (Zaragoza, Spain: International Centre for Advanced Mediterranean Agronomic Studies (CIHEAM) / Food and Agricultural Organization (FAO), 2010), 279–283, http://om.ciheam.org/om/pdf/a95/00801357.pdf.

68. United Nations, "Water For Life Decade" (2013), accessed August 12, 2013, http://www.un.org/waterforlifedecade/human_right_to_water.shtml.

69. Lauren Gelfond Feldingerm, "The Politics of Water: Palestinians Bracing for Another Dry Summer," *Haaretz*, April 13, 2013.

70. Alon Tal, "Thirsting for Pragmatism: A Constructive Alternative to Amnesty International's Report on Palestinian Access to Water," *Israel Journal of Foreign Affairs* 4 (2) (2010): 59–73.

71. U.S. Central Intelligence Agency (CIA), "West Bank—People and Society," *The World Factbook* (2013), accessed March 30, 2015, https://www.cia.gov/library/publications/the-world-factbook/geos/we.html.

72. Zafrir Rinat, "The Water Authority: Water Pollution in One-Tenth of the Groundwater in the Groundwater of the Coastal Plain," *Haaretz*, March 21, 2011.

73. Hillel Shuval, "The Agricultural Roots of Israel's Water Crisis," in *Between Ruin and Restoration*, 129–145.

74. Avraham Tenne, Israel Water Authority, personal communication, July 11, 2013; also, A. Tenne, D. Hoffman, and E. Levi, "Quantifying the Actual Benefits of Large-Scale Seawater Desalination in Israel," *Desalination and Water Treatment* 51 (1–3) (2013): 26–37.

75. Alon Tal, "Rethinking the Sustainability of Israel's Irrigation Practices in the Drylands," *Water Research* 90 (2016): 387–394. Shmuel Assouline, David Russo, Avner Silber, and Dani Or, "Balancing Water Scarcity and Quality for Sustainable Irrigated Agriculture, *Water Resources Research* 51 (5) (2015): 3419–3436.

CHAPTER 3. OF IMPAIRED PUBLIC SERVICES, POVERTY, AND POPULATION PRESSURES

1. Paul R. Ehrlich, Anne H. Ehrlich, and Gretchen C. Daily, *The Stork and the Plow: The Equity Answer to the Human Dilemma* (New York: Putnam, 1995), 17.
2. Haim Bibi, "Impact of Air Pollution on Children's Health" (paper presented at Health and Environment conference, Mount Carmel Hotel, Haifa, Israel, September 3, 2012); Nir Brender, "Air Pollution: 2.5 Times the Asthma among Children in the Haifa Region," *Ynet*, January 5, 2012, http://www.ynet.co.il/articles/0,7340,L-4171913,00.html.
3. Avi Bar-Eli, "Traffic Jams Cost Israel NIS 20 Billion a Year," *Haaretz*, October 7, 2010, http://www.haaretz.com/print-edition/business/traffic-jams-cost-israel-nis-20-billion-a-year-1.317606.
4. Ibid.
5. Dubi Ben Gedalyahu, "A Holiday for the Milkers: Vehicle Deliveries in 2015 Continue to Break Records," *Globes*, September 2, 2015, http://www.globes.co.il/news/article.aspx?did=1001065886.
6. Israel Central Bureau of Statistics (CBS), "2013—2.85 Million Motor Vehicles in Israel" (press release, March 30, 2014), http://www.cbs.gov.il/reader/newhodaot/hodaa_template.html?hodaa=201427079.
7. Israel CBS, "Population According to Groups" (updated, October 6, 2015), http://www.cbs.gov.il/reader/cw_usr_view_SHTML?ID=629.
8. Israel CBS, "Table 31: Construction of Roads and Widening and Reconstruction of Roads, by District and Type of Road," *Transport Statistics Quarterly* 2 (Jerusalem, 2013), 47.
9. Israel CBS, "Table 33: Annual Average Daily Traffic and Road Accidents with Casualties on Selected Road Sections," *Transport Statistics Quarterly* 2 (Jerusalem, 2013), 50, 51.
10. Israel CBS, "Table 24.1: Main Indices of Transportation, 1999–2013" *Israel Statistical Abstract* (Jerusalem, 2014), http://147.237.248.50/shnaton65/diag/24_01e.pdf.
11. Israel CBS, "Table 6: Import Value of Vehicles, Accessories and Spare Parts," *Transport Statistics Quarterly* 2 (Jerusalem, 2013), 21; Gedalyahu, "A Holiday for the Milkers."
12. Israel CBS, "Motor Vehicles and Level of Motorization," *Israel Statistical Abstract* (Jerusalem, 2012), 1033.
13. Aaron Kalman, "Futuristic Transport Pods to Land in TA," *Times of Israel*, July 31, 2013, http://www.timesofisrael.com/futuristic-transport-pods-coming-to-tel-aviv/.
14. Avi Bar-Eli, "Tel Aviv to Ban Trucks in Morning Rush Hour," *Haaretz*, October 7, 2010, http://www.haaretz.com/print-edition/business/tel-aviv-to-ban-trucks-in-morning-rush-hour-1.317607.
15. David Wainer, "In Tel Aviv, Nasty Traffic and Navigation Apps Go Hand in Hand," *Bloomberg Business Week*, June 20, 2013.
16. Tamar Keinan, *Promoting Public Transportation in Local Governments: First Ten Steps* (Tel Aviv: Transportation Today and Tomorrow, 2013).
17. Jonathan Leape, "The London Congestion Charge," *Journal of Economic Perspectives* 20 (4) (2006): 157–176.

18. Israel Ministry of Construction and Housing, "Households in Israel and Projections of Demand for Housing, 2013," accessed October 18, 2015, http://www.moch.gov.il /meyda_statisti/habikush_beshuk_hadiyur/Pages/mishkey_habait_beisrael.aspx.

19. Nimrod Buso, "What Is the Government Doing to Help 2 Million People Renting Apartments?" *The Marker*, August 24, 2013, http://www.themarker.com/realestate/1 .2104539.

20. Niv Ellis, "Israel Housing Forecast: Prices on the Rise," *Jerusalem Post*, August 30, 2015, http://www.jpost.com/Business-and-Innovation/Israel-Housing-Forecast-Prices -on-the-rise-413722.

21. Globes staff, "Israel Has World's Ninth Largest Home Prices Rise," *Globes*, June 20, 2013, http://www.globes.co.il/serveen/globes/docview.asp?did=1000854145&fid=1124.

22. Nimrod Bousso, "Housing Market Trends Point to Price Rises Ahead," *Haaretz*, March 12, 2013, http://www.haaretz.com/business/real-estate/housing-market-trends -point-to-price-rises-ahead-1.508788.

23. Einat Paz-Frankel, "Home Prices Double OECD Average in Salary Terms," *Globes*, March 11, 2012, http://www.globes.co.il/serveen/globes/docview.asp?did=1000732101 &fid=1124.

24. Zafrir Rinat, "Netanyahu's Flagship Land Planning Reform Runs Aground," *Haaretz*, September 9, 2012, http://www.haaretz.com/news/national/netanyahu-s-flagship-land -planning-reform-runs-aground-1.463573.

25. Moshe Golan, "Bank of Israel Keeps Interest Rate Unchanged," *Globes*, June 24, 2013, http://www.globes.co.il/serveen/globes/docview.asp?did=1000856753&fid=1725.

26. Aviad Glickman, "Judge Commits Suicide 'Due to Workload,'" *Ynet*, February 9, 2011.

27. Tova Tsimuki, "A Mountain of Files," *Yedioth Ahronot*, July 1, 2013; Aviad Glickman, "Judge Ben-Atar Committed Suicide: Feared He Would Be Fired," *Ynet*, August 2, 2011, http://www.ynet.co.il/articles/0,7340,L-4025848,00.html.

28. Esti Aharonovich, "The Widow of the Judge Morris Ben Atar Doesn't Forget and Surely Doesn't Forgive," *Haaretz*, March 18, 2011, http://www.haaretz.co.il/misc/1 .1167439.

29. Avi Ashkenazi, Nativ Nachmani, and Noam Sharvit, "The Judge That Committed Suicide, Morris Ben Atar from the Jerusalem Magistrate Court," *Maariv/NRG*, February 8, 2011, http://www.nrg.co.il/online/1/ART2/209/847.html.

30. Hila Raz, "The Rate of Plea Bargains in Israel Is among the Highest in the World— It's Disturbing," *The Marker*, May 15, 2012.

31. Oren Gazal-Ayal, "Partial Ban on Plea Bargains," *Cardozo Law Review* 27 (2006): 2295.

32. Evgenia Bystrov and Arnon Soffer, "Demography and the Deterioration of the Education System," in *Israel: Demography and Density, 2007–2020* (Haifa: University of Haifa, 2008), 59–61.

33. Noah Efron, *A Chosen Calling: Jews in Science in the Twentieth Century* (Baltimore, MD: Johns Hopkins University Press, 2014).

34. Eytan Avriel, "Joining OECD is Pure Gain for Israel," *Haaretz*, May 11, 2010, http:// www.haaretz.com/print-edition/business/joining-oecd-is-pure-gain-for-israel-1.289558.

35. Shahar Hai, Michal Margalit, and Ilana Couriel, "Crowded in Class: In These Conditions, It's Impossible to Teach," *Ynet*, March 9, 2015; Globes News Service, "OECD Report: Crowded Classrooms and Low Teacher Pay in Israel," *Globes*, June 25, 2013, http://www.ynet.co.il/articles/0,7340,L-4633327,00.html; Organisation for Economic Co-operation and Development (OECD), *Education at a Glance, 2013 OECD Indicators* (Paris, 2013), http://dx.doi.org/10.1787/eag-2013-en.

36. Lior Dattel, "Israeli Classrooms Are Most Crowded in the Western World, *Haaretz*, March 6, 2013, http://www.haaretz.com/business/israeli-classrooms-are-most-crowded -in-the-western-world.premium-1.507564.

37. Rotem Ellizera, "The Most Crowded in the World," *Yedioth Ahronot*, September 10, 2014, 9.

38. Israel CBS, 2000, as quoted in Bystrov and Soffer, "Demography and the Deterioration of the Education System," 59.

39. Gary Evans, "Child Development and the Physical Environment," *Annual Review of Psychology* 57 (2006): 423–451; also, Parveen Khan and Mohammad Iqbal, "Overcrowded Classroom: A Serious Problem for Teachers," *Elixir Educational Technology* 49 (2012): 10162–10165; Richard Needle, Tom Griffin, and Roger Svendsen, "Occupational Stress: Coping and Health Problems of Teachers," *Journal of School Health* 51 (3) (1981): 175–181; Martins Fabunmi, Peter Brai-Abu, and Isaiah Adeyinka Adenij, "Class Factors as Determinants of Secondary School Students' Academic Performance in Oyo State, Nigeria," *Journal of Social Science* 14 (3) (2007): 243–247.

40. Jean Baker, "Teacher-Student Interaction in Urban At-Risk Classrooms: Differential Behavior, Relationship Quality, and Student Satisfaction with School," *Elementary School Journal* 100 (1) (1999): 57–70.

41. Elizabeth Mackintosh, Sheree West, and Susan Saegert, "Two Studies of Crowding in Urban Public Spaces," *Environment and Behavior* 7 (1975): 159–184.

42. Amanda Ripley, *The Smartest Kids in the World: And How They Got That Way* (New York: Simon and Schuster, 2013).

43. Ben Hartman, "PISA Test Results Show Colossal Failure of Israel Schools," *Jerusalem Post*, September 9, 2010, http://www.jpost.com/National-News/PISA-test-results-show -colossal-failure-of-Israel-schools.

44. Yoav Vaknin, interview with author, August 20, 2013.

45. James McAfee, "Classroom Density and the Aggressive Behavior of Handicapped Children," *Education & Treatment of Children* 10 (2) (May 1987): 134–145.

46. C. Kennith Tanner, "The Classroom: Size versus Density," *School Business Affairs* 66 (12) (2000): 20–23.

47. Anat Zeira, Ron Avi Astor, and Rami Benbenishty, "School Violence in Israel: Findings of a National Survey," *Social Work* 48 (4) (2003): 471–482.

48. Anat Cohen, "Juvenile Crime on Rise in Israel," The International Child and Youth Care Network (CYC-NET), February 19, 2006, http://www.cyc-net.org/features /viewpoints/c-juvenilecrime.html.

49. Ezri Amram, "Youth in Israel: More Sexual Crimes, Less Physical Violence and High Alcohol Consumption," *News* 2, May 3, 2011, http://www.mako.co.il/news-israel /education/Article-eb58847a576bf21004.htm.

50. Moshe Nussbaum, "Violence by Youths at Yad Vashem," Channel 2 Central News-cast, March 7, 2013, broadcast at http://www.mako.co.il/news-channel2/Channel-2 -Newscast/Article-a115ed21e064d31004.htm.

51. Omri Maniv, "The State Comptroller Will Investigate Violence by Youths on the Social Networks," *NRG*, December 25, 2012, http://www.nrg.co.il/online/1/ART2/424/455.html.

52. Shahar Chai, "OECD: Israel Has Most Crowded Classrooms," *Ynet*, June 25, 2013.

53. Yaron Kellner, "The Illness: Crowding," *Yedioth Ahronot*, June 28, 2013.

54. Rachel Feit, interview with author, August 19, 2013.

55. Dr. Uri Givon, interview with author, August 19, 2013.

56. Dan Eden, "Report: Israel's Hospitals Are Most Crowded in the West," *Haaretz*, July 4, 2011.

57. Stanford University Medical Center, "Project Renewal," accessed October 19, 2015, http://www.sumcrenewal.org/projects/project-overview/stanford-hospital/.

58. Yaron Kelner, "Fewer Beds Relative to the Population: 2014," *Ynet*, October 28, 2014, http://www.ynet.co.il/articles/0,7340,L-4584800,00.html.

59. Kellner, "Illness: Crowding."

60. Givon, interview.

61. Kellner, "Illness: Crowding."

62. Givon, interview.

63. Efat Monshari Goren, "The Premature Baby Wards are Collapsing," *On Life*, November 1, 2011.

64. U.S. Central Intelligence Agency (CIA), "Life Expectancy at Birth," *The World Factbook* (2015), accessed October 19, 2015, https://www.cia.gov/library/publications/the -world-factbook/fields/2102.html; Ido Efrati, "L'haim//The Life Expectancy of Israeli Men Ranks Fourth Highest in the World," *Haaretz*, May 16, 2014, http://www.haaretz .com/life/health-fitness/.premium-1.590976.

65. Ilanit Bar, "Description and Analysis of Dimensions of Poverty and Inequality in Israel and Developed Countries," (Jerusalem: Knesset Center for Research and Information, 2012), http://www.knesset.gov.il/mmm/data/pdf/m03095.pdf.

66. Israel CBS, "Rahat," *The Local Authorities in Israel, 2010: Publication Number 1* (Jerusalem, 2013), 324–325.

67. Step Forward for the Promotion of Education in Rahat, accessed August 19, 2013, http://www.step4rahat.com/about.htm.

68. Etti Weisblau, "Children in the Negev Bedouin Sector—Snap Shot," report submitted to the Knesset Committee for Children's Rights, November 20, 2006, 4, http://www .knesset.gov.il/mmm/data/pdf/m01676.pdf.

69. Niri Berner, "How Am I Supposed to Feed 12 Children?" *Ynet*, September 20, 2012, http://www.ynet.co.il/articles/0,7340,L-4284212,00.html.

70. Faiz Abu Sahiban, mayor of Rahat, interview with author, June 20, 2013.

71. Ibid.

72. Omar Abu Muamar, interview with author, June 30, 2013; Mohammed Alnabari, interview with author, July 11, 2013.

73. Lee Cahaner, Nicola Yozgof-Orbach, and Arnon Soffer, *The Haredim in Israel: Space, Society and Community* (Haifa: University of Haifa, 2012), 34–35.

74. Hila Weisburg, "A Ticking Time Bomb—More than Half of the Haredis and the Arabs Live Below the Poverty Line," *The Marker*, December 11, 2012, http://www.themarker.com/news/politics/1.1883555.

75. Myers-JDC-Brookdale Institute, *Facts and Figures 2013: Poverty in Israel* (Jerusalem: Myers-Joint Distribution Committee [JDC]-Brookdale Institute, 2013), http://brookdale.jdc.org.il/_Uploads/dbsAttachedFiles/Facts-and-Figures-2013—Poverty-in-Israel.pdf.

76. Ayal Kimhi, "Income Inequality in Israel," *State of the Nation Report: Society Economy and Policy in Israel*, ed. Dan Ben-David (Jerusalem: Taub Center for Social Policy Studies in Israel, 2011), 113.

77. David W. Lawson and Ruth Mace, "Sibling Configuration and Childhood Growth in Contemporary British Families," *International Journal of Epidemiology* 37 (2008): 1408–1421.

78. Ari Shavit, *My Promised Land* (New York: Random House, 2013), 339–350.

79. OECD, "Country Note, Israel," *Divided We Stand: Why Inequality Keeps Rising* (Paris, 2011), www.oecd.org/els/social/inequality.

80. Sever Plotsker, "The Secret of Inequality," *Yedioth Ahronot—Finance*, July 12, 2013, 2.

81. Tomer Lev, personal communication, November 3, 2012.

CHAPTER 4. THE RISE AND FALL OF ALIYAH

1. Abraham Duvdevani, Chairman of the World Zionist Organization, interview with author, July 8, 2013.

2. Sergio DellaPergola, "The Global Context of Migration to Israel," in *Immigration to Israel: Sociological Perspectives*, ed. Elazar Leshem and Judith Shuval (New Brunswick, NJ: Transaction Publishers, 1998), 87–88.

3. Law of Return, para. 4, *Sefer HaChokim*, July 5, 1950, 51. English translation at http://www.refworld.org/docid/3ae6b4ea1b.html/.

4. Dov Friedlander and Calvin Goldscheider, *The Population of Israel* (New York: Columbia University Press, 1979), 84.

5. Sergio DellaPergola, *Jewish Demographic Policies: Population Trends and Options in Israel and in the Diaspora* (Jerusalem: Jewish People Policy Institute, 2011), 131, http://www.moia.gov.il/Hebrew/InformationAndAdvertising/Statistics/Pages/ImmigrationData2009.aspx.

6. Yosi Greenstein, "The Number of Émigrés from Israel Dropped Last Year to Only 15.6 Thousand," *Maariv-NRG*, August 6, 2012, http://www.nrg.co.il/online/16/ART2/392/834.html.

7. Sergio DellaPergola, Uzi Rebhun, and Mark Tolts, "Contemporary Jewish Diaspora in Global Context: Human Development Correlates of Population Trends," *Israel Studies* 11 (2005): 61–95.

8. Minutes of the Executive of the Jewish Agency, Jerusalem, December 6, 1942, as quoted in Tom Segev, *The Seventh Million: The Israelis and the Holocaust* (New York: Hill and Wang, 1993), 97.

9. David Ben-Gurion Diary, July 30, 1945, as cited in Segev, *Seventh Million*, 114.

10. David Ben-Gurion, "Eternal Israel" (1954), as quoted in Segev, *Seventh Million*, 113.
11. Walter Laqueur, A *History of Zionism* (New York: Holt, Rinehart and Winston, 1972), 372.
12. Kemal H. Karpat, "Ottoman Population Records and the Census of 1881/82–1893," *International Journal of Middle East Studies* 9 (1978): 237–274.
13. Neville Mandel, "Ottoman Policy and Restrictions on Jewish Settlement in Palestine, 1881–1908: Part I," *Middle Eastern Studies* 10 (3) (1974): 312–332.
14. Walter Laqueur, A *History of Zionism: From the French Revolution to the Establishment of the State of Israel* (New York: Schocken Books, 2003), 278–279.
15. Amos Elon, *The Israelis: Founders and Sons* (New York: Penguin, 1983), 39; Sergio Della-Pergola, "Correspondence," *Azure* (Winter 2007): 4–22.
16. Howard Sachar, A *History of Israel: From the Rise of Zionism to Our Time* (New York: Alfred Knopf, 2007), 26–30.
17. Shlomit Laskov, *The Biluim* (Jerusalem: World Zionist Organization, 1979).
18. Friedlander and Goldscheider, *Population of Israel*, 55.
19. Laqueur, *History of Zionism*, 2003 ed., 279.
20. Boaz Neumann, *Land and Desire in Early Zionism* (Lebanon, NH: University Press of New England, 2011), 5–7.
21. Ari Shavit, *My Promised Land* (New York, Random House, 2013): 25–48.
22. Gur Alroey, "The Jewish Emigration from Palestine in the Early Twentieth Century," *Journal of Modern Jewish Studies* 2 (2) (2003): 111–131.
23. David Ben-Gurion, "At the Half-Jubilee Celebration" in Habas, *The Second Aliyah*, 17–18, as quoted in Alroey, "Jewish Emigration," n. 44.
24. Sergio DellaPergola, personal communication, August 27, 2013.
25. Roberto Bachi, *The Population of Israel* (Jerusalem: Committee for International Cooperation in National Research in Demography [CICRED], 1974), 87.
26. Sergio DellaPergola, "Demography in Israel/Palestine: Trends, Prospects, Policy Implications" (International Union for the Scientific Study of Population [IUSSP] XXIV General Population Conference, Salvador de Bahia, August 2001), http://212.95.240.146/Brazil2001/s60/S64_02_dellapergola.pdf.
27. Yehoshua Ben Arieh, *Jerusalem in the 19th Century*, vol. 1: *The Old City* (Jerusalem: Ben Zvi Institute, 1984), 279.
28. Friedlander and Goldscheider, *Population of Israel*, 17.
29. Ibid.
30. E. Mills, *Census of Palestine, 1931*, vol. 1 (Alexandria, Egypt: Whitehead Morris, 1933), 44.
31. Friedlander and Goldscheider, *Population of Israel*, 23.
32. Mills, *Census of Palestine, 1931*, 42.
33. Tom Segev, *One Palestine Complete: Jews and Arabs under the British Mandate* (New York: Metropolitan Books, 1999), 185–186.
34. Ibid., 189–192, 195.
35. "Max Nordau," *Encyclopedia, Israel and Zionism, Ynet*, accessed March 31, 2015, http://www.ynet.co.il/yaan/0,7340,L-16784-MTY3ODRfMjU5MzQ5NDZfMTQ4Njg3MjAw-FreeYaan,00.html.

36. "Jabotinsky Scores Nazis as Revisionist Congress Opens," *Jewish Telegraphic Agency* (*JTA*), September 9, 1935, http://www.jta.org/1935/09/09/archive/jabotinsky-scores-nazis -as-revisionist-congress-opens#ixzz2kNe7RNT7.

37. Joseph Schectman, *The Life and Times of Vladimir Jabotinsky* (Silver Spring, MD: Eshel, 1986), 347.

38. Ezra Mendelsohn, *The Jews of East Central Europe between the World Wars* (Bloomington: Indiana University Press, 1983), 80.

39. Dan Kupfert Heller, personal communication, November 27, 2013.

40. Schectman, *Life and Times of Vladimir Jabotinsky*, 342–363; also, Shmuel Katz, *Lone Wolf: A Biography of Vladimir (Ze'ev) Jabotinsky, Book Two* (New York: Barricade Books, 1996).

41. Segev, *One Palestine Complete*, 225.

42. Laqueur, *A History of Zionism*, 1972 ed., 372.

43. Sachar, *History of Israel*, 144.

44. Peter Kenez, "The Pogroms of 1919–1921: Pogroms and White Ideology in the Russian Civil War," in *Pogroms: Anti-Jewish Violence in Modern Russian History* (Cambridge: Cambridge University Press, 2004), 293–313.

45. Elon, *Israelis: Founders and Sons*, 53–54.

46. Sachar, *History of Israel*, 154.

47. Mills, *Census of Palestine, 1931*, 144.

48. John Hope Simpson, "Chapter X: Immigration," in *Palestine: Report on Immigration, Land Settlement and Development* (London: H. M. Stationery Office, 1930), 25.

49. Arieh Avneri, *The Claim of Dispossession* (Tel Aviv: Hidekel Press, 1984), 28.

50. Mills, *Census of Palestine, 1931*, 45.

51. Joan Peters, *From Time Immemorial: The Origins of the Arab-Jewish Conflict over Palestine* (New York: Harper & Row, 1984) 230–233.

52. Yehoshua Porath, "Mrs. Peters's Palestine," *New York Review of Books*, January 16, 1986, http://www.nybooks.com/articles/archives/1986/jan/16/mrs-peterss-palestine/?page=1.

53. Mills, *Census of Palestine, 1931*, 32.

54. Fred M. Gottheil, "The Smoking Gun: Arab Immigration into Palestine, 1922–1931," *Middle East Quarterly* (Winter 2003): 53–64.

55. Avneri, *Claim of Dispossession*, 34.

56. Vladimir Jabotinsky, "The Iron Wall" (original in Russian, Razsviet, April 11,1923), http://www.marxists.de/middleast/ironwall/ironwall.htm.

57. *Palestine Royal Commission Report* (Peel Commission), presented by the Secretary of State for the Colonies to the United Kingdom Parliament by Command of His Britannic Majesty, July 1937.

58. Mathew Hughs, "The Banality of Brutality: British Armed Forces and the Repression of the Arab Revolt in Palestine, 1936–39," *English Historical Review* 74 (2009): 313–354.

59. "Emigration and the Evian Conference," *The Holocaust Encyclopedia* (Washington, DC: U.S. Holocaust Memorial Museum), accessed March 31, 2015, http://www.ushmm .org/wlc/en/article.php?ModuleId=10005520.

60. Benny Morris, *Righteous Victims: A History of the Zionist-Arab Conflict, 1981–1999* (New York: Alfred A. Knopf, 1999), 164.

61. Segev, *One Palestine Complete*, 459.

62. Morris, *Righteous Victims*, 163, 176, based on Idith Zertal, *From Catastrophe to Power: Jewish Illegal Immigration to Palestine, 1945–1948* (Tel Aviv: Am Oved, 1996).

63. Friedlander and Goldscheider, *Population of Israel*, 23.

64. Gabriel Lipshitz, *Country on the Move: Migration to and within Israel, 1948–1995* (Dordrecht, Netherlands: Kluwer, 1997), 43–44.

65. Benny Morris, *The Birth of the Palestinian Refugee Problem Revisited* (Cambridge: Cambridge University Press, 2004).

66. "Israel Declaration of Independence," May 14, 1948, Jerusalem, Israel Foreign Ministry, http://www.mfa.gov.il/mfa/foreignpolicy/peace/guide/pages/declaration%20of%20 establishment%20of%20state%20of%20israel.aspx.

67. Tom Segev, *1949: The First Israelis* (New York: Free Press, 1986), 95.

68. Bachi, *Population of Israel*, 89.

69. DellaPergola, *Jewish Demographic Policies*, 27.

70. Amir Haskel and Navah Ron, "Absorbing the Holocaust Survivors in Israel" (Jerusalem: Ministry of Education, 2009), http://cms.education.gov.il/NR/rdonlyres/627770B0 -A358-42E4-8C7E-B831EAA3FB13/104453/surviers.pdf.

71. Jewish Agency for Israel, "Ingathering of the Exiles," accessed August 31, 2013, http:// www.jafi.org.il/JewishAgency/English/About/History#t4.

72. Segev, *1949*, 118.

73. Jewish Agency for Israel, "Ingathering of the Exiles."

74. Lipshitz, *Country on the Move*, 47.

75. Jewish Agency for Israel, "Ingathering of the Exiles."

76. Bachi, *Population of Israel*, 96.

77. Alon Tal, *All the Trees of the Forest: Israel's Woodlands from the Bible to the Present* (New Haven, CT: Yale University Press, 2013), 33, 66–72.

78. Yehudah Gradus and Shaul Krakover, "The Effects of Government Policy on the Spatial Structure of Manufacturing in Israel," *Journal of Developing Areas* 11 (1977): 393–409.

79. Friedlander and Goldscheider, *Population of Israel*, 87.

80. Devorah HaCohen, *Immigrants in Turmoil: The Great Wave of Immigration to Israel and Its Absorption, 1948–1953* (Jerusalem: Yad Ben-Zvi, 1994).

81. Friedlander and Goldscheider, *Population of Israel*, 101.

82. Ruth Gabizon, *Sixty Years of the Law of Return: History, Ideology and Justification* (Jerusalem: Matzilah Center, 2009), 18.

83. Ibid., 29–35.

84. Law of Return, para. 1, *Sefer HaChokim*.

85. Yair Ettinger, "Chief Rabbi Lau to Haaretz: Law of Return a Problem," *Haaretz*, April 14, 2014, http://www.haaretz.com/news/national/.premium-1.585536.

86. Shmuel Diklo, "A Historic Decision by the High Court of Justice," *Globes*, March 31, 2005, http://www.globes.co.il/news/article.aspx?did=899802; Supreme Court Decisions, Israel, High Court of Justice (BAGATZ) 6539/03 *Liora Goldman versus The State of Israel, the Ministry of Interior and Others* (2004), as well as BAGATZ 2597/99, *Rodriguez versus Minister of Interior and Others* (2005).

87. Law of Return, para. 4A, *Sefer HaChokim*.

88. Devorah HaCohen, *Immigrants in Turmoil*, 49.
89. Yaakov Gil, *Divrei HaKnesset (Proceedings of the Knesset)*, meeting no. 160, 18th of Tamuz, 5710, July 3, 1950, 2044.
90. David Ben-Gurion, *Divrei HaKnesset (Proceedings of the Knesset)*, meeting no. 162, 18th of Tamuz, 5710, July 5, 1950, 2099.
91. Law of Return, para. 2(b)(1–3).
92. Claude Klein, "The Lansky Case," *Israel Law Review* 8 (1973): 286–295.
93. Segev, *1949*, 105–108.
94. Cable from Yitzhak Ben-Menachem to the Mosad L'aliyah, quoted in Segev, *1949*, 111.
95. Report of the Jewish Agency, Department of Immigration, March 1952, repr. in Friedlander and Goldscheider, *Population of Israel*, 99.
96. Judith Shuval ands Elazar Leshem, "The Sociology of Migration in Israel: A Critical View," in *Immigration to Israel*, 26.
97. "Jews in Riot-torn Moroccan Town Seek Refuge in European Quarters: French Troops Alerted," *JTA*, June 10, 1948, http://www.jta.org/1948/06/10/archive/jews-in-riot-torn-moroccan-town-seek-reguge-in-european-quarters-french-troops-alerted.
98. Friedlander and Goldscheider, *Population of Israel*, 105.
99. Israel Central Bureau of Statistics (CBS), "Immigrants by Period of Immigration and Last Country of Residence," *Israel Statistical Abstract* (Jerusalem, 2012), 4.2, http://www1.cbs.gov.il/shnaton63/st04_02.pdf.
100. Esther Benbassa, *The Jews of France: A History from Antiquity to the Present* (Princeton, NJ: Princeton University Press, 1999).
101. As quoted in Lipshitz, *Country on the Move*, 44.
102. Ibid., 55.
103. Daniel Sheck, interview with author, September 3, 2013.
104. Shavit, *My Promised Land*, 271–295.
105. Avi Pickar, "Immigrants in a Measuring Tube: Israel's Policy Towards the Immigration of North African Jews, 1951–1956," (Beer Sheva: Ben Gurion Institute, 2012).
106. Michael Biton, interview with author, September 12, 2013.
107. Sachar, *History of Israel*, 738.
108. Ibid., 968.
109. Fred Lazin, *The Struggle for Soviet Jewry in American Politics: Israel versus the American Jewish Establishment* (Lanham, MD: Lexington Books, 2005).
110. Fred Lazin, "Refugee Resettlement and Freedom of Choice: The Case of Soviet Jewry," *Backgrounder* (Washington, DC: Center for Immigration Studies, 2005), 3.
111. Ann Cooper, "U.S. Abruptly Closes a Route for Soviet Jews," *New York Times*, November 6, 1989, http://www.nytimes.com/1989/11/06/world/us-abruptly-closes-a-route-for-soviet-jews.html.
112. Lazin, "Refugee Resettlement," 12.
113. Sachar, *History of Israel*, 1081.
114. Sarit Cohen-Golder and Yoram Weiss, "High-Skilled Immigration in the Israeli Labor Market: Adjustment and Impact," in *High-Skilled Immigration in a Global Labor Market* (Lanham, MD: Rowman & Littlefield, 2011), 252–252.

115. Eliezer Ben-Rafael, Elite Olshtain, and Idit Geijst, "Identity and Language: The Social Insertion of Soviet Jews in Israel," in *Immigration to Israel*, 333.

116. Tamar Horowitz, "The Influence of Soviet Political Culture on Immigrant Voters in Israel: The Elections of 1992," in *Immigration to Israel*, 253–272.

117. Dan Senor and Saul Singer, *Start-up Nation: The Story of Israel's Economic Miracle* (New York: Hachette Book Group, 2009).

118. Philip Reeves, "On Multiple Fronts, Russian Jews Reshape Israel," NPR News, January 2, 2013, http://www.npr.org/2013/01/02/168457444/on-multiple-fronts-russian -jews-reshape-israel.

119. Shelley Neese, "Israel's 'Non-Jewish' Jews," Jerusalem Connection Writers Archives (2010), http://www.thejerusalemconnection.us/news-archive/2010/03/02/israels-non -jewish-jews.html.

120. Sachar, *History of Israel*, 939–940.

121. Steven Kaplan and Chaim Rosen, "Ethiopian Immigrants in Israel: Between Preservation of Culture and Invention of Tradition," in *Immigration to Israel*, 408–410.

122. Elazar Leshem, "The Israeli Public's Attitudes toward the New Immigrants of the 1990s," in *Immigration to Israel*, 318–319.

123. Majid Al-Haj, "Soviet Immigration as Viewed by Jews and Arabs: Divided Attitudes in a Divided Country," in *Population and Social Change in Israel*, ed. Calvin Goldscheider (Boulder, CO: Westview Press, 1992), 92–95.

124. A classic satirical skit by entertainers Arik Einstein and Uri Zohar about the stereotyping of different waves of immigration can be found at http://www.youtube.com /watch?v=VjDx2ZwLUso.

125. Kaplan and Rosen, "Ethiopian Immigrants in Israel," 407.

126. Pew Research Center, "How Many Jews Are There in the United States?" October 2, 2013, http://www.pewresearch.org/fact-tank/2013/10/02/how-many-jews-are-there -in-the-united-states/; The Jewish Federations of North America, *National Jewish Population Survey—Strength, Challenge and Diversity in the American Jewish Population* (New York: United Jewish Communities, 2004), http://www.jewishfederations .org/local_includes/downloads/4606.pdf; also, Egon Mayer, Barry Kosmin, and Ariela Keysar, *American Jewish Identity Survey* (New York: City University of New York, 2001), http://www.simpletoremember.com/vitals/ajisbook.pdf.

127. Israel CBS, "Immigrants by Period."

128. "Immigration to Israel: Total Immigration by Country Per Year," Jewish Virtual Library, accessed February 8, 2016, https://www.jewishvirtuallibrary.org/jsource /Immigration/immigration_by_country2.html.

129. Arie Lova Eliav, *Land of the Hart: Israelis, Arabs, the Territories and a Vision of the Future*, trans. Judy Yalon (Philadelphia: Jewish Publication Society of America, 1974), 332–333, originally published in Hebrew in 1972.

130. "Goldmann Urges New Zionist Approach at Opening of 27th Congress in Israel," *JTA*, June 10, 1968, http://www.jta.org/1968/06/10/archive/goldmann-urges-new-zionist -approach-at-opening-of-27th-congress-in-israel.

131. American Zionist Movement, "The Revised Jerusalem Program of 1968," accessed March 31, 2015, http://www.azm.org/1968.shtml.

132. Sarah Morrison, "Nefesh B'Nefesh: 'Most Profitable Non-Profit Business I've Seen,'" *Arutz Shevah, Israel National News*, accessed September 10, 2013, http://www.israelnationalnews.com/News/News.aspx/124900#.Ui5ICsbIbGA.

133. Mathew Sperber, personal communication, November 26, 2014.

134. Nefesh B'Nefesh, "Nefesh B'Nefesh Aliyah Services," accessed September 10, 2013, http://www.nbn.org.il/about/about-nbn-services.html.

135. *Haaretz* Staff, "329 North American Immigrants Arrive," *Haaretz*, July 10, 2002, http://www.haaretz.com/print-edition/news/329-north-american-immigrants-arrive-1.40122.

136. Erez Halfon, interview with author, July 9, 2013.

137. Yehoshua Fass, interview with author, July 9, 2013; *The Economic Impact of Nefesh B'Nefesh Aliyah on the State of Israel*, Deloitte Information Technologies Israel, October, 2009, http://www.bjpa.org/Publications/details.cfm?PublicationID=3948. The sum includes tourist income from visiting family members, professional skills, etc.

138. Chaim Levinson, Uri Blau, and Mordechai I. Twersky, "Nefesh B'Nefesh an Ineffective Monopoly with Overpaid Executives, Say Critics," *Haaretz*, October 20, 2012, http://www.haaretz.com/weekend/magazine/nefesh-b-nefesh-an-ineffective-monopoly-with-overpaid-executives-say-critics.premium-1.471163.

139. "U.S. Immigration to Israel Drops 13 Percent," *JTA*, December 29, 2013, http://www.jta.org/2013/12/29/news-opinion/israel-middle-east/israel-welcomes-19200-immigrants-in-2013.

140. Halfon, interview.

141. Jewish Federations, *National Jewish Population Survey*.

142. Fass, interview.

143. Birthright Israel, accessed March 31, 2015, http://www.birthrightisrael.com/Pages/Default.aspx.

144. Michael Maze, interview with author, September 11, 2013.

145. U.S. Central Intelligence Agency (CIA), "Total Fertility Rate," *The World Factbook* (2015), https://www.cia.gov/library/publications/the-world-factbook/fields/2127.html.

146. DellaPergola, *Jewish Demographic Policies*, 66–67. Based on a "core definition," in 2010 DellaPergola estimated a population of 484,000, but other definitions yield a Jewish community as large as 600,000.

147. Ariel David, "Anti-Semitic Attacks Surged in 2012, Report Claims," *Huffington Post*, July 4, 2013, http://www.huffingtonpost.com/2013/04/07/anti-semitic-attacks-2012_n_3033372.html.

148. Maia de la Baume, "Radicalism Prompts Warnings in France," *New York Times*, October 8, 2012, http://www.nytimes.com/2012/10/09/world/europe/in-france-jews-and-muslims-warn-of-anti-semitism.html?_r=0.

149. Shahar Chai, "Sharp Rise in Global Anti-Semitism, France Leads," *Ynet*, July 4, 2013, http://www.ynetnews.com/articles/0,7340,L-4364834,00.html.

150. Sam Sokol, "Four French Jews Named as Victims of Paris Kosher Deli Attack," *Jerusalem Post*, January 10, 2015.

151. Omri Efraim, "2014 a Record Breaking Year for Aliyah," *Ynet*, December 31, 2015; Joseph Strich, "Jewish Agency Chief Touts Anticipated Wave of French Olim," *Jeru-*

salem Post, June 6, 2014, http://www.jpost.com/Jewish-World/Jewish-News/Jewish-Agency-chief-touts-anticipated-wave-of-French-olim-361614; "U.S. Immigration to Israel Drops 13 Percent."

152. "Le chiffre de l'alya des Juifs de France ne décolle pas!" Blog terredisrael.com, March 1, 2012, accessed September 10, 2015, http://www.terredisrael.com/infos/le-chiffre-de-lalya-des-juifs-de-france-ne-decolle-pas/.

153. Duvdevani, interview.

154. Armand Sibony, interview with author, September 23, 2013.

155. Joseph Berger, "Israel Sees a Surge in Immigration by French Jews, but Why?" *New York Times,* July 4, 2004, http://www.nytimes.com/2004/07/04/world/israel-sees-a-surge-in-immigration-by-french-jews-but-why.html.

156. Ofer Petersberg, "Is Crisis Bringing French Jews to Israel?" *Ynet Real Estate,* May 23, 2012, http://www.ynetnews.com/articles/0,7340,L-4230253,00.html; also, Ben Sales, "As French Community Grows in Israel, Baguettes Join Pita," *JTA,* September 12, 2012, http://www.jta.org/2012/09/12/life-religion/features/as-french-community-grows-in-israel-baguettes-join-pita.

157. Sibony, interview.

158. DellaPergola, "Global Context of Migration to Israel," 88.

159. "U.S. Immigration to Israel Drops 13 Percent."

160. Shuval and Leshem, "Sociology of Migration," 16.

161. DellaPergola, "Correspondence," 10–11.

162. Israel CBS, "Israelis Who Remained Overseas for a Year or More: Selected Data, 1990–2010," (Jerusalem, 2011), accessed September 10, 2013, http://www.cbs.gov.il/www/publications/alia/t3.pdf.

163. Israel CBS, "Immigrants by Period."

164. Israel Ministry of Absorption, "Aliyah to Israel—Statistics of Aliyah By Year," accessed October 20, 2015, http://www.moia.gov.il/Hebrew/InformationAndAdvertising/Statistics/Pages/ImmigrationData2012.aspx.

165. Elon, *Israelis: Founders and Sons,* 143.

166. Shalom Hartman Institute, *Engaging Israel: Foundations for a New Relationship* (2011), http://www.hartman.org.il/Fck_Uploads/file/EI.brochure.pdf.

CHAPTER 5. BLESSED WITH CHILDREN

1. Rebecca Steinfeld, "Fruitful," *Slate Magazine,* June 20, 2011, http://www.tabletmag.com/jewish-news-and-politics/70286/fruitful.

2. Uri Misgav, "Ben Gurion: The Decline," *Haaretz,* April 4, 2012, http://www.haaretz.co.il/magazine/1.1678821.

3. Jacqueline Portugese, *Fertility Policy in Israel: The Politics of Religion, Gender, and Nation* (Westport, CT: Praeger, 1999), 82.

4. Shabtai Teveth, *The Evolution of Transfer in Zionist Thinking* (Tel Aviv: Shiloah Institute, Tel Aviv University, 1989), 48.

5. Jon Anson and Avinoam Meir, "Religiosity, Nationalism and Fertility in Israel," *European Journal of Population* 12 (1) (1996): 1–25.

6. Portugese, *Fertility Policy in Israel*, 81.
7. David Ben-Gurion, *Israel: A Personal History* (New York: Funk & Wagnalls, 1971), 839.
8. Daphna Birenbaum-Carmeli, "'Cheaper Than a Newcomer': On the Social Production of IVF Policy in Israel," *Sociology of Health and Illness* 26 (7) (2004): 901.
9. Leonard Singerman, Joel Singerman, and Janice Singerman, *The Threat Within: Israel and Population Policy* (New York: Vantage Press, 1975), 52.
10. Herschel Schacter, "Halachic Aspects of Family Planning," *Journal of Contemporary Society* 4 (1982): 5.
11. Moses Feinstein, *Iggerot Moshe, 1959–1996* (New York: Balshon, 2012), 69, 71, Institute of Microfilmed Hebrew Manuscripts (IMHM) 2: 69, 71, 73.8.
12. Dov Friedlander and Calvin Goldscheider, *The Population of Israel* (New York: Columbia University Press, 1979), 123.
13. Gary Schiff, "The Politics of Fertility Policy in Israel," in *Modern Jewish Fertility* (Leiden, Netherlands: E. J. Brill, 1981), 267.
14. Sharon Asiskovich, "Child Allowances," in "Speaking in Two Voices" (Ph.D. diss., Hebrew University, 2007), 111–113.
15. Organisation for Economic Co-operation and Development (OECD), "Better Life Index" (2013), http://www.oecdbetterlifeindex.org/topics/life-satisfaction/; Hila Weissberg, Nimrod Bousso, and Ronny Linder-Ganz, "Israelis Happy, Says OECD, Despite Low Ranking on Income and Education," *Haaretz*, April 2, 2013, http://www.haaretz.com/news/national/israelis-happy-says-oecd-despite-low-ranking-on-income-and-education.premium-1.512930.
16. Tali Heruti-Sover, "Happiness is Personal, Not National, Israelis Say," *Haaretz*, January 23, 2013, http://www.haaretz.com/news/national/happiness-is-personal-not-national-israelis-say.premium-1.495875; Allison Kaplan Sommer, "Why Are Israelis So Damn Happy?" *Haaretz*, April 3, 2013, http://www.haaretz.com/blogs/routine-emergencies/why-are-israelis-so-damn-happy.premium-1.513233.
17. Portugese, *Fertility Policy in Israel*, 56; Michal D'vir Koren, "Raising Children: Meet the New Fathers," On the Couch, Israel's Psychologists' Index, accessed March 31, 2015, http://www.alhasapa.co.il/3140.asp.
18. Friedlander and Goldscheider, *The Population of Israel*, 137.
19. Steinfeld, "Fruitful."
20. Portugese, *Fertility Policy in Israel*, 86.
21. United Nations, *Views and Policies Concerning Population Growth and Fertility among Governments in Intermediate-Fertility Countries* (New York: UN Population Division, 2002), 221, 223, http://www.un.org/esa/population/publications/completingfertility/RevisedPOPDIVPPSpaper.PDF.
22. Israel National Archives, "The Fertility Prize," *Israel the Documented Story*, July 19, 2012, accessed March 31, 2015, http://israelidocuments.blogspot.com/2012/07/blog-post_1398.html.
23. Friedlander and Goldscheider, *Population of Israel*, 126.
24. Dov Friedlander, "Population Policy in Israel," in *Population Policy in Developed Countries*, ed. Bernard Bereson (New York: McGraw Hill, 1974), 54.
25. Employment of Women Law, 1954, para. 6, *Sefer HaChokim*, no. 160, August 12, 1954.

26. Amendment 46 to the Women's Labor Law, *Sefer HaChokim*, no. 2235 (2010).

27. Jonathan Lis, "Bill: Israeli Dads to Get 8-Day Paternity Leave," *Haaretz*, October 27, 2013, http://www.haaretz.com/news/national/.premium-1.554646.

28. Miriam Rosenthal, "Nonparental Child Care in Israel: A Cultural and Historical Perspective," in *Child Care in Context: Cross-cultural Perspectives*, ed. Michael E. Lamb, Kathleen Sternberg, Carl-Philip Hwang, Anders Brober (Hillsdale, NJ: Lawrence Erlbaum, 1992), 319–320.

29. Ibid., 322.

30. Margalit Bachi-Bejarano, interview with author, September 23, 2013.

31. Tom Segev, *One Palestine Complete: Jews and Arabs under the British Mandate* (New York: Metropolitan Books, 1999), 407.

32. Sergio DellaPergola, interview with author, July 3, 2013.

33. Bachi-Bejarano interview.

34. Friedlander and Goldscheider, *Population of Israel*, 130.

35. Israel Ministry of Justice, *Report of the Committee for the Problems of Natality* ("*Bachi Report*") (Jerusalem: Ministry of Justice, 1966).

36. Israel Government Decision no, 428, regarding "Demographic Policies" by the 13th government of Israel (April 9, 1967) (copy with author).

37. Ministry of Justice, *Bachi Report*, 4.

38. Ministry of Justice, *Bachi Report*, 13.

39. Ministry of Justice, *Bachi Report*, 15–16.

40. Dov Friedlander and Carole Feldmann, "The Modern Shift to Below-Replacement Fertility: Has Israel's Population Joined the Process?" *Population Studies* 47 (1993): 296.

41. As quoted in Gabriel Lipshitz, *Country on the Move: Migration to and within Israel, 1948–1995* (Dordrecht, Netherlands: Kluwer, 1997), 44.

42. Ministry of Justice, *Bachi Report*, 14.

43. Portugese, *Fertility Policy in Israel*, 91–110.

44. Ministry of Justice, *Bachi Report*, 17.

45. Nurit Yaffe, "Population," in Israel Central Bureau of Statistics (CBS), Sixty Years of *Israel in Statistics, 1948–2007* (Jerusalem, 2009), 3, http://www.cbs.gov.il/statistical /statistical60_heb.pdf.

46. Ministry of Justice, *Bachi Report*, 25.

47. Ibid., 30.

48. Ibid., 50.

49. Ibid., 32–38.

50. Barbara Okun, "Innovation and Adaptation in Fertility Transition: Jewish Immigrants to Israel from Muslim North Africa and the Middle East," *Population Studies: A Journal of Demography* 51 (1997): 317–335.

51. Bachi-Bejarano interview.

52. Israel Government Decision no, 428 (April 9, 1967).

53. Ibid.

54. Israel Government Decision no. 1596, regarding "Demographic Trends of the Jewish People" by the twenty-first government of Israel (May 18, 1986) (copy with author).

55. Bachi-Bejarano interview.

56. William Robert Johnston, "Historical Abortion Statistics: Israel," last updated December 27, 2014, http://www.johnstonsarchive.net/policy/abortion/ab-israel.html.

57. National Insurance Institute, "Birth Grants," last updated January 1, 2015, accessed October 21, 2015, http://www.btl.gov.il/benefits/maternity/maternity_grant/Pages/default .aspx.

58. The Center for Research and Information, "Home Births in Israel and the World," submitted to the Knesset Committee for the Status of Women (Jerusalem: Knesset, 2008), 2–3, http://www.knesset.gov.il/mmm/data/pdf/m02115.pdf.

59. Israel CBS, "Mortality Rates per 1,000 Residents, by Age, Population Group and Sex," *Israel Statistical Abstract* (Jerusalem, 2013), 3.26, http://www.cbs.gov.il/shnaton64/st03 _26x.pdf.

60. OECD, "Health Status and Risk Factors," *OECD Health Data: How Does Israel Compare?* (Paris, 2013), http://www.oecd.org/els/health-systems/Briefing-Note-ISRAEL -2013.pdf.

61. Jona Schellekens, "Family Allowances and Fertility: Socioeconomic Differences," *Demography* 46 (3) (2009): 457.

62. A calculator for the public, which allows for quick computation of the precise day-care discount rate based on socioeconomic strata, number of children in family, etc., can be found on the Web site of the Ministry of Economics, last accessed November 16, 2015, http://www.moital.gov.il/NR/exeres/30F5191B-FD36-4A0C-B9AB-49D415CEBB62 .htm.

63. Meirav Arlosoroff, "How Subsidized Israeli Day Care Allows Ultra-Orthodox to Avoid Work," *Haaretz*, December 6, 2013, http://www.haaretz.com/business/.premium -1.562089.

64. The National Insurance Institute, "Education Grant," last updated January 1, 2015, accessed October 21, 2015, http://www.btl.gov.il/benefits/children/%D7%9E%D7%A2% D7%A0%D7%A7%20%D7%9C%D7%99%D7%9E%D7%95%D7%93%D7%99%D7 %9D/Pages/default.aspx.

65. "Speaker of the Knesset Scholarship Fund," Oranim College, accessed October 21, 2015, http://www.oranim.ac.il/sites/heb/about/students-dean/scholarships/kneset-scholarship /pages/default.aspx.

66. Zchouti (My Rights), "Rights: To What Are You Entitled," accessed September 28, 2013, http://www.myrights.co.il.

67. Schellekens, "Family Allowances and Fertility," 457.

68. OECD, *Doing Better for Families* (Paris, 2011), http://www.oecd.org/els/soc/doing betterforfamilies.htm.

69. Junsen Zhang, Jason Quan, and Peter van Meerbergen, "The Effect of Tax-Transfer Policies on Fertility in Canada," *Journal of Human Resources* 29 (1994): 181–201.

70. Lilach Wiseman, "Yishai Takes Care of His Voters: Increases the Discount in City Taxes for Families with Many Child by 25%; the Discount for Reservists—Only 5%," *Globes*, December 27, 2011, http://www.globes.co.il/news/article.aspx?did=1000710365.

71. Israel Defense Forces (IDF), "Questions and Answers," Chief Office of the Reserves, accessed March 31, 2015, http://www.aka.idf.il/kamlar/faq/default.asp?catId=43339 &docId=&pageNum=2.

72. Friedlander and Goldscheider, *Population of Israel*, 130.
73. The National Insurance Law, 1953, *Sefer HaChokim*, no. 137, November 27, 1953.
74. Barbara Swirski, interview with author, June 9, 2013.
75. Michal Ofir and Tami Eliav, *Child Subsidies in Israel: A Historic Look and International Perspective* (Jerusalem: Israel National Insurance Institute, 2005), 5, http://www.btl.gov.il/SiteCollectionDocuments/btl/Publications/mechkar_91.pdf.
76. Minister of Labor, Mordechai Namir, in *Divrei haKnesset* (*Knesset Minutes*), July 21, 1959, 2639, 2646.
77. Naomi Mei-Ami, "Child Subsidies: A Historical Review" (Jerusalem: Knesset Center for Research and Information, 2008), 7.
78. National Insurance Law, Amendment 4, 1959, *Sefer HaChokim*, no. 287 (August 13, 1959), 160–163.
79. Asiskovich, "Child Allowances," 114.
80. Mei-Ami, "Child Subsidies," 7.
81. Asiskovich, "Child Allowances," 114–115.
82. Ofir and Eliav, *Child Subsidies in Israel*, 5.
83. Asiskovich, "Child Allowances," 117.
84. Schiff, "Politics of Fertility Policy in Israel," 267, 269–270.
85. Mei-Ami, "Child Subsidies," 7.
86. Shahar Ilan, "When the Allowances Were Increased, the Number of Children Doubled," *Haaretz*, July 24, 2000.
87. Eli Berman, "Sect, Subsidy, and Sacrifice: An Economist's View of Ultra-Orthodox Jews," *Quarterly Journal of Economics* 115 (3) (2000): 913.
88. Yossi Nissan, "10,000 Yeshiva Students Allegedly Defraud Education Ministry," *Globes*, June 9, 2011, http://www.globes.co.il/serveen/globes/docview.asp?did=1000652787.
89. Ilan, "When the Allowances Were Increased."
90. Portugese, *Fertility Policy in Israel*, 108.
91. Mei-Ami, "Child Subsidies," 4.
92. Smadar Shmueli, "The Law for Families Blessed with Children Was Approved in the Labor and Welfare Committee," *Ynet*, July 18, 2000, http://www.ynet.co.il/articles/0,7340,L-35358,00.html.
93. Amnon Atad, "The Law of Families Blessed with Children Passed," *Ynet*, November 1, 2000, http://www.ynet.co.il/articles/0,7340,L-221211,00.html.
94. Mei-Ami, "Child Subsidies," 9.
95. Dan Ben-David, "Increase in Male Non-Employment over Past Three Decades," *Taub Center Bulletin* 2 (1) (2010), 4, http://taubcenter.org.il/tauborgilwp/wp-content/uploads/Taub_Bulletin_final.pdf.
96. Arieh O'Sullivan, "Haredi Unemployment Unsustainable," *Jerusalem Post*, July 22, 2010, http://www.jpost.com/Business/Business-News/Haredi-unemployment-unsustainable.
97. Berman, "Sect, Subsidy, and Sacrifice," 916.
98. Schiff, "Politics of Fertility Policy in Israel," 267.
99. Sever Plotsker and Gad Lior, "Netanyahu: A Woman Who Marches 200 Kilometers Can Work in Packaging," *Ynet*, July 18, 2003, http://www.ynet.co.il/articles/0,7340,L-2697456,00.html.

100. Ruth Sinai, "Netanyahu Opposed, but the Allocations from the National Insurance Were Harmed Again," *Haaretz*, September 17, 2003, http://www.haaretz.co.il/misc/1 .911172.

101. Alma Cohen, Rajeev Dehejia, and Dmitri Romanov, "Financial Incentives and Fertility," *Review of Economics and Statistics* 95 (1) (2013): 1–20, 3.

102. Herzliyah Conference, "Minister of Finance, Benjamin Netanyahu," December 14, 2004, http://www.herzliyaconference.org/?CategoryID=230&ArticleID=1636.

103. Shai Niv, "Towards the Biggest Storm: Cutbacks on Child Subsidies," *Globes*, March 28, 2013, http://www.globes.co.il/news/article.aspx?did=1000832613.

104. Jeremy Sharon, "Cuts to Haredi Sector Yield Mixed Results," *Jerusalem Post*, August 15, 2013, http://www.jpost.com/Jewish-World/Jewish-News/Cuts-to-haredi-sector-yield -mixed-results-323269.

105. Zvi Zrihiah, "At 3:10 in the Morning: The State Budget Was Approved by the Knesset in Second and Third Calls," *The Marker*, July 30, 2013, http://www.themarker.com /news/1.2083442.

106. Omri Efraim, "National Insurance Institute Head: 40,000 Families to Become Poor," *Ynet*, July 5, 2013, http://www.ynetnews.com/articles/0,7340,L-4377099,00.html.

107. Yori Yanover, "Lapid Tells Haredim 'Go Work' as Child Subsidy Cuts Go into Effect," *Jewish Press*, August 20, 2013, http://www.jewishpress.com/news/breaking -news/lapid-tells-haredim-go-work-as-child-subsidy-cuts-go-into-effect/2013/08 /20/0/.

108. Yanover, "Lapid Tells Haredim 'Go Work.'"

109. Meir Porush, interview with author, July 23, 2014.

110. Charles F. Manski and Joram Mayshar, "Private Incentives and Social Interactions: Fertility Puzzles in Israel," *Journal of the European Economic Association* 1 (1) (2003): 181, citing John Bongaarts and Susan Cotts Watkins, "Social Interactions and Contemporary Fertility Transitions," *Population and Development Review* 22 (1996): 639–682.

111. Berman, "Sect, Subsidy, and Sacrifice," 937.

112. Manski and Mayshar, "Private Incentives and Social Interactions," 182–183.

113. Schellekens, "Family Allowances and Fertility," 462.

114. Ibid., 460.

115. Esther Toledano, Roni Frish, Noam Zussman, and Daniel Gottlieb, "The Effect of Child Allowances on Fertility," *Israel Economic Review* 9 (1) (2011), 103–150; also, *The Influence of Child Allowance Levels on Fertility and Natality* (research no. 101) (Jerusalem: National Insurance Institute, 2009).

116. Noam Zussman, Roni Frish, and Daniel Gottlieb, *The Impact of the Rate of Child Allowances on Fertility and Birth Rates* (Jerusalem: Bank of Israel, 2009), http://www .boi.org.il/he/research/pages/papers_dp0913h.aspx.

117. Esther Toledano, Roni Frish, Noam Zussman, and Daniel Gottlieb, "The Effect of Child Allowances on Fertility," *Israel Economic Review* 9 (1) (2011): 103–150.

118. Cohen, Dehejia, and Romanov, "Financial Incentives and Fertility," 1–20, 3.

119. Alphabetically listed, this research from numerous countries includes Anna Cristina d'Addio and Marco Mira d'Ercole, *Trends and Determinants of Fertility Rates*

in OECD Countries: The Role of Policies (Paris: OECD, 2005), http://www.oecd.org/social/family/35304751.pdf; John Ermisch, "Econometric Analysis of Birth Rate Dynamics in Britain," *Journal of Human Resources* 23 (1988): 563–576; Anne Gauthier, "Family Policy in Industrialized Countries: Is There Convergence?" *Population* 57 (2002): 447–474; Anne Gauthier and Jan Hatzius, "Family Policy and Fertility: An Econometric Analysis," *Population Studies* 51 (1997): 295–306; Kevin Milligan, "Subsidizing the Stork: New Evidence on Tax Incentives and Fertility," *Review of Economics and Statistics* 87 (2005): 554; Leslie Whittington, "Taxes and the Family: The Impact of the Tax Exemption for Dependents on Marital Fertility," *Demography* 29 (1992): 215–226; Leslie Whittington, James Alm, and H. Elizabeth Peters, "The Personal Exemption and Fertility in the United States," *American Economic Review* 80 (1990): 545–556; Zhang, Quan, and van Meerbergen, "Effect of Tax-Transfer Policies on Fertility in Canada," 181–201.

120. Milligan, "Subsidizing the Stork," 539–555.
121. Adriaan Kalwij, "The Impact of Family Policy Expenditure on Fertility in Western Europe," *Demography* 47 (2) (2010): 503–519.
122. Sever Plotsker, "Time for Amendments," *Yedioth Ahronot, Finance* supp., May 31, 2014, 2.
123. Zvi Zarhiya, Meirav Arlozorov, "Who Will Receive How Much: Everything You Wanted to Know about the Historic Change in Child Allowances," *The Marker*, July 28, 2015, http://www.themarker.com/news/1.2693950.
124. "How Much Does It Cost Us," 3kids, accessed June 27, 2014, http://3kids.co.il/%D7%9B%D7%9E%D7%94-%D7%96%D7%94-%D7%A2%D7%95%D7%9C%D7%94-%D7%9C%D7%A0%D7%95/.
125. Misha Shauli, personal communication, April 29, 2014.

CHAPTER 6. WOMEN'S REPRODUCTIVE RIGHTS

1. "Proclamation of Tehran, International Conference on Human Rights" (1968), Human Rights Library, https://www1.umn.edu/humanrts/instree/l2ptichr.htm; Lynn Freedman and Stephen Isaacs, "Human Rights and Reproductive Choice," *Studies in Family Planning* 24 (1) (1998): 18–30.
2. L. Purdy, "Women's Reproductive Autonomy: Medicalisation and Beyond," *Journal of Medical Ethics* 32 (5) (2006): 287–291.
3. Gila Stopler, "Israel's Demographic Policies in the Area of Natality and the Rights of Women and Minorities," *Law and Administration* 11 (2008): 487.
4. "Authority for Promoting the Status of Women," Israel Prime Minister's Office Website, accessed October 21, 2015, http://www.pmo.gov.il/BranchesAndUnits/Pages/woman.aspx.
5. Tali Heruti-Sover, "Executive Pay for Israeli Women Lags Far Behind That of Their Male Counterparts, and the Gap Is Only Growing," *Haaretz*, May 1, 2013, http://www.haaretz.com/business/executive-pay-for-israeli-women-lags-far-behind-that-of-their-male-counterparts-and-the-gap-is-only-growing.premium-1.518483.

6. Susan Martha Kahn, *Reproducing Jews: A Cultural Account of Assisted Conception in Israel* (Durham, NC: Duke University Press, 2000).

7. The National Health Insurance Law, *Sefer HaChokim*, no. 1469 (1994), 156.

8. Center for Reproductive Rights, "European Standards on Subsidizing Contraceptives," *Fact Sheet* (2010), http://reproductiverights.org/sites/crr.civicactions.net/files/documents/pub_fac_slovak_european%20standards_9%2008_WEB.pdf.

9. Associated Press, "Free Birth Control Leads to Way Fewer Abortions," *CBS News*, October 5, 2012, http://www.cbsnews.com/news/study-free-birth-control-leads-to-way-fewer-abortions/.

10. Tal Amati-Nishri, chief assistant, Department of Claims and Inspection, Ministry of Health, personal communication, June 30, 2014.

11. Ibid.

12. Jacqueline Portugese, *Fertility Policy in Israel: The Politics of Religion, Gender, and Nation* (Westport, CT: Praeger, 1999), 124–125.

13. Dov Friedlander, "Family Planning in Israel: Irrationality and Ignorance," *Journal of Marriage and Family* 35 (1) (1973): 117–124.

14. Ibid., 117.

15. Calvin Goldscheider, *Israel's Changing Society: Population, Ethnicity, and Development* (Cambridge, MA: Westview 2002), 171.

16. Portugese, *Fertility Policy in Israel*, 119–120.

17. Roberto Bachi, *The Population of Israel* (Jerusalem: Committee for International Cooperation in National Research in Demography [CICRED], 1974), 221–222.

18. Dov Friedlander and Calvin Goldscheider, *The Population of Israel* (New York: Columbia University Press, 1979), 128–129.

19. Eileen Basker, "Belief Systems, Cultural Milieu and Reproductive Behavior: Women Seeking Abortions in a Hospital in Israel" (Ph.D. diss., Hebrew University, 1980), 2–3, as reported in Portugese, *Fertility Policy in Israel*, 125.

20. Portugese, *Fertility Policy in Israel*, 119–120.

21. Sami Shalom Chetrit, "Mizrahi Politics in Israel: Between Integration and Alternative," *Journal of Palestine Studies* 29 (4) (2000): 51–65.

22. Portugese, *Fertility Policy in Israel*, 121.

23. Barbara Okun, "Family Planning in the Jewish Population of Israel: Correlates of Withdrawal Use," *Studies in Family Planning* 28 (3) (1997): 217.

24. See chapter 2 in Shirley Green, *The Curious History of Contraception* (New York: St. Martin's Press, 1971).

25. Bachi, *Population of Israel*, 223–224.

26. Okun, "Family Planning in the Jewish Population of Israel," 217.

27. Barbara Okun, "Innovation and Adaptation in Fertility Transition: Jewish Immigrants to Israel from Muslim North Africa and the Middle East," *Population Studies: A Journal of Demography* 51 (1997): 317–335.

28. Abraham Doron, *Family Planning in Israel: Behavior and Attitudes of Professionals, Part I* (Jerusalem: Department of Social Welfare, 1976) as quoted in Portugese, *Fertility Policy in Israel*, 133.

29. Barbara Okun, "Religiosity and Contraceptive Method of Choice: The Jewish Population of Israel," *European Journal of Population* 16 (2000): 116.

30. Amati-Nishri, personal communication.

31. Okun, "Innovation and Adaptation in Fertility Transition," 317–335.

32. Portugese, *Fertility Policy in Israel*, 125.

33. Okun, "Innovation and Adaptation in Fertility Transition," 317–335.

34. Evgenia Bystrov, "The Second Demographic Transition in Israel: One for All?" *Demographic Research* 27 (10) (2012): 284.

35. Amati-Nishri, personal communication.

36. Sharon Orshlimi, "Numbers behind the Abortion Industry," Onlife—A Web site of Substance and Current Events for Women, August 6, 2013, http://www.onlife.co.il.

37. Ibid.

38. Portugese, *Fertility Policy in Israel*, 130.

39. Lior Dattel and Yarden Skop, "We Don't Need No Sex Education," *Haaretz*, September 3, 2013, http://www.haaretz.com/news/natioJnal/.premium-1.545015.

40. "Checkups for a Minor without Parental Accompaniment," Israel Medical Association, last accessed October 22, 2015, http://www.ima.org.il/mainsite/viewcategory.aspx?CategoryId=967. See also Yaron Kelner, "The Age When You Can Start," *Yedioth Ahronot,* May 16, 2014, 11.

41. Hedva Eyal, of Woman to Woman, interview, July 2, 2013.

42. Orr Kashti, "40% of the Schools in Israel Do Not Teach Sex Education," *Haaretz*, March 10, 2010, http://www.haaretz.co.il/news/education/1.1192721.

43. Eyal, interview.

44. Hadas Tal, interview with author, November 8, 2013.

45. Talila Nesher, "Israel Admits Ethiopian Women Were Given Birth Control Shots," *Haaretz*, January 27, 2013, http://www.haaretz.com/news/national/israel-admits-ethiopian-women-were-given-birth-control-shots.premium-1.496519.

46. Hedva Eyal, *Depo-Provera: On the Policy of Utilization among Women from the Ethiopian Community in Israel* (Haifa: Isha L'Isha, 2009), http://www.isha.org.il/upload/File/%D7%93%D7%A4%D7%95%20%D7%A2%D7%91%D7%A8%D7%99%D7%AA.pdf/.

47. Rashi commentary to Talmud, Sanhedrin, 72(A).

48. The Criminal Code Ordinance, 1936, sec. 175, no. 74, *Palestine Gazette* (1936), no. 652, supp. 1 (January 14, 1936): 399.

49. Bachi, *Population of Israel*, 222.

50. Friedlander and Goldscheider, *Population of Israel*, 129.

51. Israel Ministry of Justice, *Report of the Committee for the Problems of Natality* ("*Bachi Report*") (Jerusalem: Ministry of Justice, 1966), 44.

52. Portugese, *Fertility Policy in Israel*, 84.

53. Eyal, interview.

54. Israel's Penal Law, 1977, sec. 314, *Sefer HaChokim*, no. 226 (September 12, 1977).

55. Israel's Penal Law, 1977, sec. 320.

56. Amati-Nishri, personal communication.

57. Portugese, *Fertility Policy in Israel*, 146.

58. Ministry of Health, "List of Committees for Approving Abortions," updated November 2013, http://www.health.gov.il/Subjects/Med_Inst/abortion/Documents/abortion_committee.pdf.

59. Israel Penal Law, sec. 315.

60. Ministry of Health, Circular of the Director General, "Upholding the Law and the Regulations by the Committees for Termination of Pregnancies: Implementation Directives," November 14, 1993, 3–4, http://www.health.gov.il/hozer/mk23_1993.pdf.

61. Israel Penal Law, sec. 316(b).

62. Amati-Nishri, personal communication.

63. Israel Ministry of Health, Circular of the Deputy Director General for Oversight of Health Programs, "The Procedures or Health Funds in Cases of Pregnancy and Abortions for Girls Until Age 19," November 19, 2012, 1.1–1.4, http://www.health.gov.il/hozer/sbn13_2012.pdf.

64. Sharon Orr Shaloni, of "Open Door," personal communication, October 22, 2013.

65. The Penal Law Amendment (Termination of Pregnancy), 1977, *Sefer HaChokim* (1977): 852.

66. Ibid., sec. 5(a)5.

67. The Penal Law Amendment 9 (1979): 954; Testimony of Elli Shushheim, director of Efrat before the Knesset Committee for Promoting the Status of Women, October 7, 2003, www.knesset.gov.il/protocols/data/html/maamad/2003-10-07.html.

68. "The Vote and Its Significance," *HaModia*, November 14, 1979, as reported in Portugese, *Fertility Policy in Israel*, 140–141.

69. Portugese, *Fertility Policy in Israel*, 139–140.

70. Proposed law by MK Reshef Hen; Proposed Penal Law—Amendment; Proposed Laws 1614 (2003); Proposed law by MK Zahava Galon; Proposed Penal Law—Amendment to Return the Social Clause; *Proposed Laws* (2006): 280.

71. Minutes of a meeting of the unit for prevention of abortion in the Israel Demography Center, June 28, 1982 (copy with author).

72. Directives to the Pregnancy Termination Committees, Circular of the Ministry of Health, no. 43/88 (1988), sec. 1, www.health.gov.il/download/forms/a1723_mr43_88.pdf.

73. Protocol of meeting no. 181 of the Committee to Promote the Status of Women, 16th Knesset, May 31, 2005, www.knesset.gov.il/protocols/data/rtf/maamad/2005-05-31-02.rtf.

74. Sagit Pastman, "Abortions in Israel: Why Women Need to Lie?" *Saloona*, January 21, 2013, http://saloona.co.il/?p=126556?ref=saloona_tags.

75. Dr. Susan Warchaizer, interview with author, October 28, 2013.

76. Testimony of Dr. Amy Avger, from the Association for the Promotion of Women's Health in front of the Knesset Committee to Promote the Status of Women, Minutes of the Committee (May 19, 2003), www.knesset.gov.il/protocols/data/rtf/maamad/2003-05-19.rtf.

77. Israel Central Bureau of Statistics (CBS), "Applications for Pregnancy Termination in 2011" (press release, October 14, 2013), http://www.cbs.gov.il/reader/newhodaot/hodaa_template.html?hodaa=201305281,"

78. Ibid.

79. Goldscheider, *Israel's Changing Society,* 233.

80. Israel CBS, "Applications for Pregnancy Termination in 2011."

81. Itai Gal, "A Young Woman Underwent an Illegal Abortion and Almost Died," *Ynet,* January 15, 2013, http://www.ynet.co.il/articles/0,7340,L-4332680,00.html.

82. Tal, interview.

83. Esther Herzog, "Abortions in Israel—Deteriorating into Religious Fanaticism," *Ynet,* November 11, 2012, http://www.ynet.co.il/articles/0,7340,L-4302790,00.html.

84. Efrat, "How Efrat Began," accessed March 31, 2015, http://www.efrat.org.il/english /about/default.asp?id=64.

85. Dr. Eli J. Schussheim, interview, June 10, 2013.

86. Efrat, the Association for Encouraging Birth in the Jewish Nation, accessed October 21, 2015, http://www.efrat.org.il/hebrew/considering-abortion/?id=24.

Or the alternative English Web site: Efrat, Committee for the Rescue of Israel's Babies, https://www.efrat.org.il/english/.

87. Ruth Tedhar, interview, June 10, 2013.

88. Avishag Lev, interview, July 24, 2014.

89. Hillary Clinton, Congressional Testimony, MoveOn, April 22, 2009, http://front .moveon.org/watch-hillary-go-to-battle-with-the-gop-over-abortion-and-womens -rights/#.Un2JhfnIbTk.

90. Daphna Birenbaum-Carmeli and Martha Dirnfeld, "In Vitro Fertilisation Policy in Israel and Women's Perspectives: The More the Better?" *Reproductive Health Matters* 16 (31) (2008): 182, 184.

91. Daphna Birenbaum-Carmeli, "'Cheaper Than a Newcomer': On the Social Production of IVF Policy in Israel," *Sociology of Health and Illness* 26 (7) (2004): 913.

92. Daphna Birenbam-Carmeli and Yoram S. Carmeli, "Adoption and Assisted Reproduction Technologies: A Comparative Reading of Israeli Policies," in *Kin, Gene, Community— Reproductive Technologies among Jewish Israelis,* ed. Daphna Birenbaum-Carmeli and Yoram Carmeli (New York, Berghahn Books, 2010), 132.

93. Orna Hirshfield, Renata Gorbtuv, and Miri Ben Simchon, "Adopted Children and Adopting Families," *Research and Assessment: Review of the Social* Services (Jerusalem: Ministry of Social Affairs and Social Service, 2011), 257–259, http://www.molsa.gov .il/CommunityInfo/ResearchAndEvaluation/Pages/ReviewOfSocialServicesIn2011 .aspx.

94. U.S. Department of State, "Adoption Process, Israel," accessed November 1, 2013, http://adoption.state.gov/country_information/country_specific_info.php?country -select=israel.

95. Meital Yasur and Liat Rotem, "Romi Neumark, the First Test Tube Baby: An Exciting Day," *Ynet,* October 4, 2010, http://www.ynet.co.il/articles/0,7340,L-3963786,00 .html.

96. Birenbaum-Carmeli, "'Cheaper Than a Newcomer,'" 906.

97. Halit Yanai, "Humanity Has Lost Some of Its Fertility Abilities, but Not of Its Desire for Continuity," *Globes,* February 15, 2013, http://www.globes.co.il/news/article.aspx ?did=1000822446.

98. Birenbaum-Carmeli, "'Cheaper Than a Newcomer,'" 904.

99. Dan Even, "Israel Pioneering Fertility Treatments, but Not Legally," *Haaretz*, January 12, 2010, http://www.haaretz.com/print-edition/news/israel-pioneering-fertility -treatments-but-not-legally-1.261260.

100. Israel Government, "Guide to Fertility: Adoption and Surrogacy," accessed March 31, 2013, http://www.gov.il/FirstGov/TopNav/Situations/SSituationsInLife /SFerSurAdop/SFTreatmentEntitlement/.

101. Nivin Todd, "Infertility and In Vitro Fertilization," WebMD, http://www.webmd .com/infertility-and-reproduction/guide/in-vitro-fertilization.

102. In 2012, Israel's Ministry of Health estimated that one IVF treatment cycle costs 10,500 shekels (slightly less than $3,000).

103. Halit Yanai, "Humanity Has Lost Some of Its Fertility Abilities."

104. Birenbaum-Carmeli and Dirnfeld, "In Vitro Fertilisation Policy in Israel," 185.

105. Even, "Israel Pioneering Fertility Treatments."

106. Sarit Rosenbloom, "A Multitude of Fertility Treatments—Few Pregnancies," *Yedioth Ahronot*, November 25, 2014, 9.

107. Shlomo Mashiach, Daphna Birenbaum-Carmeli, Roy Mashiach, and Martha Dirnfeld, "The Contribution of Israeli Researchers to Reproductive Medicine: Fertility Experts' Perspectives," in *Kin, Gene, Community*, 51–61.

108. Quoted in the January 1987 edition of women's magazine *Olam Haisha* and quoted in Portugese, *Fertility Policy in Israel*, 153.

109. Elly Teman, "The Last Outpost of the Nuclear Family: A Cultural Critique of Israeli Surrogacy Policy," in *Kin, Gene, Community*, 107–126.

110. Barry Freundel, "Abortion and Jewish Law," in *Public Policy and Social Issues: Jewish Sources and Perspectives*, ed. Marshall J. Breger (Westport, CT: Praeger, 2003), 65–78.

111. *Haaretz* newspaper from March 18, 1988, as quoted by Daphna Birenbaum-Carmeli, "'Cheaper Than a Newcomer,'" 905.

112. Yali Hashash, "Medicine and the State: The Medicalization of Reproduction in Israel," in *Kin, Gene, Community*, 271–295.

113. Birenbaum-Carmeli and Dirnfeld, "In Vitro Fertilisation Policy in Israel," 189.

114. Hedva Eyal, of Woman to Woman, interview with author, July 2, 2013, personal communication.

115. Adi Niv-Yaguda, "The Movie of Orli and Guy: A Child? Not at Any Price," *Ynet*, September 12, 2012, http://www.ynet.co.il/articles/0,7340,L-4279500,00.html.

116. Yanai, "Humanity Has Lost Some of Its Fertility Abilities."

117. This Knesset hearing is extensively quoted in Daphna Birenbaum-Carmeli, "'Cheaper Than a Newcomer,'" 909–910.

118. Yanai, "Humanity Has Lost Some of Its Fertility Abilities."

119. Georgina M. Chambers, G. David Adamson, and Marinus J.C. Eijkemans, "Acceptable Cost for the Patient and Society," *Fertility and Sterility* 100 (2) (2013): 319–327.

CHAPTER 7. "BE FRUITFUL AND MULTIPLY"

1. Nathan Jeffay, "In Israel, Haredi and Muslim Women Are Having Fewer Children," *Forward*, July 5, 2011, http://forward.com/articles/139391/in-israel-haredi-and-muslim -women-are-having-fewer/.

2. Dov Friedlander and Carole Feldmann, "The Modern Shift to Below-Replacement Fertility: Has Israel's Population Joined the Process?" *Population Studies* 47 (1993): 296.

3. Yitzhak Tractingot, personal communication, May 27, 2013.

4. Lee Cahaner, Nicola Yozgof-Auerbach, and Arnon Soffer, *The Haredim in Israel: Space, Society and Community* (Haifa: University of Haifa, 2012), 36.

5. Alan Weisman, *Countdown: Our Last, Best Hope for a Future on Earth?* (New York: Little, Brown and Company 2013), 113.

6. Daniel Orenstein, "The Impact of Child Allowances on Ultra-Orthodox Jewish Fertility Rates in Israel," unpublished paper (2004), copy with author.

7. Pew Research Center, *2013 Survey of U.S. Jews* (Washington DC: Pew Research Center, 2013), 49, http://www.pewforum.org/files/2013/10/jewish-american-beliefs-attitudes -culture-survey-full-report.pdf. The study lacked sufficient respondents in the critical forty-to-fifty-nine age group (who presumably are at the end of their childbearing years) to definitively project average fertility among American ultra-Orthodox families. Liga Plaveniece, Project Director, Pew Research Center's Religion & Public Life Project, interview, October 2, 2013.

8. Jack Wertheimer, "Jews and the Jewish Birthrate," *Commentary*, October 2005, http:// www.commentarymagazine.com/articles/jews-and-the-jewish-birthrate/.

9. Jonny Paul, "Three of Four Jewish Births in UK Are Haredi," *Jerusalem Post*, January 8, 2007, http://www.jpost.com/Jewish-World/Jewish-News/Three-of-four-Jewish-births -in-UK-are-Haredi.

10. Yarden Skop, "The C.B.S.: In Another Six Years, Only About 40% of Pupils Will Be in the Jewish National Education System," *Haaretz*, August 6, 2013, http://www.haaretz .co.il/news/education/1.2090826.

11. Israel Museum, "A World Apart Next Door: Glimpses into the Life of Hasidic Jews," http://www.imjshop.com/A-World-Apart-Next-Door-Glimpses-into-the-Life-of -Hasidic-Jews-P1338.aspx#; Yair Ettinger, "Israel Museum to Introduce Sex-Segregated Visiting Hours for Haredi Exhibit," *Haaretz*, July 23, 2012, http://www.haaretz.com /news/national/israel-museum-to-introduce-sex-segregated-visiting-hours-for-haredi -exhibit-1.452849.

12. Rivka Neria-Ben Shahar, "The Learners' Society: Education and Employment among Ultra-Orthodox (Haredi) Women," *Sociological Papers, Women in Judaism* 14 (2009): 2.

13. Lawrence Kaplan, "Daas Torah: A Modern Conception of Rabbinic Authority," in *Rabbinic Authority and Personal Autonomy*, ed. M. Sokol (New Jersey and London: Orthodox Forum Series, 1992), 1–60.

14. Cahaner, Yozgof-Auerbach, and Soffer, *Haredim in Israel*, 35.

15. Emmanuel Sivan, "The Enclave Culture," in *Fundamentalism Comprehended*, ed. M. E. Marty and R. S. Appleby (Chicago: University of Chicago Press, 1991), 11–68.

16. Noah J. Efron, *Real Jews: Secular versus Ultra-Orthodox and the Struggle for Jewish Identity in Israel* (New York: Basic Book, 2003).
17. Mark Levine and Liam O'Mara, "Religion in the Palestinian-Israeli Conflict," in *One Land, Two States: Israel and Palestine as Parallel States*, ed. Mark Levine and Mathias Mossberg (Berkeley: University of California Press, 2014), 230.
18. Cahaner, Yozgof-Auerbach, and Soffer, *Haredim in Israel*, 39.
19. Dan Ben-David and Eitan Regev, as quoted in Eitan Regev, *Education and Employment in the Haredi Sector* (Jerusalem: Taub Center for Social Policy Studies in Israel, 2013), 121, http://taubcenter.org.il/tauborgilwp/wp-content/uploads/E2013.06-Haredim-2.pdf.
20. Neria-Ben Shahar, "Learners' Society," 2.
21. Babylonian Talmud, *Yoma*, 9b. Sometimes the divisions were too profound to be bridged, and groups like the Christians or the Karaites splintered off into new religious identities.
22. Efron, *Real Jews*, 19, 25; also, "Moses Mendelssohn," in *Encyclopedia Britannica* (1911), now available at http://en.wikisource.org/wiki/1911_Encyclop%C3%A6dia_Britannica/Mendelssohn,_Moses.
23. Jacob Katz, "Orthodoxy in Historical Perspective," in *Studies in Contemporary Jewry*, part 2, ed. Peter Y. Medding (Bloomington: Indiana University Press, 1986), 4.
24. Jacob Katz, *Halacha in Distress: Obstacles on the Way to Orthodoxy in Formation* (Jerusalem: Magnes, 1992).
25. Michael Silber, "The Emergence of Ultra-Orthodoxy: the Invention of a Tradition," in *The Uses of Tradition: Jewish Continuity since Emancipation*, ed. Jack Wertheimer (New York: Jewish Theological Seminary / Harvard University Press, 1992), 23–84.
26. Yosef Fund, *Separation or Participation: Agudat Yisrael versus Zionism and the State of Israel* (Jerusalem: Magnes, 1999).
27. Jacob Katz, "Da'at Torah: The Unqualified Authority Claimed for Halachists," in *The Harvard Law School Program in Jewish Studies: The Gruss Lectures—Jewish Law and Modernity: Five Interpretations* (Cambridge, MA: Harvard University Law School, 1997), repr. at http://www.juedisches-recht.de/rec_daat_tora.php.
28. Gershon Bakon, *Politics and Tradition: Agudat Yisrael in Poland, 1916–1939* (Jerusalem: Zalman Shazar Center, 2005).
29. While the Eda Haredit does not appear to actively maintain its own Web site, a description of its activities and those of Badatz can be found on the Web site Hadrei Haredim, http://www.bhol.co.il/Articlesearch.aspx?sCond=%D7%94%D7%A2%D7%93%D7%94%20%D7%94%D7%97%D7%A8%D7%93%D7%99%D7%AA&tid=368.
30. Cahaner, Yozgof-Auerbach, and Soffer, *Haredim in Israel*, 18–19.
31. Yuval Elizur and Lawrence Malkin, *The War Within: Israel's Ultra-Orthodox Threat to Democracy and the Nation* (New York: Overlook Duckworth, 2013), 60.
32. "The Decision of the Council of the Torah Scholars regarding the Partition of the Land of Israel," *HaPardes*, 6 (11) (September 1937), http://www.hebrewbooks.org/pdfpager.aspx?req=12084&st=&pgnum=9.
33. Elizur and Malkin, *War Within*, 61.

34. Meir Porush, interview with author, July 23, 2014.
35. Menachem Schneerson, "Birth Control and Contraception," in *Healthy in Body, Mind and Spirit—A Guide to Good Health*, ed. Sholom Wineberg, 2006, accessed August 14, 2014, http://www.chabad.org/therebbe/letters/default_cdo/aid/2307921 /jewish/Part-II-Reproduction-Chapter-V-Birth-Control-and-Contraception.htm.
36. Charles F. Manski and Joram Mayshar, "Private Incentives and Social Interactions: Fertility Puzzles in Israel," *Journal of the European Economic Association* 1 (1) (2003): 182–183.
37. Tamar Rotem, "To Grow Up in the Haredi World: A Wound That Does Not Mend," *Haaretz*, February 2, 2012, http://www.haaretz.co.il/magazine/1.1636898.
38. Cahaner, Yozgof-Auerbach, and Soffer, *Haredim in Israel*, 39.
39. Yonatan Less, "The Knesset Approved: The Age of Marriage in Israel Will Be Raised from 17 to 18," *Haaretz*, November 4, 2013, http://www.haaretz.co.il/news/education/1 .2157211.
40. Cahaner, Yozgof-Auerbach, and Soffer, *Haredim in Israel*, 39.
41. Neria-Ben Shahar, "Learners' Society," 3.
42. Moti Kaplan, interview with author, June 27, 2013.
43. Porush, interview.
44. Lee Cahaner, "Appendix 3-C: Table of Results of Elections to Ashkenazi Parties by Region," in *The Development of the Spatial and Hierarchic Structure of The Ultra-Orthodox Jewish Population in Israel* (Haifa: University of Haifa, October 2009), 25.
45. Amiram Gonen and Bezalel Cohen, "The Ongoing Transformation of Haredi Population in Israel: Past Developments and Future Options in Education and Employment," (Jerusalem: Jerusalem Institute for Israel Studies, 2015), 4, http://www.jiis.org/.upload /Haredi%20Education.pdf.
46. Friedlander and Feldmann, "Modern Shift to Below-Replacement Fertility," 305.
47. Leonard Singerman, Joel Singerman, and Janice Singerman, *The Threat Within: Israel and Population Policy* (New York: Vantage Press, 1975), 21–23.
48. Joshua London, "Jewish Family Values," in *Public Policy and Social Issues: Jewish Sources and Perspectives*, ed. Marshall Breger (Westport, CT: Praeger, 2003), 219.
49. *Shulhan Arukh*, Even HaEzer, 1:1.
50. Babylonian Talmud, Yevamot, 63B.
51. Maimonides (Rabbi Moshe Ben Maimon), Mishnah Torah, "Halachot Ishut," 15:2.
52. Mishnah and Babylonian Talmud, Yevamot, 63A.
53. Babylonian Talmud, Yevamot, 6:6.
54. Babylonia Talmud, Megillah, 27A. The *Shulhan Arukh* also repeats this position.
55. David Feldman, *Marital Relations, Birth Control, and Abortion in Jewish Law* (New York: Schocken, 1974), 40–41.
56. Babylonian Talmud, Ketubot, 62B–63A.
57. Babylonian Talmud, Kidushin, 29B.
58. Feldman, *Marital Relations*, 30–31.
59. Babylonian Talmud, Yevamot, 63B; Feldman, *Marital Relations*, 31.
60. Mishnah, Yevamot, 6:6; 61b.
61. Babylonian Talmud, Yevamot, 62A.

62. Ibid.

63. Maimonides (Rambam), *Personal Religious Law* (Halchot Ishiot), 15(4).

64. Babylonian Talmud, Yevamot, 62A.

65. "Rulings of Rabbi Eliezer." Mishnah, Ketubot, 61B.

66. David Feldman, "The Legitimacy of Sexual Pleasure," in *Marital Relations*, 81–105.

67. Babylonian Talmud, Sotah, 20a, Ketubot, 62B; Feldman, *Marital Relations*, 63.

68. David Boothe, personal communication, January 6, 2014.

69. Moshe Ben Nachman, *The Holy Letter: A Study in Jewish Sexual Morality*, trans. Seymour Cohen (Northvale, NJ: Jason Aronson, 1993). For example the monograph suggests ways to slow ejaculation in order to ensure women's pleasure, 110.

70. Babylonian Talmud, Ketubot, 63A.

71. Feldman, *Marital Relations*, 169.

72. Ibid., 104.

73. Barbara Okun, "Religiosity and Contraceptive Method of Choice: The Jewish Population of Israel," *European Journal of Population* 16 (2000): 114–115.

74. Babylonian Talmud, Nedarim, 35a–b; Feldman, *Marital Relations*, 176–193.

75. Jeremy Benstein, *The Way into Judaism and the Environment* (Woodstock, VT: Jewish Lights, 2006), 116–117.

76. *Mishnah*, Taanit, 11A.

77. Benstein, *Way into Judaism*, 117.

78. Peter McDonald, "Gender Equity in Theories of Fertility Transition," *Population and Development Review* 26 (3) (2000): 437–439.

79. Jeremy Sharon, "Haredi Students Fail as They Lack Secular Studies," *Jerusalem Post*, March 14, 2013, http://www.jpost.com/Jewish-World/Jewish-News/Haredi-students-fail -as-they-lack-secular-studies.

80. Haredi College Web site, http://www.mcy.org.il.

81. Porush, interview.

82. Yair Ettinger, "Shas's Leader: It is Prohibited to Pursue Academic Studies—It's Not the Way of the Torah," *Haaretz*, June 23, 2014, http://www.haaretz.co.il/news/education /.premium-1.2357007.

83. Porush, interview.

84. Shneur Rosen, interview with author, July 23, 2014.

85. Yosseph Shilhav, *Ultra-Orthodoxy in Urban Governance in Israel* (Jerusalem: Floersheimer Institute for Policy Studies, 1998), 91, 101–102, http://fips.org.il/Fips/Site/System /UpLoadFiles/DGallery/4–6englishadobe.pdf.

86. Alisa Odenheimer and Gwen Ackerman, "Israel Existential Crisis Creates Haredi Breadwomen as Men Study," *Bloomberg*, June 28, 2012, http://www.bloomberg.com /news/2012-06-27/israel-existential-crisis-creates-haredi-breadwomen-as-men-study .html.

87. Shilhav, *Ultra-Orthodoxy in Urban Governance in Israel*, 102.

88. Ibid., 101–102.

89. Esti Shoshan, "Obsession with Modesty Is Killing Us," *Ynet*, May 21, 2013 http://www .ynetnews.com/articles/0,7340,L-4382643,00.html.

90. Shmuel Halberstein, interview with author June 9, 2013.

91. Ibid.

92. Okun, "Religiosity and Contraceptive Method of Choice," 109–113.

93. Porush, interview.

94. Uziel Schmelz, "Religiosity and Fertility among Jews of Jerusalem," in *Papers in Jewish Demography, 1985* (Jerusalem: Institute of Contemporary Judaism, 1989), 157–185, as reported by Okun, "Religiosity and Contraceptive Method of Choice," 132.

95. Rosen, interview.

96. Yosef Yitzhak Neuman, interview with author, June 27, 2013.

97. Zohar Blumenkrantz, "Be Fruitful and Multiply? A Haredi Attempted to Smuggle Through Customs a Suitcase Filled with Spermicide Candles," *The Marker*, February 27, 2011, http://www.themarker.com/misc/1.597176.

98. Yitzhak Neuman, interview.

99. Ibid. Quoted reference is to Rabbi Ben Zoma in Mishnah "Nezikin" Avoth, 4:1.

100. Weisman, *Countdown*, 8–9.

101. Yosef Balmas, interview with author, June 17, 2013.

102. Israel Ministry of Interior, "Notice Regarding the Determination of the Number of Representatives on City Councils," (Jerusalem: Ministry of Interior, 2013), http://www.moin.gov.il/Subjects/Bchirot/Documents/election-yosh.pdf.

103. Paul Rivlin, *The Israeli Economy from the Foundation of the State through the 21st Century* (Cambridge: Cambridge University Press, 2010), 169.

104. Bat Sheva Fried, interview with author, July 16, 2013.

105. Shilhav, *Ultra-Orthodoxy in Urban Governance in Israel*, 101–102.

106. Idan Yosef, "The Number of Drafted Haredim Jumped by 40%," *News1*, September 7, 2014, http://www.news1.co.il/Archive/001-D-353602-00.html.

107. Gilad Malach, *New Arrangements: Strategies and Public Policies Regarding the Haredim* (Ph.D. diss., Hebrew University of Jerusalem, 2013), 5. Also see, generally, Kimmy Caplan and Nurit Stadler, eds., *From Survival to Consolidation: Changes in Israeli Haredi Society and Its Scholarly Study* (Jerusalem: Van Leer Institute, 2012); also, Kimmy Caplan and Nurit Stadler, eds., *Leadership and Authority in Israeli Haredi Society* (Tel Aviv: Hakibbutz Hameuhad and Van Leer Institute, 2009); Kimmy Caplan, "Research into the Haredi Community in Israel: Achievements and Challenges," in *Israeli Haredim: Integration without Assimilation?* ed. Emmanuel Sivan and Kimmy Caplan (Jerusalem: Van Leer Institute, 2004), 227.

108. Ahmad Hleihel, *Fertility among Jewish and Muslim Women in Israel, by Level of Religiosity, 1979–2009* (Jerusalem: CBS—Demography and Census Department, 2011), 32, http://cbs.gov.il/www/publications/pw60.pdf; Tamar Rotem, "The Fertility of Haredim: Be Fruit and Multiply, but Less," *Haaretz*, July 1, 2011, http://www.haaretz.co.il/misc/1.1179091.

109. Nurit Stadler, Eyal Ben-Ari, and Einat Mesterman, "Terror, Aid and Organization: The Haredi Disaster Victim Identification Teams (ZAKA) in Israel," *Anthropological Quarterly* 78 (3) (2005): 619–651.

110. Israel Defense Forces, "Haredi Service: All the Data on Drafting Haredim to the IDF," March 1, 2012, accessed December 18, 2013, http://www.idf.il/1133-15081-HE/Dover.aspx.

111. Mathew Wagner, "Shas Accepted into World Zionist Organization," *Jerusalem Post*, January 20, 2010, http://www.jpost.com/Jewish-World/Jewish-News/Shas-accepted-into-World-Zionist-Organization.

112. Eli Yishai, interview with author, July 9, 2013.

113. Nechumi Yaffe, interview with author, July 17, 2013.

114. Efrat Neuman, "Do Money Worries Affect People's Decision to Have Children?" *Haaretz*, December 6, 2013, http://www.haaretz.com/business/.premium-1.562098.

115. Yaffe interview.

116. Tali Farkash, "Rise in the Percentage of Divorces: Tel Aviv Holds the Record," *Ynet*, January 29, 2013, http://www.ynet.co.il/articles/0,7340,L-4338320,00.html.

117. Netta Moshe, "Selected Data Regarding Divorce in Israel," (Jerusalem: Knesset Center for Research and Information, 2013), http://www.knesset.gov.il/mmm/data/pdf/m03199.pdf; Nurit Dubrin, "Divorce in Israel: The Extent of Divorce and Factors that Influence the Likelihood of Getting Divorced," (Jerusalem: CBS, 2005), http://www.cbs.gov.il/publications/tec13.pdf.

118. Yaffe, interview.

119. Shilhav, *Ultra-Orthodoxy in Urban Governance in Israel*, 37.

120. Mathew Wagner, "More Than 30% of Haredi Teens—'Hidden Dropouts,'" *Jerusalem Post*, August 7, 2013, http://www.jpost.com/Israel/More-than-30-percent-of-haredi-teens-hidden-dropouts.

121. Tali Farkash, "Are Haredi Women Neglecting Their Health?" *Ynet*, November 11, 2014, http://www.ynetnews.com/articles/0,7340,L-4590786,00.html.

122. Shilhav, *Ultra-Orthodoxy in Urban Governance in Israel*, 54.

123. Ilana Brosch and Yochanan Peres, "Child Quantity versus Quality: A General Dilemma in Israeli Terms," *Megamot* 40 (2) (2000): 185–198.

124. Koheleth Rabbah 7:13.

125. Porush, interview.

126. Weisman, *Countdown*, 12.

127. Eilon Schwartz, interview with author, June 2, 2013.

128. Kimmy Caplan, *The Internal Popular Discourse in Israeli Haredi Society* (Jerusalem: Zalman Shazar Center, 2007).

129. Nurit Stadler, *Yeshiva Fundamentalism: Piety, Gender, and Resistance in the Ultra-Orthodox World* (New York: New York University Press, 2009).

130. Cahaner, Yozgof-Auerbach, and Soffer, *Haredim in Israel*, 40–41.

131. Ofer Petersburg, "Haredim 'Taking Over' Periphery," *Ynet*, February 23, 2011, http://www.ynetnews.com/articles/0,7340,L-4031115,00.html.

132. Lior Detel, "Partial Success in Integrating Haredim in Academia—The Most Effective Program is for Women," *The Marker*, July 16, 2015, http://www.themarker.com/news/education/1.2684989. Levi Brackman, "Poverty Drives Change among Haredi Jews," *Ynet*, November 20, 2013, http://www.ynetnews.com/articles/0,7340,L-4452433,00.html.

133. Malach, *New Arrangements*, 41. Compare Malach's old figures to updated IDF nos.: see "Haredi Service."

134. Jeremy Sharon, "Education Blamed for Low Male Haredi Employment," *Jerusalem Post*, December 11, 2012, http://www.jpost.com/Jewish-World/Jewish-Features/Education-blamed-for-low-male-haredi-employment.
135. Roee Yinovsky, "More Haredim Working? How Does It Work In Practice?" *Ynet*, March 18, 2015, http://www.ynet.co.il/articles/0,7340,L-4637534,00.html.
136. Regev, *Education and Employment in the Haredi Sector*, 134.
137. Yaffe, interview.
138. Porush, interview.

CHAPTER 8. THE DEMOGRAPHIC TRANSITION

1. Laurence Oliphant, *Life in Modern Palestine* (Edinburgh: Blackwood and Sons, 1887).
2. Tim Dyson, *Population and Development: The Demographic Transition* (London: Zed Books, 2010).
3. Warren Thompson, "Population," *American Journal of Sociology* 34 (6) (1929): 959–975.
4. Dennis Hodgson, "Warren S. Thompson," in *Encyclopedia of Population*, ed. Paul Demeny and Geoffrey McNicoll (New York: Macmillan, 2003), 939–940.
5. Ansley Coale, "The Demographic Transition," *Pakistan Development Review* 23 (4) (1984): 531–532.
6. Massimo Livi-Bacci estimated that between year 1 and 1750, the world's population grew at an annual rate of 0.064 percent. Massimo Livi-Bacci, *A Concise History of World Population* (Oxford: Blackwell, 1997).
7. David Canning, "The Causes and Consequences of Demographic Transition," *Population Studies* 65 (3) (2011): 353–361.
8. Dudley Kirk, "Demographic Transition Theory," *Population Studies: A Journal for Demography* 50 (3) (1996): 361–362.
9. U.S. Central Intelligence Agency (CIA), *The World Factbook*, accessed January 5, 2014, https://www.cia.gov/library/publications/the-world-factbook/.
10. Paul and Anne Ehrlich, *The Population Explosion* (New York: Simon & Schuster, 1990), 55–56; F. Landis Mackellar and David Horlacher, "Population, Living Standards and Sustainability: An Economic View," in *Beyond the Numbers: A Reader on Population, Consumption, and the Environment*, ed. Laurie Ann Mazur (Washington, DC: Island Press, 1994), 76–77.
11. Sharon Camp, "The Politics of U.S. Population Assistance," in *Beyond the Numbers*, 129–132.
12. Paul and Anne Ehrlich, "Population Momentum," in *The Population Explosion*, 55–56, 59–61.
13. Wang Feng, Yong Cai, and Baochang Gu, "Population, Policy, and Politics: How Will History Judge China's One-Child Policy?" *Population and Development Review* 38 (2012): 115–129.
14. Danielle Demetriou, "Japan's Population Suffers Biggest Fall in History," *Telegraph*, April 17, 2013, http://www.telegraph.co.uk/news/worldnews/asia/japan/9999591/Japans-population-suffers-biggest-fall-in-history.html. Also see "Japan GDP Per Capita,"

Trading Economics, accessed October 24, 2015, http://www.tradingeconomics.com
/japan/gdp-per-capita.

15. Paolo von Schirach, "Europe (Especially Italy and Greece) Going Towards Population Decline," *Schirach Report,* January 27, 2012.

16. See: "Japan GDP per capita, 1960–2016," *Trading Economics,* http://www.trading
economics.com/japan/gdp-per-capita. Also, Oded Galor and David Weil, "Population,
Technology, and Growth: From Malthusian Stagnation to the Demographic Transition and Beyond," *American Economic Review* 90 (4) (2000): 806–828.

17. Israel Central Bureau of Statistics (CBS), "Table B/1: Population by Population
Group," (Jerusalem, 2015), http://www.cbs.gov.il/publications15/yarhon0915/pdf/b1.pdf,
accessed October 24, 2015; also, Roberto Bachi, "Table 14.1," in *The Population of Israel* (Jerusalem: Committee for International Cooperation in National Research in
Demography [CICRED], 1974), 262.

18. Israel CBS, "Fertility Rates by Age and Religion," *Statistical Abstract of Israel,* 2013,
3.13 (Jerusalem, 2013), http://www1.cbs.gov.il/reader/shnaton/templ_shnaton_e.html
?num_tab=st03_13&CYear=2013. And, more recently, see Israel CBS, "Fertility Rates
by Age and Religion" (September 10, 2015), http://www.cbs.gov.il/reader/shnaton/templ
_shnaton.html?num_tab=st03_13&CYear=2015.

19. Israel CBS, "Table B/1: Population by Population Group," accessed November 11, 2015.

20. Efrat Neuman, "Do Money Worries Affect People's Decision to Have Children?"
Haaretz, December 6, 2013, http://www.haaretz.com/business/.premium-1.562098.

21. Gadi Elgazi, "The Deep State Talks: The Koenig Document, 1976," The Arab-Jewish
Movement for Political and Social Change, accessed October 14, 2013, http://www
.tarabut.info/he/articles/article/koenig-report-1976/.

22. Netanyahu Disseminated a Video: "The Arabs Are Arriving in Enormous Numbers to the Ballot Boxes," Walla!, March 17, 2015, http://elections.walla.co.il/item
/2838603; also, Lahav Harkov, "Netanyahu Warns: The Left Is Busing Arabs to Vote,
the Right Is in Danger," *Jerusalem Post,* March 17, 2015, http://www.jpost.com/Israel
-Elections/Netanyahu-warns-The-Left-is-busing-Arabs-to-vote-the-Right-is-in
-danger-394176.

23. Itamar Ecihner and Yuval Carrni, "The Apology," *Yedioth Ahronot,* March 24,
2015, 1–2.

24. *Reuters,* "Jerusalem Fight," *Times of London,* April 6, 1920, original article repr. at
https://en.wikipedia.org/wiki/1920_Nebi_Musa_riots#/media/File:Nebi_Musa_riots,
_The_Times,_Thursday,_Apr_08,_1920.png.

25. Tom Segev, *One Palestine Complete: Jews and Arabs under the British Mandate* (New
York: Metropolitan Books, 1999), 127–139.

26. Dan Rabinowitz and Khawla Abu-Baker, *Coffins on Our Shoulders: The Experience of
the Palestinian Citizens of Israel* (Berkeley: University of California Press, 2005), 30.

27. Amin al-Husseini, *Through the Eyes of the Mufti: The Essays of Haj Amin,* trans. Zvi
Elpeleg and Rachell Kessel (London: Valentine Mitchell, 2009).

28. Chaim Weizmann, *Trial and Error: The Autobiography of Chaim Weizmann* (London:
Hamish Hamilton, 1949), 294–298.

29. Vladimir Jabotinsky, *The Jewish War Front* (London: Allen & Unwin, 1940), 220.

30. Vladimir Jabotinsky, "The Iron Wall—We and the Arabs," essay first published in Russian in 1923, translated and available at www.marxists.de/middleast/ironwall/ironwall .htm.

31. Bachi, *Population of Israel*, 201.

32. "Israel Declaration of Independence," May 14, 1948, Jerusalem, Israel Foreign Ministry, http://www.mfa.gov.il/mfa/foreignpolicy/peace/guide/pages/declaration%20of%20 establishment%20of%20state%20of%20israel.aspx.

33. Theodor Herzl, *Old New Land (Altneuland)* (New York: Random House, 1987).

34. In a power-sharing arrangement, it was suggested that when the prime minister was Jewish, the deputy would be Arab. Jabotinsky, *Jewish War Front*, 216–217.

35. Among the more reliable descriptions of events is Benny Morris's *The Birth of the Palestinian Refugee Problem Revisited* (Cambridge: Cambridge University Press, 2004).

36. United Nations, "Report of the Technical Committee on Refugees," General Progress Report and Supplementary Report of the United Nations Conciliation Commission for Palestine, covering the period from December 11, 1949 to October 23, 1950 (New York: United Nations, 1951), sec. 15, http://domino.un.org/unispal.nsf/9a798adbf322aff 38525617b006d88d7/93037e3b939746de8525610200567883.

37. Zeidan Atashe, *Druze and Jews in Israel—A Shared Destiny?* (Brighton: Sussex Academic Press, 1995).

38. Oz Almog and Sharon Hornstein, "The Dimensions of the Arab Sector from a Historic Perspective," People Israel, 2009, http://www.peopleil.org/details.aspx?itemID =7398.

39. Ibid.

40. Israel CBS, "65th Independence Day—More than 8 Million Residents in the State of Israel" (press release, April 14, 2013), http://www1.cbs.gov.il/www/hodaot2013n/11_13 _097e.pdf.

41. Bernard Lewis, *Semites and Anti-Semites: An Inquiry into Conflict and Prejudice* (New York: Norton, 1999).

42. David Kretzmer, *The Legal Status of the Arabs in Israel* (Boulder, CO: Westview, 1992); for a historic review: Shira Robinson, *Citizen Strangers: Palestinians and the Birth of Israel's Liberal Settler State* (Stanford, CA: Stanford University Press, 2013); for ethnographies: Amina Minns and Nadia Hijab's *Citizens Apart: A Portrait of the Palestinians in Israel* (London: I. B. Taurus, 1990) 68–113; or the much more common polemical diatribes, such as Ben White's *Palestinians in Israel: Segregation, Discrimination and Democracy* (London: Pluto Press, 2012).

43. Dr. Mousa Diabat, personal communication, July 7, 2014.

44. Sammy Smooha, *Arabs and Jews in Israel*, vol. 1: *Conflicting and Shared Attitudes in a Divided Society* (Boulder, CO: Westview Press, 1989). For an opposing view: As'ad Ghanem, "The Israeli-Arab Stream," in *The Palestinian-Arab Minority in Israel, 1948–2000* (Albany: State University of New York Press, 2001), 37.

45. Ghanem, *Palestinian-Arab Minority in Israel*, 27–29.

46. Robinson, *Citizen Strangers*, 63–67.

47. Adeed Dawisha, "Requiem for Arab Nationalism," *Middle East Quarterly* 10 (1) (2003): 25–41.

48. Zachi Shalom, *The Ongoing Security Policy of Israel in Its First Decade* (Ra'anana, Israel: Open University Press, 1999); also, Rabinowitz and Abu-Baker, *Coffins on Our Shoulders*, 51.

49. Ronen Bergman, "Revealed: In 1950s Mossad Spies Married Arabs to Conceal Identity," *Ynet*, August 27, 2013, http://www.ynetnews.com/articles/0,7340,L-4422919,00 .html.

50. Rabinowitz and Abu-Baker, *Coffins on Our Shoulders*, 60.

51. Paul Ehrlich, *The Population Bomb* (New York: Ballantine Books, 1968).

52. "Reserved General Shlomo Gazith and the Journalist Amnon Dunkner: 'Israeli Arabs' Are Demographic Time Bomb," *Maariv*, April 7, 2001, http://forum.walla.co.il /viewtopic.php?f=1015&t=446582; Yoram Ettinger, "Demography Is an Asset Not a Strategic Burden," *New Directions* 16 (2007): 110, http://www.wzo.org.il/files/kivunim /kivunim_16_new.pdf.

53. "Remembering Mahmoud Darwish," Electronic Intifada, August 11, 2008, http:// electronicintifada.net/content/remembering-mahmoud-darwish/7663.

54. Rhoda Ann Kanaaneh, *Birthing the Nation: Strategies of Palestinian Women in Israel* (Berkeley: University of California Press, 2002), 60–61.

55. Ibid., 61.

56. Minns and Hijab, *Citizens Apart*.

57. Justin McCarthy, *The Population of Palestine: Population History and Statistics of the Late Ottoman Period and the Mandate* (New York: Columbia University Press, 1990). Other estimates do not agree that population exceeded 1 million people: Magen Broshi, "The Population of Western Palestine in the Roman-Byzantine Period," *Bulletin of the American Schools of Oriental Research* 236 (1979): 1–10; Yigal Shiloh, "The Population of Iron Age Palestine in the Light of a Sample Analysis of Urban Plans, Areas, and Population Density," *Bulletin of the American Schools of Oriental Research* 239 (1980): 25–35.

58. McCarthy, *Population of Palestine*, 1, 11.

59. Diabat, personal communication.

60. Baruch Kimmerling and Joel Migdal, *Palestinians: The Making of a People* (New York: Free Press, 1993), 16.

61. Bertha Spafford Vester, *Our Jerusalem: An American Family in the Holy City, 1881–1949* (Garden City, NY: Doubleday, 1950), 62.

62. Yehoshua Ben Arieh, *Jerusalem in the 19th Century*, vol. 1: *The Old City* (New York: MacMillan, 1985), 27.

63. McCarthy, *Population of Palestine*, 37.

64. Ya'akov Firestone, "The Land Equalizing Musa-Village, a Reassessment," in *Ottoman Palestine, 1800–1914: Studies in Economic and Social History*, ed. Gad Gilbar (Leiden, Netherlands: Brill Academic Publishing, 1990), 114–116.

65. Alon Tal, "Rethinking the Eradication of Malaria in Israel," *Bulletin for the History of Medicine* 82 (4) (2008): 964–966.

66. McCarthy, *Population of Palestine*, 31–32.

67. David Grossman, *Rural Arab Demography and Early Jewish Settlement in Palestine: Distribution and Population Density During the Late Ottoman and Early Mandate Periods* (New Brunswick, NJ: Transaction Publishers, 2011), 30.
68. Theodore Herzl, "Jerusalem, October 31, 1898," in *The Diaries of Theodor Herzl*, trans. and ed. Marvin Lowenthal (New York: Grosset's Universal Library, 1962), 283–284.
69. Grossman, *Rural Arab Demography and Early Jewish Settlement in Palestine*, 1–2.
70. Gad Gilbar, "Economic Involvement of Palestine with the West," in *Ottoman Palestine*, 114–116.
71. Grossman, *Rural Arab Demography and Early Jewish Settlement in Palestine*, 20–21.
72. Ibid., 17–18.
73. Mark Twain, *The Innocents Abroad or The New Pilgrim's Progress*, vol. 2 (New York: Harper and Brother, 1911), 234–235.
74. Grossman, *Rural Arab Demography and Early Jewish Settlement in Palestine*, 1–2.
75. Spafford Vester, *Our Jerusalem*, 85.
76. Ruth Kark and Michal Oren Nordheim, *Jerusalem and Its Environs: Quarters, Neighborhoods, Villages, 1800–1948* (Detroit, MI: Wayne State University Press, 2001), 34.
77. Yaron Perry and Efraim Lev, *Modern Medicine in the Holy Land: Pioneering British Medical Services in Late Ottoman Palestine* (London: Tauris Academic Studies, 2007).
78. Bachi, *Population of Israel*, 248–249.
79. Sandra M. Sufian, *Healing the Land and the Nation: Malaria and the Zionist Project in Palestine, 1920–1947* (Chicago: University of Chicago Press, 2007).
80. Alon Tal, *Pollution in a Promised Land: An Environmental History of Israel* (Berkeley: University of California Press, 2002), 58–61.
81. John Hope Simpson, *Palestine: Report on Immigration, Land Settlement and Development* (London: H. M. Stationery Office, 1930), 26.
82. Bachi, *Population of Israel*, 5.
83. Majid Al-Haj, *Education among the Arabs in Israel: Control and Social Change* (Jerusalem: Magnes, 1996), 22–26.
84. E. Mills, *Census of Palestine, 1931* (Jerusalem: Greek Convent and Goldberg Press, 1932), 134, https://cs.anu.edu.au/people/Brendan.McKay/yabber/census/Palestine Census1931.pdf.
85. E. Mills, *Census of Palestine, 1931*, 134.
86. Ari Shavit, *My Promised Land* (New York, Random House, 2013), 99–134.
87. Rabinowitz and Abu-Baker, *Coffins on Our Shoulders*, 35.
88. Bachi, *Population of Israel*; Eli Rekhess, "Arab Politics in Israel at a Crossroads: Papers and Panel Discussion Based on the Proceedings of a Conference Held at Tel Aviv University, 30–31 October 1994," Tel Aviv: The Moshe Dayan Center for Middle Eastern and African Studies, Tel Aviv University.
89. Onn Winckler, "Fertility Transition in the Middle East: The Case of the Arab Israelis," *Israel Affairs* 9 (1–2) (2002), 44.
90. Jona Schellekens and Zvi Eisenbach, "Religiosity and Marital Fertility: Israeli Arab Muslims, 1955–1972," *Journal of Family History* 35: 147–163.
91. Don Peretz, "The Arab Refugee Dilemma," *Foreign Affairs* 33 (1) (1954): 134–138, http://www.foreignaffairs.com/articles/71153/don-peretz/the-arab-refugee-dilemma.

92. Geremy Forman and Alexander Kedar, "From Arab Lands to Israeli Lands: The Legal Dispossession of the Palestinians Displaced by Israel in the Wake of 1948," *Society and Space* 22 (6) (2004): 809–830.

93. Tal, *Pollution in a Promised Land*, 87–88; also, Rassem Khamaisi, "Land Ownership as a Determinate in the Formation of Residential Areas in Arab Localities in Israel," *Geoforum* 26 (2) (1995): 211–224.

94. Ian Lustick, *Arabs in a Jewish State: Israel's Control of a National Minority* (Austin: University of Texas Press, 1980); Salman Abu Sitta, *Dividing War Spoils: Israel's Seizure, Confiscation and Sale of Palestinian Property* (London: Palestine Land Society, 2009); Robinson, *Citizen Strangers*.

95. Kimmerling and Migdal, *Palestinians*, 174–175.

96. Henry Rosenfeld, "The Class Situation of the Arab National Minority in Israel," *Comparative Studies in Society and History* 20 (3) (1978): 374–407.

97. Diabat, personal communication.

98. Kimmerling and Migdal report, surprisingly, that during this period, nearly three-quarters of the industrial workers in Arab industries were women; Kimmerling and Migdal, *Palestinians*, 176.

99. Israel CBS, "Fertility Rates by Age and Religion."

100. Yair Hasson, "Half of Workforce Earns Less Than 6,451 NIS per Month," *Ynet*, June 11, 2013; UNICEF, "Jordan—Statistics," accessed March 31, 2015, http://www.unicef.org/infobycountry/jordan_statistics.html. Minimum wage in the Palestinian Authority is less than a third of the level in Israel.

101. Israel CBS, "Life Expectancy, by Sex, Religion and Population Group," *Statistical Abstract of Israel* (Jerusalem, updated September 10, 2015), http://www.cbs.gov.il/reader/shnaton/templ_shnaton_e.html?num_tab=st03_24&CYear=2015; Ofer Aderet, "Israelis' Life Expectancy Has Risen by Two Years over Past Decade," *Haaretz*, September 16, 2013, http://www.haaretz.com/news/national/.premium-1.547293.

102. Organisation for Economic Co-operation and Development (OECD), "Life Expectancy" (2013), http://www.oecd.org/berlin/47570143.pdf.

103. Israel CBS, "Fertility Rates by Age and Religion."

104. CIA, "Total Fertility Rates," *World Factbook* (2013), https://www.cia.gov/library/publications/the-world-factbook/fields/2127.html.

105. Israel CBS, "Live Births, By Birth Order, Population Group and Mother's Religion," *Statistical Abstract of Israel* 3.16 (Jerusalem, 2013), http://www1.cbs.gov.il/shnaton64/st03_16.pdf.

106. Yaron Druckman, "Jewish Women are Giving Birth More, Arab Women Are on a Downward Trend," *Ynet*, January 14, 2013, http://www.ynet.co.il/articles/0,7340,L-4332305,00.html.

107. Mills, *Census of Palestine, 1931*, 11.

108. Israel CBS, "Population By Religion," *Statistical Abstract of Israel* 2.2 (Jerusalem, 2010), http://www1.cbs.gov.il/shnaton61/st02_02.pdf.

109. Israel CBS, "The Druze Population of Israel, a Collection of Statistics" (Jerusalem, April 24, 2015), www.cbs.gov.il/www/hodaot2015n/11_15_097b.pdf.

110. Winckler, "Fertility Transition in the Middle East," 44–46.
111. Kanaaneh, *Birthing the Nation*, 62–63.
112. Ibid., 62.
113. Rinal Shalabana-B'hote, interview with author, July 7, 2013.
114. Kanaaneh, *Birthing the Nation*, 82.
115. Smooha, *Arabs and Jews in Israel*.
116. Sammy Smooha, *Index of Arab Jewish Relations* (Haifa: University of Haifa, Jewish Arab Center, 2005), 6.
117. Nadim Rouhana, *Palestinian Citizens in an Ethnic Jewish State: Identities in Conflict* (New Haven, CT: Yale University Press, 1997), 147.
118. Suleiman Abu Bader and Daniel Gottlieb, "Poverty, Education and Employment in the Arab-Bedouin Society: A Comparative View" (working paper, Jerusalem: National Insurance Institute, 2009), 9.
119. Roni Malkai (Ministry of Welfare spokesperson), "The Minister of Welfare Appointed an Advisor from the Arab Sector to Address Matters of Welfare in the Arab Sector," Ministry of Social Affairs and Social Services, August 4, 2013, http://www.molsa.gov .il/dover/pages/newspage.aspx?listid=76c73ffb-5c7e-40f4-bdc1-20a68f9aa9e8&webid =57bafbcd-ffba-4897-85eb-c3379813c505&itemid=457.
120. The Or Commission's official name was "The State Commission of Inquiry into the Clashes between Security Forces and Israeli Civilians," and the report can be found at http://elyon1.court.gov.il/heb/veadot/or/inside_index.htm; Yair Ettinger, "92 Hearings, 377 Witnesses, 4,289 Exhibits," *Haaretz*, September 1, 2003, http:// www.haaretz.com/print-edition/news/92-hearings-377-witnesses-4-289-exhibits-1 .98822.
121. Eliezer Ben-Rafael and Yochanan Peres, *Is Israel One? Religion, Nationalism, and Multiculturalism Confounded* (Boston: Brill, 2005), 170–171.
122. Itamar Radai, Meir Elran, Yousef Makladeh, and Maya Kornberg, "The Arab Citizens in Israel: Current Trends According to Recent Opinion Polls, *Strategic Assessment* 18 (2) (2015): 102, http://www.inss.org.il/uploadImages/systemFiles/adkan18 _2ENG_4_Radai%20et%20al488551568.pdf.
123. Meirav Arlosoroff, "That Is Certainly No Way to Integrate Arab Israelis into the Workforce," *Haaretz*, January 9, 2014, http://www.haaretz.com/business/1.567704.
124. Sammy Smooha, "Contrasting Trends of Change in Arab and Jewish Attitudes toward Each Other and the State" (lecture at the 30th Annual Conference of the Association of Israel Studies, Ben-Gurion University, Sede Boqer Campus, Israel, June 24, 2014).
125. Liora Gvion, "Narrating Modernity and Tradition: The Case of Palestinian Food in Israel," *Global Studies in Culture and Power* 16 (2009): 402–403.
126. Hasan Shaalan and Ellior Levi, "Arabs Also Are Giving Up Cottage Cheese, Preparing Labaneh at Home," *Ynet*, June 16, 2011, www.ynet.co.il/articles/0,7340,L -4082923,00.html.
127. Ruta Kupfer, "Arab Israeli Wins Reality Cooking Show 'Master Chef,'" *Haaretz*, April 6, 2014, http://www.haaretz.com/life/movies-television/1.583998.

128. Hila Miro, "Rana Raslan: Once a Queen, Always a Queen," *Ynet*, January 13, 2008, http://www.ynet.co.il/articles/0,7340,L-3492669,00.html.

129. Eurovision Song Contest, "Israel: A Trilingual Duet with One Message," Eurovision Web posting, 2009, http://www.eurovision.tv/page/news?id=israel_a_trilingual _duet_with_one_message.

130. Tamir Sorek, "Between Football and Martyrdom: The Bi-Focal Localism of an Arab-Palestinian Town in Israel," *British Journal of Sociology* 56 (4) (2005): 635–660.

131. Hussein Tarbiah, "Minority Report: Environmental Challenges Facing the Arab Society in Israel," in *Between Ruin and Restoration: An Environmental History of Israel*, ed. Daniel Orenstein, Alon Tal, and Char Miller (Pittsburgh: University of Pittsburgh Press, 2013), 190–208.

132. Shmuel Grueg, "Planning Rights in Arab Settlements—A Snapshot in Israel" (Tel Aviv: Bimkom, 2003).

133. Hanadi Higress, interview with author, June 26, 2013.

134. Jamila Elnashef, "Walking on a Fine Line: Between Integration and a National-Professional Trap in Israel: Muslim Female Teachers in Jewish Schools" (lecture at the 30th Annual Conference of the Association of Israel Studies, Ben-Gurion University, Sede Boqer Campus, Israel, June 24, 2014).

135. Basel Ghattas, interview with author, June 10, 2013.

136. Banu Ergocmen, "Women's Status and Fertility in Turkey," in *Fertility Trends: Women's Status and Reproductive Expectations in Turkey* (Ankara, Turkey: Hacettepe University Institute of Population Studies, 1997), 79–104, http://dhsprogram.com /pubs/pdf/FA16/FA16.pdf.

137. S. J. Jejeebhoy, "Women's Status and Fertility: Successive Cross-sectional Evidence from Tamil Nadu, India, 1970–80," *Studies in Family Planning* 22 (4) (1991): 217–30.

138. Xiaogang Wu, Hua Ye, and Gloria Guangye He, "Fertility Decline and Women's Empowerment in China" (working paper, Washington, DC: International Center for Research on Women Fertility and Empowerment, 2012), 1–35.

139. David Shapiro, "Women's Education and Fertility Transition in Sub-Saharan Africa," *Vienna Yearbook of Population Research* 10 (2012): 9–30.

140. Ibtisam Ibrahim, "The Status of Arab Women in Israel," *Critique: Critical Middle Eastern Studies* 7 (12) (1998): 107–120.

141. Winckler, "Fertility Transition in the Middle East," 46.

142. Eran Yashiv and Nitsa Kasir, "Arab Women in the Israeli Labor Market: Characteristics and Policy Proposals," *Israel Economic Review* 10 (2) (2013): 13.

143. Barbara Okun, "Fertility and Marriage Behavior in Israel: Diversity, Change, and Stability," *Demographic Research* 28 (17) (2013): 470.

144. Higress, interview.

145. Lilian Abou-Tabickh, "Women's Masked Migration," in *Displaced at Home: Ethnicity and Gender Around Palestinians in Israel*, ed. Rhoda Ann Kanaaneh and Isis Nusair (Albany: State University of New York Press, 2010), 189–190.

146. Shalabana-B'hote, interview.
147. Robert Engelman, "Trusting Women to End Population Growth," in *Life on the Brink: Environmentalists Confront Overpopulation* (Athens: University of Georgia Press, 2012), 229.
148. Kanaaneh, *Birthing the Nation*, 71–72.
149. *Reuters*, "Palestinians See Worrisome Trend in Rise of 'Honor Killings,'" *Jerusalem Post*, November 12, 2013, http://www.jpost.com/Middle-East/Palestinian -see-worrisome-trend-in-rise-of-honor-killings-334645; also, Laura Smith-Spark, "Third of Teens in Amman, Jordan, Condone Honor Killings, Study Says," *CNN*, June 20, 2013, http://www.cnn.com/2013/06/20/world/meast/jordan-honor-crimes -study/.
150. Amalia Sa'ar, "Lonely in Your Firm Grip: Women in Israeli-Palestinian Families," *Journal of the Royal Anthropological Institute* 7 (4) (2001): 723–739.
151. Insaf Abu-Shareb, "A Conspiracy of Silence: Domestic Violence against Arab-Bedouin Women in the Negev" (Beer Sheva: Women Lawyers for Social Justice, 2013).
152. Shlomi Eldar, "Arab Women in Israel: From Oppression to Empowerment," March 7, 2013, http://www.al-monitor.com/pulse/originals/2013/03/arab-women-in-israel-from -oppression-to-empowerment.html##ixzz2qVmWF1fL.
153. Higress, interview.
154. Khawla Rihani, director, Association for Economic Empowerment for Women, interview with author, July 2, 2013.
155. Yashiv and Kasir, "Arab Women in the Israeli Labor Market," 22.
156. Naftali Bennet (presentation *at Israel Conference for Peace*, Tel Aviv, July 8, 2014).
157. Joshua Mitnick, "Why Israel Wants More Arab Women Earning a Paycheck," *Christian Science Monitor*, November 13, 2013, http://www.csmonitor.com/World/Middle -East/2013/1113/Why-Israel-wants-more-Arab-women-earning-a-paycheck.
158. Tamar Keinan and Dorit Bar, *Mobility among Arab Women in Israel* (Haifa: Kayan, 2008).
159. Yashiv and Kasir, "Arab Women in the Israeli Labor Market," 22–23.
160. Yosef Jabareen, "Employment Equity" (PowerPoint presentation, March 23, 2010), http://www.powershow.com/view4/49c569-MzQoZ/Employment_Equity _powerpoint_ppt_presentation.
161. Rihani, interview.
162. Manal Shalabi, "The Sexual Politics of Palestinian Women in Israel," in *Displaced at Home*, 153–154.
163. Abdessamad Dialmy, "Sexuality in Contemporary Arab Society," in *Judaism and Islam: Essays on Sexuality and Religion*, ed. Stephen Hunt (Surrey, UK: Ashgate, 2010), 335.
164. Manal Shalabi, "The Sexual Politics of Palestinian Women in Israel," 167.
165. Kanaaneh, *Birthing the Nation*, 78.
166. Ibid., 200.
167. Dr. Ziad Aga, interview with author, July 22, 2013.

168. Itai Gal, "Abortions: Rise among Arabs; Peak—Ethiopians," *Ynet*, September 21, 2011, http://www.ynet.co.il/articles/0,7340,L-4125154,00.html.

169. Ben-Rafael and Peres, *Is Israel One?* 171.

170. Sahih Muslim 8:337: Relevant passages can be found at http://wikiislam.net/wiki /Qur'an,_Hadith_and_Scholars:Al-'Azl.

171. Heather Boonstra, "Islam, Women and Family Planning: A Primer," *Guttmacher Report on Public Policy* 4 (6) (2001): 4–5.

172. Laithe Gnaim, interview with author, June 26, 2013.

173. Omar Abu Muamar, interview with author, June 30, 2013; Mohammed Alnabari, interview with author, July 11, 2013.

174. Akbar Aghajanian and Amir H. Merhyar, "Fertility, Contraceptive Use and Family Planning Program Activity in the Islamic Republic of Iran," *International Family Planning Perspectives* 25 (2) (1999): 98–102.

175. Israel CBS, "Fertility Rates by Age and Religion" (September 10, 2015), http://www .cbs.gov.il/reader/shnaton/templ_shnaton.html?num_tab=st03_13&CYear=2015.

176. Israel CBS, "Christians in Israel, on Christmas, 2013" (Jerusalem, December 24, 2013), http://www1.cbs.gov.il/reader/newhodaot/hodaa_template.html?hodaa=201311353.

177. Sugase Akiko, "To Be or Not to Be an Arab: The Complex Identity of Arab Christians in Israel," *Kyoto Bulletin of Islamic Area Studies* 3 (1) (2009): 232–236.

178. Elnashef, "Walking on a Fine Line."

179. For instance: Exodus, 22:22, Leviticus 19:34, and 25:35, Deuteronomy 26:12, and 27:19.

180. John Rawls, *A Theory of Justice* (Cambridge: Belknap Press, 1999).

181. Faisal Azaiza, Udi Cohen, and Ibrahim Abu-Shindi, *Index of Arab Jewish Relations* (Haifa: University of Haifa, Jewish Arab Center, 2005), 6.

182. Sammy Smooha, "Relations of Arabs and Jews in Israel as a Jewish and Democratic State," *Trends in Israeli Society*, ed. Efraim Ya'ar and Ze'ev Shavit (Ra'anana, Israel: Open University, 2001), 231.

CHAPTER 9. GROWING PAINS

1. U.S. Central Intelligence Agency (CIA), "West Bank," *The World Factbook*, updated June 20, 2014, https://www.cia.gov/library/publications/the-world-factbook/geos/we .html.

2. CIA, "Gaza Strip," *World Factbook*, updated June 20, 2014, https://www.cia.gov /library/publications/the-world-factbook/geos/gz.html.

3. Ari Paltiel, Michel Sepulcer, Irene Kornilenko, and Martin Maldonado, *Long-Range Population Projections for Israel: 2009–2059* (Jerusalem: Central Bureau of Statistics [CBS], Demography and Census Department, 2011), 11, http://www.cbs .gov.il/www/publications/tec27.pdf.

4. Gidon Kressel, interview with author, June 23, 2014; Havatzelet Yahel, Ruth Kark, and Seth J. Frantzman, "Fabricating Palestinian History—Are the Negev Bedouin an Indigenous People?" *Middle East Quarterly* 19 (3) (2012): 9–11. This position is

challenged by Oren Yiftachel and Batia Roded in "Between Rights and Denial: Indigenousness in the Negev"(unpublished manuscript, 2014).

5. Aref el-Aref, *Bedouin Love, Law and Legend: Dealing Exclusively with the Badu of Beersheba; A Version in English of the Book in Arabic* (New York: AMS Press, 1974); Clinton Bailey, *Bedouin Poetry: From Sinai and the Negev* (New York: Oxford University Press, 1991); Rohn Eloul, *Culture Change in a Bedouin Tribe: The Arab al Hgerat, Lower Galilee, A.D. 1790–1977* (Ann Arbor, MI: Museum of Anthropology, University of Michigan, 2010).
6. Sultan Abu Avid, interview with author, June 11, 2013.
7. Avinoam Meir, "Demographic Changes in Bedouin Society in the Negev," in *Proceedings of a Conference About the Bedouins, February 6, 1984* (1984), repr. by Ben-Gurion University Snunit, http://www.snunit.k12.il/beduin/arti/1501.html.
8. Meir, "Demographic Changes in Bedouin Society in the Negev."
9. Ehud Praver and Lirit Sarfus, *The Bedouin in the Negev: Policy, Difficulties and Recommendations; Position Paper* (Herzliya: National Council for Security, 2006), 4, http://www.izsvideo.org/videos/full/bed2.pdf.
10. Josef Ben-David, *The Bedouins in Israel—Land Conflicts and Social Issues* (Jerusalem: Institute for Land Policy, 2004), 55–56.
11. E. Mills, *Census of Palestine, 1931*, vol. 1 (Alexandria, Egypt: Whitehead Morris, 1933), 328–335.
12. Yifat Shani Abuhazira, *The Bedouin Population in Israel—Population Register Compared with Population Estimation as Basis of Demographic Indexes* (Jerusalem: CBS, 2010), 28, http://www.cbs.gov.il/www/publications/pw50.pdf.
13. Emanuel Marx, *Bedouin of the Negev* (Manchester, UK: Manchester University Press, 1967), 9–11; Ruth Kark and Seth Frantzman, "The Negev: Land, Settlement, the Bedouin and Ottoman and British Policy, 1871–1948," *British Journal of Middle Eastern Studies* 39 (1) (2012): 53–77; Ruth Kark, *Frontier Jewish Settlement in the Negev, 1880–1948* (Jerusalem: Ariel, 2002), 38–44.
14. Ben-David, *Bedouins in Israel*, 119.
15. Howard Sachar, *A History of Israel: From the Rise of Zionism to Our Time* (New York: Alfred Knopf, 2007), 384–385.
16. Marx, *Bedouin of the Negev*, 9–11, 18.
17. The Knesset, "Minorities in Israel: The Bedouin," accessed January 21, 2014, http://main.knesset.gov.il/About/Lexicon/Pages/bedouim.aspx.
18. Rutie Frum Aricha, Israel Ministry of Agriculture and Rural Development, personal communication, November 12, 2015; also, Silvia Boarini, "Negev Bedouin Resist Israeli Demolitions 'To Show We Exist,'" Inter Press Service New Agency, February 20, 2015, http://www.ipsnews.net/2015/02/negev-bedouin-resist-israeli-demolitions-to-show-we-exist/.
19. Israel Ministry of Education, "General Information on the Bedouin," accessed January 21, 2014, http://cms.education.gov.il/EducationCMS/Units/Mazkirut_Pedagogit/Beduim/Razional/NetunimStatistim/.
20. Suleiman Abu Bader, ed., *The Negev Bedouin: Statistical Data Book, No. 30* (Beer Sheva: Ben-Gurion University, 2010), 37, 169.

21. Abu Avid, interview; also, Chanina Porat, *The Bedouin-Arab in the Negev between Migration and Urbanization, 1948–1973* (Beer Sheva: Negev Center for Regional Development, 2009).

22. Shaul Krakover, "Urban Settlement Program and Land Dispute Resolution: The State of Israel versus the Negev Bedouin," *GeoJournal* 47 (4) (1999): 551–561.

23. Yosef Ben-David, "Adaptation Through Crisis: Social Aspects of Bedouin Urbanization in the Negev," in *The Arab Community in Israel: Geographical Processes* (Ramat Gan, Israel: Bar Ilan, 1994), 48–76.

24. Harriet Sherwood, "Israel's Plan to Forcibly Resettle Negev Bedouins Prompts Global Protests," *Guardian*, December 1, 2013, http://www.theguardian.com/world/2013/dec/01/israel-negev-bedouins-day-of-rage. Abu Bader, *Negev Bedouin*, 37.

25. Suleiman Abu Bader and Daniel Gottlieb, *Poverty, Education and Employment in the Arab-Bedouin Society: A Comparative View* (working paper, Jerusalem: National Insurance Institute, 2009), 16.

26. Abu Bader and Gottlieb, *Poverty, Education and Employment in the Arab-Bedouin Society*, 26.

27. Ibid., 37.

28. Ibid., 133.

29. Abu Avid, interview.

30. Abu Bader, *Negev Bedouin*, 110.

31. Clinton Bailey, *Bedouin Law from the Sinai and the Negev: Justice Without Government* (New Haven, CT: Yale University Press, 2009), 244–250.

32. Insaf Abu Shareb, "A Conspiracy of Silence: Domestic Violence against Arab-Bedouin Women in the Negev" (Beer Sheva: Women Lawyers for Social Justice, 2013), 12.

33. Julie Cwikel and Nurit Barak, *Health and Welfare of Bedouin Women in the Negev* (Beer Sheva: Ben Gurion University, 2002), 4; Abu Avid, interview.

34. Cwikel and Barak, *Health and Welfare of Bedouin Women in the Negev*.

35. Abu Bader, *Negev Bedouin*, 169.

36. Ibid., 173.

37. Abu Bader and Gottlieb, *Poverty, Education and Employment in the Arab-Bedouin Society*, 27.

38. Abu Bader, *Negev Bedouin*, 70.

39. Sarab Abu-Rabia-Queder, *Excluded and Loved: Educated Bedouin Women's Life Stories* (Jerusalem: Magnes, 2008).

40. Alnabari, interview with author, July 11, 2013.

41. Faiz Abu Sahiban, interview with author, June 20, 2013; Omar Abu Muamar, interview with author, June 30, 2013; Alnabari, interview.

42. *Ben Naser Saarah versus the Institute for National Insurance*, Beer Sheva Regional Labor Court, B'L 1533-09 (January 2, 2011).

43. Insaf Abu Shareb, interview with author, July 14, 2013.

44. Hassan Shaalan, "Murdered Bedouin Sisters Laid to Rest," *Ynet*, May 24, 2013, http://www.ynetnews.com/articles/0,7340,L-4383806,00.html. The officers involved were dismissed from the police.

45. Abu Shareb, interview.

46. Safa Abu-Rabia, "New Leadership among the Bedouin Arabs of the Negev" (lecture at the 30th Annual Conference of the Association of Israel Studies, Ben-Gurion University, Sede Boqer Campus, Israel, June 24, 2014).

47. Abu Shareb, interview.

48. The Penal Law, 1977, sec. 176 or, generally, part "H," "Polygamy," *Israel Law Book*, 1977, no. 864, 226.

49. Orly Almagor-Lotan, *Polygamy among the Bedouin Population in Israel: A Report Submitted to the Committee on the Status of Women* (Jerusalem: Knesset, 2006).

50. Shahar Ginosar, "The Desert Generation," *Yedioth Ahronot, Shiva Yamim Supplement*, June 17, 2011, 23–25.

51. Abu Sahiban, interview.

52. Qur'an, Sura 4 (An-Nisa), Ayah 3, http://quran.com/4/3.

53. Boaz Velinitz, "Pay and Take: Polygamy Continues and the State is Silent," *Walla! News*, September 23, 2010, http://news.walla.co.il/?w=/90/1735189.

54. Alnabari, interview.

55. Alean Al-Krenawi and John R. Graham, "A Comparison of Family Functioning, Life and Marital Satisfaction, and Mental Health of Women in Polygamous and Monogamous Marriages," *International Journal of Social Psychiatry* 52 (1) (2006): 5–17.

56. Alean Al-Krenawi, "Women from Polygamous and Monogamous Marriages in an Out-Patient Psychiatric Clinic," *Journal of Transcultural Psychology* 38 (2) (2001): 187–199.

57. "Polygamy Causes Suffering among Women, Study Finds," Shatil, May 29, 2011, http://english.shatil.org.il/polygamy-causes-suffering-among-women-study-finds/.

58. David Miller, "Israeli Anti-Polygamy Activists Run into Islamic Opposition," *Jerusalem Post*, December 23, 2010, http://www.jpost.com/Middle-East/Israeli-anti-polygamy-activists-run-into-Islamic-opposition.

59. Abu Shareb, interview.

60. Sarab Abu-Rabia-Queder interview with author, July 23, 2013.

61. Abu Sahiban, interview.

62. Alnabari, interview.

63. Yossi Klein Halevi, *Like Dreamers: The Story of the Israeli Paratroopers Who Reunited Jerusalem and Divided a Nation* (New York: HarperCollins, 2013), 113–208.

64. Yossi Beilin, *Israel: A Concise Political History* (London: Weidenfeld & Nicolson, 1992), 163.

65. Elior Levy, "Report: Palestinians to Outnumber Jews by 2020," *Ynet*, January 1, 2013, http://www.ynetnews.com/articles/0,7340,L-4327295,00.html.

66. Max Blumenthal, "How Ariel Sharon Shaped Israel's Destiny," *Nation*, January 11, 2014, http://www.thenation.com/article/177883/how-ariel-sharon-shaped-israels-destiny#.

67. Arnon Soffer, interview with author, June 3, 2013.

68. Jefferson Morley, "Israeli Withdrawal from Gaza Explained," *Washington Post*, August 10, 2005, http://www.washingtonpost.com/wp-dyn/content/article/2005/08/10/AR2005081000713.html.

69. Yoram Ettinger, interview with author, July 3, 2013.

70. Ibid.

71. Bennett Zimmerman, Roberta Seid, and Michael L. Wise, "The Million Person Gap: The Arab Population in the West Bank and Gaza," *Begin-Sadat Center for Strategic Studies, Mideast Security and Policy Studies* 65 (2006): 1–3, http://www.biu.ac.il/Besa /MSPS65.pdf.

72. Yoram Ettinger, "Israel's Jewish Demography Defies Conventions," *Israel Hayom*, April 05, 2013, http://bit.ly/16BnlKH.

73. Jeff Jacoby, "The Myth of the Inevitable Jewish Minority in Israel," *Boston Globe*, June 26, 2013; Guy Bechor, "The Number of Settlers Is Already Half of the Number of Palestinians in Judea and Sumaria," *Gplanet*, June 20, 2013, http://www.gplanet.co.il /prodetailsamewin.asp?pro_id=1684.

74. Ian Lustick, "What Counts Is the Counting: Statistical Manipulation as a Solution to Israel's 'Demographic Problem,'" *Middle East Journal* 67 (2) (2013): 185–205.

75. Nir Hasson, "How Many Palestinians Actually Live in the West Bank?" *Haaretz*, June 30, 2013, http://www.haaretz.com/israel-news/.premium-1.532703.

76. Hasson, "How Many Palestinians Actually Live in the West Bank?"

77. Palestinian CBS, Population and Social Statistics Directorate (PSSD) Demographic Statistics Department, "Comments on 'Arab Population in the West Bank and Gaza: the Million and a Half Person Gap,'" 2006, as quoted in Lustick, "What Counts Is the Counting," 2013.

78. Professor Uzi Ravhon, interview with author, July 3, 2013; Sergio DellaPergola, interview with author, July 3, 2013; Soffer, interview.

79. Sergio DellaPergola, "Correspondence," *Azure*, Winter 2007, 11–12.

80. "Summary Final Results of 1997 Census," as reported in DellaPergola, "Correspondence," 22, n. 13.

81. Ibid., 4–22.

82. Ibid., 8.

83. CIA, "Gaza Strip."

84. Manar Hasan, "The Politics of Respect: Patriarchy, the State and the Murder of Women in Honor Killings," in *Sex, Gender and Politics*, ed. Emek Yezreel (B'nei Brak, Israel: Hakibbutz Hameuchad Press, 1999), 267–294.

85. Basel Ghattas, interview with author, June 10, 2013.

86. Sylvia Foa, "Battle of the Wombs: The Future's Numbers Game," *Village Voice*, December 3, 2002, http://www.villagevoice.com/2002-12-03/news/battle-of-the-wombs/.

87. Lustick, "What Counts Is the Counting," 185–205.

CHAPTER 10. CARRYING CAPACITY—PAST AND PRESENT

1. Jeremy Benstein, *The Way into Judaism and the Environment* (Woodstock, VT: Jewish Lights, 2006), 116.

2. Jonathan Roughgarden, *Theory of Population Genetics and Evolutionary Ecology: An Introduction* (New York: Macmillan, 1979), 305.

3. Eric Pianka, *Evolutionary Ecology*, 6th ed., ed. Benjamin Cummings (San Francisco: Addison-Wesley-Longman, 2000).

4. Benstein, *Way into Judaism and the Environment*, 115–116.

5. John Vidal, "10 Ways Vegetarianism Can Help Save the Planet," *Guardian*, July 17, 2010, http://www.theguardian.com/lifeandstyle/2010/jul/18/vegetarianism-save-planet -environment.

6. Edward O. Wilson, *The Future of Life* (New York: Vintage, 2002).

7. Julian Simon, "World Population Growth: Facts and Consequences," *Atlantic Monthly*, 1981, 70–76. Simon claims in his book *The Ultimate Resource* (Princeton, NJ: Princeton University Press, 1981) that natural resources are essentially infinite. Similar voices can be heard more recently, like Erle Ellis, "Conserving a Used Planet: Embracing History as Transformers of the Earth," *Snap Magazine*, September 24, 2013, http://www.snap.is/magazine/embracing-our-history-as-transformers-of-earth/.

8. Harold Barnett and Chandler Morse, *Scarcity and Growth* (Baltimore, MD: Johns Hopkins University Press, 1963); Charles Perrings, *Economy and Environment* (Cambridge: Cambridge University Press, 1987).

9. Garett Hardin, *The Ostrich Factor: Our Population Myopia* (New York: Oxford Press, 1999), 35.

10. *Gittin*, 57a; some translate the word "*tzvi*" as "hart" rather than "gazelle." Hence Arie Lova Eliav's famous tome about Israel, *Land of the Hart* (Philadelphia: Jewish Publication Society, 1974), where this passage opens the book.

11. Babylonian Tal mud, *Yoma*, 21A.

12. Thomas Malthus, *An Essay on the Principle of Population* (New York: Norton, 1976), 68.

13. Jared Diamond, *Collapse: How Societies Choose to Fail or Succeed* (New York, Penguin, 2006).

14. William Rees, "Revisiting Carrying Capacity: Area-Based Indicators of Sustainability," *Population and Environment: A Journal of Interdisciplinary Studies* 17 (3) (1996): 195–215.

15. Flavius Josephus, "Antiquities of the Jews," in *The Works of Flavius Josephus*, trans. William Whiston, ed. A. R. Shilleto (London: George Bell, 1889), 201.

16. Flavius Josephus, "The War of the Jews," in The Complete Works of Flavius-Josephus: The Celebrated Jewish Historian (Philadelphia: Potter, 1895).

17. Tacitus, "The Jews," in *Histories*, bk. 5, 13, available at http://www.ourcivilisation.com /smartboard/shop/tacitusc/histries/chap18.htm.

18. Michael Avi-Yonah, *The Jews of Palestine: A Political History from the Bar Kokhba War* (Oxford: Blackwell, 1976), 19.

19. Ilan Troen, *Imagining Zion: Dreams, Designs, and Realities in a Century of Jewish Settlement* (New Haven, CT: Yale University Press, 2003), 173.

20. Magen Broshi, "The Population of Western Palestine in the Roman-Byzantine Period," *Bulletin of the American Schools of Oriental Research* 236 (1979): 1–10; Yigal Shiloh, "The Population of Iron Age Palestine in the Light of a Sample Analysis of Urban Plans, Areas, and Population Density," *Bulletin of the American Schools of Oriental Research* 239 (1980): 25–35.

21. Ram Gophna and Juval Portugali, "Settlement and Demographic Processes in Israel's Coastal Plain from the Chalcolithic to the Middle Bronze Age," *Bulletin of the American Schools of Oriental Research* 269 (1988): 11–28.

22. Eric Meyers, personal communication, March 7, 2013.

23. Avi-Yonah, *Jews of Palestine*, 19.

24. Roberto Bachi, *The Population of Israel* (Jerusalem: Cooperation in National Research in Demography [CICRED], 1974), 4.

25. Alexander Schölch, "The Demographic Development of Palestine, 1850–1882," *International Journal of Middle East Studies* 17 (4) (1985): 485–505.

26. Tom Segev, *One Palestine Complete: Jews and Arabs under the British Mandate* (New York: Metropolitan Books, 1999), 185–186.

27. Daniel Orenstein, "Zionist and Israeli Perspectives on Population Growth and Environmental Impact in Palestine and Israel," in *Between Ruin and Restoration: An Environmental History of Israel*, ed. Daniel Orenstein, Alon Tal, and Char Miller (Pittsburgh: University of Pittsburgh Press, 2013), 82–105.

28. Samer Alatout, "Bringing Abundance into Environmental Politics: Constructing a Zionist Network of Water Abundance, Immigration, and Colonization," *Social Studies of Science* 39 (3) (2009): 363–394.

29. Shalom Reichman, Yossi Katz, and Yair Paz, "The Absorptive Capacity of Palestine, 1992–1948," *Middle Eastern Studies* 33 (2) (1997): 338–361.

30. Charles Warren, *The Land of Promise* (London: George Bell & Sons, 1875), 5–6.

31. David Ben-Gurion and Yitzhak Ben-Zvi, *Eretz Israel in the Past and in the Present* (repr. in Hebrew) (Jerusalem: Yad Ben Zvi, 1979).

32. Ilan Troen, "Calculating the 'Economic Absorptive Capacity' of Palestine: A Study of the Political Uses of Scientific Research," *Contemporary Jewry* 10 (2) (1989): 22–23.

33. Reichman, Katz, and Paz, "Absorptive Capacity of Palestine," 341.

34. Ibid., 346.

35. Ibid., 342.

36. Michael Cohen, *Britain's Moment in Palestine: Retrospect and Perspectives, 1917–48* (Abingdon, Oxon, UK: Routledge, 2014), 133.

37. John Hope Simpson, *Palestine: Report on Immigration, Land Settlement and Development* (London: H. M. Stationery Office, 1930), 61.

38. Troen, "Calculating the 'Economic Absorptive Capacity' of Palestine," 27.

39. William Clay Lowdermilk, *Palestine: Land of Promise* (New York: Harper & Brothers, 1944), 3, 5, 6, 102.

40. Hope Simpson, *Palestine: Report*, 42.

41. E. Mills, *Census of Palestine, 1931*, vol. 1 (Alexandria, Egypt: Whitehead Morris, 1933), 46–47.

42. Arthur Ruppin, *Three Decades in Palestine: Speeches and Papers on the Upbuilding of the Jewish National Home* (Jerusalem: Chicken, 1937), 74.

43. Troen, "Calculating the 'Economic Absorptive Capacity' of Palestine," 31.

44. Ibid., 32.

45. David Ben-Gurion, *The Peel Report and the Jewish State*, vol. 10 (London: Palestine Labor Society, 1938), as quoted in Orenstein, "Zionist and Israeli Perspectives on Population Growth," 90–91.

46. Alon Tal, *Pollution in a Promised Land: An Environmental History of Israel* (Berkeley: University of California Press, 2002), chap. 3.

47. Reichman, Katz, and Paz, "Absorptive Capacity of Palestine," 350.
48. David Ben-Gurion, *The Teachings of David Ben-Gurion*, ed. Yaakov Becker (Tel Aviv: Yavneh Press, 1958), 35.
49. David Ben-Gurion, "Southbound," in *Topics in the Bible* (Tel Aviv: Am Oved, 1969), 132–144; also, Itzhak Kanev, *Population and Society in Israel and in the World* (Jerusalem: Bialik Institute, 1957), as quoted in Orenstein, "Zionist and Israeli Perspectives on Population Growth," 82–105.
50. Moshe Dayan, *Story of My Life* (New York: William Morrow, 1976), 264–272; Levi Eshkol, "Speech to the Executive of the Jewish Agency," Jerusalem, January 24, 1950, in *Levi Eshkol: Selected Documents* (Jerusalem: Israel State Archives, 2002), 251.
51. Kanev, *Population and Society in Israel and in the World*, as quoted in Orenstein, "Zionist and Israeli Perspectives on Population Growth," 94–95. More recently: Francis Moore Lappe, *Food First: Beyond the Myth of Scarcity* (New York: Houghton Mifflin, 1977); Amartya Sen, *Poverty and Famines: An Essay on Entitlements and Deprivation* (Oxford: Clarendon Press, 1981).
52. Orenstein, "Zionist and Israeli Perspectives on Population Growth," 94.
53. Kanev, *Population and Society in Israel and in the World*, 94–95.
54. Alon Tal, "Enduring Technological Optimism: Zionism's Environmental Ethic and Its Influence on Israel's Environmental History," *Journal of Environmental History* 13 (2008): 275–305.
55. Arieh Sharon, *Physical Planning for Israel* (Jerusalem: Ministry of Interior, 1951); Alon Tal, "Space Matters: Historic Drivers and Turning Points in Israel's Open Space Protection Policy," *Journal of Israel Studies* 13 (1) (2008): 122–124.
56. Oren Yiftachel, "From Sharon to Sharon: Spatial Planning and Separation Regime in Israel/Palestine," *HAGAR: Studies in Culture, Polity and Identities* 10 (1) (2010): 83.
57. Ari Shavit, *My Promised Land* (New York, Random House, 2013): 135–174.
58. Howard Sachar, *A History of Israel: From the Rise of Zionism to Our Time* (New York: Alfred Knopf, 2007), 407.
59. Index Mundi, "Israel GDP Per Capita," last accessed November 16, 2015, http://www.indexmundi.com/facts/israel/gdp-per-capita.
60. Leslie Stein, *The Making of Modern Israel, 1948–1967* (Cambridge: Polity, 2009), 125.
61. Alon Tal, "Seeking Sustainability: Israel's Evolving Water Management Strategy," *Science* 313 (2006): 1081–1084.
62. Tal, *Pollution in a Promised Land*, 212.
63. Ibid., 212–213.
64. Israel Water Authority, *The Wastewater and Treated Effluents Infrastructure Development in Israel* (presentation at the World Water Forum, Tel Aviv, 2015), http://www.water.gov.il/Hebrew/ProfessionalInfoAndData/2012/05-Water%20Sector%20in%20Israel%20-%20Zoom%20on%20Desalination.pdf.
65. Daniel Hillel, "40 Years of Drip Irrigation: Reviewing the Past, Prospects for the Future," *CSA News* 53 (2008): 3–7.
66. Alon Tal, "To Make a Desert Bloom—The Israeli Agriculture Adventure and the Quest for Sustainability," *Agricultural History* 81 (2) (2007): 228–258.

67. Yoav Kislev, personal communication, June 28, 2013 based on graph in: *Statistical Atlas of Israeli Agriculture*, ed. Yoav Kislev and Shaul Zaban (Beit Dagan, Israel: Ministry of Agriculture, 2013), 6, http://www.moag.gov.il/agri/Files/atlas_haklaut.pdf.

68. Amir Givati, "Climate Trends in Israel and Effects on Water Resources" (PowerPoint presentation, Jerusalem: Israeli Hydrological Service, Israeli Water Authority, 2011), http://www.water.gov.il/Hebrew/ProfessionalInfoAndData/2012/16-Israel-Water-Sector-Climate-Change.pdf; Lucy Michaels and Pinhas Alpert, "Anthropogenic Climate Change in Israel," in *Between Ruin and Restoration*, 309–315.

69. A. Tenne, D. Hoffman, and E. Levi, "Quantifying the Actual Benefits of Large-Scale Seawater Desalination in Israel," *Desalination and Water Treatment* 51 (1–3) (2013): 26–37.

70. Amiram Barkat, "Israel Faces Water Surplus," *Globes: Israel's Business Arena*, November 5, 2013, http://www.globes.co.il/serveen/globes/docview.asp?did=1000891490; also, Alon Tal, "The Desalination Debate—Lessons Learned Thus Far," *Environment* 53 (5) (2011): 35–49.

71. Inbal Orpaz, "Waze Will Always Be Free, Says Founder after $1 Billion Sale to Google," *Haaretz*, June 21, 2013, http://www.haaretz.com/business/.premium-1.531124.

72. See, generally, *Between Ruin and Restoration*.

73. S. Assouline, D. Russo, A. Silber, and D. Or, "Balancing Water Scarcity and Quality for Sustainable Irrigated Agriculture," *Water Resources Research* 51 (5) (2015): 3419–3436. Zafrir Rinat, "The Price of Water Recycling: Use of Effluents Is Destroying Israel's Agricultural Land," *Haaretz*, March 11, 2014, http://www.haaretz.co.il/news/science/.premium-1.2266941.

74. Alon Tal, "Management of Transboundary Wastewater Discharges," in *Shared Borders, Shared Waters*, ed. S. B. Megdal, R. G. Varady and S. Eden (Paris, Leiden: CRC Press, 2013), 221–232.

75. Joel Cohen, *How Many People Can the Earth Support?* (New York: Norton, 1995).

76. Joel Cohen, "Population Growth and Earth's Human Carrying Capacity," *Science* 269 (5222) (1995): 343.

77. Cohen, *How Many People Can the Earth Support?* 223–224.

78. Cohen, "Population Growth and Earth's Human Carrying Capacity," 342–343.

79. Justus Freiherr von Liebig, *Principles of Agricultural Chemistry* (New York: John Wiley, 1855); also, William Brock, *Justus von Liebig: The Chemical Gatekeeper* (Cambridge: Cambridge University Press, 2002).

80. Tal, "To Make a Desert Bloom," 228–258.

81. For instance: Sino-Israeli Global Network, "Introduction to Agriculture in Israel," http://en.sino-israel.org/irc/agriculture/into_agriculture/.

82. John Fedler, "Focus on Israel: Israel's Agriculture in the 21st Century," (Jerusalem: Ministry of Foreign Affairs, 2002), repr. on Ministry of Foreign Affairs Web site, http://mfa.gov.il/MFA/AboutIsrael/Economy/Pages/Focus%20on%20Israel-%20Israel-s%20Agriculture%20in%20the%2021st.aspx.

83. S. Buchwald and Hillel Shuval, "The Role of the Import of Virtual Water in the Israel Food Supply" (unpublished study, Division of Environmental Sciences, Hebrew University of Jerusalem, 2003).

84. Tal, *Pollution in a Promised Land*, 237.

85. Buchwald and Shuval, *Role of the Import*.

86. Israel Central Bureau of Statistics (CBS), "Food Supply Balance Sheet" (Jerusalem, 2012), http://www.cbs.gov.il/webpub/pub/text_page_eng.html?publ=45&CYear=2012 &CMonth=1.

87. Shaul Zaban, interview with author, July 7, 2013.

88. Efrat Hadas, Director, Economy & Quality Management Investment Financing Department, Israel Ministry of Agriculture and Rural Development, personal communication, June 30, 2014.

89. Food and Agriculture Organization of the United Nations, "Israel Country Profile," 2014, accessed April 2, 2015, http://faostat.fao.org/desktopdefault.aspx?pageid=342 &lang=en&country=105.

90. Ministry of Tourism, *Tourism in Israel, 2012: Statistical Findings* (Jerusalem, 2013), 28, http://www.tourism.gov.il/GOVheb/Ministry%20of%20Tourism/Statistics /Documents/DOH-2012.pdf.

91. Ministry of Agriculture, "National Plan for Agriculture and Rural Development in Israel—Import of Food," (PowerPoint presentation, 2013), available from author.

92. Worker's Hotline, "Agricultural Workers," accessed April 2, 2014, http://www.kavlaoved .org.il.

93. Arie Regev, "Israel's Agriculture at a Glance," in *Israel's Agriculture* (Tel Aviv: Israel Export and International Cooperation Institute, 2012), 8.

94. Aliza Stark, Hebrew University Department of Nutrition, personal communication, February 22, 2014.

95. Efrat Hadas and Yoav Gal, "Barriers Preventing Food Security in Israel, 2015," *Managing Global Transitions* 12 (1) (2014), 3–22, at 13.

CHAPTER 11. TOWARD AN OPTIMAL POPULATION SIZE

1. Joel Cohen, "Population Growth and Earth's Human Carrying Capacity," *Science* 269 (5222) (1995): 343.

2. Adlai Stevenson, "Speech to the Economic and Social Council of the United Nations," Geneva, Switzerland, July 9, 1965: *Adlai Stevenson of the United Nations*, ed. Albert Roland, Richard Wilson, and Michael Rahill (Manila: Free Asia Press, 1965), 224.

3. Cohen, "Population Growth and Earth's Human Carrying Capacity," 342–343.

4. Moti Kaplan, interview with author, June 27, 2013.

5. John Holdren, "Population and the Energy Problem," *Population and Environment* 12 (3) (1991): 231–255.

6. BBC, "Energy That We Use," *BBC World News*, 2013, http://www.bbc.com/special features/horizonsbusiness/wp-content/uploads/2013/04/Energy1.pdf.

7. Holdren, "Population and the Energy Problem," 252.

8. Gretchen Daily, Anne Ehrlich, and Paul Ehrlich, "Optimum Human Population Size," *Population and Environment* 14 (6) (1994): 474–475.

9. David Pimental and Marcia Pimentel, "Land Energy and Water: The Constraints Governing Ideal U.S. Population Size," *Focus: Carrying Capacity Selections* 1 (113) (1991), repr. in *Social Contract* (Fall/Winter 2008): 50–58, http://www.thesocialcontract .com/pdf/nineteen-one/tsc_19_1_pimentel.pdf.

10. Daily, Ehrlich, and Ehrlich, "Optimum Human Population Size," 469–475.

11. All figures based on U.S. Central Intelligence Agency (CIA), "Israel," *The World Factbook*, https://www.cia.gov/library/publications/the-world-factbook/rankorder/2233rank .html.

12. Yael Bar-Ilan, David Pearlmutter, and Alon Tal, *Building Green: Policy Mechanisms for Promoting Energy Efficiency in Buildings in Israel* (Haifa: Technion, Center for Urban and Regional Studies Press, 2010).

13. Israel Ministry of Infrastructure, "Policy of the Ministry of Infrastructure for Integrating Renewable Energies into Israel's Electricity Production System," (Jerusalem, 2010), http://energy.gov.il/GxmsMniPublications/renewables.pdf.

14. Naomi Lipsten and Alon Tal, "Renewable-Energy Policy in Israel: Past and Present," *Jewish Energy Guide* (New York: Jewish Council for Public Affairs, 2014), 25–34.

15. Zafrir Rinat and Barak Ravid, "Netanyahu: Israel 'Rethinking' Nuclear Power Plant in Negev," *Haaretz*, March 18, 2011, http://www.haaretz.com/print-edition /news/netanyahu-israel-rethinking-nuclear-power-plant-in-negev-1.349895.

16. Ernest Scheyder, "Israeli Natural Gas Fields Hold Big Promise for Noble Energy," *Reuters*, February 10, 2014, http://www.reuters.com/article/2014/02/10/us-nobleenergy -israel-idUSBREA191SC20140210.

17. "Leviathan Gas Field, Levantine Basin, Mediterranean Sea, Israel," OffshoreTechnology.com, http://www.offshore-technology.com/projects/leviathan-gas-field-evantine -israel/; also U.S. Geological Service, "Assessment of Undiscovered Oil and Gas Resources of the Levant Basin Province, Eastern Mediterranean," World Petroleum Resources Project (March, 2010), http://pubs.usgs.gov/fs/2010/3014/pdf/FS10-3014.pdf.

18. Martin Fletcher, "Israel's Big Gusher," *Moment Magazine*, February 2014, http://www .slate.com/articles/news_and_politics/moment/2014/02/israel_s_natural_gas _deposits_tel_aviv_s_offshore_gas_fields_will_make_it.html.

19. Steven Scheer, "Nothing Will Stop Israel's Natural Gas Development—Netanyahu," *Reuters*, May 26, 2015, http://www.reuters.com/article/2015/05/26/israel-natgas-idUSL5 N0YH2GA20150526; "Israel Takes Step towards Becoming a Gas Exporter," *Reuters*, February 7, 2014, http://www.reuters.com/article/2014/02/07/woodside-leviathan-idUSL3 N0LB5KU20140207. For a review of less-sanguine assessments, see Naomi Klein, *This Changes Everything, Capitalism versus Climate Change* (New York: Simon & Schuster, 2014), 128–130, 144, 213–215.

20. David Kashi, "Coal-To-Natural-Gas Switch for Power Generation Is Paying Off in Smaller Carbon Footprint," *International Business Times*, January 13, 2014, http://www .ibtimes.com/coal-natural-gas-switch-power-generation-paying-smaller-carbon -footprint-1537662; also, Daniel Orenstein, "Is Gas Really Greener?" *Haaretz*, September 16, 2011, http://www.haaretz.com/print-edition/opinion/is-gas-really-greener-1 .384759.19. Robert W. Howarth, Renee Santoro, and Anthony Ingraffea, "Methane and the Greenhouse-Gas Footprint of Natural Gas from Shale Formations," *Climatic*

Change 106 (2011): 679–690; also, Scot Miller, et al., "Anthropogenic Emissions of Methane in the United States," *Proceedings of the National Academy of Science* 110 (5) (2013): 20018–20022.

21. Alon Tal, "Natural-Gas Exports: A Debate over Values, Not Numbers," *Jerusalem Post*, May 16, 2013, http://www.jpost.com/Business/Commentary/Natural-gas-exports-A -debate-over-values-not-numbers-313561.

22. Meidad Kissinger and Abraham Haim, "Urban Hinterlands: The Case of an Israeli Town Ecological Footprint," *Environmental Development and Sustainability* 10 (2008): 391–405.

23. Ibid.

24. Millennium Ecosystem Assessment, *Living Beyond Our Means: Natural Assets and Human Well-Being* (Washington, DC: Island Press, 2005).

25. Food and Agriculture Organization, "What Lands Are Prone to Desertification?" in *Sustainable Development of Drylands and Combating Desertification* (Rome: FAO, 1993).

26. William Rees, "Ecological Footprints and Appropriated Carrying Capacity: What Urban Economics Leaves Out," *Environment and Urbanisation* 4 (2) (1992): 121–130.

27. Thora Amend, Bree Barbeau, Bert Beyers, Susan Burs, Stefanie Eißing, Andrea Fleis- chhauer, Barbara Kus, and Pati Poblete, *A Big Foot on a Small Planet? Accounting with the Ecological Footprint; Succeeding in a World with Growing Resource Restraints* (Hei- delberg, Germany: Federal Ministry for Economic Cooperation and Development, 2010), 23.

28. This is defined as "the annual productivity of one hectare of biologically productive land or sea with world-average productivity."

29. Global Footwork Network, "Definitions," accessed April 2, 2015, http://www .footprintnetwork.org/en/index.php/gfn/page/glossary/.

30. Mathis Wackernagel, "The Global Auction: Risks and Opportunities in the New Era of Ecological Constraints" (PowerPoint presentation, November 2013), available from author.

31. Global Footprint Network, "Facts," *Living Planet Report*, 2014, http://www .footprintnetwork.org/en/index.php/GFN/page/living_panet_report_2014_facts/.

32. Mathis Wackernagel, interview with author, February 19, 2014.

33. Sharon Udasin, "Fishermen, Environmentalists Band Together to Demand Reforms in Fishing Industry," *Jerusalem Post*, February 7, 2014, http://www.jpost.com/Enviro -Tech/Fishermen-environmentalists-band-together-to-demand-reforms-for-Israels -fishing-industry-340632.

34. Israel Ministry of Foreign Affairs, "Israel's Chronic Water Problem," Jerusalem, ac- cessed February 27, 2014, http://mfa.gov.il/MFA/IsraelExperience/AboutIsrael /Spotlight/Pages/Israel-s%20Chronic%20Water%20Problem.aspx.

35. Dan Zaslavsky, Rami Guhteh, and Ayal Sahar, *Policies for Utilizing Sewage in Israel— Sewage Treatment for Effluent Irrigation or Desalinating Effluents to Drinking Water Quality* (Haifa: Technion, 2004).

36. Global Footprint Network, *Mediterranean Ecological Footprint Trends* (Geneva: Global Footprint Network, 2012), 18.

37. Alessandro Galli, Martin Halle, Nicole Grunewald, "Physical Limits to Resource Access and Utilisation and Their Economic Implications in Mediterranean Economies," *Environmental Science and Policy* 51 (2015): 125–136.
38. Kissinger and Haim, "Urban Hinterlands," 391–405.
39. Meidad Kissinger and Dan Gottlieb, "Place Oriented Ecological Footprint Analysis— The Case of Israel's Grain Supply," *Ecological Economics* 69 (2010): 1639–1645; also, Meidad Kissinger and Dan Gottlieb, "From Global to Place Oriented Hectares—The Case of Israel's Wheat Ecological Footprint and Its Implications for Sustainable Resource Supply," *Ecological Indicators* 16 (2012): 51–57.
40. Kissinger and Haim, "Urban Hinterlands," 396.
41. Tamara Traubmann, "Israel Needs 10 Times Its Own Area to Sustain Itself," *Haaretz*, July 9, 2007, http://www.haaretz.com/print-edition/news/israel-needs-10-times-its-own-area-to-sustain-itself-1.225153.
42. Israel Ministry of National Infrastructures, Energy and Water Resources, "The National Electricity Sector in Israel," accessed February 27, 2014, http://energy.gov.il/English/Subjects/Electricity/Pages/GxmsMniElectricitySector.asp.
43. Stephanie Joyce, "On Denmark's Road to Renewable Power," Inside Energy, June 24, 2015, http://insideenergy.org/2015/06/24/on-denmarks-road-to-renewable-power/.
44. Edmund Ramsden and Jon Adams, "Escaping the Laboratory: The Rodent Experiments of John B. Calhoun and Their Cultural Influence," *Journal of Social History* 42 (3) (2009): 761–792.
45. John B. Calhoun, "Population Density and Social Pathology," *Scientific American* 206 (2) (1962): 139–150.
46. Edmund Ramsden, "The Urban Animal: Population Density and Social Pathology in Rodents and Humans," *Bulletin of the World Health Organization* 87 (2009): 82.
47. Ramsden and Adams, "Escaping the Laboratory," 761–792.
48. Charles Southwick, "An Experimental Study of Intragroup Agonistic Behavior in Rhesus Monkeys (*Macaca mulatta*)," *Behaviour* 28 (1, 2) (1967): 182–209; K. Alexander and E. M. Roth, "The Effects of Acute Crowding on Aggressive Behavior of Japanese Monkeys," *Behaviour* 39 (2) (1971): 73–90; Peter Judge and F. B. M. de Waal, "Rhesus Monkey Behaviour under Diverse Population Densities: Coping with Long-Term Crowding," *Animal Behavior* 54 (3) (1997): 643–662; Adinda Sannen, Linda Van Elsacker, and Marcel Eens, "Effect of Spatial Crowding on Aggressive Behavior in a Bonobo Colony," *Zoo Biology* 23 (2004): 383–395.
49. Megan L. van Wolkenten, Jason M. Davis, May Lee Gong, and Frans B. M. de Waal, "Coping with Acute Crowding by *Cebus paella*," *International Journal of Primatology* 27 (5) (2006): 1241–1256.
50. Bill Slott, personal communication, February 12, 2014.
51. Jonathan Freedman, "Reconciling Apparent Differences between the Responses of Humans and Other Animals to Crowding," *Psychological Review* 86 (1) (1979): 80–85.
52. Edward T. Hall, *The Hidden Dimension* (New York: Anchor Books, 1990). Alexander and Roth, "Effects of Acute Crowding on Aggressive Behavior of Japanese Monkeys," 73–90.

53. Ian Wanyeki, Sherry Olson, Paul Brassard, Dick Menzies, Nancy Ross, Marcel Behr, and Kevin Schartzman, "Dwellings, Crowding, and Tuberculosis in Montreal," *Social Science and Medicine* 63 (2006): 501–511.

54. Daniel Stokols, "On the Distinction between Density and Crowding," *Psychological Review* 79 (1972): 275–277.

55. Mary Curtis, "2 Killed, 95 Injured at Rock Concert in Israel: Accident: A Southland Teen-ager Is among the Dead," *Los Angeles Times*, July 20, 1995, http://articles.latimes.com/1995-07-20/news/mn-26071_1_rock-concert.

56. Elena Bilotta and Gary Evans, "Environmental Stress," in *Environmental Psychology: An Introduction* (West Sussex, UK: BPS Blackwell, 2013), 31.

57. Irwin Altman, *The Environment and Social Behavior: Privacy, Personal Space, Territory, Crowding* (Monterey, CA: Brooks, 1975).

58. Russell Veitch and Daniel Arkkelin, *Environmental Psychology: An Interdisciplinary Perspective* (New York: Prentice Hall, 1995).

59. Radya Dyson-Hudson and Eric Alden Smith, "Human Territoriality: An Ecological Reassessment," *American Anthropologist* 80 (1971): 21–41.

60. Gary Evans and Sheldon Cohen, "Environmental Stress," in *Handbook of Environmental Psychology*, vol. 1, ed. Daniel. Stokols and Irwin Altman (New York: Wiley, 1987) 571–610.

61. Gary Evans, "Environmental Stress and Health," in *Handbook of Health Psychology*, ed. Andrew Baum, Tracey Revenson, and Jerome Singer (Hillsdale, NJ: Erlbaum, 2001).

62. Gary Evans and Richard Werner, "Rail Commuting Duration and Passenger Stress," *Health Psychology* 25 (3) (2006): 408–412.

63. Gary Evans, Stephen Lepore, S. J. Shejwal, and M. N. Palsane, "Chronic Residential Crowding and Children's Well-being: An Ecological Perspective," *Child Development* 69 (1998): 1514–1523.

64. Graham Brown, Thomas Lawrence, and Sandra Robinson, "Territoriality in Organizations," *Academy of Management Review* 30 (3) (2005): 577–594.

65. Jonathan Freedman, Simon Klevansky, and Paul Ehrlich, "The Effect of Crowding on Human Task Performance," *Journal of Applied Social Psychology* 1 (1) (1971): 7–25.

66. Bruce McEwen, *The End of Stress as We Know It* (Washington, DC: Joseph Henry Press, 2002).

67. LSE Cities, "Urban Stress and Mental Health" (November 2011), http://lsecities.net/media/objects/articles/urban-stress-and-mental-health/en-gb/.

68. Florian Lederbogen Peter Kirsch, Leila Haddad, Fabian Streit, Heike Tost, Philipp Schuch, Stefan Wüst, et al., "City Living and Urban Upbringing Affect Neural Social Processing in Humans," *Nature* 474 (2011): 498–501.

69. Raymond Novaco, Wendy Kliewer, and Alexander Broquet, "Home Environmental Consequences of Commute Travel Impedance," *American Journal of Community Psychology* 19 (1991): 881–909.

70. Meni Kozlowsky, Avraham Kluger, and Mordechai Reich, *Commuting Stress* (New York: Plenum, 1995).

71. Ministry of Transportation, *Developing Public Transportation: A Strategic Program* (Jerusalem: Ministry of Transportation and Ministry of Finance, 2012), 11.

72. Arline Bronzaft, "The Effect of a Noise Abatement Program on Reading Ability," *Journal of Environmental Psychology* 1 (1981): 215–222.

73. Francisco L. Rivera-Retie and Lilian Marti, "A School System At Risk: A Study of the Consequences Of Overcrowding in New York City Public Schools," report prepared for the New York City Citizen's Commission on Planning for Enrollment Growth, January 1995, Institute for Urban and Minority Education Research Report no. 95-1.

74. Tel Aviv Municipality, "Beaches," 2012, http://www.tel-aviv.gov.il/english/Documents /Beaches%20_2_.pdf.

75. CIA *World Factbook*, "Israel."

76. Arnon Soffer, "Introduction" in Michael Burt, *The Marine Option: The Need to Head to the Sea* (Haifa: University of Haifa, 2014), http://hevra.haifa.ac.il/~ch-strategy/index .php/books/45-2015-03-09-12-05-47.

77. Avner de-Shalit, interview with author, July 3, 2013.

78. Edward Glaeser, *Triumph of the City: How Urban Spaces Make Us Human* (London: Pan, 2012), 6.

79. Ibid., 94.

80. Ibid., 7–8.

81. Sheldon Cohen, David Glass, and Susan Phillips, "Environmental Health," in *Handbook of Medical Sociology*, ed. Howard Freeman, Sol Levine, and Leo Reeder (Englewood Cliffs, NJ: Prentice-Hall, 1979), 135.

82. Omer R. Galley, "Population Density and Pathology: What Are the Relationships for Man?" *American Sociological Review* 36 (1971): 18–29.

83. Kate Walters, Elizabeth Breeze, Paul Wilkinson, Gill M. Price, Chris J. Bulpitt, and Astrid Fletcher, "Local Area Deprivation and Urban-Rural Differences in Anxiety and Depression among People Older Than 75 Years in Britain," *American Journal of Public Health* 94 (10) (2004): 1772.

84. George Jarvis, Roberta Ferrence, Paul Whitehead, and F. Gordon Johnson, "The Ecology of Self-Injury: A Multivariate Approach," *Suicide and Life-Threatening Behavior* 12 (2) (1982): 90–102.

85. R. O. Straub, *Health and Psychology*, 2nd ed. (New York: Worth, 2007).

86. Ari Paltiel, Michel Sepulcer, Irene Kornilenko, and Martin Maldonado, *Long-Range Population Projections for Israel: 2009–2059* (Jerusalem: CBS, Demography and Census Department, 2011), 47–48.

87. Arnon Soffer, "Introduction," 7.

88. C. T. De Wit, "Photosynthesis: Its Relationship to Overpopulation," in *Harvesting the Sun: Photosynthesis in Plant Life* (New York: Academic Press, 1967), 315–320, as quoted in Joel Cohen, *How Many People Can the Earth Support?* (New York: Norton, 1995), 172–175.

89. Yodan Rofeh, "Urbanism Sustainability and Public Parks: Towards a New Perspective on Open Spaces in the City," in *Sustainability Considerations in Design of Public Parks in Israeli Cities*, ed. Y. Schnell (Tel Aviv: Pardes, 2014); also, T. Efrati and

A. Churchman, "Guide for Planning and Allocation of Open Spaces for Public Needs" (Tel Aviv: Ministry of Education, 2005).

90. Institute for Research and Development for Educational and Welfare Institutions, *Planning Guide for Land Allocation for Public Use* (Jerusalem: Israel Ministry of Interior, 2005), 50–52. Israel Ministry of Interior (presentation by the Strategic Branch of the Planning Authority, February 9, 2013), http://www.moin.gov.il /SubjectDocuments/haktzat_karka/Present_vaadat_iguy_9.10.13.pdf.

91. Israel Ministry of Environmental Protection, "Survey of Open Spaces in Givatayim," (Tel Aviv: Ministry of Environmental Protection, 2013), http://www.sviva .gov.il/InfoServices/ReservoirInfo/DocLib2/Publications/P0701-P0800/P0733.pdf.

92. Daniel Orenstein, interview with author, June 2, 2013.

93. Yaniv Kubovich, Shirly Seidler, Eli Ashkenazi, and Zafrir Rinat, "Tourist Sites Overflow as Holiday Visitors Turned Away from Kinneret," *Haaretz*, April 17, 2014, http://www.haaretz.com/news/national/.premium=1.585923.

94. Moti Kaplan, interview with author, June 27, 2013.

95. Jim Moore, "Population Density, Social Pathology, and Behavior Ecology," *Primates* 40 (1) (1999): 3.

96. Orenstein, interview.

97. Gretchen Daily and Paul Ehrlich, "Population, Sustainability and the Earth's Carrying Capacity," *Biosciences* 42 (10) (1992): 761–762.

98. Mill, *Principles of Political Economy*, 129.

99. Population Reference Bureau, "Data Finder" (based on 2013 figures); accordingly, Denmark has 130 people per square kilometer; the Netherlands, 404 people per square kilometer; and Japan, 337 people per square kilometer, http://www.prb.org /DataFinder/Geography.aspx?loct=3.

100. Israel Ministry of Interior, "Comprehensive, Integrated Planning for the State of Israel" (National Masterplan 35), accessed January 2015, http://www.moin.gov.il /Subjects/GeneralPlaning/Pages/default.aspx.

101. Yosef Yitzhak Neuman, interview with author, June 27, 2013.

102. Jeremy Benstein, interview with author, July 23, 2013.

103. Garett Hardin, *The Ostrich Factor: Our Population Myopia* (New York: Oxford Press, 1999), 2.

CHAPTER 12. WE CAN DO IT — AN AGENDA FOR STABILIZING ISRAEL'S POPULATION

1. United Nations (UN), *World Population Prospects: 2015 Revision* (New York: UN, Department of Economic and Social Affairs, Population Division, 2015), http://esa.un.org /unpd/wpp/Publications/Files/Key_Findings_WPP_2015.pdf.

2. Data from UN Population Division, http://www.un.org/en/development/desa /population/, and U.S. Central Intelligence Agency (CIA) *The World Factbook*, accessed October 26, 2015, https://www.cia.gov/library/publications/the-world-factbook /rankorder/2127rank.html.

3. Paul Demeny, "Population and the Invisible Hand," *Demography* 23 (4) (1986): 473.

4. Garret Hardin, *Living with Limits: Ecology, Economics, and Population Taboos* (New York: Oxford, 1993), 218–220.

5. Garrett Hardin, "The Tragedy of the Commons," *Science* 162 (1968): 1248.

6. Adam Werbach, interview with author, March 13, 2014.

7. Adam Werbach, "The End of the Population Movement," *American Prospect* 16 (2005): 10, http://prospect.org/article/end-population-movement.

8. Don Weeden and Charmayne Palomba, "A Post-Cairo Paradigm: Both Numbers and Women Matter," in *Life on the Brink: Environmentalists Confront Overpopulation* (Athens: University of Georgia Press, 2012), 240–254.

9. Kathryn Hansen, "NASA Reveals New Results from Inside the Ozone Hole," (Greenbelt, MD: NASA, December 11, 2013), http://www.nasa.gov/content/goddard/new-results-from-inside-the-ozone-hole/#.UzMOUPmSy64.

10. International Whaling Commission, "Status of Whales," accessed March 23, 2014, http://iwc.int/status.

11. Intergovernmental Panel on Climate Change, "No Regrets Options," in *Climate Change 2001: Mitigation* (Geneva, Switzerland, 2001), 7.3.4.2, http://www.ipcc.ch/ipccreports/tar/wg3/index.php?idp=292.

12. Alon Tal, "Tried and True: Reducing Greenhouse Gas Emissions in New Zealand through Conventional Environmental Legislative Modalities," *Otago University Law Journal* 12 (2009): 1–47; Suzanne Martin, "Examples of 'No-Regret,' 'Low-Regret' and 'Win-Win' Adaptation Actions," *Climate Change* (Edinburgh, Scotland, 2011), http://www.climatexchange.org.uk/files/6713/7365/7183/adaptation_noregret_actions.pdf.

13. Philip Cohen, "Let's Not Panic Over Women with More Education Having Fewer Kids," *Atlantic*, February 12, 2013, http://www.theatlantic.com/sexes/archive/2013/02/lets-not-panic-over-women-with-more-education-having-fewer-kids/273070/.

14. Steven Rattner, "The Lessons of Japan's Economy," *New York Times*, October 19, 2013, http://www.nytimes.com/2013/10/20/opinion/sunday/rattner-the-lessons-of-japans-economy.html?_r=0.

15. Justin McDonnell, "Japan Struggles with Women in the Workforce," *Diplomat*, December 10, 2013, http://thediplomat.com/2013/12/japan-struggles-with-women-in-the-workforce.

16. Japanese women earn 72 percent less than Japanese men for the same job. Laura D'Andrea Tyson, "Japan's Women to the Rescue," *New York Times*, August 23, 2013, http://economix.blogs.nytimes.com/2013/08/23/japans-women-to-the-rescue/?_php=true&_type=blogs&_r=0.

17. Karen Anderson, *Wartime Women: Sex Roles, Family Relations, and the Status of Women During World War II* (New York: Berkley Books, 2001).

18. Susan Hartman, *The Home Front and Beyond: American Women in the 1940s* (Boston: Twayne Publishers, 1982).

19. Gary Becker, "An Economic Analysis of Fertility," in *Demographic and Economic Change in Developed Countries* (New York: Columbia University Press, 1960), repr. at http://www.nber.org/chapters/c2387.pdf.

20. Thomas Malthus, *An Essay on the Principle of Population* (New York: Norton, 1976), 105–107.
21. Ibid.
22. Becker, "An Economic Analysis of Fertility."
23. Gary Becker, *A Treatise on the Family,* enlarged ed. (Cambridge, MA: Harvard University Press, 1991), 138–139.
24. Ibid., 144.
25. Namkee Ahn and Pedro Mira, "A Note on the Changing Relationship between Fertility and Female Employment Rates in Developed Countries," *Journal of Population Economics* 15 (2002): 667–682.
26. Shelly Simone, "Employment of Women" (Jerusalem: Knesset Research Branch, 2015), 4, http://main.knesset.gov.il/Activity/Info/MMMSummaries19/Women.pdf.
27. Meirav Arlosoroff, "Women in the Workforce Are Saving Israel's Economy," *Haaretz,* September 25, 2012, http://www.haaretz.com/business/women-in-the-workforce-are-saving-israel-s-economy-1.466785.
28. Simone, "Employment of women," 4.
29. Ronald Rindfuss and Larry Bumpass, "Education and Fertility: Implications for the Roles Women Occupy" (presented at the American Sociological Association Meeting, San Francisco, September 1978), http://www.ssc.wisc.edu/cde/cdewp/79-7.pdf.
30. Teresa Castro Martin, "Women's Education and Fertility: Results from 26 Demographic and Health Surveys," *Studies in Family Planning* 26 (4) (1995): 187–202.
31. Theresa Castro Martin and Fatima Juarez, "The Impact on Women's Education on Fertility in Latin America: Searching for Explanations," *International Family Planning Perspectives* 21 (2) (1995): 52–57.
32. Eitan Regev, *Education and Employment in the Haredi Sector,* Taub Center Policy Paper no. 2013.06 (Jerusalem: Taub Center for Social Policy Studies in Israel, 2013), 5–6.
33. Hila Weisberg, "Ultra-Orthodox Jewish Women Hit Glass Ceiling in Higher Education," *Haaretz,* February 21, 2013, http://www.haaretz.com/news/national/ultra-orthodox-jewish-women-hit-glass-ceiling-in-higher-education.premium-1.504815.
34. Eitan Regev, *Education and Employment in the Haredi Sector,* 11.
35. Khawla Rihani, director, Economic Empowerment for Women, Haifa, interview with author, July 2, 2013.
36. Ari Shavit, *My Promised Land* (New York, Random House, 2013): 410–411.
37. Aviad Glickman, "High Court Says Law Encourages Haredim Not to Learn Core Studies," *Ynet,* April 10, 2011, http://www.ynetnews.com/articles/0,7340,L-4131128,00.html.
38. Eitan Regev, *Education and Employment in the Haredi Sector,* 9.
39. Roby Nathanson and Hadar Wiseman, "Occupational Absorption of the Haredi and Arab Sector through Training Centers: Analysis of Recommendations for Policies" (Tel Aviv: Macro Center for Political Economics, 2013).
40. Dan Ben-David, "Outline for Systemic Treatment of Israel's Primary Socioeconomic Challenges," *Policy Brief* (Jerusalem: Taub Center for Social Policy Studies in Israel, 2014), 3.

41. Eran Yashiv and Nitsa Kasir, *The Labor Market of Israeli Arabs—Key Features and Policy Solutions* (Tel Aviv: Tel Aviv University, 2014), 34.

42. Eran Yashiv and Nitsa Kasir, *Arab Women in the Israeli Labor Market: Characteristics and Policy Measures* (Jerusalem: Research Department, Bank of Israel, 2012), 2–5.

43. Inbal Orpaz, "Arabs Taking Their Place in Startup Nation," *Haaretz*, January 24, 2014, http://www.haaretz.com/business/.premium-1.570280.

44. Yashiv and Kasir, *Arab Women in the Israeli Labor Market*, 10.

45. Ibid., 13.

46. David Brodet, "Plans to Promote Israel's Arab Population Socially and Economically under Israel 2028," in *The Economic Benefits of Equality between Arabs and Jews in Israel* (Haifa: Neeman Institute, 2009); Sharon Rabin Margalioth, "Labor Market Discrimination against Arab Israeli Citizens: Can Something Be Done?" *NYU Journal of International Law and Politics* 36 (2004): 845–884; Talia Steiner, "Addressing Discrimination against Arabs in the Israeli Job Market," in *Parliament* (Jerusalem: Israel Institute for Democracy, 2013); Manuel Trajtenberg, *Report of the Committee for Social and Economic Reform* (Jerusalem: Prime Minister's Office, 2011); Sami Miari, Ula Nabuani, and Nabil Hatab, "Bench Players: Arab Workers in Israel," (Jerusalem: Israeli Institute of Democracy, 2011), http://hidavrut.gov.il/sites/default/files/%20%D7%A1%D7%95%D7%A4%D7%99.pdf; Orly Almagor-Lotan, *Public Programs to Encourage Employment among Arab Women* (Jerusalem: Knesset Research Branch, 2009).

47. Yashiv and Kasir, *Arab Women in the Israeli Labor Market*, 30–31.

48. Almagor-Lotan, *Public Programs to Encourage Employment Among Arab Women*, 16.

49. Kate Rogers, "Would Subsidized Child Care Boost U.S. Labor Participation Rates?" *Fox Business*, April 23, 2013, http://www.foxbusiness.com/personal-finance/2013/04/23/subsidizing-childcare-german-study/.

50. D'Andrea Tyson, "Japan's Women to the Rescue."

51. Claire Lundberg, "Trapped by European-style Socialism and I Love It," *Slate*, November 2, 2012, http://www.slate.com/articles/life/family/2012/11/socialist_child_care_in_europe_creche_ecole_maternelle_and_french_child.2.html.

52. World Bank, "Labor Participation Rate, Female (% of female population ages 15+)," http://data.worldbank.org/indicator/SL.TLF.CACT.FE.ZS.

53. Rihani, interview.

54. Ibid.

55. Amalia Sa'ar, *A Business of One's Own* (Jerusalem: Israel National Insurance, 2007), 42–43.

56. Michal Raz-Haimovitz and Daphna Harel Kfir, "The Middle Class is Collapsing: Preschool Education Until Age 3 Costs 3,000 Shekels a Month," *Globes*, February 20, 2013, http://www.globes.co.il/news/article.aspx?did=1000823513.

57. Lynn Karoly, Peter Greenwood, Susan Everingham, Jill Houbé, Rebecca Kilburn, Peter Rydell, Matthew Sanders, and James Chiesa, *Investing in Our Children: What We Know and Don't Know about the Costs and Benefits of Early Childhood Interventions* (Santa Monica, CA: RAND, 1998); Jane Waldfogel, "Child Care, Women's Employment, and Child Outcomes," *Journal of Population Economics* 15 (2002): 531.

58. Analia Schlosser, "The Impact of Free Preschool Education on the Employment of Arab Mothers: Findings of a Natural Experiment," *Economics Quarterly* 3 (2006): 517–553.

59. Meirav Arlosoroff, "How Subsidized Israeli Day Care Allows Ultra-Orthodox to Avoid Work," Haaretz, December 6, 2013, http://www.haaretz.com/business/.premium-1 .562089.

60. Amal Ayoub, "Arab Citizens in the Start-Up Nation: High Tech in Israel's Arab Society and Arab Citizens in Israel's Tech Sector" (lecture at Jewish Funders Network Conference, Miami, FL, March 10, 2014).

61. Amal Ayoub, founder and CEO of Metallo Therapy, "The Gold Standard in Cancer Treatment," TedMed Live, 2014, http://www.tedmed.co.il/portfolio/dr-amal-ayoub -founder-and-ceo-of-metallo-therapy/.

62. Lidar Grave-Lazi and Niv Elis, "Women Earn 30 Percent Less Than Men, Says CBS Report," *Jerusalem Post*, March 4, 2014, http://www.jpost.com/Business/Business -Features/Only-356-percent-of-high-tech-workers-are-women-344252.

63. Hila Weissberg, Haim Bior, and Ora Coren, "Survey: More Israeli Women Becoming Top Managers," *Haaretz*, March 6, 2013, http://www.haaretz.com/business/survey -more-israeli-women-becoming-top-managers.premium-1.507728.

64. "The State Commission of Inquiry into the Clashes between Security Forces and Israeli Civilians," *Report* (Jerusalem: Israel Supreme Court, 2003), http://elyon1.court .gov.il/heb/veadot/or/inside_index.htm.

65. Gil Klian, "The Arabs Gallop, but Not to Work in the Civil Service," *Kalklaist*, August 19, 2015.

66. Neeman Institute, "Haredi Employment—An Information Booklet" (Haifa: Technion, 2012), 10.

67. Tal Tamir, *Guide for Equal Opportunity at Work* (Jerusalem: Ministry of Trade and Industry, n.d.), http://www.moital.gov.il/NR/rdonlyres/9AB286FD-0523-488B-B6D5 -6E918E4EE7D3/0/shivyonhizdamnuyot_inside_171.pdf.

68. Ruth Eglash, "Tziona Koenig-Yair: Lady Liberty," *Jerusalem Post*, September 25, 2008, http://www.jpost.com/Magazine/Features/Social-Affairs-Tziona-Koenig-Yair-Lady -liberty.

69. Tziona Koenig-Yair, Equal Employment Opportunity Commissioner, "Arab Citizens in the Start-Up Nation: High Tech in Israel's Arab Society and Arab Citizens in Israel's Tech Sector" (presentation at Jewish Funders Network Conference, Miami, FL, March 10, 2014).

70. Jonathan Lis, "Knesset Passes New Draft Law, Which Includes Haredi Conscription," *Haaretz*, March 12, 2014, http://www.haaretz.com/news/national/.premium-1 .579362; also, Lahav Harkov, "Knesset Approves Haredi Conscription Law," *Jerusalem Post*, March 13, 2014, http://www.jpost.com/Diplomacy-and-Politics/Haredi -conscription-bill-passes-67-1-345110.

71. Dan Senor and Saul Singer, *Start-up Nation: The Story of Israel's Economic Miracle* (New York: Hachette Book Group, 2009).

72. Hussein Tarabieh, interview with author, June 26, 2013.

73. William Ryerson, "How Do We Solve the Population Problem?" in *Life on the Brink: Environmentalists Confront Overpopulation* (Athens: University of Georgia Press, 2012), 243.

74. Lawrence B. Finer and Mia R. Zolna, "Shifts in Intended and Unintended Pregnancies in the United States, 2001–2008," *American Journal of Public Health* 104 (1) (2014): 43–48.

75. Gilda Sedgh, Susheela Singh, Iqbal Shah, Elisabeth Ahman, Stanley Henshaw, and Akinrinola Bankole, "Induced Abortion: Incidence and Trends Worldwide from 1995 to 2008," *Lancet* 379 (9816) (2012): 625–632.

76. Robert Engelman, "Trusting Women to End Population Growth," in *Life on the Brink*, 223–239.

77. S. Sanandakumar, "Rubber Prices to Make Condoms a Costly Affair," *Economic Times*, September 13, 2010, http://articles.economictimes.indiatimes.com/2010-09-13/news/27625568_1_condom-manufacturers-m-ayyappan-price-hike.

78. AIDS Healthcare Foundation, "What Price Condoms?" *AHF News*, 2012, http://takeaction.aidshealth.org/site/MessageViewer?em_id=11181.0.

79. Ilana Tsigler, Director, "Open Door," interview with author, April 29, 2015.

80. Alan Weisman, *Countdown: Our Last, Best Hope for a Future on Earth?* (New York: Little, Brown, 2013), 366.

81. Apiradee Treerutkuarkul, "Thailand's New Condom Crusade," *Bulletin of the World Health Organization* 88 (2010): 404–405.

82. Alan Weisman, "Safe Sex," in *Countdown*, 368.

83. Zohar Mor, Tamy Shohat, Yael Goor, and Michael Dan, "Risk Behaviors and Sexually Transmitted Diseases in Gay and Heterosexual Men Attending an STD clinic in Tel Aviv, Israel: A Cross-sectional Study," *Israel Medical Association Journal* 14 (2012): 147–151; Yoav Fisher, "Russian Roulette—Israeli Style," *Jerusalem Post*, November 13, 2008, http://www.jpost.com/Local-Israel/Around-Israel/Russian-roulette-Israeli-style.

84. Tyson Vandament, "It's the Incentives Stupid," *Policy Options*, September 2013, http://www.irpp.org/en/po/the-age-of-man/its-the-incentives-stupid/.

85. U.S. Congress, "Endangered Farmers and Ranchers: The Unintended Consequences of the Endangered Species Act," Hearing before the Subcommittee on Rural Enterprise, Agriculture, and Technology, July 17, 2003, http://www.gpo.gov/fdsys/pkg/CHRG-108hhrg92898/html/CHRG-108hhrg92898.htm.

86. Adriaan Kalwij, "The Impact of Family Policy Expenditure on Fertility in Western Europe," *Demography* 47 (2) (2010): 503–519.

87. Alan Weisman, "Shrink and Prosper," in *Countdown*, 297–329.

88. Alma Cohen, Rajeev Dehejia, and Dmitri Romanov, "Financial Incentives and Fertility," *Review of Economics and Statistics* 95 (1) (2013): 1–20.

89. Noam Zussman, Roni Frish, and Daniel Gottlieb, *The Impact of the Rate of Child Allowances on Fertility and Birth Rates* (Jerusalem: Bank of Israel, 2009), http://www.boi.org.il/he/research/pages/papers_dp0913h.aspx.

90. Ibid.

91. Taub Center, "Unequal and Unsustainable," *News Bulletin*, February 2, 2010, http://taubcenter.org.il/index.php/e-bulletin/unequal-and-unsustainable/lang/he/.

92. Dan Ben-David and Haim Bleikh, *Poverty and Inequality over Time in Israel and the OECD*, Policy Paper no. 2013.03 (2013), 3–4, http://taubcenter.org.il/tauborgilwp/wp-content/uploads/E2013.03-Poverty-4.pdf.

93. Malthus, *Essay on the Principle of Population*, 54–55.

94. As quoted in Swee-Hock Saw, *Population Policies and Programmes in Singapore* (Singapore: Institute of Southeast Asian Studies, 2005), 25.

95. Shirley Hsaio-Li Sun, *Population Policy and Reproduction in Singapore: Making Future Citizens* (London: Routledge, 2012), 63.

96. Swee-Hock Saw, *The Population of Singapore*, 3rd ed. (Singapore: Institute of Southeast Asian Studies, 2012), 173, 177.

97. "The general abortion rate in 1970 was only 4.2 percent but by 1985 it had reached 31 percent." Saw, *Population of Singapore*, 199.

98. CIA "Country Comparison, GDP," *World Factbook* (2014), accessed March 8, 2015, https://www.cia.gov/library/publications/the-world-factbook/rankorder/2004rank.html.

99. Hossein Malek-Afzali, Amir Mehryar, and Mohammad Jalal Abbasi-Shavazi, "Iran," in *No Vacancy: Global Responses to the Human Population Explosion*, ed. Michael Tobias, Bob Gillespie, Elizabeth Hughes, and Jane Gray Morrison (Pasadena, CA: Hope Publishing, 2006), 1–5.

100. Ben-David, "Outline for Systemic Treatment of Israel's Primary Socioeconomic Challenges," 2.

101. Arlosoroff, "How Subsidized Israeli Day Care Allows Ultra-Orthodox to Avoid Work."

102. Natan Lipso, "Beer Sheva Mayor: By 2020, We Will Cancel the Concept of Periphery," *The Marker*, April 6, 2011, http://www.themarker.com/news/1.620485.

103. Gudmund Hernes, "The Process of Entry into First Marriage," *American Sociological Review* 37 (2) (1972): 174.

104. Ibid., 173–182.

105. Robert Pollak and Susan Watkins, "Cultural and Economic Approaches to Fertility: Proper Marriage or Misalliance?" *Population and Development Review* 19 (3) (1993): 467–496.

106. Hans-Peter Kohler, Francesco C. Billari, and José Antonio Ortega, "The Emergence of Lowest—Low Fertility in Europe during the 1990s," *Population and Development Review* 28 (4) (2002): 641–680.

107. Mikko Myrskylä and Joshua R. Goldstein, "Probabilistic Forecasting Using Stochastic Diffusion Models, with Applications to Cohort Processes of Marriage and Fertility," *Demography* 50 (1) (2013): 237–260.

108. Nitza Berkovitch, "Motherhood as a National Mission: The Construction of Womanhood in the Legal Discourse in Israel," *Women's Studies International Forum* 20 (5–6) (1997): 605–619; also, Sylvie Fogiel-Bijaoui, "Familism, Postmodernity and the State: The Case of Israel," *Journal of Israeli History* 21 (1) (2002): 8–62.

109. Laura Bernardi, "Channels of Social Influence on Reproduction," *Population Research and Policy, Review* 22 (5–6) (2003): 527–528.
110. Israel Central Bureau of Statistics (CBS), "Selected Data on the Occasion of 'Tu B'av'" (press release, July 29, 2015), http://www.cbs.gov.il/www/hodaot2015n/11_15_200b.pdf.
111. Evgenia Bystrov, "The Second Demographic Transition in Israel: One for All?" *Demographic Research* 27 (10) (2012): 278–279.
112. Virginia Deane Abernethy, "Population Dynamics Revisited: Lessons for Foreign Aid and U.S. Immigration Policy," in *People and Their Planet: Searching for Balance*, ed. Barbara Sundberg Baudot and William Moomow (New York: Macmillan, 1999), 144, 153.
113. Bystrov, "The Second Demographic Transition in Israel," 263.
114. Ibid., 271–272.
115. "Rate of Single Mothers Doubles since 2000," *Ynet*, February 22, 2012, http://www.ynetnews.com/articles/0,7340,L-4192981,00.html.
116. Bystrov, "The Second Demographic Transition in Israel," 279–280.
117. Roger Hardy, "The Iran-Iraq War: 25 Years On," *BBC News*, September 22, 2005, http://news.bbc.co.uk/2/hi/4260420.stm.
118. Abrahamian Ervand, *A History of Modern Iran* (Cambridge: Cambridge University Press, 2008), 173–174.
119. Weisman, "Safe Sex," 270–271.
120. Elaine Sciolino, *Persian Mirrors: The Elusive Face of Iran* (New York: Free Press, 2000), 282.
121. Amir Mehrayar, "The Revolution," in *No Vacancy*, 6.
122. Malek-Afzali, Mehryar, and Abbasi-Shavazi, "Iran," 1–5.
123. Mohammad Jalal Abbasi-Shavazi, "Recent Changes and the Future of Fertility in Iran," *Population Bulletin of the United Nations: Completing the Fertility Transition* (New York: United Nations Publishers, 2002) 425–433.
124. Mohammad Jalal Abbasi-Shavazi, "Iran's Fertility Decline," in *No Vacancy*, 7.
125. CIA, "Total Fertility Rate," *World Factbook* (2014), https://www.cia.gov/library/publications/the-world-factbook/fields/2127.html.
126. Lester Rowntree, Martin Lewis, Marie Price, and William Wyckoff, "South Asia," in *Diversity Amid Globalization: World Regions, Environment, Development*, 5th ed. (Boston: Prentice Hall, 2012), 548.
127. Tom Strode, "Bangladesh Imitates China's 1-Child Policy," *Baptist News*, January 18, 2010, http://www.bpnews.net/printerfriendly.asp?id=32070.
128. Bystrov, "Second Demographic Transition in Israel," 287.
129. William Ryerson and Dobrah Sopariwala, "A Report on a Series of Three Surveys in the Hindi-Speaking Region to Test the Effect of the Television Serial Humraahi, as a Vehicle of Social Change," (Shelburne, VT: Population Media Center 1992).
130. William Ryerson, "How Do We Solve the Population Problem?" in *Life on the Brink*, 245–247.
131. Alon Tal, *Pollution in a Promised Land: An Environmental History of Israel* (Berkeley: University of California Press, 2002), 172–174.

132. William Ryerson, "How Do We Solve the Population Problem?" 248.

133. Alon Tal, "Two Sides of the Same Rectangle: The Environmental Movement and the Population Explosion," *Ecology and Environment* 3 (2012): 273–283.

134. Robert Engelman, "Population as a Scale Factor, Impact on Environment and Development," in *People and Their Planet, Searching for Balance*, ed. Barbara Sundberg Baudot and William Moomaw (New York, MacMillan Press, 1999), 126.

INDEX

Page numbers in *italics* refer to illustrations.

Haredim (continued)
stigmatizing of, 93; unemployment among, 96, 134, 153, 268; working women among, 266, 268; Zionists and, 134–138. *See also* Orthodox Jews
Har Tuv transit camp, 57
HaShomer, 50
Hasidim, 132, 137, 137–138, 157
Hasina, Sheikh, 290
health care, 39, 41, 42. *See also* hospitals
health insurance, 106–107, 109, 116, 122, 126
Hebrew language, 50, 62, 193, 206
Hebron, 26, 136
Hernes, Gudmund, 285
Herod I, king of Judea, 23
Herodian well, 26
Herzl, Theodore, 46, 51, 173, 179
Herzog, Esther, 122
Herzog, Isaac, 81
Hillel (rabbi), 144, 157
Hiriya, 14, 15
Hitler, Adolf, 48, 54, 136
HIV (human immune deficiency virus), 278–279
Holdren, John, 238–239
Holocaust, xvii, 3, 7, 48, 55, 57, 60, 75, 81, 87, 183, 227
Holy Letter (Ramban), 145
homosexuality, 114
Hong Kong, 220
honor killings, 204
Hope-Simpson Commission, 225–227
hospitals, xvii, 9, 13; abortion in, 110, 115, 116, 119, 120, 122; crowding in, 39–42
Hotovely, Tzipi, 214
housing, xvii, 13, 18, 31–33, 59; in Bedouin towns, 202; family size and, 90, 103, 283
How Many People Can the Earth Support? (Cohen), 232
Hunah (rabbi), 144
Hungary, 52, 60
hunting, 16, 18

Huntington, Ellsworth, 225
Husseini, Haj Amin al-, 173

Iceland, 42, 266
Ichilov Hospital, 40
Ilan, Shahar, 94
illiteracy, 183, 204
immigration, 2, 4, 46–78, 261, 292; as founding principle, 56, 60; prestige attached to, 6, 47; from Soviet Union, 35, 47, 64–65, 66–67, 132, 139, 288
India, 59, 80, 191, 259, 291
industrialization, 169
infant mortality, 53, 55, 90, 179, 203, 265
infectious disease, 247
inflation, 60
infrastructure, 9, 18, 27, 180
interest rates, 33
intifada, 196
intrauterine devices (IUDs), 108, 109, 110, 111, 146, 151, 194, 207
in vitro fertilization (IVF), 125–127
Iran, 58, 259, 283, 289–290
Iraq, 173, 289; immigration from, 58; population growth in, x
Ireland, 60, 259
Iron Dome, xviii
irrigation, 24, 26, 180, 181, 226, 231, 243
Isaac (biblical figure), 143, 147
Isaiah, book of, 145
Isha L'Isha (feminist group), 113, 129
Islamic law, 106
Islamic Movement, 43
Israel Defense Forces (IDF), 67, 94, 199
Israel Family Planning Association, 278
Israelization, 187–190
Itach (NGO), 205
Italy, 4–5, 65, 66, 170, 288

Jabareen, Yosef, 193
Jabotinsky, Vladimir "Zeev," 52, 173, 226
Jacob (biblical figure), 143, 146
Jaffa, 51, 181, 183